THE IMPERIAL WAR MUSEUM BOOK OF

MODERN WARFARE

Julian Thompson joined the Royal Marines a month after his eighteenth birthday and served for thirty-four years, retiring as Major General. His service, mainly for the Royal Marines Commandos, took him to seven continents. He commanded 3rd Commando Brigade, which carried out the initial landings to repossess the Falkland Islands in 1982 and fought most of the subsequent land battles.

He is now Visiting Professor in the Department of War Studies, King's College, London. He has presented a series of short Second World War commemorative films on BBC1 and has written books on military strategy, the Commandos and the Parachute Regiment.

D1438334

THE IMPERIAL WAR MUSEUM BOOK OF

MODERN WARFARE

BRITISH AND COMMONWEALTH FORCES AT WAR

1945–2000

Edited by

Major General Julian Thompson

PAN BOOKS

in association with

The Imperial War Museum

First published 2002 by Sidgwick & Jackson

This edition published 2003 by Pan Books
an imprint of Pan Macmillan Ltd
Pan Macmillan, 20 New Wharf Road, London N1 9RR
Basingstoke and Oxford
Associated companies throughout the world
www.panmacmillan.com

ISBN 0 330 39304 9

A CIP catalogue record for this book is available from
the British Library.

Typeset by SetSystems Ltd, Saffron Walden, Essex
Printed and bound in Great Britain by
Mackays of Chatham plc, Chatham, Kent

Preface

This Imperial War Museum book looks back over the period from the end of the Second World War to the close of the twentieth century, a time which saw the British armed forces, and sometimes those from the Commonwealth, engaged in operations without pause. I was asked to edit this book by the Imperial War Museum, and they gave me discretion to choose the campaigns it would cover. So the responsibility for selection is mine and mine alone. I picked what I judged were the fifteen major campaigns, operations and wars in which the British were involved since 1945. Commonwealth contingents, often substantial, participated in some of them, notably in Malaya, Korea, and Borneo. In the Netherlands East Indies from 1945 to 1947, units from the old pre-independence Indian Army, soon to be the armies of Pakistan and India, played a major part. In Kenya from 1952 to 1956, African troops from the King's African Rifles and the Kenya Regiment were indispensable to the successful outcome of the emergency.

Of course Australians and New Zealanders fought in Vietnam, and, as one would expect, their impact was out of all proportion to the size of their contribution. But no British troops took part, hence Vietnam does not feature in this book. Neither have I included a multitude of other operations, or potential operations, which involved British troops, ships or aircraft over the years between 1945 and 2000, such as deployments to British Honduras/Belize from 1948 to 1983, Eritrea 1948–51, British Guiana 1953–64, the Cameroons 1960–61, the East African Army mutinies in 1964, the New Hebrides 1980, and Beirut 1983; and these are but a tiny sample from a list of around eighty-three operations and deployments since 1945.

The author of each chapter is either an expert on the campaign, or took part in some capacity (sometimes at senior level), or both. I am extremely grateful to all the authors for their contributions. They are without exception very busy and gave generously of their time and advice. It is a great sadness to me that General Sir Walter Walker, who played such a key part in the successful Borneo campaign, has not lived to see his chapter in print.

I must pay tribute to Laurie Milner of the Research and Information Department of the Imperial War Museum for his indefatigable assistance and wise advice, especially, but not exclusively, in the selection of photographs to illustrate the book and maps. The Photographic Archive of the Imperial War Museum was, as always, an incomparable source of material. Their patience and forbearance in the face of short-notice requests was outstanding.

Julian Thompson
2001

Contents

List of Maps

List of Illustrations

Netherlands East Indies

1. The burnt-out car of Brigadier Mallaby in Surabaya. *(Imperial War Museum)*
2. Soldiers of the 8th/13th Frontier Force Rifles guard suspected Indonesian terrorists. *(Imperial War Museum)*
3. A 3.7 in gun of the 24th Indian Mountain Battery firing at Indonesian mortar positions in the hills beyond Grissee. *(Imperial War Museum)*

Palestine

4. A Haganah mortar bomb hits Haifa Docks. *(David Gilbert)*
5. Arab refugees massed outside the Docks after the shelling of the Souk by Haganah. *(David Gilbert)*
6. A Staghound armoured car covering the mass influx of Arab refugees. *(David Gilbert)*
7. The last British troops to leave Palestine, 40 Commando Royal Marines, march on board the LST *Striker*, 30 June 1948. *(David Gilbert)*

Malaya

8. Admiral Lord Louis Mountbatten, Supreme Allied Commander South East Asia, shakes hands with Chin Peng, the leader of the Malayan Peoples' Anti-Japanese Army. *(Imperial War Museum)*
9. A patrol of the 1st Battalion the Cameronians displaying caps and flags taken in a 'bandit' camp. *(Imperial War Museum)*
10. A British soldier checks a rubber tapper's identity on a rubber plantation in 1950. *(Imperial War Museum)*

Korea

11. Hawker Sea Furies and Fairey Fireflies ranged on the flight deck of HMS *Ocean*. *(Imperial War Museum)*
12. Marines of 41 Independent Commando Royal Marines on the long fighting

Borneo

South Arabia and Aden

Dhofar

Northern Ireland

Glossary

25-pounder – British Second World War artillery piece, maximum range 12,250 yards (seven miles), firing a 25 lb shell.

76 mm – Main-armament gun mounted on the Saracen armoured car.

AAV – Amphibious Assault Vehicle: swimming tracked armoured vehicle.

Aermacchi – A light jet aircraft, armed with guns and bombs.

Alarm missile – The British equivalent of the **Harm** missile but with the capability to be used at low level; also able to loiter for a few minutes on a parachute. Used for the first time during the Gulf War.

Alouette – Light helicopter of French design.

Anson – British Second World War coastal command aircraft.

Armalite – Generic name for the rifle based on the original AR-15 American-designed 5.56 mm calibre weapon, which became the AR-16 issued to the US armed services. Many marks and 'clones' have been produced.

Battalian – see **Regiment.**

B-29 – Superfortress: a four-engined American heavy bomber, which first saw service in June 1944, and in the Second World War served solely in the Far East. Carried double the bomb load of the famous B-17 Flying Fortress over twice the distance.

B-52 – Stratofortress: an eight-engined American long-range bomber with an exceptional bomb load of about 70,000 lb (31.25 tons). It first flew in 1954, and was used widely to attack and harass the Iraqi army in and around Kuwait, and its logistic installations. Also used to deliver cruise missiles.

Bell 212 – Light, armed helicopter, of US manufacture.

Belvedere – A not wholly successful British designed twin-rotor helicopter (it looked somewhat like a mini-Chinook). Dubbed the 'Widow maker' by marines and soldiers because of its unfortunate propensity to crash.

BL 755 – An RAF anti-armour weapon, deploying bomblets. It was little used in the Gulf because it had to be released from very low level. It has subsequently been modified for medium-level use.

Bren – The British light machine gun of the Second World War and until the late 1950s. Fired a standard .303 in round from a 28-round magazine. Modified to fire 7.62 mm ammunition with the introduction of the **SLR** in the late 1950s. Replaced by the **GPMG** in the mid-1960s.

Browning – A belt-fed .30 in light machine gun. Many marks produced, including water-cooled versions; some units in the British army were issued with the air-cooled version, which was the Browning fitted in armoured fighting vehicles.

Buccaneer – A former Royal Navy low-level bomber which was brought into RAF service. Approaching its end of service life in 1991, it was used both as a laser designator for **Paveway Two** bombs, using a US system called **Pave Spike**, and as a bomber.

BV 202 – Bandwagon, a tracked oversnow vehicle made by Volvo.

Carl Gustav – 84 mm shoulder-held recoilless medium anti-armour weapon.

C-130 – Four-engined short take-off and landing transport aircraft. Still a great workhorse, despite being largely 1950s technology, although uprated in the latest marks such as the C-130J.

Canberra – Jet medium bomber of British design.

CAP – Combat Air Patrol, the equivalent of the old 'cab rank'. The CAP can consist of fighters positioned to defend against intruding enemy aircraft, or ground-attack aircraft ready to carry out strikes in support of ground forces.

CBU-87 – The US equivalent of the **BL 755**, which is dropped from medium level. It was used extensively by the Americans, and by RAF **Jaguars**.

Chinook – Large, twin-rotor helicopter with a payload of ten tons.

Glossary

CRV-7 – A Canadian-built high-velocity rocket. RAF **Jaguars** carried two pods of such weapons, mostly on anti-shipping operations.

CTF – Commander Task Force.

CVRT – Combat Vehicle Reconnaissance Tracked: **Scorpion** or **Scimitar** light tank.

DSO – Distinguished Service Order. Instituted in 1886; until the awards system was changed in 1994 it was a dual-role decoration, recognizing gallantry at a level below that qualifying for the VC by junior officers, and exceptional leadership by senior officers in battle. Officers of all three services were and are eligible. Since 1994, it is a less prestigious decoration, awarded for successful command in 'operational circumstances'.

DZ – Dropping Zone (British), Drop Zone (US); the area chosen for landing by parachute troops.

F-4G – Wild Weasel: a late version of the Phantom fighter-bomber used to attack surface to air missiles (**SAM**) and anti-aircraft artillery (AAA) sites by the use of **Harm** missiles.

F-16 – Fighting Falcon: one of the world's most successful single-seat fighter-bombers, it is the workhorse of the USAF and has been sold all over the world. More sorties were flown in the Gulf War by F-16s than by any other aircraft.

F-111 – Aardvark: a swing-wing bomber similar in capability to the RAF's **Tornado.** Used at low and medium level during the Gulf War to attack a wide variety of targets including armoured vehicles using 500 lb laser-guided bombs.

F-117A – Nighthawk: the first US stealth fighter, although actually flown as a bomber. It was used extensively in the Gulf War to attack key targets. None were lost on operations despite penetrating the most heavily defended points.

Ferret – British light armoured car.

Gazelle – French-designed light helicopter. A good battlefield helicopter, fast and excellent for command and observation. Still in service.

GBU-27 – An advanced 2,000 lb laser guided bomb, two of which were carried on the **F-117A**.

GPMG – General Purpose Machine Gun: belt-fed, 7.62 mm calibre, it replaced the **Bren** in the mid-1960s.

GPS – The Global Positioning System. It is a means of highly accurate navigation around the world using a constellation of 22 satellites in geostationary earth orbit.

GR-3 – RAF version of the Harrier. Had no on-board radar, unlike the **SHAR.**

Halifax – Second World War British heavy bomber.

Harm missile – A US missile, launched from medium altitude, which homes onto the radar signal of an emitting anti-aircraft radar. Hundreds were fired during the Gulf War.

Hunter – A highly successful British single-seater jet fighter/bomber. Fulfilled the airman's old adage, 'if it looks good, it is good'. It was.

Jaguar – A joint Anglo-French fighter-bomber aircraft. The RAF and French Air Force deployed one squadron each to the Gulf.

JP 233 – An anti-airfield weapon carried exclusively by the **Tornado.** Two weapons can be carried on each aircraft, giving a combination of 60 cratering munitions and 430 minelets. About 100 such weapons were dropped during the Gulf War.

Kalashnikov – Soviet assault rifle, originally 7.62 mm calibre; there are many variants and many 'clones' based on the original AK-47 design of 1949. Highly successful, perhaps the best assault rifle in the world even today. Sometimes known as the 'banana gun' after its distinctive curved magazine.

Lancaster – Second World War British heavy bomber.

LMG – Light Machine Gun. In the British service this was the **Bren.**

LPD – Landing Platform Dock – assault ship. Britain still has two, *Fearless* and *Intrepid*, although the latter has now been so cannibalized for spares that the chance of her being operational again is remote. Two replacements have recently been launched: HM Ships *Albion* and *Bulwark* will come into service in 2003.

LPH – Landing Platform Helicopter – in the British service, originally an aircraft carrier converted to carry an RM Commando and helicopters to fly them ashore. The US Navy has had purpose-built LPHs for years. The first ever British purpose-built LPH is HMS *Ocean*, launched in 1995.

LSL – Landing Ship Logistic – roll-on, roll-off ships manned by the Royal Fleet Auxiliary.

In the fifty-six years that have passed since 1945 to the time of writing, much else has changed. The British armed forces are tiny compared with those at the end of the Second World War, and for some years after. The Royal Navy now has 42,698 people, 3 carriers, 2 amphibious ships, 32 destroyers and frigates, 50 miscellaneous small vessels, and 22 auxiliaries. At the war's end, over 850,000 men and women were in the Royal Navy, which had some 2,000 warships, and over 1,000 landing craft and minor vessels, deployed all over the world. Now its strike aircraft, the Sea Harrier (SHAR), total a mere 24 compared with nearly 1,500 varied combat aircraft in 73 squadrons in 1945, and around 150 assorted helicopters complete Britain's maritime armoury. Today the British army is 108,916 strong compared with over 3 million men and women in 1945, with 6 armoured divisions, 18 infantry divisions, and 2 airborne divisions, and a host of other units. The Royal Air Force now has 241 combat aircraft and 54,436 personnel, compared with a 1945 strength of over 1 million men and women and 408 combat squadrons comprising over 10,000 combat aircraft.

For the reasons touched on above, the defence scene in the early twenty-first century would, in many respects, be totally incomprehensible to the inhabitants of these islands in 1945, and especially the soldiers, sailors and airmen on whose shoulders the defence of the realm then rested. So will service people be prepared to die for politically correct causes? What damage is being done to cohesion? What will the morrow bring?

*

All these and a host of other questions lay in the future when on 9 August 1945 a B-29 bomber of the United States Army Air Force (USAAF) dropped an atomic bomb, code-named 'Fat Man', on the Japanese city of Nagasaki. Three days earlier, the first nuclear weapon in history, 'Little Boy', had been dropped on Hiroshima. Aircraft from the fast carriers of the United States Third Fleet and the USAAF's Pacific islands-based bomb groups continued with their raids on Japanese cities until 14 August, when, following the personal intervention of the Japanese Emperor, Hirohito, the Japanese government accepted the Allied terms of unconditional surrender. The war against Japan was at an end, months, if not years, before the expected date. In a replay of Victory in Europe day three months previously, the people of the United

Kingdom danced in the streets. Now ended almost six years of war in which Britain, and her Empire and Commonwealth, had fought from the first day to the last, and for just over a year of that time alone. There was indeed reason for rejoicing.

In the world war just finished, the British had mobilized manpower resources proportionately greater than any other country, Allied or Axis.[9] Her armies, fleets and air forces had fought in every theatre of that war except on the German–Soviet front, and even there Britain had supported the Soviet Union with vast quantities of materiel carried in Arctic convoys at great cost in lives and ships. From the end of 1940 Britain's war effort had been increasingly financed and equipped by the United States, under the system of Lend-Lease initiated by President Roosevelt.[10] A week after the Japanese surrender, President Truman announced the end of Lend-Lease. The dollar had superseded the pound as the world's main currency. British industry was worn out and devoted almost entirely to war production. In the great crusade against tyranny, the British had spent most of their overseas assets, a loss according to John Maynard Keynes thirty-five times greater than that of the United States. Britain was broke.

Paradoxically, the Empire and Commonwealth, and areas around the globe occupied by British troops, had never been larger in her history. The whole of the Empire had been restored. With their allies, the British occupied Germany, Austria, and Italy. The British presence in the Mediterranean was more extensive than ever before, with troops stationed in North Africa from the Suez Canal to Tunisia, in the Levant, and in Greece. The British also found themselves committed, albeit temporarily, in the colonies of their allies; very briefly in French Indo-China and for over a year in the Netherlands East Indies. Both these colonies had been occupied by the Japanese and the majority of the population were set against welcoming back their former masters. After the British had withdrawn, both colonies were to be the scene of considerable fighting; in Indo-China for thirty years, in the Netherlands East Indies for rather less.

Although the strength of all three services began to be reduced following the end of the war, Britain's global commitments still demanded huge numbers of ships, aircraft and equipment and the sailors, soldiers and airmen to man them. By June 1946, there were still over 2 million men and women in the armed forces. For example, the small British contingent in Japan alone consisted of 3,000 soldiers,

1,200 airmen and fifty-two aircraft. The First Sea Lord argued in the Chiefs of Staff Committee that it was necessary to maintain a 'comparatively large' fleet in the Pacific, consisting of two battleships, two aircraft carriers, seven cruisers, sixteen destroyers, and thirty-four other vessels. The Chief of the Air Staff pressed for at least twelve squadrons of bombers to be retained in the Mediterranean Theatre. There was a small occupation force in Iran, and a very much larger one of 20,000 soldiers plus an air component in Libya. Three divisions were deployed in and around Trieste deterring Yugoslav aggression. The British contributions to the Allied occupation forces in Germany and Austria were 200,000 and 60,000 soldiers respectively, plus over 200 aircraft and 20,000 airmen. Stationed in the UK were some 200,000 soldiers and about the same number of airmen together with about 1,000 aircraft. The Home Fleet comprised two battleships, four carriers, seven cruisers, sixteen destroyers, twenty-five submarines, and sixty-two other vessels. Deployed to meet commitments in the Mediterranean, the Middle East, India, South-east Asia and the Pacific were around 140,000 soldiers, 78,000 airmen, and 700 aircraft. To these figures should be added two battleships, five carriers, twenty cruisers, forty destroyers, twenty submarines, and 102 other vessels, not to mention four cruisers and four escorts on the America and West Indies and Africa stations.[11]

Despite this global spread, and the largest empire the world had ever seen, Britain was no longer what would later be called a superpower: that distinction was reserved for the USA and later the USSR. Without these two, the Axis, and Germany in particular, would never have been defeated, and the world would be a different place today, let alone in 1945. Both the USA and USSR were well aware of this fact, and attempted to use the influence that flowed from their status to their own advantage, but in different ways.

The Americans, especially those from New England, felt an affinity to the British. In 1945 there was still a sense in North America of a common Anglo-Saxon inheritance, a perception that has diminished, or even disappeared, in large parts of the subcontinent today. In 1945 General MacArthur could say in a message to the British Prime Minister, referring to the Commonwealth troops (largely Australians and New Zealanders) who fought under his command in the South-West Pacific, that they proved themselves 'fully worthy of our race'.[12] American attitudes to the Empire, on the other hand, were a combination of prejudice and ignorance. As a union of mostly ex-British colonies, the United States was not disposed to look kindly on Britain retaining any part of her Empire and was certainly not going to lift a finger to assist her in remaining a colonial power. The ignorance is perhaps illustrated by a question posed to the author in the United States as late as the early 1980s to the effect of when the British were going to withdraw their troops from Dublin.[13] Although it may seem almost unbelievable at the beginning of the twenty-first century, in 1945 Britain was in no hurry to give up her Empire. The Labour government, elected in July that year, had as its first priority social reform at home. 'The British Empire was held momentarily in abeyance so to speak, while the new rulers of Great Britain decided what best to do with it.'[14]

This somewhat laissez-faire attitude reflected the opinion of the vast majority of the British electorate in the 1940s who, finding no reason to be ashamed of the Empire, saw little reason for hastening its demise. This is not to say that there was a widespread appetite for fighting a bloody war to maintain the status quo, and there were of course a substantial number of people who campaigned for, or wished to see, an end to colonialism, mainly in the Labour Party and among its supporters. Servicemen, especially those returning from India, were probably the least enamoured of keeping the 'jewel in the crown'. In the majority of colonies, the desire for independence was felt most acutely by the handful of intellectuals and professionals; teachers, lawyers and doctors. They led the independence movements, and were the principal beneficiaries when it came. Although it is unfashionable to say so, the majority of the inhabitants of the colonies, and in Africa especially, were better off in almost every way as part of the British Empire than they are today. Heaven forfend that this statement should be taken as hankering after a return to those days, it is merely the truth, and no amount of hand-wringing and bogus guilt about the past on the part of some sections of present-day British society can alter that reality.

In a sense the British Empire was a confidence trick on a global scale. The Victorian British army was not large, just over twice the size of today's shrunken force, but Britain ruled over a quarter of the world's land surface. Most of the world's oceans were a British lake, thanks to the Royal Navy, which at the time of Queen Victoria's Diamond Jubilee was equal in size to the next five navies combined. The secret of the trick was immense Victorian self-confidence embedded in a belief that what

we were doing was right. Looking back over the century since Victoria's
death in 1901, it is hard to detect the exact moment when that self-
confidence began to ebb. But the tide was running out fast by 1945, and
some events in the years that followed hastened the flow.

American distaste for colonialism did not deter them from establishing spheres of influence and meddling in the affairs of others, in South
America, Africa, the Middle East and in Asia, nowhere more than in
China where they considered themselves to have special interests. American support and encouragement for the British reconquest of Burma
in 1943–5 had everything to do with opening up the supply route to
Chiang Kai-shek, the Nationalist ruler of China and supporting him
against the Japanese, and nothing to do with Britain regaining part of
her Empire. In 1941 the United States suggested that the British give
Hong Kong to Chiang Kai-shek, at one point offering to buy the port
off them if necessary, and Roosevelt raised the subject at least twice more
at Allied conferences during the course of the war. American enthusiasm
for the British to hand over Hong Kong diminished rapidly, however,
after the Chinese communists defeated the Nationalists and Chiang
Kai-shek fled with the remnants of his army and followers to the island
of Formosa (Taiwan).

The Soviet Union, exhausted by the war, reserved her efforts immediately afterwards for imposing control over the eastern European territory
she had overrun in the course of defeating Germany, in the process
establishing what Churchill was to call the 'Iron Curtain'. A decade
passed before Russian influence was felt outside Europe, except for the
export of communist ideology, though communist books and pamphlets
had been circulating in Asia and Africa since well before the Second
World War. Some African and Asian leaders, for example Jomo Kenyatta from Kenya and Kwame Nkrumah from the Gold Coast (Ghana),
had studied in Moscow in the 1930s. Now the war had ended, a new
generation of leaders was learning and spreading Marxist ideas. The first
Pan-African Congress was held in 1945 in Chorlton-on-Medlock, a
suburb of Manchester, where delegates from most African countries, all
still European colonies or administered from Europe, passed a resolution
demanding autonomy and independence for all black Africa.

The seeds of one of the biggest post-Second World War conflicts were
sown by the Soviet Union in Korea, which had been a Japanese colony
since 1910. After the first atom bomb was dropped on Hiroshima, the

Soviet Union, which until now had not been at war with Japan, sensed that the end of the war could not be far off, and made moves to establish its place as one of the victors in the Far East. The United States realized that Soviet operations against Japan were imminent, and that the likely area for them was Korea, whose border was contiguous with the USSR. The US had no formations that could get there before the Russians. Accordingly a hasty agreement was reached designating the 38th parallel as the demarcation between the Soviet and US zones of occupation. Four days before Japan surrendered, the Soviet Army invaded Korea, occupying the country as far south as Pyongyang. The US XXIV Corps did not arrive until 8 September, by which time the Soviets had completed their occupation down to the 38th parallel. While the Soviets steadily built up their influence in the northern half of the country, the USA seemed unable to decide on a firm policy for their occupation of the south. From the beginning the Soviets governed through an Interim People's Committee with hand-picked Korean surrogates as their mouth-pieces. The most promising was Kim Il-sung (a nom de guerre), who had been heavily involved in the anti-Japanese partisan movement after the invasion of Manchuria in 1931. He had attended political and military training in Moscow from 1941 to 1945, when he returned to Korea as an officer in the Red Army.

The Americans, on the other hand, had made no such preparations and were unable to communicate in Korean. They found themselves forced to administer their zone of occupation through the highly effi-cient Japanese military and civil service they found when they arrived, as those few Koreans who had been involved in the administration during the Japanese occupation were so loathed by their fellow countrymen as collaborators that they had to be removed. Furthermore, although they had been the hated enemy a month earlier, the Americans found the disciplined, well-mannered, and highly efficient Japanese infinitely pref-erable to the Koreans. This of course was deeply offensive to the Koreans, who had suffered greatly under Japanese occupation. Eventually it was found expedient to replace the Japanese with American civil servants, who spoke no Korean and knew absolutely nothing about the country. The Americans allowed the leader of the Korean government in exile, Syngman Rhee, to return to his native land. He had been forced to flee to America in 1919 after an abortive rising against the Japanese.

Although Koreans on both sides of the 38th parallel pressed for reunification of the country, moves to bring this about were continually frustrated by the USSR. Eventually the Americans proceeded with plans for a self-governing South Korea, under Syngman Rhee. However, neither he nor Kim Il-sung was content to see the country divided for the foreseeable future and thus the seeds were sown for the war that was to follow in 1950.

In 1945, China, portrayed in Allied Second World War propaganda as one of the 'big four' (the other three being the USA, USSR, and Great Britain – France did not qualify, having opted out of the war for three years after her defeat in the Battle of France), was in a state of total exhaustion. For her the Second World War had begun in July 1937, when a minor skirmish near the Marco Polo bridge near Peking (Beijing) led to all-out war between Japan and the Chinese Nationalists led by Chiang Kai-shek, and soon involved the communists led by Mao Tse-tung. Over the following eight years the Japanese succeeded in occupying a broad swathe southwards across China from Manchuria to Indo-China. The surrender of Japan left China as a survivor rather than a winner, and at a huge cost in human life; probably only the Soviet Union suffered greater casualties. The available figures are unreliable, but Chinese military casualties between 1937 and 1945, both Nationalist and communist, could have been in the order of 5 million, with perhaps another 10–20 million civilian deaths from starvation, disease, and Japanese action. The stage was now set for the showdown between Mao's People's Liberation Army and Chiang's Nationalists, ending in the latter's defeat in 1949. Communist victory in China was to have repercussions elsewhere, first in Asia, and later in Africa.

Despite the growing influence of the Soviet Union, and later China, outside their borders, it would be mistaken to imagine that the wars in which the British engaged between 1945 and 1999 were the result of an orchestrated anti-imperialist/capitalist plan. As James Morris has remarked about the world in 1945:

> It was not simply a new world, as it had been after the First World War. Now it was *several* [sic] new worlds, surrounding the perimeters of the British Empire, and erupting within. This great movement of change and discontent was more organic than deliberate. No universal conspiracy linked the scattered patriots. Some were Communists, some tribalists, some men of religion, some cultural irredentists. Some were pursuing old grudges, or evolving new ambitions.[15]

As the years after 1945 passed, the conditions set out in this perceptive assessment became less and less pertinent to the theme of this book, and anyway four of the wars which feature in this work had no connection with Britain's imperial past. But Morris's analysis neatly summarizes the condition of many former overseas possessions in the aftermath of the Second World War, not only the British ones, but also those of other colonial powers, of whom the French, Dutch and Portuguese were the most important.

India in 1945 was no nearer to independence than she had been in 1935, when the Government of India Act was passed by the British Parliament as a first step towards self-government. Independence was generations away in the British perception but could not come quickly enough for the Indian Congress Party. Only two years later a *partitioned* Indian subcontinent was independent. Although few people would disagree that by 1945 the time for the transfer of power had come, the manner in which it was implemented was a humiliation to Britain, despite it being depicted by what we now call 'spin doctoring' as a triumph of diplomacy and pragmatism. As the withdrawal of British troops did not involve them in any fighting, the period from August 1945 to August 1947 does not merit a chapter in this book, but deserves mention here.

The creation of Pakistan as an independent Muslim state had been formally aspired to since 1940 by Mohammed Ali Jinnah, leader of the Muslim League. When the borders of West Pakistan (present-day Pakistan) and East Pakistan (Bangladesh) were announced in 1947, masses of Muslims and Hindus who found themselves on the wrong side of the religious divide tried to cross over; many made it, large numbers did not, killed by Indians of the opposite religious persuasion. Although there was abundant bloodshed both before and after partition into India and Pakistan, except for isolated incidents it mostly passed the British by. A poisonous combination of personalities and overweening ambition combined to make the prelude to, and aftermath of, independence a bitter, and often deadly, time of massacre, mass rape, and violence for hundreds of thousands of the unfortunate people of the subcontinent and the uprooting of millions more. The critical flaw in the plan was lack of time, the result of the British Labour government's earnest desire to divest themselves of an increasingly troublesome possession, which led them to announce a date of 3 June 1948 for independence. The unseemly haste of the Viceroy, the 'mendacious and intellectually limited hustler' Lord Mountbatten, in forcing through independence in seventy-three days, far short of the deadline of sixteen months set by the Attlee government which had sent him there, was the principal cause of the mayhem. He selected 14/15 August 1947 for the transfer of power, purely because it was the second anniversary of the Japanese surrender, announcing it 'out of the blue' in answer to a question at a press conference. Others also played their part. Nehru, the brilliant Harrow-educated barrister, who was so plainly Mountbatten's favourite and who completely dominated him, led the Congress Party and became the first Prime Minister of an independent India. The arrogant Jinnah, dying of cancer, who saw through Mountbatten at their first meeting, and thought even 3 June 1948 too early a date for independence, eventually became Governor General of Pakistan. The machiavellian Gandhi concealed his guile under a saintly aura, and was rigidly opposed to partition. He had acted with serene irresponsibility during the war, when with the Japanese poised on the eastern border he called for the British to quit India, based on the quaint supposition that the Japanese would call off the attack. If they did not the Indians could resist non-violently, he pontificated: 'the resisters may find that the Japanese are utterly heartless and they do not care how many they kill. The non-violent resisters will have won the day inasmuch as they will have preferred extermination to submission.'[16]

As Lawrence James remarks, both Gandhi and Jinnah 'had the same relaxed attitude to other people's lives': after massacres in Calcutta, Gandhi said that if India wanted a bloodbath, it could have it, while Jinnah opined that Pakistan was worth the sacrifice of ten million Muslims.[17]

In the background, but sometimes too far into the foreground for some tastes, the mega-rich, pro-Soviet and anti-capitalist Lady Mountbatten openly flaunted her relationship with Nehru. Their intimacy, which they made no effort to conceal, signalled that the Mountbattens were partial, and furthermore that Nehru, and therefore the Congress Party, was privy to information denied to Jinnah and the Muslims. Whether these confidences were imparted on the pillow or in the drawing room was unimportant.

Mountbatten's greatest error was not allowing time for the reorganization of the Indian and Pakistani armed forces well *before* partition and the announcement of the boundary delineation, and insisting that these forces, alongside British troops if necessary, policed the movement of refugees across the boundaries. Instead, the boundary decisions were announced only days before independence, and complete road convoys, and trainloads, of refugees, both Muslim and Hindu, were massacred, villages were devastated, and utter chaos ensued for months. During this period of transition, Mountbatten, now Governor General of India, found time to return to England for the wedding of Princess Elizabeth, and spent many of his evenings in the Residence in Delhi drawing up his family tree. He had hoped to be Governor General of Pakistan too, but Jinnah would not have him at any price.[18]

The Japanese defeat of the British in Malaya, culminating in the humiliating surrender of the garrison of Singapore to a Japanese force one-third of its strength, sent shock waves throughout South-East Asia and sounded the death knell of British prestige in the region. Although the British comeback in 1944–5 saved some 'face', it did nothing to reverse the desire for independence in Burma, Ceylon, and Malaya. Burma gained independence at the same time as India, and elected to leave the Commonwealth. At the time of writing the British media carries reports from time to time about Sun Aung San, a political prisoner of the Burmese fascist regime in Rangoon. She is the daughter of U Aung San, the Burmese Nationalist leader who in March 1945, when Slim's Fourteenth Army definitely looked like winning, changed overnight from fighting for the Japanese to an 'anti-fascist'. U Aung San's Burma National Army (BNA) was hated by villagers more than the Japanese. The Karens, Kachins, and Chins, hill tribes who had fought on the British side, had no wish to be ruled by the Burmese, who on the whole supported the Japanese, engaged in a guerrilla war against the Burmese from 1947, which continues to this day.

Ceylon, now Sri Lanka, remained within the Commonwealth. Neither Burma (now Myanmar) nor Sri Lanka figures in our story hereafter.

Malaya, on the other hand, does feature, as do Borneo and Brunei, for reasons which will be made clear in the relevant chapters. When the Japanese in Malaya surrendered in August 1945, the Malayan Peoples' Anti-Japanese Army (MPAJA), based on the Malayan Peoples' Communist Party (MCP), which was recruited exclusively from the Chinese population and trained and equipped by the British, was some 7,000 strong. In December 1945 the MPAJA was disbanded and ordered to hand in its weapons. Some members did, but about 4,000 did not. Their leader, Chin Peng, was awarded the OBE and took part in the Victory Parade in London in 1946. The Chinese formed about 38 per cent of the population of Malaya, the Malays around 49 per cent, and Indian immigrants some 12 per cent. The remaining 1 per cent were aborigines and Europeans, the latter mostly British rubber planters and business-men. In general the somewhat easy-going Malays, most of whom had supported the Japanese, or at best had avoided taking sides, resented the near monopoly the hardworking and entrepreneurial Chinese exerted on the economy. By 1945 most of the Chinese population had been born in Malaya, but regarded China, soon to become communist, as their cultural and political home. The Chinese not only inhabited Chinatown in every Malayan city and town, but some 600,000 of them farmed 'squats' on the jungle fringes, where they had moved during the Japanese occupation to avoid persecution.

Palestine, once part of the Ottoman Empire and a British Mandate since the end of the First World War, had been the scene of Arab–Jewish strife before the outbreak of the Second. The roots of discord went back to 1917, when the British government announced in a letter from Lord Balfour, the Foreign Secretary, to Lord Rothschild that it would look with sympathy on the concept of a national home for the Jews. The 'Balfour Declaration' included a caveat which is often forgotten: 'it being clearly understood that nothing shall be done which may prejudice the civil and religious rights of existing non-Jewish communities in Palestine . . .' By 1939 the Jewish population living in Palestine was 500,000, a tenfold increase over the twenty years since the end of the Ottoman Empire. The British response to inter-communal violence and Arab pressure was to limit Jewish immigration to a maximum of 75,000 over five years, after which there would be no more without the consent of the Arabs. By 1945 the terrible experiences of the Jews at the hands of the Nazis and the consequent worldwide sympathy for the Jews, especially in the United States, placed the British, still responsible for Palestine, in an impossible position. The decision of the Jewish Agency, which was responsible for Jewish affairs in Palestine, to mount a campaign of violence and propaganda to persuade the British to lift immigration restrictions, and to gain worldwide support for the concept of a Jewish national home in Palestine, marked the beginning of the events described in Chapter 3.

The British had had even longer involvement in two other countries at the eastern end of the Mediterranean, Egypt and Cyprus. As will become apparent, the British withdrawal from Egypt was to have an effect on the situation in Cyprus, but in 1945 that lay some ten years ahead. Both had once been part of the Ottoman Empire. Cyprus had been ceded to Britain by Turkey in 1878, and had since then been a colony of little importance. It lacked a deep-water port, so the Royal Navy used either Alexandria or Malta as a base. Even during the Second World War it played no part in Britain's strategic plans. Although the Greek population on the island outnumbered the Turks by four to one, Cyprus had never in its history been part of Greece. This was not, however, to deter the Greek majority from hankering after union with Greece, *enosis*. The Turks would have none of it. Both communities detested each other, and herein lay the root of the strife which surfaced ten years later.

Egypt on the other hand had played a key part in British strategy since the opening of the Suez Canal in 1869. Following the Anglo-Egyptian war of 1882, the British ruled Egypt for the next seventy years, and used Egypt as a critical strategic and logistic base in both world wars. In the First it provided the crucial launching point from which operations were conducted against the Turks in the Near East, Balkans, and Arabia; in the Second it was vital, as the base for the huge Middle East Command, including the Mediterranean Fleet in the years when Malta lay under the lash of the Luftwaffe and the Italian Air Force. In the first years of the twenty-first century it is easy to forget how important the Suez Canal was in British eyes less than halfway through the twentieth. In 1945 Egypt housed extensive logistical installations, several airfields and a garrison of around 80,000 British troops. Not only did Egypt lie across the sea route to India and the Empire east of Suez, it was centrally positioned as the springboard from which the large British strategic reserve could deploy to trouble spots worldwide.

British interest in Kenya began in the last years of the nineteenth century with the building of a railway from Mombasa to Uganda, linking with the Sudan (another British colony ruled nominally with Egypt, as Anglo-Egyptian Sudan, from 1899). Most European settlement in Kenya dates from the inter-war period, and increased after the Second World War. The colony had been an important stepping stone for the campaign against the Italians in the Horn of Africa and Ethiopia in the early years of the war, and after the fall of Singapore, Mombasa was for a time the base for the Eastern Fleet. By 1945 its strategic importance was minimal. However, the Second World War had impinged on Kenya's African people in another way. Along with large numbers of other East and West Africans they had served in Burma, and, having seen something of the world outside Africa, were no longer content with their former lot. The end of the Second World War also saw the return to Kenya of the General Secretary of the Kikuyu Central Association (KCA), Jomo Kenyatta. He was a member of the Communist Party, and had twice visited the Soviet Union during his fifteen years in England. The Kikuyu were the largest and most sophisticated and politically astute tribe in Kenya, who greatly resented the European settlement of the best farming land, which they claimed had been wrested from them by the white settlers; the KCA's publicly declared aim was to take it back.

Aden's importance dated from the opening of the Suez Canal, when it became a coaling, and later oiling, station and garrison for British troops at the southern approaches to the Canal. It served in that capacity in both world wars. In 1945 it remained important as a staging post to the Empire, and to the Persian Gulf, where British strategic interests centred on the Persian oilfields, and the possibility of oil finds elsewhere in the region, most of them yet to be exploited. By 1945 oil had been discovered in Saudi Arabia, but its exploitation was monopolized by American companies.

In 1945, Northern Ireland was an integral part of the United Kingdom, as it is today. The population had played a full part in the Second World War: in particular the province had been a vital base in the Battle of the Atlantic, and as a training ground for over 100,000 US troops preparing for the Normandy landings. Éire, formerly the Irish Free State, independent and partitioned from Northern Ireland since 1922, had been neutral in the Second World War, although over 38,000 southern Irish had voluntarily enlisted in the British forces and fought with great gallantry. The Irish Republican Army (IRA) had not accepted the partition of Ireland, and although its members had been interned, and in some cases executed, by the Free State government, they continued to dream of a united Ireland. The beginning of the Second World War had seen a flurry of activity by the IRA, taking advantage of Britain's attention being engaged elsewhere, but by the end of 1939 these pinprick attacks died away. The Free State south, Éire, was in every sense a backwater presided over by the Anglophobe de Valera, who had personally signed the book of condolence in the German Embassy in Dublin when he learned of Hitler's death.

In 1945 the Balkans, including Yugoslavia, were firmly in the Soviet Union's sphere of influence. Yugoslavia, an uncomfortable creation of the post-First World War peace arrangements, was a hotch-potch of by no means compatible countries all of which at one time had formed part of either the Austro-Hungarian or Ottoman Empire, and some, in turn, of both. In 1945 the country was held together by the iron will of Marshal Tito, a Croat and a communist. Backed initially by the British, and subsequently by the Red Army, as well as engaging the Germans, he had eliminated all rival partisan groups – the latter rather more vigorously than the former. The proof of the priorities of most Yugoslavs of any persuasion lay in the fact that most of the 1.2 million Yugoslavs who died in the Second World War did so at the hands of other Yugoslavs. The seeds were thus sown for the hatred that was to manifest itself some thirty-five years later.

It can be seen that the world in 1945 contained a number of areas ripe for further conflict, which came to pass in some of them very quickly indeed.

1

PETER DENNIS

Netherlands East Indies, 1945–1947:
An Unwelcome Commitment

Peter Dennis is Professor of History at University College, Australian Defence Force Academy, Canberra. His publications include *The Territorial Army, 1906–1940* (1987); *Troubled Days of Peace: Mountbatten and South East Asia Command, 1945–46* (1987); as joint editor and author, *The Oxford Companion to Australian Military History* (1995); and, with Jeffrey Grey, *Emergency and Confrontation: Australian Military Operations in Malaya and Borneo, 1950–1966* (1996). He is also the joint editor (with Lieutenant General John Coates (Rtd)) of the seven-volume *Australian Centenary History of Defence* series (2001).

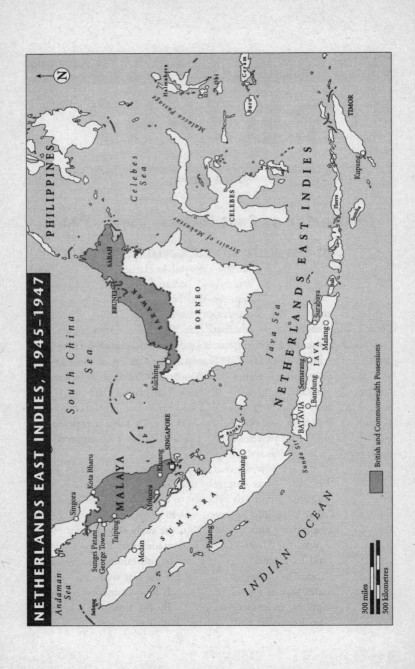

NETHERLANDS EAST INDIES, 1945–1947

Andaman Sea

PHILIPPINES

South China Sea

Malacca Passage

Halmahera

Buru   Ceram

Obi

TIMOR

Kupang

Celebes Sea

CELEBES

Straits of Makassar

Sumba   Flores   Bali

NETHERLANDS EAST INDIES

Java Sea

BORNEO

SABAH

BRUNEI   SARAWAK

Kuching

Surabaya

Malang

Semarang

Bandung   JAVA

BATAVIA

Sunda St

BANKA

Palembang

SUMATRA

Padang

INDIAN OCEAN

MALAYA

Singora

Kota Bharu

Sungei Patani   Taiping

George Town

Medan

Molocca   Kluang

SINGAPORE

Setul

N

300 miles

500 kilometres

British and Commonwealth Possessions

At the surrender ceremony in Singapore on 12 September 1945 the Supreme Allied Commander, South East Asia Command, Admiral Lord Louis Mountbatten, stressed that the Japanese had given in to overwhelming force. In the wider sphere, especially in the shadow of the atomic attacks on Hiroshima and Nagasaki, preceded by the bitter fighting as Allied forces drew closer to the Japanese home islands, that was undoubtedly true, but at the regional level the picture was much less convincing. Although British and Indian forces had won crushing victories in Burma, the Philippines had been liberated by MacArthur's campaigns, and in the most important areas of British, Dutch and French possessions in South-East Asia (Burma, Borneo and Dutch New Guinea excepted) the Japanese had not encountered any significant Allied military pressure. Consequently the signing of the surrender was more the result of events distant from South-East Asia than the triumphant conclusion to a theatre-wide campaign. That reality, and the circumstances underlying the Allied return to South-East Asia, created for Britain in particular a situation that she neither expected nor welcomed, and confronted her with a military problem of unprecedented complexity.

Each of the major colonial powers in South-East Asia – Britain, France and the Netherlands – was determined to reassert its colonial position once the war against Japan was brought to a successful conclusion. The fulfilment of that intention, however, was to prove much more difficult than any of the parties anticipated. From the early stages of its participation in the war, the United States had made clear its opposition to colonialism, and its intention to bring about substantial changes in the political conditions in the region. The longer the war went on, the more the United States was in a position, through its ever-increasing control of military supplies, to enforce its policy. By the time the war ended, Franklin Delano Roosevelt had died and had been succeeded by Harry

S. Truman, and whereas Roosevelt's long-standing opposition to French policy in Indo-China had gradually weakened as Indo-China became more important to US plans to defeat Japan, and his views on Dutch colonialism had been somewhat ameliorated by his own Dutch ancestry, Truman was quite different: he had a barely concealed antipathy to the new French leader, Charles de Gaulle, and his pretensions in Indo-China, and he had no intention of allowing American materiel, let alone manpower, to be diverted from the task of defeating Japan and used to restore European colonial empires. As a result, when the Japanese surrender was announced – much more suddenly than any of the Allied leaders, especially the military, had expected – Britain was the only colonial power with significant forces available, for whatever task they might be required in the post-surrender period. Neither the Dutch nor the French had reliable forces at hand to deal with the situation that confronted them nor was there the prospect of such forces readily becoming available.

That situation, especially in the Netherlands East Indies (NEI), was quite unlike what the colonial powers had anticipated and planned for. The Allies had intended to return to their South-East Asian colonies as victors in battle, clearly demonstrating their military superiority over the Japanese and thereby, to some degree at least, recovering from the humiliating defeats of 1942. The dropping of the atomic bombs and the surrender that quickly followed robbed them of that redemptive victory, and left in place, largely untouched, the hollowness of the promise that at the very least colonial rule gave peace and security to colonial peoples. When the Allies returned, therefore, the assumed moral authority that had underpinned colonial rule had in no sense been recovered. Instead, to their utter surprise, they found themselves confronted with independence movements that rejected their claims of imperial control; and instead of being welcomed back as liberators from Japanese oppression, they were regarded as discredited opponents of the forward march to independence. Nowhere was this more so than in Java, the most heavily populated and politically important island of the vast archipelago that made up the NEI.

The lack of awareness of the Allies over developments in the NEI was the result of several factors. The wartime Dutch government in exile in London had had few contacts with the NEI, whose own administration had relocated to Australia following the collapse of the American-British-

Dutch-Australian Command in February 1942. Thereafter the Dutch had only minimal intelligence links with the NEI. The British had even fewer links, and when in July 1945 the boundaries of Mountbatten's SEAC were extended to include southern Indo-China, Java, Borneo and Dutch New Guinea (i.e. the areas that no longer interested MacArthur in his exclusive focus on his promise to return to the Philippines), they relied on MacArthur's undertaking to give them all the intelligence he had on the situation in the NEI. It transpired that he had very little, and he never delivered on the promised handover. The Dutch themselves were torn between a recognition that some change was necessary and a reluctance, both during and after the war, to make any changes. Under intense political pressure from the United States the Dutch government had promised such change (albeit in very vague terms) in a speech by Queen Wilhelmina broadcast in December 1942, but by mid-1945 opinion was hardening. In any case there was stark failure on the part of the Dutch to appreciate that the war had fundamentally changed power and the perceptions of power, and that it would take much more than the mere assertion of authority for that authority to be accepted.

The nub of the problem facing British forces in 1945–6 in Java was that they were engaged simultaneously in three separate but overlapping operations. First, there was the task of ending the war against Japan, which entailed disarming, concentrating and eventually removing back to Japan several hundred thousand Japanese troops. Second, there was the task of locating and repatriating scores of thousands of Allied prisoners of war and civilian internees whose whereabouts were not known with any certainty. Third, in the absence of Dutch troops in substantial numbers, British forces had to reimpose control pending the arrival of the Dutch civil authorities. These would have been difficult enough in themselves, but the situation was immensely complicated by two developments: the emergence of a strong nationalist movement that established itself as a functioning government before the arrival of Allied forces, and the willingness of the Japanese, certainly at the local level, to defy the terms of the pre-surrender agreement by giving material assistance to the nationalists who were pledged to resist not only the return of the Dutch but any forces they regarded as acting as Dutch proxies.

Originally, planning in SEAC for the post-surrender period had been based on the assumption that Japanese forces would maintain law and order until the arrival of Allied troops, and that British forces would work closely with the Netherland Indies Civil Administration (NICA) to ensure a swift and smooth transition to full Dutch control. What no one had anticipated was the proclamation, on 17 August 1945, of the Republic of Indonesia by the veteran nationalist leaders, Sukarno and Mohammed Hatta. The Japanese in Java chose not to resist this development, even though the timing preceded their own preferred date, and turned over the bulk of their weapons to the nationalists then interned themselves in camps to await the arrival of Allied forces. The first Allied contact was made on 8 September, when a small party of Special Operations Executive/Force 136 personnel was parachuted into Batavia to make a preliminary assessment of the POW situation. Although his mission was strictly limited in scope, it is surprising that the group's leader, Major A. G. Greenhalgh, dismissed the growing power of the nationalists, because by the time he arrived in Batavia, nationalist forces effectively controlled most of the main towns and cities in Java and were thus able, if they chose, to hamper attempts to rescue POWs and internees, whose situation, Greenhalgh had emphasized, was precarious. Mountbatten's plans had called for a steady, measured occupation of Java, with the first British forces (26th Division) not scheduled to land on the island until early October, and then only if SEAC was assured that the Japanese were complying with the terms of the surrender and had taken steps to clear the sea approaches to Batavia of mines and if the designated division was not required for more urgent tasks elsewhere.

Even before Greenhalgh's report reached Mountbatten, the Supreme Commander had realized that the situation in the NEI into which SEAC forces were being inexorably drawn required more than a purely military response, since the third task given to him was to establish and maintain peaceful conditions preparatory to the reinstitution of Dutch rule. The Lieutenant-Governor of the NEI, Dr Hubertus van Mook, who was also head of the Civil Affairs Bureau, was determined that nothing should be done to imply any hint of recognition of the new republic, and requested Mountbatten to instruct the staff of Repatriation of Allied Prisoners of War and Internees (RAPWI) teams not to have any dealings with the nationalists. While he did not yet fully appreciate the degree of nationalist support, Mountbatten realized that on purely practical grounds there would have to be contact of some sort with the nationalists if the

POWs and internees were to be rescued. A much more realistic picture was provided to Mountbatten once British naval forces arrived at the port of Batavia on 15 September, and first-hand accounts of both the POW and internee situation and the extent of nationalist support were given by the recently liberated Lieutenant Colonel Laurens van der Post, whose comments on the strength of Republican sentiment were echoed by Major General Yamamoto Moichiro, Chief of Staff of the Japanese Military Government in Java.

Faced with the tension between the increasingly intransigent position of the Dutch, who insisted that Mountbatten abide by the strict letter of the inter-Allied agreement, and the emerging reality of the situation on the ground, Mountbatten decided to speed up the schedule for the insertion of Allied troops into Java. On 19 September General Sir William Slim, C-in-C, Allied Land Forces, South-East Asia, ordered a brigade group plus headquarters from 23rd Division to leave Malaya for Batavia by 1 October, with a second brigade group to follow shortly thereafter, bound for Surabaya in eastern Java, the other stronghold of Republican support. Lieutenant General Sir Philip Christison, who had distinguished himself with XV Indian Corps in the Arakan campaign, was appointed C-in-C, Allied Land Forces, NEI (ALFNEI, which subsequently became AFNEI when Christison's command was extended to include sea and air forces), with the promise that he would ultimately have at his disposal 23rd Division, less one brigade group, a brigade group from 26th Division in Sumatra pending the gradual build-up of the entire division, and another division to replace Australian forces that had taken control in Borneo.

Developments in Java, however, had moved ahead of this accelerated plan, and a day after Slim had ordered elements of 23rd Division to Batavia, he was forced to send in whatever troops were available as an emergency measure to forestall what appeared likely to be a complete breakdown of law and order in the city. As a result, on 29 September, 1st Seaforth Highlanders, accompanied by some 500 marines and other naval personnel, were landed in Batavia where they spent two days controlling outbreaks of arson, looting and rioting, with four demonstrators being killed. The day after the Seaforth Highlanders landed in Batavia, Christison arrived and gave a press conference. His remarks were subsequently the subject of much interpretation and accusation, but it seems clear that he stated his intention to hold talks with the nationalist leaders in order to gain their support in helping him carry out his main tasks of disarming and removing the Japanese and, in particular, in rescuing Allied POWs and internees. This was a sensible approach to a pressing practical problem, but in the overheated circumstances of the post-17 August republican declaration it caused a sensation. Certainly in Dutch eyes it seemed to imply a de facto recognition of the republic, and was therefore completely unacceptable.

The Dutch themselves, however, presented a confused and confusing picture of their position. Upon his arrival in Batavia on 15 September, the Deputy Governor of the NEI, Dr Charles van der Plas, had rebroadcast Queen Wilhelmina's speech, which had been welcomed by the nationalist leaders as a sign that the Dutch were prepared to arrive at some sort of political compromise with the newly declared republic. For the British, it meant that the nationalists undertook to cooperate in the fulfilment of the two main tasks allotted SEAC, repatriating the Japanese forces and locating and evacuating the POWs and internees. Furthermore, the nationalist leaders accepted that British forces were not acting as the vanguard for the reimposition of Dutch control, and they agreed to try to restrain the extremist elements in the nationalist camp who were threatening to use armed force against any Allied troops, British or Dutch. This promising development was completely scuppered by van Mook, who on his arrival in Batavia on 7 October repudiated van der Plas's broadcast and rejected any political concessions, least of all to the nationalist leaders whose authority over their own forces he doubted. Thereupon the nationalists pledged total resistance to the Dutch, and to the British, whom they now regarded as agents of the Dutch intention to restore Dutch authority in full. It was a tragic turn of events, and could have been avoided. Once van Mook's position became known it seemed inevitable that British forces would become embroiled in a violent struggle with nationalist forces.

Mountbatten had quickly become aware that the deteriorating situation presented him with a difficult choice, which he put before the Chiefs of Staff on 5 October. He argued that either he should be directed to limit his force deployment strictly to fulfilling the first two tasks originally allotted him (thereby inevitably drawing criticism from the Dutch that he had abandoned the third task of establishing law and order pending the return of Dutch forces), or he should be directed to accept responsibility for law and order in the entire NEI. Such a course would require a substantial increase in the requirement for British troops, which he detailed as one corps of two divisions and an armoured brigade, a naval lift for one brigade, four RAF fighter-bomber squadrons, a medium-range transport squadron, and a Dutch flying-boat squadron – this at the time when the British government was under intense domestic pressure to demobilize its wartime forces as quickly as possible. The only alternative – the use of Indian troops – seemed even less acceptable, with the Government of India and the C-in-C, India, Field Marshal Sir Claude Auchinleck, pressing Mountbatten to speed up the return of Indian forces to the subcontinent. On the other hand, the adoption of the first course threatened to sour post-war relations with the Netherlands (and with France, which had similar concerns over British actions in southern Indo-China) just when a united European front seemed increasingly important in the face of the emerging difficulties with the Soviet Union.

In the absence of a speedy response from the Chiefs of Staff, who had sought further information on the situation in Java, and who in the Defence Committee were coming under criticism from the Foreign Office for appearing to accept Mountbatten's assessment, which was thought to have conceded too much to the nationalist position, Mountbatten proceeded to build up his forces in Batavia. By the end of October, with the arrival of the remainder of the first brigade group, Headquarters of XV Corps and 23rd Division, and 904 Wing RAAF (two squadrons of Thunderbolts, one of Dakotas, and a detachment of Mosquitos), British forces were sufficiently strong to impose a measure of order on Batavia. Although the infantry battalions quickly gained control of the docks in Batavia and the areas within the city where evacuated POWs and internees were to be concentrated, nationalist forces established roadblocks in the outer areas, attacked trains carrying internees to the safety of Batavia, and took over control of several internee camps. Sporadic violence broke out across the western half of Java, and British forces were hard-pressed to control it.

It was in the eastern half of Java, however, that the most serious opposition was encountered. On 25 October Headquarters 49th Brigade (Brigadier A. W. S. Mallaby) arrived at Surabaya, and two Indian battalions (6/5th Mahrattas and 5/6th Rajputana Rifles) landed without immediate resistance. Taken by surprise, the local nationalist leaders insisted that no more troops were to be landed, and nationalist supporters proceeded to throw up barricades to impede the progress of the Indian troops through the city to take control of key points. Resistance was ineffective – a flight over the city of twelve Thunderbolts from Batavia had underscored British determination to brook no opposition – and by the end of the first day much of the city was patrolled by the troops of 49th Brigade, although the nationalist forces, backed by an increasingly threatening population, retained control of a key bridge, the electricity power station and the airfield. The following day Mallaby met the nationalist leaders and it was agreed that while the nationalists would seek to disarm the unruly mobs, their own forces would retain their weapons and would assist him in maintaining law and order so that POWs and internees could be safely evacuated. In an atmosphere of great tension and suspicion, with the nationalists remaining to be convinced that British forces were not using the POW and internee operation as a prelude to bringing in Dutch forces, it was a workable plan that seemed to allow the fulfilment of Mountbatten's main objectives at minimal cost.

It went tragically wrong when, without Mallaby's knowledge and in the absence of any understanding of the local conditions in Surabaya, let alone of the agreement reached there on the 26th, a Dakota from Batavia, under orders from Christison's headquarters, dropped thousands of leaflets over Surabaya as part of a campaign to assert British control that had begun in western Java in early October. It seems to have been entirely coincidental that the leaflets, which had been prepared with the general situation in Java in mind and before the extent of nationalist support had become clear, and certainly without any knowledge of the working agreement that Mallaby and his deputy (Colonel L. H. O. Pugh) had reached in Surabaya, were dropped within hours of the apparently successful talks. Inevitably, the leaflet's demands that all arms be surrendered to British forces on pain of death, and that British authority be acknowledged, brought charges of bad faith. The nationalist leaders who had reached an agreement with Pugh and Mallaby were replaced by less amenable Indonesians, and on 29 October attacks were mounted on the positions held by 49th Brigade and on convoys bringing internees to the safety of the British-held areas of Surabaya. An attempt by Sukarno, who was flown to Surabaya on Christison's orders, to broker a new truce failed, Mallaby's brigade major and a Force 136 representative were abducted (and subsequently tortured and murdered) when they tried to reopen talks with the nationalists, and on the evening of 30 October Mallaby himself was killed by gunfire when, accompanied by moderate nationalist leaders, he tried to calm the crowds.[1]

The situation rapidly reached crisis point. The small British force – about 1,500 troops – was now faced by a mob of 100,000, well armed with weapons handed over by the Japanese and backed by armoured cars and light tanks. Originally dispersed throughout the city, 49th Brigade was withdrawn from its exposed positions and concentrated around the vital dock area, the airfield (which had been occupied by British troops as part of the ultimately abortive settlement negotiated by Sukarno) and the main (known) internment camps. On 31 October Christison warned that unless attacks on British forces stopped, the full military weight of Allied power would be deployed against the nationalists, and this warning was given substance by the arrival of 5th Indian Division (Major General E. C. Mansergh) off Surabaya on 1 November, having been ordered there on 17 October; by 9 November the division was fully landed. The critical situation that had developed in Surabaya, together with deteriorating conditions in central Java around Semarang, required Mountbatten to find additional troops from somewhere, and there was a feeling in London that Auchinleck had exaggerated the possibility of disaffection if Indian troops were retained in the NEI, while there was an unspoken commitment to maintaining the pace of the repatriation of British forces.

The fact was that, in Mountbatten's mind at least, it was preferable to use – and possibly lose – Indian rather than British troops: 'he did not want British troops widowed [sic] at this time so long after the war', to which Christison's representative at the meeting where Mountbatten made this remark, Lieutenant Colonel W. Ridley, courageously replied: 'Sir, do you really think it is different if Mrs Poop Singh is made a widow?'[2]

When there was no satisfactory answer to the British ultimatum by the evening of the 9th, the order was given to begin the forcible occupation of the city early the following morning. In the sector to the west of the canal which broadly divided the city into two, 49th Brigade (less one battalion), supported by elements of 11th Cavalry, was charged with clearing the area south of the docks and airfield, while to the east of the canal, 123rd Brigade, supported by B Squadron 11th Cavalry (less one troop) was gradually to reoccupy the rest of the city, with 9th Brigade detailed to hold the perimeter east of the canal. In the face of fierce resistance from nationalist forces, progress was slow and costly, and Mansergh felt obliged to call in naval and air support in addition to the artillery of 3rd Field Regiment. On 10 November bombing attacks by aircraft (a composite flight of eight Thunderbolts and two Mosquitos were called in from Batavia, although more aircraft were available if required) and naval artillery fire from the three destroyers anchored off Surabaya commenced, and continued for several days. Air attacks caused considerable damage to public buildings in the city, but utterly failed to daunt the nationalists, who charged British tanks with rifles, knives and, in some cases, bare hands. Concerned by the worldwide adverse publicity, which was completely disproportionate to any advantage on the ground that the British had gained, Mountbatten directed that henceforth air strikes be used on a very restricted basis. One-third of the city had been occupied by the end of the first day's fighting, but resistance continued for many weeks, and it was not until late December, and only after protracted street-by-street fighting, that, in the words of the official British historian, 'comparative peace ... descended on Surabaya'.[3] Estimates of Indonesian losses vary considerably, from the AFNEI report of about 2,500 to a historian's figure of 15,000.[4] Whatever the final cost, nationalist supporters regarded the outcome as a huge victory for their cause (and still celebrate it more than fifty years later). Although British and Indian casualties were very much lower, the operation was costly in that it might have been avoided had Mallaby been better briefed on the situation in Surabaya and had there been better coordination between Mallaby and HQ AFNEI. This is not to apportion blame, but to underline the fact that so many of the difficulties that British forces faced in Java arose, as much as anything, from a lack of good intelligence and from the failure, especially at higher military and political levels, to appreciate the complexities of the situation and to respond rapidly to the shifting circumstances in which British forces had to operate.

The second area of concern to British forces was Semarang, on the central north coast of Java. Semarang was an important point for the concentration of POWs and internees from the interior of the island, and there were increasing signs that the nationalists intended to use control of transit routes in their campaign to assert political independence. Fears that extremist elements in the nationalist camp were about to seize control led to the despatch from Batavia of 3/10th Gurkhas, the third battalion of 37th Brigade, to Semarang, where they landed early in the morning of 10 October. The situation that developed was a curious comment on the tangled circumstances that confronted British forces in Java. Following the Japanese surrender, the Japanese Kido Battalion in the vicinity of Semarang had handed over its weapons to nationalist elements, who promptly placed most of the battalion in the local jail. Over time a number of Japanese soldiers were removed by the nationalists, tortured and killed. This eventually provoked the rest of the battalion into storming their captors, even though they had only sticks and their bare hands to use in their attack. They overpowered the nationalists, and proceeded to establish Japanese control over most of the town, this action occurring on the very day that 3/10th Gurkhas landed. Working from opposite ends of Surabaya, the Gurkhas and the Japanese ran into each other and briefly exchanged fire until both sides realized that they were in fact clearing out a common enemy. Thereafter the Kido Battalion operated under British command and was included on 49th Brigade's order of battle.

Although British troops assisted by the Kido Battalion (which was subsequently described as having done 'sterling work'[5]) managed with great difficulty and at the cost of some casualties to keep the road from Magelang (central Java) open for the purpose of concentrating POWs and internees in Semarang, they were unable to prevent nationalist forces committing atrocities against isolated pockets of internees who had not yet reached the comparative safety of the British perimeter in Semarang. News of the nationalist resistance to British forces in Surabaya spurred the nationalists around Semarang into more vigorous attacks on British forces from 23 November, which were only repulsed by gunfire from the British naval ships anchored off the city. Four days later, 49th Brigade less one battalion deplaned from Surabaya and moved out south of the city to cover the withdrawal to Surabaya of 3/10th Gurkhas and the internees they were protecting. Systematic sweeps of the surrounding countryside were carried out, and 49th Brigade again relied on naval guns to silence nationalist artillery and mortars. 49th Brigade was relieved by 5th Parachute Brigade, which was deployed to Semarang on 11–14 January 1946, following its successes in systematically clearing the kampongs around Batavia, and 49th Brigade returned to Batavia. Over the next several weeks the Paras encountered little resistance, with the result that in late February AFNEI was able to advise SEAC that Dutch forces would shortly be able to relieve the British garrison.

It must be said that while British forces had undoubtedly gained the upper hand in direct military contact with nationalist forces, they also benefited from considerable cooperation from moderate nationalist elements in moving internees to Surabaya, a policy initiated in December by Christison, with Mountbatten's support, which infuriated the Dutch, who complained that while the British were willing to deal with nationalist military forces they seemed simultaneously to be doing everything in their power to hamper the re-entry of Dutch troops to the NEI. To some extent this was true, and on one level there was a considerable element of inconsistency in the British approach, but Mountbatten's overriding concern was always the pragmatic one of rescuing POWs and internees. If that entailed inconsistency, so be it.

The nationalist stand against British and Indian troops in Surabaya boosted nationalist resistance to and attacks on Allied troops in the western end of Java, especially on routes leading to Batavia, the main evacuation point in that part of the island. Sporadic shooting broke out in the suburbs of Batavia, and while there was a demonstrable failure on the part of the Indonesian police to control the situation, Christison felt that Dutch Ambonese troops had contributed to the overheated atmosphere by their 'trigger happy' approach. (Native troops from Ambon were largely Christian, and were customarily awarded extra pay for 'foreign service' in Java and Sumatra. They remained loyal to the Dutch after the Dutch surrender to the Japanese, and were therefore imprisoned along with Dutch troops, while other native troops were disarmed and then allowed to go free. In the post-Japanese surrender situation that developed in Java, the use of Ambonese troops – in the absence of Dutch forces – was bound to cause trouble.) At Christison's insistence, they were withdrawn, and replaced in January 1946 by a Dutch battalion that arrived from training in Malaya. It subsequently transpired that the Dutch troops were hardly more capable of restraint than the troops they had replaced, but by then Mountbatten's options, if he was to stick to his policy of gradually withdrawing British and Indian forces, were rapidly disappearing.

The scattered outbreaks of violence that had begun in early November took on a more threatening note on the 9th, when a force of 500 Indonesians attacked an internee camp; they were repulsed and lost ten of their number, but again there were signs that the police had virtually sided with the nationalists. The most serious incident occurred on

24 November, when a search party looking for the known survivors of a Dakota crash was attacked by a known extremist group, the 'Black Buffaloes', and tortured and killed along with the crash survivors. Pursued by British troops, about sixty of the extremists fled to the small town of Bekasi where all were killed in a firefight. Christison thereupon ordered the burning of the huts on the outskirts of the town, not, as he explained to Mountbatten, as a deterrent but as an 'operational necessity'. While Mountbatten duly accepted that Christison's action had not been in retaliation against the murder of the air crew and search party, he was concerned at the adverse publicity this action had caused, and strengthened his earlier restrictions on the use of air strikes, adding that due warning had to be given before any building that was being used by snipers could be destroyed.

Attacks on military positions, and on convoys of surrendered Japanese and internees, continued in the area around Bandung throughout November. As a result of the situation in Surabaya, a new group of Indonesians had emerged, the so-called IFTUs, or Inhabitants Friendly To Us, i.e. local people who either by conviction or from terror at the tactics of the nationalists preferred to throw their lot in with the Dutch cause. By the end of November the number of IFTUs seeking Allied protection had swelled to scores of thousands (in early December Mountbatten estimated 147,000 in Surabaya alone), in turn presenting a further tempting target for nationalist attacks. Mosquito bombers were used at the beginning of December to support 37th Brigade Gurkha troops in escorting internees and IFTUs from Bandung to Batavia, but even though the attacks by nationalist forces were repelled, it was not without cost, the Gurkhas losing thirteen killed and wounded. A week later, on 8 December, a large convoy heading to Bandung and escorted by armoured cars was ambushed by a nationalist force. In the ensuing hand-to-hand fighting the three companies of 5/9th Jats lost twenty-five killed and forty-two wounded.

Continuing nationalist attempts to cut communications between Batavia and outlying towns were largely frustrated by a firm British response, at times backed by Stuart tanks from 13th Lancers, but casualties mounted, so that by early December British and Indian forces had lost more than 1,000 killed and wounded. Such losses could not be sustained, not least for political reasons both in the United Kingdom and in India, and pressure grew for a political solution to be found, if only to enable

British and Indian forces to be withdrawn having evacuated Allied POWs and internees. The relative calm of January and February 1946, with the encouraging instance of republican forces escorting a convoy to Batavia suggesting that the worst was over, was shattered in March when another convoy took five days to cover the hundred miles from Buitenzorg to Batavia. Under constant fire from snipers and some mortars, it only reached its destination with the aid of medium tanks from 'A' Squadron 13th Lancers, light tanks of 11th Cavalry, a troop of 25-pounders, a motorized infantry company of Bombay Grenadiers, and troops from four infantry battalions; casualties were seventeen killed and eighty-eight wounded. 36th Brigade was ordered to leave Batavia and establish itself just west of Bandung, to protect the Bandung–Batavia route.

To Mountbatten and Lieutenant General Sir Montagu Stopford (who on 1 February 1946 had succeeded Christison in command of AFNEI, the latter returning to the United Kingdom to become C-in-C, Northern Command) it became ever more essential to find a way of disengaging British and Indian troops from the deteriorating situation. This seemed to become a more realistic possibility with the arrival on 9 March of the first Dutch troops. Mountbatten proposed that with the gradual build-up of Dutch strength in Java it would become practicable to withdraw British and Indian forces: 5th Division from Surabaya in the second week of April, 5th Parachute Brigade from Semarang in the third week of April, and 36th Brigade and 161st Brigade in mid-April. By then he could claim that his two primary tasks had been largely achieved, and that Dutch forces could deal with the political–military situation that had developed, although Headquarters XV Corps and 23rd Division would remain in west Java until the autumn pending the arrival of a Dutch division.

These proposals were eventually accepted by the Chiefs of Staff, but not without objections from the Dutch, who argued that by insisting on what they regarded as a premature withdrawal the British were failing to fulfil their third mission, that of maintaining law and order until the Dutch were in a position to assume control. It was an argument that held less and less sway in British military and political circles, not least because of what seemed to be the intransigent opposition of the Dutch to dealing with the situation that existed. Having pushed for months for the deployment of Dutch troops in Java, the Dutch were now hardly in a position to complain when the British saw the arrival of those troops as the justification for the withdrawal of their own forces. Mountbatten's schedule was therefore accepted, and by May 1946 British and Indian forces had left eastern and central Java. Mountbatten left SEAC on 31 May to attend the Victory Parade in London, and relinquished his command on 1 June.

In western Java, where 23rd Division remained after the withdrawal of British and Indian forces from central and eastern Java in April and May, there were further outbreaks of violence as the number of Dutch troops increased and as both the nationalists and the Dutch sought to assert their control. There were also attacks on Surabaya and Semarang in June, thus reinforcing Dutch criticism of the timing of the British departure, but nothing was allowed to impede the final British withdrawal, which was accomplished on 29 November when Rear Headquarters XV Corps left Batavia. On the following day South East Asia Command was abolished.

*

The situation that confronted British and Indian forces in Sumatra was similar to that which they encountered in Java, though generally on a lesser scale. Elements of 26th Indian Division (Major General H. M. Chambers) left Madras on 4 October 1945, splitting en route and arriving on 10 October at Medan on the north-east coast and Padang on the south-west coast. HQ Allied Forces Sumatra was established at Padang two days later. From the beginning, in marked contrast to Java, where many Japanese troops had flagrantly disobeyed the terms of the surrender and handed over their weapons to nationalists, the Japanese forces in Sumatra (the 25th Army) largely cooperated, and in addition to assisting with the recovery of POWs and internees, helped maintain the security of the oil fields and law and order in the main centres. Support for the nationalist cause was clearly evident in the local population, but following a second lift of troops at the end of October it was matched by a growing strength of British and Indian forces, infantry (1st Lincolnshire Regiment, 6th South Wales Borderers, and a number of Indian battalions), artillery (7th Indian Field Artillery Regiment and Headquarters Royal Artillery 26th Division), and armoured cars ('A' Squadron 146th Regiment RAC) and machine guns (12th Frontier Force Machine Gun Battalion).

Although in the first two months of the Allied presence there were outbreaks of violence between nationalist supporters and those they perceived to be opponents, British and Indian forces were not involved, and Mountbatten thought it was possible to draw troops from Sumatra to bolster the deteriorating situation in Java. That seemed slightly premature when the brigade major of 71st Brigade and his accompanying female Red Cross worker were kidnapped: both were murdered. Indian reinforcements were rushed to the area, arrests were made and a strict curfew imposed. There were no more incidents until February, by which time the first Dutch troops had landed on Bangka Island, off the south-east coast of Sumatra. This was regarded by the nationalists as provoca-tive and threatening, and as a sign that British forces were the vanguard of a full-scale Dutch re-entry. On 25 February 1946, three British naval officers who had been visiting the moderate nationalist leader in the town of Pelambang were ambushed, one being killed on the spot and another subsequently murdered. Thereafter attacks on Allied forces became more common. On 30 March a company of 1st Lincolns, who with Headquarters 71st Brigade had been moved to Pelambang following the attack on the naval officers, used mortar support to rescue a sixteen-man patrol from the regiment that had been attacked and charged by nationalist followers. The Lincolns suffered thirteen casualties, including two killed; the nationalists sustained over one hundred casualties.

Nationalist strength steadily increased, but Allied forces never encoun-tered the level of sustained resistance that was found in Java. In mid-June General Stopford advised the Chiefs of Staff that if the planned evacuation of Japanese troops went ahead, an additional eight battalions would be needed to maintain control in Sumatra. Given the situation in Java, and the increasingly strong opposition of the Indian government to the retention of Indian forces in the NEI, this requirement could only be met through the use of Dutch troops. Although they were regarded by the British command as aggressive and unnecessarily provocative, there was no alternative to the build-up of Dutch forces if the British and Indian withdrawal was to proceed, especially once Allied POWs and internees had been rescued and the overwhelming bulk of Japanese troops repatriated. Dutch forces therefore began landing at the port of Medan on 26 October and encountered strong resistance until a truce was brokered on 4 November. British and Indian troops were swift to respond to attempts to cut vital roads, and the Dutch build-up continued largely unhampered by the nationalists.

British and Indian forces were withdrawn from Pelambang on 9 November, from Medan on 26 November, and from Padang on 28 November. In the course of the deployment in Sumatra, where over 13,000 POWs and internees were evacuated and over 68,000 Japanese repatriated, 26th Division lost five officers and fifty other ranks killed and five missing, with a further 253 non-fatal casualties. By comparison with Java, these were relatively light losses, but they demonstrated again the costs of bringing the war against Japan to an end.

*

British involvement in the NEI following the Japanese surrender was both unexpected and unwelcome. Plans for the gradual reoccupation of Allied colonial possessions were thrown into disarray by the suddenness of the surrender, and by the emergence of strong nationalist movements whose political agendas were completely at odds with those of the returning colonial powers. The complexity of the situation that British forces encountered was unprecedented in the experience of the British army. Ending the war in the sense of returning to peace turned out to be a far more difficult process than anyone had anticipated. The task of evacuating POWs and internees was daunting enough, but willingly undertaken for humanitarian purposes. Beyond that, however, the picture was much less clear. British forces were hardly inexperienced in dealing with politically charged situations, but what distinguished the campaign in Java was the fact that the military campaign was undertaken not in British territory but in the colonial empire of another power. Wartime sympathy for the Dutch became increasingly strained as the Dutch refused to acknowledge, let alone negotiate with, the new Indonesian Republic, and insisted that British and Indian troops suppress the nationalist forces. Once Indonesian attacks on POW and internee camps and convoys began, British and Indian forces were inevitably drawn into the military (and political) conflict between the Dutch and the nationalists. In carrying out their primary tasks they suffered some 2,136 casualties. Most of those were sustained in the course of protecting POWs and internees and as such were an unavoidable part of the process of ending the war against Japan, but they were also a bitter price to pay for being dragged into a war between a colonial regime and an emerging nationalist movement. In retrospect it can be said that the commanders on the spot, and the troops they led, came to a better understanding of the realities of the situation more quickly than their masters – political or military – in London. The circumstances that prevailed in November 1946, circumstances that helped pave the way for the November Agreement between the Dutch government and the nationalist leaders which gave de facto recognition to the Republic of Indonesia, had been created in part by the efforts of British and Indian forces. In the turmoil of the immediate post-war period in South-East Asia, that was no mean achievement.[6]

2

TREVOR ROYLE

Palestine, 1945–1948:
A No-Win Situation

Trevor Royle's most recent publications are *Crimea: The Great Crimean War 1854–1856* (Little, Brown) and *Orde Wingate: Irregular Soldier* (Weidenfeld and Nicolson), a biography of the controversial Chindit leader. As a journalist he is Associate Editor of the *Sunday Herald* and is a regular commentator on defence matters and international affairs for the BBC. He is a Fellow of the Royal Society of Edinburgh and was until recently a Visiting Fellow at the Institute for Advanced Studies in the Humanities in the University of Edinburgh.

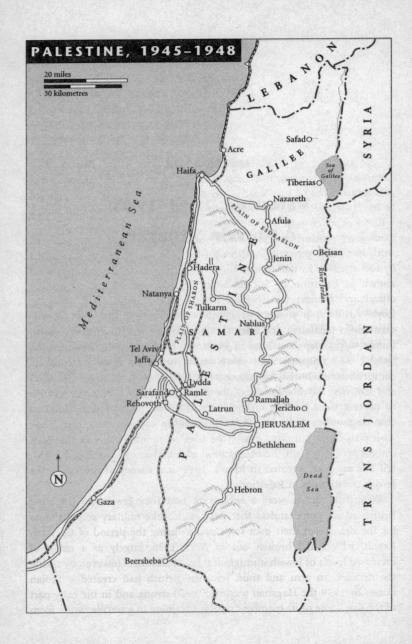

PALESTINE, 1945–1948

20 miles
30 kilometres

LEBANON

SYRIA

GALILEE

Safad

Acre

Haifa

Sea of Galilee

Tiberias

Nazareth

PLAIN OF ESDRAELON

Afula

Beisan

Jenin

Mediterranean Sea

Hadera

River Jordan

Natanya

PLAIN OF SHARON

Tulkarm

Nablus

S A M A R I A

Tel Aviv

Jaffa

P A L E S T I N E

Lydda

Sarafand

Ramle

Rehovoth

Latrun

Ramallah

Jericho

JERUSALEM

Bethlehem

T R A N S   J O R D A N

N

Hebron

Dead Sea

Gaza

Beersheba

In the summer of 1938 Sir Harold MacMichael, the British High Commissioner to Palestine, sent a despatch to London advising the government that he had 'sanctioned the employment of a small column of Jewish and British troops operating under the command of a British officer in Galilee both to afford better protection to the [Iraq Petroleum Company] pipeline and also when the occasion demands for ambush work in Galilee generally'.[1] Although the columns were not mentioned by name, either in that despatch or in others which followed, they were known in Palestine as 'Special Night Squads' and their commanding officer and founder was Captain (later Major General) Orde Wingate, Royal Artillery, a young intelligence officer with British army headquarters in Jerusalem and later the founder of the Chindit force which fought behind Japanese lines in Burma in 1943 and 1944. Basically, the Special Night Squads were small units (originally three in number) comprising ten Jewish volunteers, ten British soldiers, a British NCO and a British subaltern, which operated from Jewish settlements, both to protect them from raids by Arab guerrillas and to guard lines of communication. Each squad had a training capacity to create more all-Jewish units but what made the idea so radical was that they had come into being with the cooperation of the Haganah, an illegal Jewish self-defence force created in March 1921 as a means of defending the Jewish community in Palestine.

Wingate's squads were a success in that they proved to doubting British senior commanders that Jews could take military responsibility for the defence of their own settlements during the period of the Arab Revolt, which had broken out in April 1936, largely as a result of increased levels of Jewish immigration into Palestine. However, by taking the decision to arm and train Jews the British had created a Trojan horse. By 1939 the Haganah was over 2,000 strong and in the early part of the war some of its members received training in guerrilla tactics from the Special Operations Executive (SOE), which had been established to promote subversive warfare in enemy territory.

During the Second World War the Jews supported the British war effort by providing a full-time commando force, the Palmach, to fight alongside Allied forces in Syria in 1941 and by creating a Jewish Brigade Group for service in Italy, but that assistance turned into armed opposition in 1945 when Palestine became the focus of a new revolt against British rule. By then the Haganah had spawned two breakaway terrorist units, both of which excelled in guerrilla warfare, the Irgun Zvai Leumi and the Loerut Yisra'el, better known as the Lehi or the Stern Gang. One of Wingate's subalterns in the Special Night Squads was Lieutenant (later Major-General) H. E. N. 'Bala' Bredin and when he returned to Palestine in 1946 with the 6th Airborne Division he was not surprised to find that the terrorists attacking the security forces were 'by and large Jews whom we had trained'.[2]

That Britain should have been involved in Palestine was due to a remarkable blend of imperial realpolitik and historical romanticism. After the First World War Britain had undertaken to rule Palestine through the mandate of the League of Nations, a form of trust by which the country was administered under the supervision of a Permanent Mandates Commission. Under its terms Britain had also included the Balfour Declaration of 1917, a wartime pledge of support for the creation of a Jewish homeland in Palestine. The region contained 600,000 Arabs as opposed to 56,000 Jewish settlers who had been there since biblical times; any post-war immigration would alter the ratio to the disadvantage of the Arabs but at the time Britain's wartime government believed that the empire would benefit economically and strategically from the creation of a Jewish Palestine.

In 1922, aware of mounting Arab resistance to the declaration and the growing importance of the region's oil supplies, Britain distanced itself from its wartime policy by laying down economic guidelines for immigration and excluding neighbouring Transjordan, an importantally, from the areas available for resettlement. As tensions mounted between the rival populations in the 1930s, and spurred on by the events of the Arab Revolt, the British produced two Royal Commissions to investigate the causes of the unrest and to recommend a workable settlement for the Jewish and Arab populations. The first, led by Lord Peel in 1937, was rejected by the Arabs and accepted reluctantly by the Jewish Agency, the Jewish population's governing body. The second, led by Sir John Woodhead in the following year, took evidence to implement the Peel plan but it also failed to reach any workable conclusions. Although the British had initiated the partition proposals they could not afford to offend Arab opinion and on 17 May 1939 a White Paper was published which effectively annulled the Balfour Declaration, restricting immigration to 15,000 a year for the coming five years after which Palestine would be granted independence with national institutions reflecting the permanent Arab majority and Jewish minority.

The onset of the war and the need to defeat Hitler's Germany meant that the Palestine problem was shelved temporarily, but it did not cool passions. 'We will fight with the British against Hitler as if there was no white paper,' said David Ben-Gurion, Chairman of the Jewish Agency. 'We will fight the white paper as if there were no war.' As a result the Haganah was strengthened and it began to adopt the offensive ethos embedded in the philosophy of Ze'ev Jabotinsky, the founder of Revisionist Zionism, who believed that if a Jewish state were created in Palestine confrontation with the Arabs would be inevitable and that the Jews would be forced to fight for, and then defend, their homeland 'behind an iron wall which they [the Arabs] will be powerless to break down.'[3]

The change of direction was not long in coming. In 1940 Abraham Stern broke away from the Irgun to form his eponymous gang, which started attacking and killing British police and military personnel as well as Jewish moderates. By 1943 they had killed eight Jews, six Arabs and eleven British policemen and although Stern had been killed in a shootout in 1942 his successor, David Friedman-Yellin, announced that he was committed to continuing a policy of 'unrestricted and indiscriminate terror'. The first serious blow came in November 1944 when two members of the Stern Gang assassinated Lord Moyne, the British Minister of State in Cairo, thereby setting in train the cycle of terrorist attack followed by reprisal which dominated the immediate post-war period. There was another pointer: the two murderers who were hanged both admitted to being influenced by Michael Collins, one of the founding fathers of the Irish Republican Army whose hit-and-run tactics in 1919 had created a reign of terror which made Ireland all but ungovernable. At the same time ammunition and weapons were being stockpiled for all three groups in the struggle which would break the wartime truce between the Jews and the British. It was known as 'the movement of the Hebrew revolt'.

On the Arab side preparations were also being taken. Forces loyal to Haj Amin el Husseini, the Mufti of Jerusalem and the leader of the Palestinian Arabs, were led by his cousin Abdul Khader el Husseini, a capable soldier, and an Arab Liberation Army commanded by Fawzi al Kaukji was formed at Qatanah near Damascus. All received military support and funds from the countries of the Arab League – Egypt, Iraq, Saudi Arabia, Transjordan, Yemen, Syria and Lebanon – which was formed in Cairo in March 1945 to promote pan-Arab unity. Although the British commander of Transjordan's Arab Legion, Brigadier (later Lieutenant General Sir) John Bagot Glubb, advised the British War Office in 1945 that the Mufti's force was 'a gang . . . unpaid and therefore relied on scavenging and pillaging' while the Arab Liberation Army was only 'semi-disciplined', they proved that they could give a good account of themselves in the first fighting of the revolt, characterized by Chaim Herzog, a Haganah staff officer, as 'a series of city riots, bloody urban encounters, hit-and-run operations that left scores of dead, maimed and wounded civilians on both sides.'[4]

Standing between the two sides were the 20,000 men of the Palestinian police force backed by 80,000 soldiers of the British army's 1st Division, 6th Airborne Division and (from March 1947, when it was deployed in southern Palestine) 3rd Division. It was a deployment which Britain was hard pressed to make and throughout the period the military units involved in internal security duties were severely overstretched. There was, though, a sizeable Royal Air Force presence with five squadrons of Halifax, Lancaster and Warwick maritime aircraft flying anti-immigrant patrols over the sea area between Cyprus and Egypt. Other units, equipped with Hurricanes, Spitfires and Mustangs, flew in support of the anti-terrorist operations from Ramat David near Haifa, Petach Tiqva and Ein Shemer. Ships of the Royal Navy operated patrols off the coast of Palestine to prevent illegal immigration, a difficult and dangerous task: 'The brunt fell on the destroyers whose boarding parties were issued with cricketer's boxes as an essential item of equipment – hat-pins being a weapon of choice for the oppositions.'[5] During the period forty-nine illegal immigrant vessels were seized and some 66,000 people detained.

Despite the strain on successive post-war defence budgets, the Chiefs of Staff argued that there was a strategic imperative for Britain's presence in Palestine. It housed the British army's strategic reserve for the Middle East: together with the naval base at Haifa and the air force bases these assets were regarded as being essential for maintaining Britain's presence and prestige in the region and for protecting the country's all-important oil supplies. For the British Foreign Secretary, Ernest Bevin, it was vital to find a solution in Palestine not just to harmonize relations between Jew and Arab without upsetting the neighbouring Arab states but also to underpin the country's position in the post-war world. As he told the Cabinet's Defence Committee in March 1946 the reasons for staying in the region were economic and political: to protect oil supplies and to counter the threat from the Soviet Union.

> The Mediterranean is the area through which we bring influence to bear in Southern Europe, the soft underbelly of France, Italy, Yugoslavia, Greece and Turkey. Without our physical presence in the Mediterranean, we should cut little ice with these states which would fall, like Eastern Europe, under the totalitarian yoke.[6]

Although Bevin faced opposition from some of his Cabinet colleagues, including the Prime Minister, Clement Attlee, who was inclined to reduce Britain's international commitments, his argument prevailed. He also claimed that he would stake his career on negotiating a settlement in Palestine but he went about it in a curious way, often alienating the United States which had its own strategic interests in the Middle East. American Jews formed an influential sector of the electorate and one of President Truman's first pronouncements on the problem was to demand the admission into Palestine of 100,000 Jewish immigrants, whereas Britain wanted to limit Jewish immigration to a ceiling of 1,500 a month on the lines of the 1939 White Paper. The revelation of the Holocaust also gave a moral impetus to the idea that Palestine should provide a home for the European Jews displaced by the war. In an attempt to resolve the situation an Anglo-American Commission was formed in November 1945 but the following year it upheld Truman's figure, adding the hope that neither side should dominate the other.

It was, in fact, already too late. On 31 October 1945 the Jewish revolt had begun with all three underground groups in action and the following day Haganah's free radio station Kol Israel (Voice of Israel) revealed the extent of the damage: 'Palmach troops sank three small naval craft and wrecked railway lines in fifty different places; Irgun attacked the railway station at Lydda, and the Sternists attacked the Haifa oil refinery. The attacks were accomplished with great skill and little loss of life, probably none intentionally.' There was further trouble a fortnight later after Bevin announced that Britain would maintain its levels of immigration; rioting broke out all over the country, a number of government buildings were damaged and scores of security personnel were injured.

Early the following year (1946), the new British High Commissioner, General Sir Alan Cunningham, passed emergency laws which made death the maximum penalty, not just for taking part in terrorism but also for belonging to a terrorist group. However, even those extreme measures could not prevent further trouble as the Irgun started targeting British military bases. On 28 January, ten men dressed in British uniforms broke into RAF Agadir and stole 600 Sten guns; then on 20 February another group attacked the radar station on Mount Carmel which was used for coordinating sea–air operations and succeeded in making it unserviceable. Five days later, the RAF suffered its biggest losses on the ground since the German offensive in the Ardennes a - year earlier when the Irgun attacked three bases and destroyed eleven Halifaxes, seven Spitfires, two Ansons and three light aircraft. In his subsequent report, the Air Officer Commanding Palestine, Air Commodore H. D. Macgregor, pointed out that the terrorists had been successful because they were using techniques in which they had been trained by the wartime SOE.

The level of personal violence also escalated. On 25 April seven soldiers of the 6th Airborne Division were murdered in Tel Aviv and their weapons stolen. Two months later there was the first of several kidnappings when five British officers were captured at gunpoint in the officers' club at the Hotel Yarkon in Tel Aviv on 18 June and taken hostage for two Jews facing execution. They were released unharmed a few days later after the sentences had been commuted. Throughout the month there was a succession of successful attacks on coastguard stations as part of the campaign to hinder the Royal Navy's operations against illegal immigrant ships. Roads and bridges also became targets – at one point Palestine was entirely cut off from its neighbours – and the security forces seemed unable to counter the attacks.

When the British did react, on 29 June, the results were inconclusive. In an attempt to halt the violence Cunningham agreed to a plan, Operation AGATHA, which would break the power of the Haganah by arresting its leading personalities, while police and troops would simultaneously raid forty-nine Jewish towns and settlements suspected of sheltering terrorists and housing arms dumps. During the operation the headquarters of the Jewish Agency was sealed off and 2,718 Jewish leaders were detained, including Israel Gazili and Itzhak Sadeh, both senior Haganah commanders, but many of the most important names managed to avoid arrest – Ben-Gurion, by then the Jewish Agency's guiding force, was in Paris. Unfortunately for the British the plans had been revealed to the Haganah and the operation went off at half-cock. Despite strict security some of the planning documents had been leaked and a fortnight before the arrests the Kol Israel radio station had broadcast a warning which ended on a note of defiance: 'The document is now public property. Let the Yishuv [the Jewish community of Palestine], the Diaspora and the whole world know what Bevin, Attlee and their henchmen are preparing for us, and let the world know that we will fight.'

Breaches in security also meant that the raids on the settlements failed to meet their objectives. Most had received advance warning and when the police and troops arrived to begin their searches they usually found 'men and women lying on the ground with legs and arms locked, and refusing to move'. The scenes which followed next did nothing for Britain's reputation, smacking as they did of recent events in Nazi-occupied Europe: soldiers forcibly removing protesters, ring-leaders being arrested and barricades being broken down. In some instances, such as the search of the settlement at Meshek Yagur, Lieutenant General Sir Evelyn Barker, GOC Palestine and Transjordan, reported that his troops were forced to use sterner measures.

> The Cheshires who carried out the roundup of the people at this settlement had the devil of a time with women trying to hold on to the men to prevent them being taken away and refusing to obey orders. After collecting them all into the main dining hall they had to use tear gas in order to get them out again on to the vehicles. The heavy oil projectors were very useful also in this.[7]

Tear gas, oil jets and forcible removal: their use was not the best advertisement for the British army, especially in the United States, where public opinion had swung against Britain. Predictably, too, the tactics led to allegations of brutality and accusations that the soldiers used the operations to loot property from the settlements. In an attempt to be even-handed the army responded by instituting its own body searches of all personnel involved in the operations but the charges still stuck. To add to the frustration, the operations did not yield much in terms of arrests of suspected terrorists or finds of arms caches. Ieshek Yagur was an exception – 325 rifles, 94 2in mortars and nearly half a million rounds of ammunition were uncovered – but otherwise Operation AGATHA failed to achieve the Cabinet's orders of 20 June 'to break up illegal organisations'.

It also added to the sense of grievance felt by many Jews and as happens so often in a struggle between security forces and resistance movements action was followed by reprisal. During the search of the Jewish Agency offices the police took away its papers and files, some of which proved that the Haganah had been involved in previous terrorist operations. Partly to try to destroy those documents and partly to maintain the impetus, Haganah commanders sanctioned an attack by Irgun on the King David Hotel in Jerusalem, the building housing the Secretariat of the Government of Palestine and the Headquarters of the British Forces in Palestine and Transjordan.

On the morning of 22 July, a group of fifteen to twenty Irgun terrorists dressed as Arab workmen entered the hotel and placed several milk churns, each filled with 225kg of explosives, in the basement of the wing of the hotel occupied by the Secretariat. A British army officer, Captain A. D. Mackintosh, and a policeman became suspicious; when they approached the men there was a brief gun battle but the presence of the bombs remained undetected. Twenty minutes later the bombs went off, blowing up and destroying the entire wing. Although sappers of the Royal Engineers worked late into the night and for the next three days they found few survivors. The death toll was ninety-one and another forty-one were badly injured; fifteen of the casualties were Jewish secretaries working for the administration.

The atrocity caused widespread revulsion not just in the British camp but also in the Jewish community. It was condemned by the Jewish Agency and the Haganah broke off its links with Irgun. Afterwards it was found that a warning had been given but it had been ignored and no steps had been taken to evacuate the hotel. Even so, the Jewish political leadership was badly shaken and it cooperated with the police force's CID to provide information about suspects. In the 'cordon and search' operations which followed in Tel Aviv (thought to house Irgun's headquarters) five major arms dumps were discovered, but the lasting effect of the incident was the permanent souring of relations between the British and the Jews.

It also led to increased local support for the Irgun and the Stern Gang, which remained covert organizations, anonymous, invisible and seemingly able to strike at will. The police knew the names of the leaders but whenever they had a lead or had built up sufficient evidence for an arrest the people concerned were spirited away. By then the Haganah had around 40,000 members in the towns and settlements and they acted as an underground militia, a resistance movement which proved difficult to defeat by conventional military means. They also provided useful intelligence. For example, at 120 Maintenance Unit, Ras-el-in, the RAF employed Jewish secretaries and Arab labourers, making it difficult to keep all information secure. Many soldiers and airmen had Jewish girlfriends, some of whom were in the Haganah or were Haganah sympathizers: as one senior officer put it, 'every civilian was a potential danger'.

Inevitably, fighting an unseen enemy had a demoralizing effect on the members of the British security forces. They were able to disrupt terrorist activities and in some cases forestall them, as they did during Operation ELEPHANT in March 1947, when martial law was declared for three weeks in Tel Aviv, Petach Tikva and Ramat Gan, but the successes were overshadowed by the knowledge that the activities of the Haganah were not being disrupted. An attempt at offensive operations was mounted by two undercover squads under police control and commanded by Roy Farran, formerly of the SAS Regiment, and Alistair McGregor, who had served in the SOE, but these were disbanded when a young Jewish boy was abducted by Farran's squad in May 1947 and was never seen again. Farran fled to Syria but eventually he returned to face trial by court martial and was acquitted due to lack of evidence.

The failure to evolve an effective counter-insurgency doctrine helped to breed a siege mentality best expressed by the military historian Correlli Barnett, who served as a National Service conscript in Palestine in 1946: 'two British divisions and support troops, some 60,000 soldiers, were stuck in Palestine adding to the balance of payments deficit, carrying out clumsy and ineffective sweeps against the Jewish terrorists who were murdering their comrades, and otherwise doing nothing but guard their own barbed wire.' Another soldier-historian, Lieutenant Colonel (later General Sir) John Hackett, was more blunt, asking why 'three thousand third-class Jewish lunatics could incarcerate and render impotent the flower of the British Army.'[8]

The sense of inadequacy was exacerbated by the Jewish Agency's policy of encouraging illegal immigration of Jews from Europe. To begin with the British placed all illegal immigrants in detention camps in Palestine but in August 1946 the government agreed to deport immigrants and to forcibly prevent the ships, most of them unseaworthy and overloaded, from reaching Palestinian territorial waters. The task fell to the Royal Navy and the Royal Air Force, whose maritime aircraft flew sorties to identify suspect vessels which were then intercepted by warships, a technique perfected during the Second World War. However, the operations were carried out under the eyes of the world's press and the sight of immigrants being detained created further allegations of Nazi-like behaviour. In fact the operations were difficult and dangerous for both sides. Boarding parties were usually opposed, clubs, iron bars and hatpins being used in the scuffles, and there were casualties. The captains of the immigrant ships also manoeuvred violently or stopped their engines when approached by British warships, making it difficult for them to get alongside, and because they were often overcrowded there was the ever-present danger of capsizing.

Illegal immigrants were taken to Haifa, where they were transferred to British transport ships and taken to camps in Cyprus or Mauritius. In one incident a badly overcrowded Jewish ship sank and its survivors owed their lives to the prompt assistance offered by the crews of the fleet minesweeper HMS *Providence* and the destroyer HMS *Chevron*. Incidents of that kind were not only disliked by those who manned the boarding parties but they passed the propaganda initiative to the Jewish Agency. This was particularly true in the case of a flat-bottomed river steamer called the SS *President Warfield* which attempted to bring in 4,500 immigrants in July 1947.

Bought by the Haganah from a yard in Norfolk, Virginia, and christened the *Exodus 1947* it left the French port of Sète with the intention of running ashore near Haifa and releasing its passengers onto the beach. As it approached Palestine it was picked up by a naval force led by Captain Dymock Watson (HMS *Chequers*), and two destroyers, HMS *Childers* and HMS *Chieftain*, were eventually able to run alongside the *Exodus 1947* to allow boarding parties to go on board. After a long-running struggle the captain surrendered his ship which was taken into Haifa. The immigrants were then put on board transports and under a new policy of *refoulement*, by which they were to be taken back to the port of embarkation, they were returned to Sète. At that stage of the operation world opinion was generally on Britain's side as Jewish lives had been risked on an overcrowded and unseaworthy vessel but all that changed when the French government announced that it would only take those who disembarked of their own free will. The majority refused, leaving the British to find homes for them, but the only place with sufficient accommodation was the British Zone in Germany and the transports set sail for Hamburg. The whole voyage took forty-six days to complete and it was followed in its entirety by the world's press.

The *Exodus* incident was another propaganda humiliation for the British and combined with the almost daily terrorist outrages it led some senior commanders to argue that the revolt could only be put down by using more forceful tactics. On a fact-finding visit to the area in December 1946 the Chief of the Imperial General Staff, Field Marshal Lord Montgomery, supported General Sir Miles Dempsey, C-in-C Middle East Land Forces, who had reported earlier that 'the actual arrangements for dealing with violence are totally inadequate.' Montgomery had served in Palestine during the Arab Revolt, which had been suppressed by the security forces, and he wanted Cunningham to 'stop lawlessness by offensive action'. The High Commissioner countered that the army could only do that if they had reliable intelligence or when there was a direct link between an outrage and an illegal armed organization. At the end of the visit Montgomery sent a signal back to London informing the government that in his opinion the military situation was 'a dog's breakfast'.

> Every thinking British person in this country realises that the thing is being handled in a gutless and spineless manner and the whole business is just nonsense. There will always be lawlessness in Palestine until the forces at the disposal of the government are organised properly and are used properly.[9]

In taking that view Montgomery was out of step with the times, for the government was not prepared to rule Palestine with full military force and could not afford to alienate the Jews further by using the army as an instrument of policy. That did not stop some servicemen from arguing that more forceful measures should be used. One staff officer in the 6th Airborne Division told his commanding officer that the only way to deal with violence in Tel Aviv was 'to go in with guns roaring' and Dempsey himself admitted that the army in Palestine 'had lost the initiative'. Others were more pragmatic: following a series of attacks on air force bases in April 1946 the AOC Palestine noted that airmen who had risked their lives in the war were 'not always willing to do so merely in order to safeguard an aircraft or equipment against attack by a Jewish gangster.' Echoing that overall sense of frustration the commanding officer of 1st Argyll and Sutherland Highlanders called in journalists after one of his men had been killed and eight injured by an explosive device in Jerusalem and asked them if this was the Jews' way of thanking Britain for winning the war.[10]

Although there was never any likelihood that the British would use full military force against the civilian population, captured terrorists were not treated leniently. Under mandate law they could be sentenced to flogging and the punishment was used with a regularity which added to Britain's international unpopularity. In retaliation for two Haganah members who received eighteen strokes of the cane on 27 December 1946, Irgun captured two British soldiers and flogged them before sending them back to their units. A few terrorists were hanged but the executions only attracted equally savage retaliation. In April 1947 four terrorists were executed in Acre jail, amongst them a young man called Dov Gruner who was hailed as a martyr for the dignified way he met his end. This was followed by a wave of violence and by a daring attack on the old Napoleonic fortress on the night of 4 May. The raiders, dressed in British army uniforms, blew a hole in the main wall which allowed 255 of the prison's 623 inmates to escape, including some Arabs.

It was not the end of the matter. Two months later three more Jews were hanged and their executions exacted a terrible revenge: two British sergeants in the Intelligence Corps, Clifford Martin and Mervyn Paice, were taken hostage in Nathanya and hanged by Irgun. Then their bodies were hung upside down in a eucalyptus grove near the government forestry station at Tal Azur and the area was booby-trapped. In Britain the incident aroused widespread revulsion – there were anti-Semitic riots in London, Liverpool, Manchester and Glasgow – and, as a result, public opinion swung behind the government's decision to extricate itself from

Palestine, now no longer seen as a possible British base in the Middle East but rather as an expensive and dangerous liability. More than that, many members of the security forces, including senior commanders such as Colonel W. N. Gray, Inspector-General of the Palestine Police, believed that they were incapable of stopping the violence. 'When the underground killed our men, we could treat it as murder; but when they erected gallows and executed our men, it was as if they were saying, "We rule here as much as you do", and that no administration can bear. Either total suppression or get out, and we chose the latter.'[11]

Under sustained international pressure to retrieve the situation, the British government had finally admitted defeat in February 1947 when it announced that the problem would be handed over to the stewardship of the United Nations. The result was the formation of the United Nations' Special Committee on Palestine (UNSCOP), which was established on 15 May 1947 and got down to work immediately, taking evidence from the interested parties in Palestine. Three months later, at the end of August, UNSCOP submitted its report, which came down on the side of arbitration and ending the British mandate as soon as possible. Palestine would be partitioned into Jewish and Arab areas while Jerusalem would become an international zone safeguarded by the UN. It was a compromise but one which the Jewish Agency was prepared to accept, if with a heavy heart, because it safeguarded the concept of a Jewish state. This would comprise the fertile coastal strip between Haifa and Jaffa, the Negev and eastern Galilee, while Palestinian Arabs would be granted western and central Galilee, Samaria, the Judaean Hills and the Gaza Strip.

UNSCOP also hoped that there would be an economic union between the two territories and that Britain would continue to supply the necessary forces during the period of UN administration. In other words, Britain would have to continue semi-mandatory responsibilities while at the same time appearing to play a leading role in the creation of a permanent Jewish home. Such a position was untenable as it would endanger Britain's position in the Arab world at a time when it was necessary to safeguard oil supplies and other trading rights: realizing that the UNSCOP proposal was inimical to British interests, the government decided to adopt a neutral position and to withdraw from any further involvement in the settlement of the Palestine issue. On 17 October, while the proposal was being debated by the UN, Arthur Creech Jones, the British Colonial Secretary, announced that 'His Majesty's Government would not accept responsibility for the enforcement, either alone or in co-operation with other nations, of a settlement antagonistic to either Jews or the Arabs, or both, which was likely to necessitate the use of force.'

On 29 November the General Assembly of the United Nations passed Resolution 181 in favour of the partition, the agreement having won the support of both the United States and the Soviet Union. The mandate would come to an end on 15 May 1948, Britain having already stated on 26 September that it would withdraw all its forces by that date. At the same time the British government insisted that it would take no further responsibility for any political or military action which implied support for the policy of partition, a decision which left them, as Cunningham put it, 'holding the ring' between the two opposing sides. It proved to be no easy task. By the end of 1947 the forces had already been reduced in size: the RAF had only five squadrons remaining (although it could rely on back-up from its bases in the Suez Canal Zone and Cyprus) and the army had withdrawn one brigade from each of its divisions. Because Britain was unwilling to enforce the partition and because the UN refused to provide a supervising force the British forces would withdraw gradually, leaving Arab and Jew to divide the spoils.

In February 1947 command of the garrison had passed to Lieutenant General Sir Gordon MacMillan and he was responsible for overseeing the withdrawal, which was conducted in four timed phases beginning in October with Haifa as the main exit. Responsibility for the port area's security fell to 40 Commando Royal Marines (reinforced in the final stages by 42 and 45 Commando) and they would be the last to leave, on board the tank landing ship HMS *Striker* on 27 June. Their duties extended from protecting Arab workers as Haganah attempted to seize Haifa to checking the manifests of incoming merchant ships for illegal weapons. The cargo of one vessel, SS *Flying Arrow*, was supposed to consist of agricultural tractors but on inspection these were found to be armoured half-track vehicles.

Throughout the phased withdrawal the reductions in manpower left many bases exposed to attack from Jewish and Arab forces; depots and fuel dumps were raided by both sides and pilots of 32 Squadron RAF found themselves being asked to hand over their Spitfires in return for large sums of Jewish money and implausible stories to prove that they had ditched in the Mediterranean. As Palestine became an armed camp arms searches were also stopped, Cunningham having accepted that taking the decision would allow both sides to defend themselves in the anarchy which would follow the British withdrawal.

Early in 1948 elements of the Arab Liberation Army began infiltrating over the border from Syria and by the middle of January had established themselves in central Galilee. Their strategy was not just to assist the protection of the Arab population but also to prevent the emergence of the Jewish state which Menachim Begin, one of the wartime leaders of the Irgun Zvai Leumi and a future prime minister of Israel, had promised would come into being. 'The partition of Palestine is illegal. It will never be recognised,' he had claimed on the day following the UN vote. 'Jerusalem was and will for ever be our capital. Eretz Israel will be restored to the people of Israel. All of it and for ever.' In pursuit of that aim Haganah commanders advocated a policy of 'aggressive defence', taking the initiative and securing Jewish territory and the corridors leading to them, even if that meant going on the offensive against Arab-held towns and villages. By February the Arab irregular forces led by Abdul Khader el Husseini had gained control of the road from Tel Aviv to Jerusalem and were stifling Jewish traffic movements. As a result convoys were attacked and the Haganah found it difficult to supply and guard the more remote and unprotected settlements in Galilee and the Negev.

This was open warfare and the British forces often found themselves caught up in it while keeping open their lines of communication during the phased withdrawal. Because protection of the Jewish convoys would have implied acceptance of the policy of partition, Cunningham had refused to permit military escorts, but even when British troops did intervene their offers of help were often ignored. On 15 April, as a convoy of medical personnel from the Hadassah Hospital made its way to Mount Scopus, it was ambushed and its vehicles were set on fire. Alerted by the firing, a British officer arrived with an armoured car and an armoured personnel carrier but despite his pleas to transfer to his vehicles the doctors and nurses preferred to wait for the arrival of the Haganah. As a result seventy-eight were killed and twenty were badly wounded as the firing started up again. The savageness of the attack was

prompted by an incident a week earlier when members of the Stern
Gang massacred 245 Arabs at the village of Deir Yassin to the east of
Jerusalem.

The succession of atrocities not only made life difficult for senior
British officers who wanted to get out of Palestine with as few casualties
as possible, but also prompted allegations that the army was colluding
in the violence by ignoring it. Only once did the British forces inter-
vene decisively in the communal violence. Towards the end of April the
port of Jaffa was being attacked by Haganah forces but as it had been
allocated to the Arabs Bevin ordered the army to prevent it falling into
Jewish hands. If that happened the Arabs would be denied access to the
Mediterranean – a fortnight earlier Haifa had fallen to Haganah as
British forces withdrew into their enclave in the port area – and
Montgomery ordered General Sir John Crocker, the new GOC Middle
East, that 'it was up to us to see that it [Jaffa] did not change hands
before 15 May'.

> The Jewish forces which are attacking JAFFA must be attacked heavily by
> us with all the military force that can be made available. Use aircraft and
> bomb the Jews and shoot them up. Use British troops even if this entails
> casualties to our forces. The more armed members of the IZL [Irgun] and
> Stern gangs that you kill the better.[12]

The order was carried out – the Jewish forces were driven off by
aircraft and artillery fire and British infantrymen moved into the line
between the two sides – but all attempts to reach mediation failed and
Jaffa was eventually surrendered to the Jews after the mandate ended.
The Jewish forces were proving to be skilled infantry soldiers and, backed
up by superior heavy weapons, they were able to exploit to their
advantage the vacuum left as the British withdrew. In so doing they set
in train the expulsion of large numbers of Palestinians – by the end of
the year the figure had reached 700,000 – which was one of the most
tragic legacies of the mandate's collapse and a cause of subsequent unrest
in the region. This had not been foreseen by the British but neither had
the fighting qualities of the Jews been recognized. At the end of 1947
MacMillan had told Montgomery that the Jews 'did not like fighting for
any length of time and he did not think that they would have much
stomach for a prolonged struggle.'[13]

He was wrong but during the last six months of the mandate not much went right for the British forces. As the commanding officer of 2nd Royal Scots admitted before taking his battalion to Malta, there had been little satisfaction for his men in being forced to act as armed policemen in a struggle not of their making. Most other British sailors, soldiers and airmen felt the same. Their task had been to try to fulfil the government's policy of bringing the two peoples together in order to achieve a compromise which would have suited Britain's strategic interests. In so doing they managed to please neither side.

Many reasons combined to explain the failure of Britain's post-war role in Palestine. The government, the people and the armed forces were exhausted by the six years of the Second World War. They also found themselves at loggerheads with their closest ally, the United States, where they lost the propaganda battle especially over the issue of stopping the illegal immigrant ships. In addition, there were too many other political and economic problems happening concurrently. There was also India to consider: it became independent with Pakistan in August 1947 and the partition was marred by communal violence in which thousands of lives were lost. At home in Britain there was rationing and food shortages, and the bitter winter of 1947 put a further strain on an already weakened economy. For the military, the decision not to use direct force made it impossible to counter the Jewish attacks: instead of being allowed to take the initiative British commanders were forced to adopt half measures which only produced meagre results. In such a conflict, the first well-organized urban guerrilla war of the post-war period, they found, too, that there was no place for the traditional British virtues of patience and compromise.

Cunningham had promised that he would not leave Jerusalem until the last minute and he was as good as his word. On 14 May, having inspected a guard of honour found from the Highland Light Infantry, he went by car to the airfield at Kalindra and was flown to Haifa where he boarded the cruiser HMS *Euryalus*. At midnight the Union flag was lowered, the state of Israel came into being and the opposing factions emerged into the open to plunge the country into open warfare. Cunningham's last words were indicative of the whole muddled approach to the intractable problem of Jew and Arab living together in harmony in the Holy Land: 'I have never believed, and do not believe now, that the seed of agreement between Jews and Arabs does not exist, even though in all our efforts we have failed to find the soil in which it would germinate.' During the three years of that futile attempt at achieving harmony 338 British subjects were killed by Jewish terrorists.

3

DR JEFFREY GREY

Malaya, 1948–1960:
Defeating Communist Insurgency

Dr Jeffrey Grey is Associate Professor of History at the Australian Defence Force Academy, and in 2000–2001 held the Major General Matthew C. Horner Chair in Military Theory at the Marine Corps University at Quantico, Virginia. He holds degrees from the Australian National University and the University of New South Wales and is the author or editor of fifteen books, including *The Australian Army* (2001), *A Military History of Australia* (1990, 1999), *Up Top: The Royal Australian Navy and South-East Asian Conflicts 1955–1972* (1998) and, with others, *The Oxford Companion to Australian Military History* (1995) and *Emergency and Confrontation: Australian Military Operations in Malaya and Borneo 1950–1966* (1996). He lives in Canberra, and knows that rugby is the game they play in heaven.

MALAYA, 1948–1960

Gulf of Thailand

N

THAILAND

KEDAH

Kota Bahru

Penang

Grik
Lenggong

Kuala Kangsar

Taiping

Ipoh

KELANTAN

TRENGGANU

PERAK

Tapah

MALAYA

Kuala Lipis

Kuantan

SELANGOR

PAHANG

Port Swettenham
Kuala Lumpur

Strait of Malacca

NEGRI
SEMBILAN

(MALACCA)

JOHORE

SINGAPORE

Johore Bahru

Kota Tinggi

SUMATRA

100 miles

150 kilometres

Railways

The two most important factors in shaping post-war South-East Asia were the Cold War and the decolonization of the European empires. Both influenced the course, nature and outcome of the Malayan Emergency. Its origins lay in the pre-war growth of Malayan communism, the resistance to the Japanese occupation between 1942 and 1945, and the constitutional, economic and community politics prompted by British proposals for the Malayan Union immediately after the war's end. It furnishes an excellent example of a successful counter-insurgency campaign, while illustrating how difficult it is to wage protracted war successfully against a revolutionary insurgent movement in the Third World.

The Malayan Communist Party (MCP) had developed strong links with mainland Chinese communism before the Second World War, and was never to lose this Chinese orientation. At the time of the Japanese invasion it was a minority party without a strong mass base, although it successfully harnessed anti-Japanese sentiment among Malayan Chinese following the outbreak of the Sino-Japanese war in 1937. During the Japanese occupation the MCP formed the Malayan Peoples' Anti-Japanese Army (MPAJA), giving the party a military organization for the first time. The MPAJA received training, advice, equipment and medical supplies through the British officers sent from Force 136, and the communist leadership undertook to follow the instructions from South East Asia Command in so far as these related to the war against Japan. Its activities against the Japanese were, necessarily, limited and episodic, but the MCP used the power that its own armed force gave it to build a mass base in the countryside, in part through the effective use of terror. At the war's end the MPAJA was disbanded and arrangements were made for it to surrender its arms. There is a strong presumption that some of the equipment was in fact stockpiled for later use, while the MPAJA Ex-Service Comrades' Association helped to maintain party control and influence among the rural squatter population in the early post-war years.

Under its Secretary, Loi Tek (who had collaborated with the Japanese during the war and was a British agent both before and after the war until his defection in March 1947), the MCP initially adopted a moderate post-war policy of opting to work through its labour organizations rather than moving at once to insurrection and armed struggle. Chinese nationalism within Malaya increasingly expressed itself through the MCP and its affiliate organizations, such as the New Democratic Youth League. Malay nationalism was intensified significantly by British plans for the formation of a Malayan Union and separate Crown Colony of Singapore, an arrangement in which the Chinese population would attain citizenship rights. Heightened dissatisfaction with this proposal led to the formation of the United Malay Nationalist Organisation (UMNO) in March 1946, and to growing tension between the British and the Malay political elite. The British conceded the issue and in February 1948 announced the replacement of the Malayan Union with a Federation of Malaya, in which Chinese rights were sacrificed to the interests of the traditional Malay rulers. Although the MCP continued to extend its financial and political control of organized labour organizations, it failed to exploit dissatisfaction within the Chinese community with the Federation proposals while at no stage did it ever manage to cross the divide between the three major ethnic communities (Malay, Chinese, Indian) and broaden its political appeal. It can be argued that the shift to armed struggle in 1948 represented the last option remaining to a party that had enjoyed several important advantages at the end of the war but had failed to capitalize on them.

Neither the MCP nor the British colonial authorities were prepared for the insurgency that began with the murder of three European planters by a squad from the 5th Regiment of the Malayan Peoples' Anti-British Army (from February 1949 renamed the Malayan Races' Liberation Army (MRLA)) at Sungei Siput on 16 June 1948 (the MPAJA, the MPABA and the MRLA were the military arm of the MCP under different names). Loi Tek's successor as Secretary, Chin Peng, has subsequently admitted that this action was a mistake since it provoked the authorities into declaring a state of emergency before the MCP had completed its preparations or coordinated its units. He has also claimed that the attack was carried out without orders from the Central Committee.[1] Some party members were rounded up at once by the Malayan police, but the hard-core cadres and the trained rank and file of the MRLA took to the jungle in pre-arranged manner. The struggle that they initiated lasted twelve years.

The British conduct of the Malayan Emergency has come to be seen as a model for the suppression of communist insurgency, but it certainly did not appear that way at its outset. The British suffered a number of serious reverses, of which the murder of the High Commissioner, Sir Henry Gurney, in his car in October 1951 was the most potent symbolically. Initially they approached the situation in Malaya with something of the mindset, and some of the same personalities, that had operated in Palestine between 1946 and 1948 and which had proved a failure. Within days of the Emergency's declaration the GOC Malaya District, Major General Sir Charles Boucher, declared that 'this is by far the easiest problem that I have ever tackled. In spite of the appalling country and ease with which he can hide, the enemy is far weaker in technique and courage than either the Greek or Indian Reds'. Until Gurney's arrival in November 1948 there was confusion over the relationship between the army and the police, with suggestions that the police should operate under military control and be bound by the provisions of the Army Act. Malaya is the first modern counter-insurgency campaign associated with the policy of 'winning hearts and minds', but this approach took time to evolve and was certainly absent at the outset: the burning of the village of Kachau in Selangor in November 1948 by police and the murder of twenty-four Chinese rural workers by a patrol of the Scots Guards at Batang Kali the following month were uncharacteristic of the British conduct of the campaign as a whole, but symptomatic of the confusion and inexperience within the security forces at the outset.

The communist forces were divided essentially into two parts: the MRLA, whose members were known colloquially to the security forces as 'Communist Terrorists' or 'CTs', and the Min Yuen, the 'People's Movement'. The MRLA was organized nominally into twelve regiments; those in Perak and Johore were the best organized and prepared while the 11th Regiment, based in upper Trengganu, was never fully formed. The 10th Regiment, based in central Pahang, was designated an all-Malay regiment but it was essentially a propaganda exercise and had largely ceased to exist by late 1951 because of widespread desertion. (The MCP paid a severe price in military as well as political terms for its

failure to appeal to the population as a whole.) There were also a number
of independent companies and platoons in the various states. Accurate
figures are difficult to produce but at its height the force numbered
between 5,000 and 8,000. The rank and file was overwhelmingly Chinese,
while the officer corps was drawn extensively from veterans of the
wartime MPAJA. Weapons and equipment varied enormously. Some
of it was drawn from stockpiles of British gear hidden after demobiliza-
tion in 1945, some had been captured from surrendering Japanese
forces, while still more was captured or stolen from the security forces
themselves. One of the cardinal weaknesses that faced the MCP was
the absence of an external source of supply. Despite vague claims to the
contrary, there is no evidence that weapons, ammunition or other equipment was ever shipped to the communists from outside the country.
Early attempts to purchase radios and signals equipment on the black
market failed because the MCP did not have the funds needed and could
not match the prices offered for such items by the Indonesian nationalist
forces, who did.[2] The Min Yuen comprised those civilians organized to
assist the MRLA in supporting and ancillary functions. It numbered
some 60,000 members at the outset and ranged widely in effectiveness.
Critical to sustaining the early impetus of the insurgency was the support
obtained from a significant proportion of the rural Chinese population,
whether through conviction or coercion.[3]

At the outset the security forces seemed to enjoy the advantage on
paper, but they were not without problems of their own. In June 1948
there were at least ten infantry battalions stationed in Malaya (two of
them battalions of the Malay Regiment), with others in Singapore. The
police numbered about 9,000. Six of the infantry battalions were Gurkha,
almost all were understrength and the Gurkha battalions contained some
3,500 partially trained, recent recruits. Although the army was reinforced
in August and September with the arrival of a battalion from Hong
Kong and the 2nd Guards Brigade from Britain, the battalions were not
trained for counter-insurgency or internal security duties. The soldiers
were often young National Servicemen, prompting one company commander to observe that they were 'so young and so incredibly innocent,
boys of nineteen most of them ... Most of the older men had been with
me in Greece ... but there were only a few of these'.[4] Turnover within
units was also a problem, since although a tour in the Far East was for
three years most members of a unit were replaced at least once in that

1. The burnt-out car of Brigadier Mallaby on the spot in Surabaya where he was murdered.

2. Soldiers of the 8th/13th Frontier Force Rifles of the 36th Indian Infantry Brigade guard suspected Indonesian terrorists after clearing the route from Batavia to Bandoeng.

3. A 3.7in gun of the 24th Indian Mountain Battery firing at Indonesian mortar positions in the hills beyond Grissee.

4. A Haganah mortar bomb hits Haifa Docks. Its arrival was so sudden that the marines on the left are still standing about unconerned.

5. Following the shelling of the Arab Souk by Haganah an officer wrote: 'Confusion broke out among the Arabs and many panic-stricken men, women and children carrying pathetic bundles of belongings massed outside number 3 Gate begging to be let in. I will never forget nor forgive the Jews who had already won the battle for Haifa, for sending down a murderous fire on the unprotected mass. The CO ordered the gate opened on humanitarian grounds. While helping these refugees, Lt Peter Pitman and our Doctor Surgeon Lt Mike Cox were both wounded.'

6. A Staghound armoured car covering the mass influx of Arab refugees. The same officer wrote, 'I brought up a Staghound . . . and fired a number of rounds of HE at a row of binoculars watching from the GPO building. The firing stopped and the CO said that lines to Commando HQ were hot asking us to desist . . . the commander of the local Haganah broke his leg running downstairs.'

7. The last British troops to leave Palestine, 40 Commando Royal Marines, march on board the LST *Striker*, 30 June 1948. On the right of the picture the CO, Lieutenant Colonel R. D. Houghton MC RM.

8. After the Japanese surrender Admiral Lord Louis Mountbatten, Supreme Allied Commander South East Asia, shakes hands with Chin Peng, the leader of the Malayan Peoples' Anti-Japanese Army, after decorating him. Chin Peng led the subsequent Communist insurgency in Malaya.

9. A patrol of the 1st Battalion the Cameronians displaying caps and flags taken in a 'bandit' camp. The man crouching in front with the parang and No. 4 Lee Enfield rifle is an Iban tracker – the Ibans played an important part in the campaign. The man on the left of the picture is carrying an Owen gun without a magazine, and the man to his left is carrying a 'jungle carbine', a cut-down version of the No. 4 rifle.

10. A British soldier checks a rubber tapper's identity on a rubber plantation in 1950. He is carrying the Australian designed Owen sub-machine gun.

11. Hawker Sea Furies and Fairey Fireflies ranged on the flight deck of HMS *Ocean*. Sorties from the *Ocean* were flown against P'yongyang, the North Korean capital, and on marshalling yards and lines of communication, as well as in support of ground forces.

12. Marines of 41 Independent Commando Royal Marines as part of the 1st United States Marines Division on the long fighting withdrawal from Hagaru-Ri to Hungnam in December 1950. 'Gentlemen,' said the divisional commander, 'we are not retreating. We are merely advancing in another direction.'

13. On 7 June 1951, the day that the US Secretary of State Dean Acheson announced to the Senate that UN forces in Korea would accept an armistice on the 38th parallel, soldiers of the 3rd Battalion the Royal Australian Regiment advance towards the Imjin River on a Centurion tank of the 8th King's Royal Irish Hussars.

14. British troops search a captured Mau Mau in the forest.

15. Dedan Kimathi – self-styled Field Marshal. The photo was possibly found on a prisoner.

16. Kikuyu Guard.

time because of expiration of engagements or the completion of national service obligations. The Malayan Police Force, meanwhile, was nearly 2,000 under strength and was short of equipment, particularly vehicles and radios, while police detachments were scattered around the country in small groups – rural police stations, which might provide the only security force presence in much of Malaya, rarely numbered more than seven men at this time. The force was also riven by various factions – between 'Malaya hands' and those who transferred from Palestine in late 1948, between those who had been captured by the Japanese and those who had escaped – and this did little to improve its effectiveness. Intelligence was often poor, as was security.

Nor in the early phase of the Emergency was government strategy clear, or consistent. Under General Boucher the security forces attempted to drive the CTs into the jungle and away from settled populations; under his successor, Lieutenant General Sir Harold Briggs, they attempted to force them back out of the jungle by attacking their logistic support. The government's 'Anti-Bandit month' in February 1950 which it pronounced a great success was immediately undercut by the increase in CT attacks, which in June 1950 stood at five times the level of the previous year.[5] The authorities were on the defensive (whatever they might claim in public) and if the MCP had been better prepared when the Emergency began it might have made much deeper inroads into the government's position in the early months of the conflict.

Attacks on people and property increased between 1949 and 1951. In the second half of 1948 there were 1,274 separate incidents in which 360 members of the security forces were killed (149) or wounded (211) and 315 civilians were killed for a cost to the CTs of 693, killed (374), captured (263) or surrendered (56). In the following year the cost to the CTs almost doubled, to 1,207, but the numbers of soldiers, police and civilians also climbed, to 476 and 694 respectively in a total of 1,442 incidents. (This, however, was consistent with the incident rate the previous year.) Then in 1950 the number of incidents increased sharply, to 4,739. Losses to the CTs were 942, among the security forces 889, with 1,161 killed, wounded and missing among the civilian population. In 1951 there were more than 6,000 incidents, resulting in the deaths of 504 soldiers and police and 668 civilians for a total of 1,401 CTs eliminated.[6] In response to the increase in CT attacks, another infantry brigade was sent to Malaya from Hong Kong in March 1950, and requests for additional reinforcement were sent to Singapore. As well as attacks on civilians and on economic targets, the communists became more emboldened in early 1950 and made several large-scale attacks on Malay elements of the security forces: against police at Bukit Kepong in Johore in February, and against soldiers of the 3rd Battalion, the Malay Regiment at the Semur River in Kelantan in March.

The insurgents' actions could not disguise the longer-term disadvantages under which the MCP laboured. The retreat into the jungle lessened the communists' influence among the civilian population, notwithstanding the activities of the Min Yuen, although they retained a presence among the Chinese rural squatters, a dispossessed and aggrieved section of the community that often dwelt on the fringes of the cultivated land. Basing itself in the jungle exacerbated the MRLA's already difficult communications and this in turn further weakened command and control. The result was that companies and platoons operated with little central direction or connection to an overall strategic concept. Chin Peng aside, there were few leaders with real political or military skills. The capable among the leading cadre were often killed in skirmishes with the security forces, as in the case of Yau Lew, military commander of the MRLA, who was killed in July 1948 or Lliew Kon Kim, Leader of the 'Kajang gang' (the 4th Independent Company in south Selangor), who was shot by a patrol in July 1952. Nor was the MRLA able to recruit the necessary replacements for the losses that it suffered. As the military and police organizations against which it fought expanded to deal with the insurgency, the insurgent forces themselves shrank.

Notwithstanding the structural weaknesses of the MCP's position, the government had to defeat the insurgency, not merely wait it out. The orthodoxy concerning insurgent warfare held true in Malaya: if the government didn't win, it lost; if the insurgents didn't lose, they would win. However, there were a number of factors, and a number of individuals, that taken together gave the government the advantages it needed in order to defeat the CTs and end the Emergency.

In keeping with one of the tenets of British thinking on counter-insurgency – an emphasis on constitutionality and the rule of civil law – one of the most important weapons in the fight against the MCP was the Emergency Regulations. Introduced in 1948, they defined and greatly expanded police powers, reintroduced the death penalty for carrying arms unlawfully, and required newspapers to have a permit in order to publish. The most important regulations covered the detention of persons and the introduction of a system of national registration. In the first six months of the Emergency approximately 5,000 people were detained either because they were judged to be security risks or because the police did not (yet) have sufficient material evidence to place them before a court. Registration took some time to get underway, and the CTs urged villagers to refuse to register or to destroy their identity cards in a bid to frustrate this move. Over time and taken with other measures, the registration process was an important element in the fight to isolate the insurgents from the civil population. The Emergency Regulations also permitted the deportation of detainees who were not citizens of the Federation or British subjects, which most Chinese in Malaya were not. Many of the measures that they sanctioned were illiberal in nature and would not be tolerated in peacetime, but the point was that they provided a legal framework within which the security forces could act, and which was subject to judicial oversight.

The second measure of practical importance was structural. While some authorities in Malaya itself regarded the insurgency with a measure of complacency, this view was not shared by the Defence Coordination Committee, Far East in Singapore or by sections of the British government in London. With heightened insecurity reflected in the increased number of CT incidents in the first months of 1950, Gurney asked London for the appointment of a Director of Operations. The High Commissioner would have preferred a civilian, but the British government selected a retired soldier in recognition of local opinion among the expatriate community in Malaya and on the advice of the Chief of the Imperial General Staff, Field Marshal Sir William Slim. The officer concerned, Lieutenant General Sir Harold Briggs, had commanded the 5th Indian Division in Burma under Slim. He had also held the post of GOC-in-C Burma Command during Burma's transition to independence in 1946–7. He was widely experienced, possessed a tactful manner, and took a broader view of the complex issues which counter-insurgency threw up. Credit for breaking the back of the Emergency is popularly ascribed to Field Marshal Sir Gerald Templer, Briggs' successor. Without in any way diminishing Templer's achievement, it was Briggs who laid the basis on which Templer built so successfully.

Briggs' great contribution to the winning of the Emergency was the Briggs Plan, tendered to the Defence Coordination Committee, Far East,

within weeks of his arrival in Malaya. The communists, he saw, 'had the
initiative which had to be wrested from them'.[7] This required both short-
term and long-term solutions. The short-term plan involved a sizeable
increase in the number of troops concentrated in southern Malaya.

The long-term objective lay in breaking the link between the MRLA
and the Min Yuen upon which they relied so heavily.

> The Min Yuen is able to exist and function in populated areas mainly
> because the population as a whole lacks confidence in the ability of the
> forces of law and order to protect them against gangster Communist
> extortion and terrorism. In consequence, information, which is essential
> if the Min Yuen and the bandits are to be eliminated, is quite inadequate.[8]

The government had to demonstrate to the population at large that
it possessed both the means and the resolve to defend Malaya both
internally and externally. The rule of law and the administration of
good government had to be extended throughout the country, especially
to those sections of the population – specifically the rural squatters – to
whom these were largely unknown. This would involve, among other
things, resettling the squatters and extending to them a stake in the
country's future, strengthening local government, improving communications infrastructure to isolated parts of Malaya, and improving security
through a regular police presence. The Min Yuen was to be targeted by
the security forces and its hold on the population broken. This would
undermine the MRLA's logistic support and intelligence systems, and
would finally force them either to surrender or to engage the security
forces openly, where they could be destroyed. The overall process was
designated 'Framework Operations'.

This is not to suggest that offensive operations now ceased. Striking
forces were maintained and deployed in priority areas, in effect super-
imposed over the framework operation in a given state in order to apply
pressure directly on the CTs. The idea was that the enemy would be so
weakened through combat and the erosion of its supply and reinforcement base that it would be unable to rebuild quickly, if at all, when the
striking force moved to a new locality, and the police would then be able
to handle the remaining threat. To be successful, Briggs' conception
relied on a number of interdependent considerations: 'the judicious use
of troops; the close cooperation of troops and police; accurate and timely

intelligence above all from Special Branch, and finally, as an earnest of long term government aims, the revitalization of local government'.[9]

At Briggs' instigation the High Commissioner set up the Federal War Council in April 1950. This consisted of the Director of Operations as chairman, the Chief Secretary of the Federation, the GOC and AOC Malaya, the Commissioner of Police, the Secretary of Defence and, when required, a liaison officer for the navy. The Director of Operations issued his own directives governing the conduct of operations at all levels but he did not exercise command of either troops or police directly. The Federal War Council had ultimate responsibility for waging war against the MCP at the national level. Beneath it Briggs created the State and District War Executive Committees (SWECs and DWECs), which exercised similar responsibilities at those levels, and whose membership reflected that of the War Council itself. At the state level, for example, the Chief Minister or Mentri Besar chaired the committee, whose membership included the chief police officer, the senior military commander, the state financial officer, and representatives of local community leaders; at the district level, the committee was chaired by the district officer and included the senior police officer and senior military commander in the district, a Home Guard officer, and community leaders. Each committee also had an Operations Subcommittee, responsible for the day-to-day conduct of Emergency operations in its locality. This system continued in place until the end of the Emergency in 1960.

In one of his earliest directives, Briggs ordered the expansion and revitalization of the police. The police were responsible for the major share of operations, and in the main years of the Emergency between 1948 and 1954 lost many more men killed (regular, auxiliary and special police combined) than did the military forces, as shown in the following table.

	1948	1949	1950	1951	1952	1953	1954
Police	86	160	304	354	202	39	41
Military	60	65	79	124	56	34	34

The police initially operated under a number of disadvantages, and suffered from low morale because of shortcomings in equipment, training and overall pay and conditions. The decision to provide the police with armoured vehicles was taken reluctantly and in the face of opposition from within senior ranks of the force itself, despite the obvious utility in helping police patrols to survive road ambushes. The single greatest shortcoming in the police was a lack of experienced and qualified leadership in the field, and when the force was expanded from 1951 the authorities sought to recruit ex-servicemen from Britain and Australia as police lieutenants operating with the Police Field Force. Crucially, the police also made substantial gains in the number of Chinese recruited into the Special Branch.[10] The regular police consisted of the uniformed and detective branches, charged with orthodox police duties, the Police Field Force, paramilitary formations that operated throughout the country in the same manner as army units, the Special Branch, charged with the collection and analysis of intelligence, and the Special Constabulary, which provided Area Security Units and Police Special Squads for anti-CT patrols, enforced food denial measures and provided static defence of public utilities. The temporary and volunteer police included the Special Constables and others for use on Framework Operations in local areas. These were supplemented by the Home Guard, responsible for the close defence of their own villages. The morale of the force and its standing in the community was slowly improved following the appointment as Commissioner of A. E. Young, who was seconded from the City of London early in 1952 and who deliberately set out to rebuild trust between the police and the civil community.

One of the developments that made it possible for the government to intensify its operations against the CTs, improve government services and resettle the squatter population on productive land was the Korean War. Specifically, the prices boom for strategic materials fuelled by the Korean War and Western rearmament greatly increased the financial resources available to pay for waging the counter-insurgency in Malaya. Malayan rubber and tin paid for the soldiers, police and services that helped to beat the communists. The creation of an intended 550 New Villages, and the resettlement of 650,000 people into economically viable communities, was an expensive exercise and a critical factor in depriving the MCP of its links to the population. Much of the cost of this was met by the proceeds of the commodities boom; Anglo-Malay capitalism played a direct part in the defeat of the Malayan communist challenge.

Briggs left Malaya in December 1951. The reforms to the police were only just beginning, and the force was still short of 341 armoured vehicles. Materials for the New Villages were as yet in short supply. The tide of intelligence on CT activities had begun to flow, but the inefficiency of the police still hampered its full utilization. The incident rate in Johore, the worst area in the country for CT attacks, actually rose in the face of the early implementation of Briggs' methods. Briggs had been unhappy with the ways in which his powers were circumscribed, particularly with regard to the internal affairs of the police, and before his departure recommended that his successor be delegated executive powers over the police and Emergency affairs. The new Director of Operations, General Sir Gerald Templer, implemented these recommendations and benefited from them accordingly.[11]

The High Commissioner, Gurney, had been killed in an ambush shortly before Briggs' departure; the Director of Intelligence resigned because of differences with the Commissioner of Police; the Commissioner himself resigned at the beginning of 1952. Templer thus inherited a situation in which the principal centres of administrative and operational authority were vacant. His appointment came about from the recommendations of the Secretary of State for the Colonies, Oliver Lyttelton, following the latter's tour of Malaya in December 1951. Lyttelton was appalled by what he described as the 'tangle' of delegations and jurisdictions in Malaya, and determined that in the crisis then facing Malaya the conduct of civil and military affairs should be placed in a single set of hands, and that 'he would have to be a general'. Templer's appointment as High Commissioner with full responsibility for military and police operations as well as civil affairs was announced in January 1952.

In combining the highest powers in both civil and military affairs under one man, Templer aroused considerable nervousness among some civilian authorities in Britain and Malaya. His position was highly unusual, and was not persisted with after his return to Britain in 1954 — it can be fairly added that by then there was no need. Templer himself was not well known outside the British army of the time; his is now the name most commonly associated with the Emergency. One of his former subordinates, the historian Cyril Falls, summed him up acutely at the time: 'There is no doubt about the energy or about the flair, or about the administrative ability. He is determined, quick minded and wary . . . he has a way of getting to the heart of his problems and he has a great capacity for business'.[12] Templer himself demonstrated a grasp of the issues facing him and of the 'hearts and minds' process which would become closely associated with him: 'The shooting side of the business is only 25 per cent of the trouble', he wrote, 'and the other 75 per cent lies in getting the people of this country behind US'.[13]

Templer travelled tirelessly around Malaya, closely monitoring and supervising every stage of the fight with the communists. He paid direct, personal and practical attention to the 'hearts and minds' campaign, as his interventions involving collective punishments at Tanjong Malim, Yong Peng and Bahau, among others, illustrated.[14] All three were heavily dominated by the MCP and considered completely uncooperative and recalcitrant in their dealings with the security forces and the government. Templer's methods were direct, occasionally harsh, and usually effective. His use of collective punishment has been criticized more recently, and while it is probably true that the aboriginal inhabitants of Malaya, the Orang Asli, were coerced as often as persuaded to support the government,[15] it is equally true that Templer abolished Emergency Regulation 17D, which authorized collective detention and deportation. He visited every one of the 439 New Villages at least once, many more often than that. British officers and civilian officials who did not meet his standards were sacked; units that performed well in the field received congratulations, those that did not were chastised. He also endeavoured to reduce the polarization between the three main ethnic communities of Malaya through, for example, the formation of the Federation Regiment in the Malayan army. The hallmarks of Templer's period of command in Malaya were energy, direction and purpose. The first areas of Malaya were declared 'white' (that is, largely free of CT activity) in Malacca in September 1953. In the history of the Emergency no area that was declared 'white' reverted in status. (Areas of high CT activity were listed 'black', those in an intermediate stage were 'grey'.)

However able and energetic, Templer did not achieve the defeat of the communists on his own. The Framework Operations in his time were matched by considerable military activity against the MRLA, employing regular army units, the Police Field Force, squadrons of the SAS and units of the Royal Air Force and Royal Australian Air Force in offensive operations. In this period the army developed deep jungle operations, designed to extend government rule and protection to the aboriginal population and to strike at and disrupt the MRLA. Chin Peng and the leadership of the MCP were a particular target of deep jungle operations, such as those launched in Pahang in 1953 or Operation GALWAY/VALIANT along the border intersection of the states of Perak–Kelantan–Pahang in late 1953 to early 1954. The use of bomber aircraft to attack communist positions, known or suspected, in the deep jungle aroused some controversy. Heavy bomb loads were expended for negligible returns in enemy casualties in Operation FIREDOG, while flying in the tropics presented its usual hazards and challenges to flight crews. The air forces' most useful roles in Malaya were undoubtedly air supply, airlift, communications and casualty evacuation. On one occasion in 1955, however, aircraft of No. 1 Squadron RAAF came very close to killing Chin Peng in a jungle camp (entirely unbeknown to them at the time), while the argument about the psychological effect of 'jungle bombing' on an already demoralized and depleted enemy will find proponents on each side.[16] Several high-ranking leaders, such as Tan Fuk Leong, leader of the 3rd Independent Platoon, and Goh Peng Tuan, commissar of the 7th Independent Platoon, were killed in air raids in the course of 1956 and the effect on the units they led was devastating. In these two cases, however, efficient targeting was the result of accurate prior intelligence furnished through the Special Branch. Ships of the Royal Navy and the Malayan, Australian and New Zealand services operated offshore, but in the complete absence of attempts at seaborne infiltration and resupply by the communists their role in the emergency was marginal.[17]

The security forces ultimately numbered 40,000 British, Malayan and Commonwealth troops, 65,000 regular and special police and around 250,000 part-time members of the Home Guard.[18] As well as British and Gurkha units, there was a battalion from Fiji, a battalion of the Rhodesian African Rifles and a detachment of Rhodesian SAS, battalions of the King's African Rifles and, in the second half of the 1950s, units from Australia and New Zealand.[19] The Malayan armed forces expanded like the police. Living conditions in the field were often fairly primitive, especially earlier on. One British officer wrote that conditions for his men, accommodated in tents not far from 'rather squalid labourers' huts' were 'far from pleasant, though it is some compensation that for much of the time our men [will] be out on patrol in the rubber fields and in the jungle'.[20] From 1950 the lessons of jungle warfare and successful counter-insurgency were taught at the Far East Land Forces

Training Centre at Kota Tinggi, and disseminated throughout the Commonwealth armies in one of the classic training manuals of its kind, *The Conduct of Anti-Terrorist Operations in Malaya*, known colloquially as the 'ATOM pamphlet'.[21]

One other dimension of Emergency operations is worth discussing, and that relates to psychological warfare, propaganda and the waging of political warfare, all of which the British won comprehensively. A psychological warfare section was formed in Malaya in 1950 and worked closely with the Special Branch. It used voice aircraft and leaflet drops, among other techniques, in undermining CT morale and inducing surrenders, and the more desperate the communists' position became in the second half of the 1950s the more successful these techniques proved. In this area, and in propaganda more generally, the government made good use of surrendered enemy personnel (SEPs, to be distinguished from captured enemy personnel, or CEPs). Extra effort was made to assure those still in the jungle that SEPs were well treated after their surrender, and most were given new identities and the means to re-establish themselves in civilian life elsewhere in the country. The willingness of SEPs to betray their former comrades startled many, as did the seniority of some of those who opted to throw in their lot with the government: Lam Swee, former commissar of the 4th Regiment who changed sides in early 1951, must stand for all, but he was certainly not alone. The MCP countered the temptations to surrender among its own rank and file with show trials and executions of suspected defectors, which can have done little to reassure the waverers.

The most effective weapon in the political contest between democracy and communism was national independence, which ostensibly was what the MCP had launched the insurgency to attain. Municipal and local elections were held in 1952, in which the communists of course did not participate. By the end of 1955 there were elected local majorities in the federal and state legislatures, the first federal election having been held in July, and while the finer constitutional details had still to be negotiated it was clear that independence itself was an inevitable outcome. The MCP now attempted a 'peace offensive', but the terms it sought belied the weakness of its political and military position, and negotiations between Chin Peng and Tunku Abdul Rahman, Chief Minister of the Federation, at Baling in December 1955 came to nothing. Britain granted independence to Malaya in August 1957.

In late 1955, and largely as a result of wider Cold War concerns, ground units from Australia and New Zealand were based in Malaya as part of a Commonwealth Brigade for regional duties under the provisions of the South-East Asia Treaty Organisation (SEATO). They were never in fact deployed in that manner, but between 1955 and 1960 were used extensively in countering the CTs in the deep and rugged jungle country in the north of Malaya and along the Thai border in particular.[22] Units of the MRLA were now smaller, a result both of casualties and defections and of their inability to support large units because of pressure on their logistic system. Contacts were less frequent, and the CTs usually avoided contact when they could or broke it off as quickly as possible when they could not. In the course of 1956 one CT in five still in the jungle was killed, captured or surrendered. A continuous belt of 'white' areas was established across Malaya in August that year, splitting the MRLA in half. Enemy resistance in Perak and Johore, which had been the states with the largest and most vigorous concentrations of enemy forces, began to fall apart in 1958 with mass surrenders brought about through demoralization and relentless military pressure, together with a promise of amnesty.[23] Operational focus now shifted to the area along the Thai border, where the remaining CTs were successfully penned by Commonwealth army and Malayan Police Field Force units. By October 1959 intelligence estimates placed the strength of the MRLA at 698, of whom just 243 were still in Malaya; by March 1960 these figures had fallen further, to 609 and 117 respectively. The Emergency was declared at an end on 31 July 1960.

In the course of the Emergency 10,704 CTs were killed, captured or surrendered. The security forces lost 1,865 (1,346 police and 519 military), while 3,283 civilians were killed or otherwise missing. The successful defeat of the insurgency owed at least as much to weaknesses in the communist side as strengths on the government one. The critical factors for the government were the police and the New Villages programme, the key individuals were Briggs and Templer, and the financial benefits to the British and Malayan exchequer brought about by the Korean War were fundamental to Britain's ability to sustain the massive effort involved in mounting a twelve-year-long counter-insurgency campaign. Community politics were important also: 'the largely Chinese insurrection was met by largely Malay resistance'.[24] The last remnants of the MRLA eked out an existence along the Thai border until finally negotiating a surrender through the good offices of the Thai government in December 1989. Field Marshal Sir Gerald Templer died in 1979 and was accorded a funeral with full military honours at St George's Chapel, Windsor. After several decades living in Beijing, Chin Peng retired to Bangkok and is writing his memoirs.

4

GENERAL SIR ANTHONY FARRAR-HOCKLEY

Korea, 1950–1953:
The Far Side of the World

General Sir Anthony Farrar-Hockley joined the army as a private soldier in the Second World War. Commissioned in 1942, he served with the Parachute Regiment in North Africa, Italy, southern France, and Greece, and in post-war Palestine. Adjutant of the Glosters in Korea, he was taken prisoner on the Imjin River, becoming a persistent though unsuccessful escaper. He later related these experiences in *The Edge of the Sword*. In 1956 and 1958 he served as brigade major of 16th (Parachute) Brigade in Cyprus, Port Said and Jordan, subsequently commanding 3rd Battalion The Parachute Regiment in the Radfan. He ended his career as C-in-C Northern Europe. He has written fourteen military histories and biographies including the British *Official History of the Korean War*.

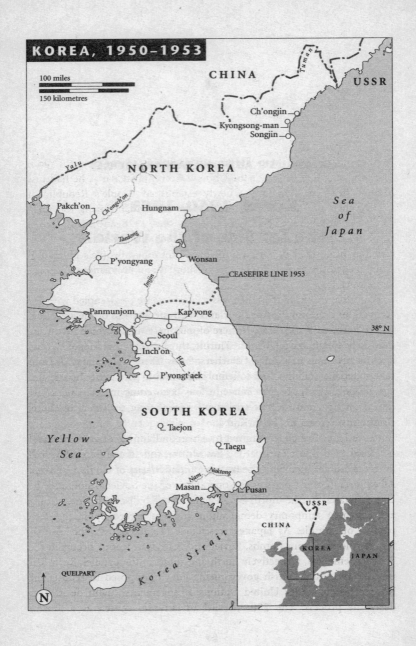

KOREA, 1950–1953

100 miles
150 kilometres

CHINA

USSR

Tumen

Ch'ongjin
Kyongsong-man
Songjin

NORTH KOREA

Yalu

Pakch'on
Ch'ongch'on
Hungnam

Sea
of
Japan

Taedong

P'yongyang
Wonsan

Imjin

CEASEFIRE LINE 1953

Panmunjom
Kap'yong

38° N

Seoul
Inch'on
Han

P'yongt'aek

SOUTH KOREA

Taejon

Yellow
Sea

Taegu

Nam *Naktong*

Masan
Pusan

Korea Strait

QUELPART

N

USSR
CHINA
KOREA
JAPAN

At the end of 1949, Mao Tse-tung paid a visit to the Soviet Union. The long-standing leader of the Chinese Communist Party, he had just become head of state in the newly established People's Republic of China. The Communists, and the Nationalists under Chiang Kai-shek, had been fighting each other intermittently since 1928, and against Japan since 1937. When Japan was defeated throughout the Pacific in 1945, civil war intensified in China until the Communist People's Liberation Army ousted the Nationalists to the offshore island of Formosa (Taiwan) in October 1949.

From that point, Mao and his associates became preoccupied with the recovery of their nation from war and the restructuring of the state. Aid was required in almost every sphere of national life, for which he turned inevitably to the Soviet Union. During three months in Moscow, Mao laid out his needs in specialist teachers and workers, in capital goods and raw materials. Stalin agreed to supply them – but at a price; he enjoyed a monopoly of supply. By chance he was negotiating military aid at the same time with another fraternal client, Kim Il-sung, leader of the ruling communist regime in North Korea.

Korea had been overshadowed by Japan and China for centuries, and occupied by Japan since 1910. Towards the end of the Second World War the Korean peninsula became a potential area of overlap between Allied aircraft and troops as the operations of the Soviet Union and the United States in the north-east Pacific moved discreetly into China and Japan. A temporary demarcation line was agreed upon, the 38th parallel of latitude. As Japanese resistance crumbled with the detonation of the two atom bombs, Soviet and American troops occupied the Korean peninsula, respectively north and south of the parallel. But when the American and British governments jointly proposed to reunite the Korean people under United Nations arrangements, Stalin decided to delay the process. The 38th parallel of latitude, chosen as a line of strategic convenience, became a political fieldwork. By 1949, two Korean states had emerged: one in the north, styled the Democratic People's Republic of Korea, and its neighbour in the south, the Republic of Korea.

The latter was governed by a right-wing coalition – fascists to centrists – under the ageing but fiery Syngman Rhee, victor in elections held under scrutiny of a United Nations Commission. The Koreans had no experience of democracy, however. Rhee expected to advance his country into the twentieth-century world as he pleased, and that included toppling Kim Il-sung and his cronies by force. The United States, mentor and paymaster to Rhee's government, was prepared to defend South Korea on a limited basis only: to secure the border with the north, and to maintain order in cooperation with the civil police against guerrillas, retainers of communism. Warships, aircraft, tanks and modern artillery were withheld from his forces. Funds were voted by the United States Congress sufficient to raise, train and equip six – later, eight – constabulary divisions.

Kim Il-sung was no less anxious to bring the southern half of Korea under his authority. A Soviet military aid mission, more than twice the size of the American Military Advisory Group in the south, controlled equipment priorities, operational plans and the training of his forces in the use of modern weapons. Well informed as to Syngman Rhee's plans and resources, Kim aimed to destabilize South Korea by guerrilla warfare while his many agents there in the army, civil service and industry undermined support for the government of the south. When this promoted widespread insurrection, he intended to march in his army to complete the conquest. Towards this objective, China and the Soviet Union were returning groups of Koreans who had fought with their respective armies during the Second World War. These were veteran soldiers, primarily infantrymen; candidates for training in the armour, artillery, and signals tended to be selected from those formerly serving in the Soviet Army. Limited aircrew training was in progress under Soviet instructors: a number of operational Yak fighters and Ilyushin light bombers had been provided within the aid programme.

In 1948, Stalin had confirmed Kim's position as leader of the Korean Workers' – Communist – Party, and as head of the Democratic People's Republic of Korea. But this did not mean that he had a free hand to invade South Korea. Capture of the south would have certain advantages for the Soviet Union but Stalin felt under no pressure to realize them casually, particularly as he had no intention of being engaged in a war with America as a consequence of appropriating South Korea.

Kim's anxiety was that he would be held back too long. Following a reception in P'yongyang, his capital, on 18 January 1950, he pressed the Soviet Ambassador to request a personal interview with Stalin on this matter, excusing a return to the subject by explaining that his situation had changed in recent months.

The security forces in South Korea had broken up the majority of his guerrillas based in the southern mountains. On the other hand, the numbers of Korean veterans still available to him from China would be sufficient to expand his army to fourteen divisions. Given additional tanks and self-propelled artillery, aircraft, oil and ammunition, he had no doubt that he would overcome the eight divisions of Syngman Rhee's constabulary – light infantry at best – in a matter of days. In January 1950, Stalin agreed in principle to the seizure of South Korea. Arrangements were set in hand from 9 February.

Aside from local circumstances, the Korean move now seemed opportune to Stalin in global terms. His attempts to overawe the nations of north-west Europe by the military power of the Soviet bloc had failed in Denmark and Norway, in Austria and France, in the isolation of Berlin. The North Atlantic Treaty was developing a considerable alliance, the more formidable as it involved North America. He intended to inhibit this by a widespread propaganda campaign for peace but it would take time to influence public opinion in the European democracies. In Korea, using a surrogate, concealing even the least participation of the Soviet Union, he would demonstrate nonetheless his intercontinental power. The capture of South Korea would extend his frontiers to the Sea of Japan. The Americans would be slighted. The United Nations would be more inclined to heed his opinions.

Certainly, some risks remained, principally the reaction of the United States, but he did not intend to be identifiable as an aggressor. Kim's war stocks would be delivered over the trans-Siberian railway into Korea via north-east China before the first shot was fired. No ship registered in the USSR, let alone submarines, would enter Korean waters. No member of the Soviet armed forces would be permitted in the battle arena – none indeed south of P'yongyang. Requests by Kim to retain Soviet advisers within operational divisions were refused with a caution to the Ambassador in P'yongyang: 'I desire that our advisers should go to the front line HQ and to the Army Groups in civilian dress as correspondents of *Pravda* in the numbers required. You will be personally responsible to the Soviet Government for ensuring that they are not captured.'

Within his own organization, Kim followed the 'advice' of the Soviet planning team in security policies. Any order or document or discussion relating in any way to the impending operations would be carried exclusively by hand of officer. Radio or telephonic means would not be employed. The mass of the North Korean People's Army (the NKPA) moved into their forming-up positions along the 38th parallel believing that they were taking part in an exercise. When live ammunition was broken out, word was passed that a South Korean attack was imminent. From 0400 on Sunday 25 June 1950 an artillery bombardment was opened across the peninsula by the NKPA artillery.

Fighting opened rapidly along the line. In the mountains, the ROK infantry resisted the early assaults of the day but were at once vulnerable in the open valleys in the west to the tanks and self-propelled artillery of the NKPA. Two fundamental problems weakened the defence operations of the Republic of Korea's army (the ROK Army). Its supporting artillery was based on an obsolete 105mm American gun with a maximum range of 7,600 yards. Each division was equipped with three batteries only. Each NKPA division possessed nine batteries of the uprated 76mm, backed by the numerous 155mm howitzers under corps direction. In anti-tank engagements, the ROK Army's weaponry was incapable of penetrating the NKPA T-34 tank armour. Their best hope was to knock off a track, but that would not of itself stop the tank firing its gun or secondary weapons. The NKPA armoured groups possessed also the highly effective SU 76mm self-propelled artillery capable of firing with equal effect both directly and indirectly. This was the first cause of NKPA success and the rapid weakening of the ROK forces.

The second was that the ROK high command, shocked, inexperienced, and lacking in confidence, scrapped the matured national war plan to resist an invasion from the north. In simple terms, it failed to trade ground for time in which to concentrate the divisions from the south to counter-attack en masse. Instead, they distributed piecemeal those sent to swell the national reserve. Units in or arriving in the battle line were ordered to hold their positions to the death.

It might be said that the ROK Army was in any case doomed on

25 June. With inferior weapons and numbers, lacking a proper chain of battle command, it was only a matter of time before the army was defeated. But this would only have been true if there had been no help forthcoming. President Rhee indeed begged the United States government from the outset of invasion to render military assistance. It was only a matter of a few days before assistance was in course of delivery, but by that time the high command made the worst of things. Issuing a stream of impracticable orders, they contributed to an almost total loss of control, particularly on the route into Seoul and across the Han bridges leading to the south. Between 2 and 3 a.m. on 28 June, when the principal crossing site was choked with troops, government officials and civilian refugees, the ROK military engineers were ordered to demolish the bridge.

The structure was at once wrecked. Hundreds of people were killed. Almost half the army, with more than half of the army's transport, heavy weapons and military supplies, was isolated on the northern side of the river.

*

When Kim's troops attacked on Sunday morning, 25 June, those in Washington DC were engaged in Saturday afternoon activities. As soon as President Truman received the news from Seoul he requested a meeting of the Security Council. This determined next day (25 June New York time) that the North Korean aggression was 'a breach of the peace'. As a consequence, by majority vote, the Council called for 'the immediate cessation of hostilities' and the withdrawal by North Korea of her armed forces to the 38th parallel.

Those voting for the resolution were: (Nationalist) China, India, Cuba, Norway, Ecuador, the United Kingdom, Egypt, the United States, and France. Yugoslavia abstained; Tito had broken with the USSR but he made it a rule just then not to vex Stalin gratuitously. More strikingly, the Soviet delegate, Yakov Malik, was absent.

He had been absent since January 1950, demonstrating a Soviet bloc protest against the retention of China's seat in the United Nations by the Nationalists. It may well be that Stalin continued to leave the Soviet seat vacant as a means of disempowering the Security Council when Kim invaded South Korea. If that was the case, he had made an error. The rules of procedure for the United Nations did not require suspension of the Security Council if one of its members remained absent following notice of a meeting.

On the 27th (New York time), the Council met again and by majority vote took note that the North Korean attack on the South continued, and that the latter had asked for assistance as a matter of urgency – it was already 28th June in Korea – and recommended 'that the Members of the United Nations furnish such assistance to the Republic of Korea as may be necessary to repel the armed attack and to restore international peace and security in the area.'

This was passed by seven votes: (Nationalist) China, Cuba, Ecuador, France, Norway, United Kingdom, United States.

Yugoslavia passed from the abstention of the previous day to a vote against active assistance to South Korea, proposing instead a contrary resolution, 'reiterating the call for a cease fire, initiating mediation, and inviting the attendance of a representative from North Korea'. India and Egypt failed to vote at all, preferring to give an impression of dithering rather than offend the Soviet Union. In Washington as in London there was unanimity that they were faced by the first post-war case of international aggression, almost certainly initiated by the Soviet Union. It had to be resisted. Air Chief Marshal Lord Tedder, head of the British Joint Services Mission in Washington, reported military and diplomatic opinions that Stalin might be using Korean aggression as a diversion. 'The next move might well be in Iran and that the sooner our governments decided what action they would take in such circumstances the better'. The State Department and Foreign Office had the same apprehensions. The only notable point that divided them at this stage was that the Americans believed the invasion of South Korea was part of 'centrally directed Communist imperialism'; the British did not. President Truman agreed that they should not use this phrase publicly.

*

As June came to an end, the march of the North Korean People's Army on the principal thrust line through Seoul came temporarily to a halt. A bridge had to be reinstated across the Han River and boats found to put infantry across to clear the southern bank. The capital meantime was to be made politically secure. During this time, General MacArthur arrived by air at Suwon, twenty miles to the south, and met President Rhee, the

United States Ambassador, and members of the South Korean high command, to discuss the situation. Surviving attack by North Korean aircraft he drove to the south bank of the Han, from where he was able to view the city and artillery actions.

At seventy, he was still an active commander – Supreme Commander of the Allied Power occupation forces in Japan, United States Commander-in-Chief of national forces in the Far East region, though his naval component did not command the Seventh Fleet. Vain, headstrong, politically manipulative, he was nonetheless an outstanding military leader, ready to take risks as here at Suwon to discover the situation for himself.

Returning to Tokyo on the evening of 29 June, his report to Washington concluded: 'Unless provision is made for the full utilization of the Army-Navy-Air team in this shattered area, our mission will be needlessly costly in life money and prestige. At worst it might even be doomed to failure.'

This prompted action in Washington which, otherwise delayed, would have led to the forcible reunion of Korea under Kim Il-sung. Necessarily, the first and main relief forces were supplied by the United States. MacArthur was appointed commander-in-chief; all contingents from other United Nations countries would be under his command. The United States Joint Chiefs of Staff became an executive agency of the Security Council. These arrangements attracted the derision of the Soviet Union and its camp followers but the NKPA, advancing steadily on the broken ROK Army, left no time for the selection of an international commander and the assembly of a headquarters from a group of strangers with differing notions concerning the conduct of a war. Besides, it was clear that military costs ahead would be underwritten largely by America; 'he who pays the piper . . .'

MacArthur omitted to mention in his report that he had already ordered the United States Far East Air Force to make ready attacks on North Korean airfields, though at that stage he had not received an operational directive from Washington authorizing such measures. Still, he knew that if his aircraft stayed on the ground, there would be no intervention at all: the port of Pusan and the railway and road communications of South Korea would be open to attack by Kim's air force: the Yaks and Ilyushins were beginning to range widely. All intervention began with the assumption of air superiority. President, Joint Chiefs of

Staff, the State Department, recognized the imperative. It was also accepted that North Korean mobile forces might shortly break through by surprise to Pusan or any other of the lesser ports, such as Masan. He pressed for and received permission to bring a regimental combat team – equivalent to a British brigade group – to establish a guard force at Pusan.

*

From these beginnings, the American national forces began to mobilize a variety of resources in pursuit of the Security Council resolution on 27 June, '. . . to repel the armed attack and to restore international peace and security in the area'. American war stocks in Japan would be tapped for the South Koreans. Warships would be used to bombard North Korean targets on the coasts though, as in the case of air attacks, maintaining a stipulated distance from the Korean borders with China and the Soviet Union. Units of the Seventh Fleet would pass to operational command of General MacArthur while committed to the neutralization of Formosa.

These were the incipient American measures, but the Security Council had opened the door to action by other members of the United Nations. Who would join the United States to validate the claim to international intervention? From 29 June, almost a dozen gave notice that they agreed in principle to do so. Seven of these made an unequivocal promise to contribute. Foremost among them was the United Kingdom.

The British Prime Minister, Clement Attlee, and his Foreign Secretary, Ernest Bevin, were in agreement with President Truman that Kim Il-sung's invasion was unquestionably an act of aggression, even though it was also a civil war. On this common perception, the alliance between Britain and America, revived already within the Atlantic Treaty, returned to the levels of their former wartime partnership. The United States retained supremacy in economic resources, was widely influential politically, but for all her financial weakness the United Kingdom was the leading power among the European democracies, and still maintained a unique relationship with the sovereign nations of the Commonwealth. The USA and UK possessed individually the product of highly secret intelligence which was more valuable when it was shared. English was their common language; they were attached to common notions concerning liberties and obligations. The sum of these factors did not deliver their political leaders and supporters from disagreement any more than they did through the greater difficulties of the Second World War, but they enabled both parties to search out mutually acceptable solutions or, where circumstances permitted, agreements to differ. For example, the British government believed throughout the Korean war that Mao Tse-tung might be weaned from the Soviet bloc; the Americans did not. The former maintained a diplomatic mission in Peking; the Americans recognized Chiang's regime in Formosa as the government of China.

From the outset, then, the American and British policy towards South Korea was identical. As their partner's contribution of military assistance began to flow into Pusan, the British had to consider what they could afford themselves.

Impoverished by the Second World War, the United Kingdom was hampered in her efforts to recover by high defence costs. Her ships, troops and aircraft were employed across the world in residual commitments – occupation forces and colonial obligations. Where possible, responsibilities were shed: in the Indian subcontinent, in Greece and Palestine. But Stalin's expansionism had necessitated foundation costs in NATO. Beyond these in 1950, the equivalent of two British divisions was engaged with communist guerrillas in Malaya. Hong Kong needed but lacked a strong garrison to deter Mao from encroaching upon the territory. As in Washington, the UK Chiefs of Staff were apprehensive that the attack in Korea might be a diversion to pin down American and British forces as a prelude to attacks elsewhere.

These demands employed 700,000 servicemen. Despite a rise of national military service to eighteen months, the Chief of the General Staff had but one operational reserve in hand. The Chief of the Air Staff was adamant that he could spare nothing from his undermanned and underequipped squadrons in Europe for Korea. The only option they advised the Cabinet on 27 June was a squadron from the Far East Fleet, a proposal at once adopted.

Early in July it became apparent that the first relief measures taken following MacArthur's report were insufficient to halt the retiring remnant of the ROK Army. American air forces were attacking the North Koreans widely but summer rain clouds reduced their target options. The south would be lost unless United States ground forces entered the battle. The 24th Division under Major General William F. Dean, one of the four American occupation divisions in Japan, embarked for Korea. He sent on by air an infantry battalion with heavy mortar and anti-tank support to stem temporarily the enemy advanced guard thirty miles south of the River Han. This was Task Force Smith. 'The first show must be good,' General Dean remarked. 'We must get food and bullets and not go off half-cocked'.

Unfortunately, Task Force Smith had been employed in occupation tasks at the expense of field training. They had food and they had bullets but they were routed as much by the battle skills of the North Korean veterans at Osan on 5 July as by their tanks and artillery. So was the 34th Infantry Regiment, following into the line during the next few days, and the 215th Regiment on 12 July after a somewhat longer struggle. On the 20th, the 24th Division as a whole was pushed out of the Taejon area. General Dean was captured. In this period, the division had withdrawn over 100 miles, losing 2,400 men and much equipment.

The 25th Infantry and 1st Cavalry Divisions – also from Japan, the latter a mechanized infantry division – took to the field, augmented by tanks. They slowed but could not halt the enemy until, at the beginning of August, a firm line was established on the Naktong River, comprehending the ports of Masan and Pusan in the south and Pohang in the north-east. About one third of the defences were held by the ROK Army, swollen by press gangs active among the southern towns and villages. Members of the Korean Military Advisory Group – the American training teams – remained with their units.

Reports of the fighting reaching Washington from Japan tended to swing between despair and hope. During days of anxiety, the American Joint Chiefs tended understandably to call upon their allies for military contributions where, earlier, they had been inclined to rely on their own forces, fearing that the standards of some national forces might be below their own. Offers of help from Chiang Kai-shek in Formosa were not accepted for political reasons.

Yet even when reports from the Korean theatre were promising as reinforcements, stripped out from the entire United States Army, flowed to Korea, it was recognized that there was a limit to national resources. American public opinion began widely to look for the deployment of British and Commonwealth forces. Sir Oliver Franks, British Ambassador in Washington, wrote directly to the Prime Minister on 15 July,

For some ten days now there has been a steady increase [in interest] on
this subject. It spreads through all departments of government and press
. . . Too often in the past we have taken our time to make a decision with
the result that, often, when we have done what was in line with American
ideas, we have got no credit or approval for it, the decision has followed
upon and seemed to be extracted from us by the massive discussion,
criticism and pressure that has been built up in the US . . .

Putting this to his colleagues, the Prime Minister wondered whether
Britain could go on in close partnership with the Americans in making
political decisions, in direct exchanges and consultations on military
proceedings, while herself taking no part beyond naval support. Useful
though that was it was not able to affect critically the land battle.
Answering for all the chiefs of staff, Field Marshal Sir William Slim said
that the military objections were still valid, but they recognized the
strong political arguments for committing a British army component.
They should send a brigade group – the 29th Infantry Brigade, with an
armoured complement and a complete slice of supporting and logistic
units. This decision being taken in a period of hope, Cabinet and Chiefs
agreed to despatch the brigade in September, when they might join a
counter-offensive. Meantime, measures must be taken to call out some
2,000 reservists, while suspending the release of regulars at the end of
their contract. Troops in Hong Kong would not be taken for the 29th
Brigade.

This outcome was almost inevitable since it was promoted by Mr
Attlee and Mr Bevin, an unassailable combination in the cabinet and the
Labour Party in and out of parliament. The Conservative Party also
supported intervention in Korea. Even so, Prime Minister and Foreign
Secretary had to define the consequences of their policy: the cost was
high. There would be pay increases to encourage regular recruiting – the
Chief of the Air Staff reminded the Defence Committee on 21 July that
the Royal Air Force lacked 20,000 men. Taken with the requirements of
the other two services, it soon became apparent that they would have
to increase the term of conscription from eighteen months to two
years. New or revived procurements in weapons and equipment would
add 50 per cent to the predicted defence costings by 1953–54. Some
benefits would flow from United States subventions but the balance
would necessarily be met from tax increases and reductions in other
government spending.

These were measures advancing in London in late July. In Korea, the run of operations seemed again threatening to the United Nations.

*

Carried away by his opening success, Kim Il-sung reinforced and diverted his 6th Division to sweep unopposed into the south-west corner of Korea, empty of forces. It seemed a brilliant stroke, likely to hasten victory. Actually, it was a blunder. The 6th Division should have been reinforcing the 4th moving to capture Pusan. If that had taken place, Pusan would probably have fallen in the third week of July. When the two divisions combined at the end of the month, the approaches were blocked by the 25th Division and a brigade of US Marines. The 2nd Division was arriving from Hawaii. Kim's hook failed to deliver a knock-out blow. Even so, heavy attacks were being pressed by the NKPA along the Naktong River to the north and down the east coast road. Thus while the American Joint Chiefs were glad to know that a British brigade would join them in October, they had to say that they needed soldiers more urgently. As General Omar Bradley, their chairman, put it, 'A platoon today would be worth a company tomorrow.'

The British responded to the crisis. Previous decisions notwithstanding, the 27th Brigade headquarters in Hong Kong was ordered to move with two under-strength battalions at once to Korea. HMS *Unicorn* and *Ceylon* carried them to Pusan on 29 August. It was understood that an Australian battalion would join them as soon as possible and a New Zealand detachment at a later date. Meantime, the British battalions were put into the line on 4 September as the North Koreans renewed their offensive west, north and east of Taegu. The army commander, Lieutenant General Walton H. Walker, committed his last reserve to securing the highway between Taegu and Pusan.

The reason for this resurgence of offensive action was that Kim foresaw the dreadful danger of failure. The NKPA had suffered 60,000 casualties by ground and air action in the battles of late July and early August. Dead and seriously wounded were replaced by 20,000 South Koreans pressed into their ranks, raising battle strength to 68,000. The ROK Army had lost 70,000 but mustered 73,000. However, half at least were newcomers scarcely able to fire a rifle shot in the desired direction. The Americans had lost 10,000 but they retained 35,000 and their numbers were slowly rising again. The Far East Air Force and the naval air, American and British, were flying whenever weather allowed, striking at troops, supplies, rail and road movements. Air intervention helped to balance the North Koreans' advantage of being able to attack en masse at any point while the UN forces were obliged to defend the whole line.

On the latter account, it seemed to those in defence that they were still fighting superior numbers, as in June and July. The balance of capabilities was, however, swinging in their favour if they could but preserve the integrity of a defensive line. If no one else recognized this, it was evident to General MacArthur.

In August, he judged shrewdly that the line would indeed hold, even though further territory might be lost. Over General Walker's protests, he withdrew the Marines from the Pusan bridgehead. Day by day he was advancing plans to land a force 300 miles north of Pusan at Inch'on on the west coast of Korea. An armada including Royal Navy and Commonwealth contingents had been assembled. A new amphibious American corps had been created which included the 1st Marine and the 7th Infantry Divisions.

On the west coast of Korea the tide falls some thirty feet twice a day. The winding channel into Inch'on runs through shifting mud flats exposed at half tide. Access to the shore batteries and other surrounds was limited in approach and time. Mines aside, the burden of risk fell upon the first wave of the US marines. While respecting General MacArthur's wide experience of seaborne assault across the Pacific, and the prize if the risks were overcome, the Chiefs in Washington were so apprehensive of a costly failure that they sent Admiral Forrest Sherman and General Joe Collins from their number to Japan to offer an escape line: a site closer to the Naktong line.

'For a five dollar ante,' MacArthur told them, 'I have an opportunity to win $50,000, and I have decided that is what I am going to do.'

'I wish I had that man's confidence,' said Admiral Sherman privily.

Sailing through a typhoon, Rear Admiral W. G. Andrewes, commanding the British naval squadron, was not alone in believing that the plan was going to be tested in every particular. His own task group was charged with protection of the sea stream during the middle passage, and cover of the forces at Inch'on from the sea, north and west thereafter. The British light fleet carrier was drawn into the naval gunfire programme as the battle developed towards Seoul.

The operation was called CHROMITE. It opened on 15 September. In hard fighting, the Marine division seized and held a bridgehead against a North Korean division. By 28 September, X Corps was in command of the capital, Seoul, the Han crossings to the south, and the airfield of Kimpo. It was a famous victory.

Meantime, the British 27th Brigade had been operating on a ten-mile front on the Naktong, an extraordinary distance for its two infantry units, the 1st Battalions of the Middlesex Regiment and the Argyll and Sutherland Highlanders, each 645 strong, a complement gathered by extensive cross-posting within the Hong Kong garrison. With these numbers alone Brigadier B. A. Coad, their commander, would at best have been able to dispose a weak outpost line. He was delivered from this necessity by an attachment of ROK police and porters, numbering perhaps 1,000 men with a variety of small arms and grenades. Communication was difficult; the best of it lay with Corporal Field of the Middlesex, who had a smattering of Japanese. With these supplementaries, the brigadier established six company bases, relying on police observation of the Naktong crossing sites between them. He had been loaned five tanks and two artillery batteries by the Americans, having none of his own. His battalions possessed six 3 in mortars and six Vickers medium machine guns. If the NKPA had attacked this sector decisively the 27th Brigade would not have been able to hold its ground.

Fortunately, due to repeated drubbing by artillery and air attack on the 4th and 5th, the North Korean 3rd Division west of the river and the 10th Mechanized to the east, advancing towards Taegu, were of a mind to be cautious. Both decided to investigate this new force in September which they would have taken at full tilt in the high aggression of the summer months. Middlesex police sweeps, 27th Brigade patrolling and opportune artillery engagements persuaded both NKPA formations to favour inaction disguised as reconnaissance.

North of 27th Brigade, the 1st Cavalry Division was unfortunately driven out of various positions covering Taegu. Fire power, ground and air, underwrote recovery of the American line. But these were not encouraging circumstances in which to receive orders for a break-out north-west from the Naktong to effect a junction with X Corps, landing imminently by sea at Inch'on. The American divisions which had survived the crises of the summer were not ready to abandon in a few days a defensive outlook, as was evident in the hesitancy of orders to the

British brigade: from 17 to 19 September the brigade was ordered out of its defences, then back again. The North Korean 10th Division was said to be advancing but this was a falsehood soon apparent. The line was moving: air and artillery concentrations were driving the enemy back across the Naktong. The Americans began belatedly to seize bridgeheads on the western bank but hung back when fire was opened from local hilltops. On the 22nd, the 27th Brigade crossed the Naktong to clear enemy positions blocking the road west from Taegu. The two battalions dislodged the North Koreans by night approaches, a success that was marred by an American air strike on the Argylls, and the withdrawal without warning of all artillery support.

Fortunately, in a period of excellent flying weather, NKPA units in the open by day were devastated by bombs, rockets, and napalm – gelatinized petroleum. Lacking supplies, without coherent orders, their line was progressively breaking up from 22 September. The hard core of North Korean survivors escaped northwards, killing arbitrarily their South Korean conscripts whose political loyalties were suspect. But many military leaders and political cadres had left their departure too late. Combing out escape routes west of the Naktong, the British took numerous prisoners from stragglers and deserters. On 27 September, news came that troops advancing from the Naktong had linked up with those round Seoul at Osan, site of Task Force Smith's reverse. A huge programme of logistic rehabilitation was instituted by Eighth Army to open road and rail communications. The 27th Brigade, clearing and stabilizing their sector north-west of Taegu, were delighted to be joined in their work by the 3rd Battalion, Royal Australian Regiment. The brigade title was at once changed by Brigadier Coad on his own initiative to '27th Commonwealth Brigade'.

It was an expression of solidarity. Base units for the Canadian and New Zealand contingents, respectively an infantry battalion and a field artillery regiment, were due to enter operations in Korea in the New Year. On the battlefield, differences between the four were rare. In the base in Japan, however, in course of expansion, intra-Commonwealth relationships sometimes required delicate handling. The British were the chief offenders at the outset. Staff officers in Whitehall tended to treat the other partners as if they were still subject to imperial authority. General Sir William Slim quickly checked this source of vexation and supported the proposal, as all contingents expanded, that the senior

Australian officer in the Japan/Korea region – Lieutenant General Sir
Horace Robertson – should be responsible for non-operational matters:
administration, political representation and protocol with General Mac-
Arthur on behalf of all Commonwealth units serving within the com-
mand. With some misgivings among the Australians, Air Vice-Marshal
C. A. Bouchier of the Royal Air Force was appointed to represent the
British Chiefs at MacArthur's headquarters.

Meantime, the 27th Brigade moved to Kimpo airfield through the first
week of October. This change of location intensified rumours of a return
to Hong Kong. A question debated throughout the UN force was: are we
going to cross the 38th parallel?

The same question occupied the governments supporting the United
Nations action in Korea. If the UN pursued the remnant to the northern
border of Korea to disarm it, to conduct democratic elections as an
essential step to reunification of the peninsula, there was a danger that
the Soviet Union and or China might take some overt military action
where now they hung back. The Soviet Union had now returned to the
Security Council, asserting her neutrality in this matter while taking
the part of North Korea. Among those seeking sincerely if ingenuously
in the Council to promote peace, India might be persuaded to support a
settlement under a UN commission. The alternative was to throw up
defences on the 38th parallel, permitting Kim Il-sung to rebuild forces
for a second invasion at a time of his choosing. This course would run
also against the several UN resolutions to bring about the reunion of
Korea by democratic process.

While the discussions proceeded, the Chinese Prime Minister, Chou
En-lai, sent for the Indian Ambassador at midnight on 3 October, and
in the course of the meeting made this point: 'If the Americans decided
to cross the [38th parallel], then it will be clear that they have elected for
war and not for peace and China will be forced to act accordingly.'

Mr Bevin believed that warnings of intervention were a form of bluff.
He drafted a catch-all resolution which reflected American views: once
the North Koreans had laid down their arms, the reunion of Korea
would be left to the UN. The resolution was passed by the General
Assembly on 7 October.

Yet the decision left many matters unsettled. Among the Koreans,
there was a danger that President Rhee and South Korean elements

would take revenge upon opponents in the north during the UN interregnum. As is now known, Kim had no intention of being a caretaker president during the election process. The requirement for UN policing of the whole territory loomed. Such horrific prospects with others occupied the UN alliance as General MacArthur called upon North Korea finally to cease hostilities and disarm, to which there was no response.

The UN advance was resumed. It was slow and uneven; every road was blocked by NKPA detachments, albeit each mostly a tank or two, a gun of sorts, a truckload of infantry. Sweeping the countryside of enemy stragglers, the 27th Brigade was plucked on 15 October from Kaesong, on the parallel, by the commander of 1st Cavalry Division and posted as his advanced guard to accelerate the onrush to P'yongyang. American tanks, artillery, and engineers were attached, trucks for infantry. Dodging press visitors by day, surprising North Koreans marching by night, the brigade won 1st Cavalry priority on the road into P'yongyang, taking almost 4,000 prisoners, 1,982 marked to the Australians. This success prompted the corps commander to speed them on to the Ch'ongch'on River, fifty miles to the north.

The pace of advance accelerated. Crossing rivers lacking bridges involved comical improvisation with a variety of boats. Literally out of the blue an American parachute brigade briefly overtook the brigade, joining forces to maintain the momentum of the advance. By 25 October, 3 RAR had survived an armoured counter-attack at Pakch'on, almost twenty miles beyond the Ch'ongch'on. The Middlesex returned to lead through what turned out to be an enemy ammunition dump concealed in burning houses. In turn the Argylls led the advance on the 28th, skirmishing at random, closing that evening to within four miles of Chongju. On the 30th, this important road and rail junction fell after a concerted effort against 200 North Koreans supported by tanks and self-propelled artillery. They were then forty miles from the Chinese border and not sorry to give way to an American regimental combat team. Next day, they buried their dead and evacuated their wounded; among them, mortally stricken, was the Australian commanding officer, Lieutenant Colonel C. H. Green.

The Middlesex were already moving that day to support the 24th Division's northern axis. Backtracking some fifty miles, they met their advanced party at Taech'on, escorting two prisoners. One was a North Korean lieutenant, the other a Chinese soldier.

*

Meantime, the 29th Independent Infantry Brigade Group – its full title as a force of all arms and services – was arriving under command of Brigadier Tom Brodie. It was at full war strength, and included a pool of '1st Reinforcements' located in the base for each unit. Each infantry battalion had 1,168 all ranks; excepting 3 RAR, numbering 1,000, each battalion in 27th Brigade averaged 600. The 29th was well armed and equipped, though the majority of its weapons and accoutrements, apart from the Centurion tank gun, were of Second World War origin. But its artillery could not have been equipped with a better gun than the 25-pounder in range, accuracy, sustained fire capability and reliability in all weathers. A battery of 4.2 in mortars was also in the complement, of which the chief weakness, like the infantry's 3 in mortar, was the cast casing and tail, known for a tendency to separate during projection. All units were issued on arrival with the American 3.5 in rocket launcher.

First to arrive were representatives to be attached to American fighting units of their respective arms and corps. The aim was to give them 'battle inoculation'. The group was then flown home to pass first-hand information of fighting conditions and practices to their units during the six-week sea voyage to Korea. Next came the advanced parties, those who would prepare reception sites for the main bodies on arrival at Suwon. Ships were due to arrive in Pusan between 1 October and 2 December, the lattermost carrying reserve vehicles, base and line of communication organizations. This programme was successful despite chaotic entrainment arrangements in Pusan.

To the 29th Brigade, however, it seemed that they had arrived too late to join the war. The Eighth and ROK Armies were already north of P'yongyang. X Corps, including 41 Royal Marine Commando with the US Marine division, was about to land on the north-east coast, from which General MacArthur hoped to manoeuvre brilliantly through the barest of mountains in that most impenetrable region. At Wake Island in mid-October, President Truman was assured by General MacArthur that the war in Korea was over. Some items of stores and supplies were already earmarked for backloading to Japan. The old – often fatal

– military catchphrase throughout Eighth Army was, 'Home for Christmas!'

The Chinese had other ideas. Communist China had been preparing to intervene in Korea since the first week in October. P'eng Te-huai was appointed to command a force of 330,000, formed in seven armies – posing as 'international volunteers' ('the Chinese People's Volunteers') – to avoid political difficulties. He made a brief reconnaissance along the southern approaches to the Yalu River, gave peremptory instructions to Kim Il-sung, and returned to issue orders to his waiting soldiers. He had worked out a scheme for circumventing Mao's strategic directive, which he judged to be unenterprising. He bore robustly the news that Stalin was not, after all, going to give him air cover by day – his columns would move exclusively by night, a tactic familiar to the People's Liberation Army – and took up position just inside Korea to direct operations.

In the last week of October the Chinese armies attacked first the ROK Army on several successive nights, breaking into their positions, shattering their fragile confidence won in the late summer battles. Night fighting spread from central Korea across the American front echeloned northwest to Chongiu. Observing the Eighth Army positions by day, Chinese divisional commanders selected the most exposed positions for attack each evening. Severely stung, the foremost UN formations were drawn back to avoid fragmentation, among them 27th Brigade, which fought its way back to the Ch'ongch'on River supported by American tanks and guns on 5 November. Next day was quiet: the Chinese had disengaged across the front.

Lacking proper maps of Korea, reliant below divisional level on telephones for intercommunication, P'eng's subordinate commanders had progressively lost control of their formations. Units had run out of contact partially because they had engaged in an orgy of looting – food, weapons and ammunition, transport and oil. In any case, P'eng had launched a trial operation; its success had surprised him but now fed his ambitions. General MacArthur announced widely that his forces, overwhelmed by 'Chinese perfidy', would return, reinforced by land, sea, and air, to defeat his foes in North Korea. The British authorities advised against a war conducted across the widest span of Korea, including a frontier with the Soviet Union. They proposed withdrawal to the narrow neck of the peninsula, an option supported by the four Commonwealth participants. The Americans objected that this would smack of concession. It would be better to negotiate following a successful advance by MacArthur. Discussions were not helped by rumours that the Chinese price for a ceasefire would include abandonment of Formosa and the Nationalists. American opinion began to favour the British proposal. All agreed that any solution must assure the Chinese that their territory would not be at risk. Indecision persisted. Once again, the policy choice was left to General MacArthur due to his standing.

On 24 November he reopened his offensive to capture and stabilize the broadest span of North Korea. Much delayed by coastal mines, X Corps had at last landed on the east coast to protect the right flank of the Eighth Army. The Marine Division with the British 41 Commando and a regiment of the 7th Division were pushing round the Changjin reservoirs; to their right the remainder of the 7th had advanced unopposed, speeding one company by the 24th to the Yalu bank at Hyesanjin. The ROK I Corps felt out the seemingly undefended east coast.

Air cover was extensive, verifiable targets were few. Across the front P'eng's soldiers lay back from the main roads, packed in remote villages or among the boulders of deep river beds. From 25 November, they began to concentrate in night actions against ROK divisions in the central mountains. On the 26th these crumbled. As in October, their dispersion opened the American IX Corps's right flank, but with greater effect. The Chinese struck now deeper and in greater numbers, breaking the cohesion of the defence. From this development, the Eighth Army was ejected from its positions. By 28 November, General Walker recognized that he no longer had control of his front. He ordered all units to break contact with the enemy and withdraw south. X and I ROK Corps, likewise, severely exposed, were ordered to re-embark at Hungnam. The epic 'march to the sea' by the US 1st Marine Division with 41 Royal Marine Commando, bringing all their equipment, wounded and dead with them, was perhaps the only creditable American performance in that dark winter of 1950.

It was a wretched winter for the UN and ROK forces, morally and physically, defeated and running in bitter weather in which the daytime air temperature of 20 degrees Celsius often fell below 30 degrees at night. Snowfalls obscured enemy movement in daylight. 29th Brigade was disposed as rearguard to the American I Corps in the western sector,

27th Brigade to IX in the centre. Falling back through P'yongyang, the two brigades crossed briefly at the central crossroads. The well-equipped 29th, mobile, with its own tanks, guns and administrative support, known to the 27th as the 'Woolworth Brigade', received derisory greetings. Jibes of 'scruffy!' were returned amiably to the travel-worn 27th. The two formations continued in this role until they reached Seoul as Christmas approached.

Glad of a breather, the I and IX Corps were disposed between the Imjin and Han rivers. Their withdrawal on wheels and tracks had outpaced the enemy, marching on foot, many still without full winter clothing due to supply muddles, a circumstance that the Chinese, hardy and confident, bore stoically. They had begun the Korean expedition in awe of the Americans but believed they now had their measure; American soldiers did not care for close fighting. On New Year's morning 1951, UN reconnaissance observed P'eng's infantry advancing between the ROK 1st and 6th Divisions.

Both these divisions had abandoned defences covering the lower Imjin River. Air and ground observation convinced I Corps commander, General 'Shrimp' Milburn, that strong enemy columns were moving round the western face of Seoul to cut escape routes across the Han. 29th Brigade was posted to cover the ground evacuated by 1st ROK Division, particularly the several mountain tracks running directly into the western suburbs of the capital, fifteen miles distant. Brigadier Brodie hastened to deploy his three battalions. The ground was like iron. Fire positions had to be built as sangars, upwards with stones.

None too soon. At 03.15 on 3 January, the advanced guards of two Chinese divisions – one of which had been drawn unwittingly southward – attacked in succession the Royal Ulster Rifles and the Northumberland Fusiliers. They took ground but were wholly ejected by the afternoon. As this news reached brigade headquarters, orders were received from I Corps that Seoul was to be evacuated; 29th Brigade was told to join the column falling back across the Han. The Fusiliers and Glosters withdrew down one route to the main road, the RUR by a second. On this latter track the Chinese had been building up since dusk a huge ambush, which rained a hail of fire upon the battalion as it passed, killing or mortally wounding fifty-seven, the commanding officer, Major Blake, among them. Gradually, over several hours in many small actions, groups escaped the bloody melee. The Chinese did not follow. Recovery occupied the remainder of the night. On 4 January, regimental parties sent out in helicopters by General Milburn found seven more survivors.

To the east, the premature withdrawal of the ROK 6th Division had threatened the movements of IX Corps's left flank, for a time denying free use of the road running north–south through Seoul. 27th Brigade was instructed to stabilize this corridor while the decision was taken as to whether the Eighth Army would fight an action before abandoning the capital.

The first task was to capture or drive off Chinese reconnaissance parties, several dozen of whom were discovered marching in civilian clothes amongst the endless columns of refugees trudging south. This accomplished, the Middlesex and Argylls were able to hold open the northern end of IX Corps's main supply route for ROK Army stragglers. Clearing back, 3 RAR broke up an expanding roadblock. As the brigade concentrated, all reports indicated that Chinese numbers were mounting round the perimeter, and it seemed likely that a move out of Seoul was impending. Even so, there were several missions to perform, not least the collection by 3 RAR of American units lost on the edge of the city, a good deed vexed by a friendly air strike en route. From the evening of 3 January the brigade maintained watch and ward on the city's edge through a cold night, agonizingly cold in positions too exposed to permit the simple comfort of a company fire. To a man, on 4 January, the brigade was infinitely relieved to be ordered to the Han from 07.30 hours.

They caught the 24th Division headquarters up on the road to I'chon. General Church remarked famously to Brigadier Coad that he 'liked to have the British undertake rearguards as they have a steadying influence on American soldiers.'

*

During the next three months President Truman and Mr Attlee, with their principal foreign and defence advisers, passed from a period of anxiety – occasionally despair – to a prospect of survival. In their darkest discussions, they foresaw their armed forces being ejected from the peninsula, leaving Koreans opposed to Communism to death or imprisonment. In December, contemplation of a defeat in arms started rumour of an atomic counterstroke impending against the Chinese. In January many of the soldiers in Korea hoped simply to be permitted to retire whenever the enemy advanced. A number of general officers shared that ambition. Yet by March the combined UN and ROK land forces had overcome the enemy in a succession of modest operations and were moving northwards to recover South Korea's territory to the 38th parallel. One man may claim the credit for this improvement: General Matthew Bunker Ridgway.

Briefly, General Walker was mortally injured in a motor accident on 23 December 1950. Ridgway took his place and began at once pacing the battle area to discover why his command – including the ROK Army – was unable to stand against the Chinese. The answer was simple, his American soldiers had lost belief in their fighting qualities. Poorly trained occupation divisions had begun the war. Others, skeleton structures, had been brought to strength by individuals posted in from all over the American army and replaced as death and wounds demanded. Day by day, many of those in the firing line were strangers to one another.

Yet other national contingents were ready to fight, a condition due to a variety of factors. National pride, and among the British and Commonwealth units also regimental pride, were among them, the more effective because their numbers were smaller and more distinct among the mass of Americans deployed. In these circumstances the essential ingredient to high morale, comradeship, flourished. Ridgway remarked the readiness for combat he found in a young British cavalry subaltern during his travels by comparison with that of an American senior noncommissioned officer earlier in the day.

The ROK Army's confidence was low because the majority of its officers and men were levies, unfledged. At best, some had completed company training by June 1950; 70 per cent had picked up marginal skills on the battlefield. Officers were commissioned in the summer of 1950 after fourteen days' instruction.

General Ridgway had first to convince his senior officers that the phase of retirement was over. He reminded them of their immense fire potential in ground, air, and sea bombardment. He had to convince all ranks that the communist Chinese soldiers were as vulnerable as themselves in combat – probably more vulnerable due to the mobility and power of their weapons. Exercising a fine calculation, he put his regiments to small-scale offensive tasks abundantly within their capabilities. A run of petty successes boosted confidence. The situation did not change overnight – the Chinese broke into IX and X Corps in February

– but fortune now favoured the commander-in-chief. The breaches were not exploited; Mao was overplaying his hand, pressing against P'eng's advice his enfeebled divisions round Seoul and south of the Han River. Supply was indeed difficult due to American air attack, and reinforcement, Mao observed, but the 'volunteers' had a revolutionary spirit to sustain them.

Perhaps they had. However, the mass of young political officers, guardians of the sacred political flame, were again depleted in February and March 1951 and the revolutionary spirit did not protect men lacking overcoats against frostbite. Vexed, Mao accepted the view of the Central Military Commission in Peking that P'eng's columns must retire.

Growing bolder, the UN and ROK armies pushed north from March into April through positions littered with Chinese dead of cold and neglect. The 27th and 29th Brigades, the former now joined by 2nd Battalion, Princess Patricia's Canadian Light Infantry, the 16th Field Regiment, Royal New Zealand Artillery, and a detachment of the Royal New Zealand Army Service Corps, were engaged respectively in IX and I Corps's advances back to Seoul and exploitation to the 38th parallel.

During the first part of April, the army commander ordered the construction of a main defence line, preceded by outposts, supported by reserve positions. Renewal of a Chinese offensive was believed to be imminent, became indeed so repetitious a topic as to lose interest. It was certainly overshadowed on the 11th by news that General MacArthur had been dismissed by President Truman for corresponding privately with members of the Republican Party. General Ridgway was appointed to the several commands vacated in Japan; Lieutenant General James Van Fleet took command in Korea. The changes were untimely.

On the other side of the line, preparations for an offensive were advancing. P'eng's resources had been raised to forty divisions – half a million troops – including six of the NKPA. Other divisions were put aside to cover a United Nations sea and airborne landing, long apprehended in the north-west. The possibility of a Nationalist Chinese intervention also persisted. Even so, P'eng did not doubt his ability to break into the UN and ROK line. What concerned him was the possibility that in an adverse air environment he would run out of supplies and transport before he had breached the UN line to its full depth. Novel schemes were introduced for the collection and redistribution of abandoned vehicles, fuel, ammunition, and food. He reckoned upon enemy stocks contributing to his own supply chain after three days.

Prime sectors to be 'wiped out' first, all offering short runs to the Han crossings, from west to west central were 1 ROK Division, 29th Brigade, 3rd US Division, the Turkish Brigade, 6th ROK Division, and 27th Brigade. Thereafter, the American 24th and 25th Divisions would become prime targets. The 29th Brigade frontage followed fourteen miles of the winding Imjin River. The 27th Brigade, unknown to P'eng, was out of the line at Kapy'ong, behind 6th ROK Division and engaged in relief by the 28th Brigade. An expectant calm spread across the Eighth and ROK Army fronts on the night of 21/22 April. In 29th Brigade a listening post of the Glosters ambushed successfully a detachment of the Chinese Sixty-Third Army, one of hundreds crossing that night to infiltrate the UN line or to reconnoitre crossing sites and assembly areas on the northern bank. Next morning, random parties appeared along the river. Captives taken and the appearance of widespread smoke screens during daylight suggested the offensive was opening. Higher commanders anticipated a final march of some twenty miles to the river on the 22nd, with the first assault on the 23rd. Actually, P'eng's leading divisions had marched the previous night to concealed sites about ten miles distant.

Ten miles was nothing to the volunteers: they attacked off the line of march all along the lower Imjin on the night of the 22nd. On the 29th Brigade front attacks were attempted by surprise, hoping to assault the British trenches within grenade-throwing range. Few succeeded; at dawn most company positions held firm though frequently pressed. Where ground was lost it was due largely due to the overwhelming enemy numbers engaged.

Left, the Glosters were separated from the remainder of the brigade by the mountain mass of Kamak-san. The battalion was sited to deny the Chinese access to sideroads 5Y and 11 since these offered a means of blocking the eventual withdrawal of the brigade and the American 3rd Division. However, the battalion's two foremost companies were in danger of being inundated after eight hours of fighting. Lieutenant Colonel Carne brought them back into a close perimeter. Right, Brigadier Brodie's task was to guard the western flank of the 3rd Division as it 'rolled with the punches' – General Ridgway's strategy – and thereafter to draw back his own force. But his attached Belgian battalion was still disposed on the northern Imjin bank. His gaping central position had been driven in. There was an acute risk that he had insufficient troops to secure at least three of the key hill features in the battle zone and to maintain control of the pass on Route 11, the ultimate line of withdrawal to all those in the right sector. Fortunately, the enemy failed to grasp the lie of the ground, engaging widely – and dangerously – but lacking coordination due to customary lack of adequate maps and radio communication below divisional headquarters. Distant orders within battalions relied upon whistles and trumpets.

The Northumberland Fusiliers established positions on the northeastern shoulder of Kamak-san; the Royal Ulster Rifles assumed a variety of tasks, including manning a keep midway down the pass. By one means and another the Belgians broke out of their positions successfully. These were the rewards of the intense struggle to hold the Chinese along the southern edge of the Imjin River. The brigade was thus free to break back to the next reserve line as ordered by General Milburn, free but fragmented amongst a depleted but still numerous and dynamic foe. By that time, on 25 April, the Glosters were too deeply isolated to fight their way alone up the pass on Route 5Y. Several forces had been assembled to relieve them and their Royal Artillery heavy mortar troop, but none was adequate to the task. All efforts to resupply ammunition to them had foundered. In new locations, the guns of 45th Field Regiment lacked the range to support the Glosters' positions.

In these circumstances, Brigadier Brodie gave Colonel Carne instructions to abandon his position, hoping that in a massed movement southward some would succeed in avoiding capture. The medical officer, chaplain and medical staff volunteered to stay with the wounded. The remainder broke away, a fraction successfully. The others became prisoners. Across the hills to the east, the greater number of 29th Brigade rejoined the main United Nations line.

Meantime, behind the central front at Kap'yong-ni, 27th Commonwealth Brigade (now under Brigadier B. A. Burke) was in the process of passing its responsibilities to 28th Brigade. This activity was shielded by the 6th ROK Division to the north. On the night of 22/23 April, part of the Chinese 60th Division silently overran the foremost positions, driving a stream of ROK troops back past the New Zealand gunners placed to support them. Three miles back fragments of the division were collected on 23 April but, with his flanking divisions under pressure,

General Hoge commanding IX Corps ordered 27th Brigade to block the north-western and northern approaches to Kap'yong.

It was an important road junction; one offshoot encircled Seoul. The brigadier had three battalions to offer for its defence: 2 PPCLI, 3 RAR, and 1 Middlesex, plus the New Zealand 16th Field Regiment – the latter two were travelling back to Kap'yong-ni at that moment. It was scarcely adequate to defeat a Chinese division, 10,000 strong, enjoying choice of ground for engagement. The corps commander sent two heavy mortar companies (which took no part in the battle) to support him, a company of Sherman tanks, two engineer companies to fight as infantry, and a howitzer battalion.

Over an arc of six miles, Brigadier Burke set out 2 PPCLI on and round the north-west height, 6 Point 677, while 3 RAR covered the junction of both north-western and northern approaches from the area of Point 504. On the valley floor between the two, 3 RAR's headquarters, augmented to control 6 ROK stragglers and refugees, was further reinforced by two platoons of the American Shermans covering both approach routes. The Middlesex and 25-pounders of 16th Field would deploy in tandem one mile behind this position.

At 20.00, Lieutenant Colonel Ferguson closed the 3 RAR check line. The Middlesex and 16th Field arrived with the American howitzer battalion, all amidst fleeing ROK detachments, flashing lights and racing engines. Random small arms fire swelled in sound and frequency as the Chinese 118th Division emerged from pools of shadow about 22.00 to attack the Australians under a rising moon. The first thrusts were easily borne; the ground was unfamiliar to the enemy. They began discovery of the defences, during which they were made aware of the American tanks under First Lieutenant Kenneth W. Koch, who broke up this process round the headquarters position.

Other Chinese groups of company or platoon size were soon engaged on the heels of reconnaissance. Strong parties scrambling round the feature topped by Point 504 were directed to one or another of the four Australian rifle companies by commanders blowing whistle signals. Attacks of increasing weight continued through the night. The defence, frequently aided by the artillery and battalion mortars, held together, but at a price. On the morning of 24 April, their casualties became evident – one company had lost fifty of a hundred, for example. Moreover, residual Chinese detachments had yet to be clawed out from random occupancy

of the Australian perimeter. Friendly air strikes after first light drove off
Chinese reinforcements arriving to extend the battle.

Notwithstanding the tenacity of 3 RAR's companies round Point 504,
Colonel Ferguson decided after dawn that he must pull back. He was
perched with his headquarters company on the front line. His casualties
were such as to threaten extinction in another day and night action; his
own position was becoming increasingly encircled. A Middlesex company sent to reinforce him was rapidly becoming isolated. Brigadier
Burke agreed. He was already concerned that ammunition resupply was
still delayed. If 3 RAR did not move shortly, they might be unable to
move at all. Through the afternoon, 3 RAR and its tanks drew back
behind the Middlesex. They settled behind brigade headquarters.

Dead bodies observed after daylight on 24 April suggest a ratio of
Chinese losses to Australian and American as 6:1. Even so, one at least
of 118th Division's regiments had not been committed on that day:
Lieutenant Colonel Stone commanding 2 PPCLI was aware that enemy
reconnaissance patrols had surveyed his positions on the 23rd and
expected an attempt to overwhelm his battalion. Curiously, having
considerable numbers in hand, the enemy commander did not attack
3 RAR and 2 PPCLI simultaneously or sidestep to the Chunch'on–Seoul
main road. Recognizing that he was probably the next target, Colonel
Stone moved his B Company from the north of Hill 677 to a spur almost
due south. Suppressive fire fell upon the new site from 22.15 on the 24th
and two assaults were made with limited success, the latter extending to
battalion headquarters, from which the Canadian mortars and .50 calibre
machine guns 'blew the Chinese back down the ravine.'

After midnight, greater Chinese numbers were engaged. A complete
battalion attacked D Company, whose foremost positions were displaced
'by sheer weight of numbers'. Captain J. G. W. Mills brought artillery
fire down on the whole position. Two further major attacks and many
on a smaller scale were defeated by fire or counter-attack during the day
in which, again, Lieutenant Koch's tanks cooperated. Against the contin-
gency of isolation four C-119 air transports dropped supplies during
the afternoon but by that time Kapy'ong was fully secure once more, its
defences boosted by the arrival of 5th Cavalry.

The 27th and 29th Brigades had held the line successfully for three
days, denying a breach to the Chinese thrusts, denying supplies and
transport to the scavengers. As early as 26th April P'eng recognized that

his thrust lines had miscarried but, shifting sectors, he maintained the weight and pace of operations to preserve his reputation for revolutionary zeal. On 22 May, he informed the Central Military Commission that 'the Fifth Campaign is about to come to an end for the time being . . .' The reason was obvious. From early May, Van Fleet had been exploiting the mobility and striking power of his artillery and aircraft intensively. Road interdiction was such that 8,000 Chinese wounded had been awaiting evacuation for over a week. The Commission agreed – Mao grudgingly – that the 'volunteers' should retire while they retained the means to give their opponents a bloody nose if they followed too fast and too far beyond the 38th parallel.

*

During June 1951, Generals Ridgway and Van Fleet advanced the UN and ROK armies up to the 38th parallel, crossing it in places to a depth of twenty miles. Following this achievement, the Soviet representative on the Security Council used a public broadcast in the United States to suggest that an armistice should be instituted on the Korean battlefield. Negotiators met at Kaesong on 8 July.

The Chinese and North Korean representatives took a high and hectoring line from the outset, claiming in all their discussions to represent the 'the peace-loving peoples of the world'. Nevertheless, after a short delay, an agenda was agreed comprehending three essential items: the establishment of a demilitarized zone between the respective armed forces; concrete arrangement for a ceasefire and armistice that would ensure against a resumption of hostilities and acts of armed force in Korea; arrangements relating to prisoners of war.

Two years would pass before these requirements were satisfied mutually. Meantime, the war continued, but no longer as a war of grand manoeuvre, rather a static environment such as that experienced on the Western Front during 1914–18.

Still, while the war continued, apprehensions and anxieties ebbed and flowed among the parties on both sides. The first was that the other side was using the negotiations as a distraction while preparing to reopen an offensive action of devastating power. The communists continued to expect a landing on the north-west coast of Korea. The Americans and British boosted their intelligence collection and analysis. The air commanders were never quite at ease with the political ruling that UN aircraft should not approach let alone cross over into north-east China, where some believed that a powerful communist air component was being prepared for renewed intervention.

The UN commanders were anxious to maintain morale and physical fitness for a long term in defence. This led as months passed to the development of plans to advance into areas vulnerable to attack, though Ridgway and Van Fleet could not agree as to objectives. Within divisions, patrol operations, even battalion raiding operations were mounted, officially to capture prisoners but more often to preserve battle fitness. As time passed, the Chinese intensified their own raiding activities, which were extended to localized struggles for possession of advantageous ground.

The British and Commonwealth soldiers were shielded substantially from such policies from August 1951 by the formation of the Commonwealth Division under Major-General A. J. H. Cassels. The policy to uprate the Commonwealth command had been proposed at the end of 1950 in order to take full advantage of the supporting 'tail' in South Korea and Japan. The commanders already in the field wished to be screened from what they believed to be, from experience during the winter of 1950–51, an American tendency to make impulsive decisions. Brigadier Coad had felt it with 24th Division, Brigadier Brodie with the 3rd Division on the Imjin. The Canadians in sending a brigade to Korea, and the Australians raising periodically the numbers of their infantry in 28th Brigade, relished the interpolation of a Commonwealth divisional commander. The advantages of support from a dedicated divisional artillery and engineer regiment were manifest across all those employed in the line.

When General Cassels took up his post the peace talks were faltering but, incidentally, local tactical enterprise was rising on the battlefield. A tour of his area had convinced him of the advantages of moving the division north across the Imjin River: he was too far back from the enemy, and the seizure of certain high points would deny the Chinese observation over his forward supply routes. This was plan 'Minden', completed in September. 'Commando', a similar plan involving the whole of I Corps, followed. It began after a series of rainstorms which required devoted engineer work across the swollen Imjin waters and finished successfully on 19 October, extended beyond expectations. Chinese tenacity was due to the fact that the UN objectives included unwittingly a section of their main battle line. From this time on, both sides were engaged in the development of continuous entrenchments – many parts of which were necessarily blasted into the rocky surface on the high ground and built up in valleys such as that of the Samich'on on the Commonwealth left flank. The consumption of sandbags soared.

October and November were difficult months. Both sides anticipated covertly the dangers of drifting into a ceasefire. Some members of the American high command and State Department could not understand why negotiations took so long to achieve so little, why 'our side' did not encourage the communists by offering concessions as incentives tied to an acceptance date. Members of the diplomatic contact points in London and Washington became petulant. Some British officials believed that the Americans were inhibited by false perspectives of communist aims, of pursuing national rather than Allied aims. Some Americans thought the British were looking for an escape route from the war. Such notions were the product of frustration and were not universal. The UN alliance had expected that agreement to negotiations would bring a quick end to the war. Fortunately, the principals maintained their aims and methods, among them Mr Churchill, in office as Prime Minister from 25 October, who was no less dedicated to a common policy with the United States in Korea than Mr Attlee, his predecessor.

It is possible that the communist hierarchies were also disappointed at the lack of progress. Some in General Ridgway's headquarters believed that an upsurge in Chinese aggression at this time was linked to the negotiations at Panmunjom. Maryang-san among other heights was stormed in November by five regiments of 'volunteers', seeking to displace severally the King's Own Scottish Borderers, the King's Shropshire Light Infantry, the Leicesters, and 3 RAR during periods of intensive shelling and close quarter actions. P'eng may simply have wished to pick up this site for its value to the final armistice line. If so, he paid a high price, over 3,000 casualties to 417 among the British Commonwealth defenders, some of whom remained in their original positions at the conclusion of the struggle. Thereafter, during the winter, the battle line quietened.

In the winter of 1951–52 there was expectation that an armistice would be in sight by the spring; and in the spring there was hope that negotiations would have been completed by the following winter. Fighting waxed and waned on the ground. Commonwealth warships under command of Vice Admiral (recently promoted from Rear Admiral) Sir William Andrewes, Royal Navy, and later his successor Sir Alan Scott-Moncrieff, mounted operations on the Heinz basis – the squadron's claim – of '57 Varieties' including air reconnaissance, capture or destruction of enemy shipping, bombardment of shore targets, minesweeping, dropping and collecting of intelligence agents, and rescuing aircrew shot down. But nothing undertaken on sea or land at that time, as it seemed to the air forces, would break the politico-military deadlock. Successive American air force commanders judged that aircraft could do it. General Ridgway and his successor General Mark Clark gave them the opportunity.

In brief, every form of conventional air warfare was brought to destroy enemy internal power sources, irrigation reserves and war manufactures above and below ground, to cut communications southwards from the Yalu River, to destroy enemy aircraft flying over Korean territory. Many tasks had been undertaken at one level or another since the beginning of the war but now they were redoubled. As a consequence, villages and towns, even cities like P'yongyang, were ruined. Against the wishes of the British government, attacks upon the previously sacrosanct hydraulic power plants astride the Yalu River were permitted. Due to British views, the only localities denied to the UN air forces were the clusters of Chinese air bases inside north-east China. The British took the view that the bombing of Chinese territory might prompt disproportionate Sino-Soviet countermeasures such as the capture of Hong Kong. In any case, the UN had the means to maintain air supremacy over the whole of North Korea, so the destruction of the airfields in north-east China was scarcely worth the risk of retaliation.

All in all, the evidence suggests that attempts to end the war by air power alone were not likely to be successful. The option of atomic weapons was aired occasionally. There was flirtation with actions preparatory to deployment but General Eisenhower, on succession to the presidency in 1953, evidently had no plans to proceed further.

In their resentment of restraint at any level, the air commanders undervalued their contribution to the land battle, in which air to ground strikes were often crucial to the preservation of UN soldiers. The communist side had no doubts in this matter, as the North Korean General Nam Il remarked at Panmunjom in August 1951: 'Without the support of the indiscriminate bombing and bombardment by your air and naval forces, your ground forces would have long ago been driven out from the Korean peninsula.'

The outcome of the negotiations was in Stalin's hands. Sometimes he seems to have thought that it would pay him to conclude an armistice yet, month by month, he let hostilities run on. However, when he died, on 5 March 1953, the Chinese political hierarchy reasserted its authority. The chief financiers of the war, Mao and his associates, judged that the costs of maintaining it were becoming intolerable. Stalin's successor agreed. From that point it was simply a matter of making a plan which suggested a balance of advantage to the communist camp.

A British proposal to exchange sick and wounded prisoners of war was gathering support in the United Nations from February 1953. Persuaded to end hostilities, it suited Moscow and Peking to take up the idea. The exchange took place on 20 April.

China and the Soviet Union now carried further their plans to end hostilities. The exchange, 'Little Switch', was used as a means to reopen negotiations, suspended earlier by the communists, who were unwilling to allow prisoners to choose their destinations on release – many Chinese and North Korean prisoners had forcibly expressed wishes not to go back to their homes. On 30 March, Chou and Kim issued a statement accepting the principle of choice. Though the UN authorities did not know it, all that remained to complete the armistice agreement was a form of implementation which shielded the Chinese from loss of face. From April, the two sides negotiated to this end.

Still, the communists were not prepared to embrace peace unreservedly. They planned to end by demonstrating a triumph in arms. 'The Hook' was chosen early as an exemplary locality, a collection of features overlooking the Samich'on in which Commonwealth units – infantry, armour, gunners and engineers, and the United States Marine Corps – had all earned reputations for valour. It was stormed again in May 1953. The Duke of Wellington's, Black Watch, Royal Fusiliers, the King's (Liverpool) Regiment, and Royal Tanks were all drawn into and around the sector. After a week of heavy shelling, a major assault was launched on 28 May which continued through the night until the Hook was cleared of the remnant of seven Chinese battalions by 04.30 on the 29th.

Across the Korean peninsula, the Chinese hierarchy indulged their readiness to accept high losses similarly against the United States and ROK armies. At the same time they shook their fists at President

Syngman Rhee, who had released North Korean prisoners of war prematurely.

The ceasefire became effective at 22.00 hours on 27 July 1953. The prisoners returned, in all 978 from the United Kingdom, 68 from other Commonwealth forces. At best, they had been treated indifferently, sometimes cruelly, by the Chinese in the interests of political subversion, and inhumanly as a rule by the North Koreans: 82 British prisoners lost their lives while captives.

Who won?

Stalin and Mao agreed that Kim Il-sung should capture South Korea. This principal objective was not realized. A majority in the United Nations wished to reunite Korea under its auspices. That was not realized. Equally, the post-war attempts to bring about a negotiated peace and reunion foundered. But the republic in the south remained free to develop into a modern, democratic state while its northern neighbour sank into bankruptcy.

From the outset the British government maintained a contribution to the Korean War second only to that of the United States. It sent forces without obligation, acting on the principle with others that aggression would not be tolerated by one state against another. Collective action against the aggressors was enforced successfully in Korea, the only war fought under the United Nations' flag.

The costs of the British contribution were burdensome. It is sometimes alleged that they set back the recovery of the economy for a decade and more, but this is doubtful. The greater portion of the war material consumed was drawn from the ageing stockpiles of the Second World War. Oil stocks were provided by the United States on account – an account it must be confessed in which the vouchers for items drawn, together with those for other services, were mislaid among all parties. The figure finally agreed was exceedingly favourable to the United Kingdom.

Most importantly, the operational contribution of the British servicemen in company with their Commonwealth partners was of a high order. The numbers, 66,000 British seamen, marines, and soldiers, and a handful of aircrew, regulars, reservists recalled, and national service men, tend to be overshadowed by those of the United States forces at 1,000,000. Nevertheless, the fielding of a division was of itself important at a time when American military manpower was severely strained. Not least, the quality of the British and Commonwealth forces was judged by American commanders such as General Ridgway to be first rate.

Some may judge that this evaluation by Britain's closest international partner encouraged successive British governments to punch beyond their weight. This may be true: the debacle of the Suez operation was shortly to follow the Korean War. But one swallow does not make a summer: the campaigns for the recovery of the Falklands and Kuwait sustain the reputation won for the United Kingdom in Korea by her military forces.

5

GENERAL SIR FRANK KITSON

Kenya, 1952–1956: Mau Mau

General Sir Frank Kitson first made a name for himself during the Mau Mau campaign in Kenya, after which he wrote about his experiences in *Gangs and Counter Gangs*. He subsequently served in many post-1945 campaigns. While still serving he published *Low Intensity Operations*, which he followed up with *Bunch of Five*. He ended his army career as C-in-C United Kingdom Land Forces. Since retiring he has published a biography of Prince Rupert.

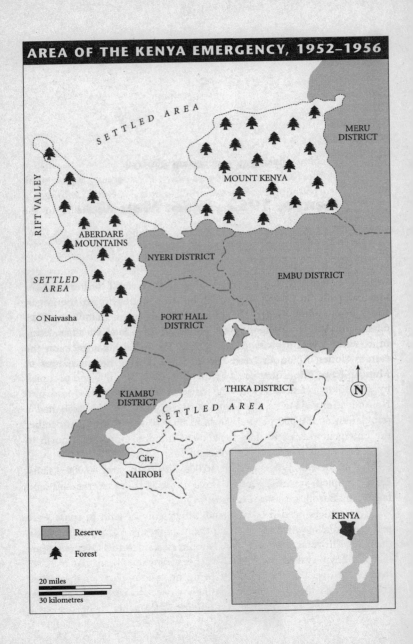

AREA OF THE KENYA EMERGENCY, 1952–1956

SETTLED AREA

MERU DISTRICT

MOUNT KENYA

RIFT VALLEY

ABERDARE MOUNTAINS

NYERI DISTRICT

EMBU DISTRICT

SETTLED AREA

○ Naivasha

FORT HALL DISTRICT

THIKA DISTRICT

KIAMBU DISTRICT

SETTLED AREA

N

City

NAIROBI

Reserve

Forest

20 miles

30 kilometres

KENYA

Of all the counter-insurgency operations undertaken by the British since 1945, the Emergency in Kenya was the bloodiest. It also took place in surroundings of outstanding natural beauty amongst a people gripped by terror accentuated by a widespread belief in the supernatural.

Kenya lies in an area of East Africa that is roughly 600 miles from north to south and 500 miles from east to west. Within it are twenty-seven main tribal groups, only one of which, the Kikuyu, was concerned with the Emergency that was declared in October 1952. But the Kikuyu together with the closely related Embu and Meru formed the largest tribal group, amounting at that time to slightly over 1.5 million of the 6.5 million Africans living in Kenya. They were subsistence farmers living in a twenty-mile strip along the edge of the forests that grew on the eastern slopes of the Aberdare mountains and the southern slopes of Mount Kenya. The area affected by the Emergency was the land occupied by the Kikuyu together with the adjacent European farms and also Nairobi, a city lying to the south of the Kikuyu lands, which had a population of 110,000 people of whom 65,000 were Kikuyu. Altogether the Emergency area stretched for about a hundred miles from north to south and rather less from east to west.

Also in the colony were about 40,000 Europeans and 80,000 Asians. Land occupied by African tribes was known as tribal reserve and land farmed by Europeans as settled area.

These settlers needed labour, and with plenty of land to spare were prepared to allow Africans to bring their families and animals to live on their farm in return for a certain amount of paid work. Over the years many Kikuyu availed themselves of this arrangement, so that by 1945 there were over 120,000 of them living in various parts of the settled area, although they became increasingly subject to irksome regulations as their growing families and multiplying stock came to be seen as a threat to the prosperity of European farmers on whose produce and taxes the economy of the colony depended.

When the British first arrived they chose a number of the most sensible Africans with whom they came in contact to help them control the various tribes, appointing them chiefs, although no such appointments had formerly existed. The British also divided the country up into provinces and districts run by British colonial officers called commissioners and into locations run by chiefs. The three Kikuyu districts from north to south were Nyeri, Fort Hall and Kiambu. Embu and Meru districts lay to the east of Nyeri.

In 1946 Jomo Kenyatta, who had been living in England for the past sixteen years, returned to Kenya and shortly afterwards became President of the Kenya African Union (KAU), an African political association. Kenyatta, who was widely known as a result of the skill with which he brought the grievances of the Kikuyu to the attention of politicians in England, set about establishing branches of the KAU throughout the colony. His policy at this time was to set right some of the genuine grievances felt by the Africans, especially the Kikuyu. Land hunger was increasing, and a small area in Kiambu district which had originally been mistakenly settled had not been returned although some compensation had been received by the tribe. The Kikuyu found it difficult to grow cash crops that might compete with the settlers', because of the way in which tribal land was held. Another grievance concerned the direction of labour for terracing designed to prevent soil erosion, and there was discontent at the way in which the 75,000 soldiers of all tribes returning from the war were being treated. The KAU rank and file was becoming impatient.

Next Kenyatta started to spread clandestinely an oath of unity to a few key supporters within the Kikuyu tribe, first in the reserve and later to the labour on European farms and finally in 1948 to Nairobi. During the summer of 1951 the Nairobi branch of the KAU set up a secret Central Committee to supervise the oathing of the Kikuyu. With or without Kenyatta's consent this committee sent out seventy-five oath administrators to extend greatly the number of Kikuyu bound to the movement known as Mau Mau which lay concealed within the KAU. This widespread oathing required strong-arm groups to collect the money levied with the oath and to force the reluctant into taking it, often killing and mutilating those who refused.

At this point it is necessary to explain the significance of the oath. It must be remembered that fifty years earlier most of the Kikuyu had never seen a European: they had not even seen animals harnessed together or ridden nor had they heard of the wheel or the plough. They had no experience of money or writing. All misfortune was put down to malignant spirits or the anger of their god. Witch doctors were usually relied on to cure bodily ills by providing concoctions that would appease the spirit or counter the spell that had caused it. Disputes were settled by councils of elders usually on the basis of compensation and one of the methods of determining a dispute was to get the parties to it to take an oath. Providing that the oath was administered in such a way as to persuade the person taking it that he would die if he lied, he would either tell the truth or keep silent. The oath therefore consisted of two parts. First there were the actions necessary for summoning the supernatural power. Certain acts, which would now be regarded as unpleasant such as suffocating a goat and using its stomach contents and other parts, would invoke this power and were in accordance with tribal custom, but certain other acts that were decidedly repulsive were not. The second part concerned what was being said. For example, the person taking the oath might be swearing that he did not steal something or he might be undertaking to do something. No one who believed in the power of the oath would take it unless he was intending to honour it and in 1950 when many had grown up before the arrival of Europeans and when the rest had been brought up by such people, nearly all Kikuyu did believe, despite the spread of Christianity. Consciously many had forsaken the old ways, but the spiritual awareness of their forebears and their attitude to life and death remained strong in the depths of their minds. They were totally different from the present generation of Kenyan Africans.

The oathing that was going on at this time was designed to ensure secrecy, obedience, unity and mutual assistance amongst the followers of the movement. As time went by methods of invoking the supernatural were extended to include activities that were taboo to the tribe so that those taking it were pushed irrevocably beyond the pale and away for ever from the influence of the elders. Naturally this was strongly resisted by the chiefs and tribal elders who had no desire to lose control in this way and the new oath and the coercion that went with it alienated many people, even though most supported the aims of the KAU.

Soon the chairman of the Nairobi branch found that he could not control the situation as the oath inflamed the impatience of the people. Murders of those opposed to the movement and general violence increased and spread to the European farms. Since 1950 the Central Committee had been systematically collecting weapons and a general insurrection throughout the Kikuyu tribe was inevitable. On the day that the Emergency was declared, 20 October 1952, 183 KAU members were detained including Kenyatta, most of the leadership and nearly all of the branch chairmen. By this time many of the Kikuyu working on European farms had been evicted and were flooding into the reserves and Nairobi. Some, finding nowhere to go, took to the forests where they were soon joined by the oath administrators and their hardcore supporters together with others who were bent on insurrection and a number of criminals on the run. Within a few weeks many gangs of several hundred each were living in forest camps in the Aberdares and Mount Kenya, being supplied by groups in the reserve. They were there to fight for the return of the land 'stolen' from the Kikuyu and for freedom to live unhampered by laws designed to safeguard European interests. They called themselves the Kenya Land and Freedom Army.

The immediate problem was to control the violence, and the ultimate responsibility for this rested with the United Kingdom government headed by Winston Churchill who in his long career had been both Undersecretary and Secretary of State for the Colonies. But it is unlikely that the problems of Kenya were uppermost in his mind at this time. Confrontation with the Soviet Union was at its most dangerous and British forces were fighting in Korea and Malaya. Against this background the murder of a few people in East Africa would have attracted little interest, although in early October the potential danger of the situation had been starkly presented to the Colonial Secretary by the new governor, Sir Evelyn Baring. And in the same way as the Kikuyu of the 1950s were very different from their counterparts today, so too was the average Englishman. The Second World War had finished a mere seven years earlier and most of the population were accustomed to death and destruction on a large scale. In war casualties amongst our own people were regarded as inevitable and the destruction of enemy forces was accepted with satisfaction. In the army all the company commanders and commanding officers had fought in the war and some of the longest serving officers had been through the First World War as well. In Kenya itself the settlers, many of whom had served in the forces during these wars, were furious that the situation had been allowed to deteriorate to this extent since they had been warning of the dangers for several years. Now they wanted the governor to crush the rebellion without delay.

Situated in Kenya was the headquarters of the general officer commanding East Africa, Lieutenant General Sir Alexander Cameron. Under his command were a brigade headquarters and seven battalions of the King's African Rifles (KAR), five of which were made available to Kenya when the Emergency was declared, at which time a British battalion, 1st Lancashire Fusiliers, was also flown in from Egypt. The only other military units available were an armoured car squadron, an anti-aircraft battery and the Kenya Regiment, a European Territorial Army battalion made up largely of young settlers. The general, not wanting to get tied down in Kenya, appointed the brigade commander to act as the governor's military adviser. At this time the Kenya Police, 7,100 strong, operated in the towns and settled area under the direction of the Commissioner of Police. Tribal police, who took their orders from the district commissioners and chiefs, operated in the reserves.

Following the declaration of Emergency there was an increase in Mau Mau activity. Another chief was murdered together with numerous loyalists and some cattle were killed by cutting open their bellies, or by leaving them hamstrung and bellowing, which greatly enraged the European community. Within two weeks the first settler was murdered. There was virtually no intelligence about the Mau Mau because the Special Branch of the Kenya Police, which might have been adequate for watching a few subversives within the KAU, was totally unable to keep track of the gangs in the forest or of the numerous Mau Mau committees supporting them (known as the passive wing). Initially all that could be done was to deploy the KAR battalions in the most active parts of the reserve and the British battalion and the Kenya Regiment in the settled area to react to incidents as they occurred.

The next priority was to provide some coordinating machinery to harness together the efforts of the loyal members of the Kikuyu tribe with the expatriate-run agencies such as the army and police. Then it would be necessary for a programme of administrative measures to be combined with the operations of the security forces in order to persuade or force those Kikuyu supporting the Mau Mau to abandon violence as a method of achieving their aims. Meanwhile the Mau Mau had to use the support it had gained, as a result of the past few years of oathing, to kill those still loyal to the government or persuade them to join the movement before the government's counter-measures could take effect.

On the government side three important developments occurred within the next two months. First, a number of loyal Kikuyu were recruited in each location to act as a Home Guard and as a focus for resistance to the Mau Mau: they were known as Kikuyu Guard. Small fortified posts were erected throughout the reserve as bases for these people whose activities were overseen by a British officer of the administration in each location, known as a District Officer (Kikuyu Guard) and answerable to the district commissioner. This force, which was initially armed with spears and swords, grew to a strength of around 30,000 men and was eventually incorporated into the Tribal Police. From the start it was in the forefront of the battle and the main target for Mau Mau attack. Second, the Kenya Police Reserve was enlarged by the recruitment of Europeans and Asians to help the regular police in the towns and settled areas on a part-time basis, which brought the total strength of the Kenya Police to around 20,000. Third, the governor insisted that a senior army officer should be appointed to his staff to coordinate action against the terrorists. Major General W. R. N. Hinde was appointed to the post, which was designated Director of Operations in April 1953. He set about installing a chain of committees at the head of which was a Colony Emergency Committee presided over by the governor. Under it was a Director of Operations Committee, and below that were Provincial and District Emergency Committees, each chaired by the relevant commissioner and including representatives of the army and police, who were thus able to coordinate their operations.

Meanwhile, in the Aberdare forest opposite Nyeri district, Stanley Mathenge was trying to organize the large numbers of Kikuyu who had taken to the forest into some sort of a military force. Mathenge had joined the KAR early in the war and had fought with them in Burma. He was a natural leader who had been in charge of collecting weapons in Nairobi, and from early in 1952, when a war council attached to the Nairobi Central Committee was formed, he was recognized as the 'chairman of Mau Mau'. His drawback was that he was illiterate. Soon after entering the forest Mathenge was joined by Dedan Kimathi, another Nyeri man and a very different sort of person. Kimathi had no military experience, having been thrown out of the KAR for repeated misconduct within a few weeks of joining. But he was well educated and could speak and read English. He had held numerous jobs in the settled area around the northern end of the Aberdares and was a known criminal. He was a powerful orator at KAU meetings and an oath administrator. In the early days in the forest he handled administrative and political matters and worked well with Mathenge.

Further south in the Aberdares, gangs of fighters from Fort Hall district were forming under their own leaders, of whom the best known was Kago. This man had served in the war and risen to the rank of corporal. He was reasonably well educated, and had worked as a house servant before moving as a labourer to the Rift Valley. Other gangs from Nyeri, Embu and Meru were forming up in the Mount Kenya forest, where the overall leader was another ex-corporal in the KAR formerly active in Nairobi as an oath administrator, known as China. (It was common practice for some fighters to assume forest names such as Kago and China.) As time went on the Fort Hall gangs accepted the overall leadership of Mathenge and Kimathi but the Mount Kenya gangs retained their independence.

In the most southern of the Kikuyu districts, Kiambu, there was less emphasis on the formation of forest gangs, because the Mau Mau wanted to keep the district quiet so that recruits and supplies collected there and in Nairobi could pass to the fighters further north without the harassment that would accompany military operations against forest terrorists. But as in other districts small gangs existed in the reserve to carry out tasks as required by the passive wing committees.

In the early months of 1953 the Mau Mau made most of the running, debouching from the forest to attack Kikuyu Guard posts and kill as many loyalists as they could. They also perfected their system for collecting recruits and supplies from Nairobi and their local committees. At this time the gang leaders still accepted instructions from their local passive wing which in turn took orders from that part of the central committee in Nairobi that was composed of people from their district of the reserve and who symbolically represented the detained political leaders.[1]

Matters came to a head on 26 March when the police station at Naivasha, deep in the settled area to the west of the Aberdares, was overrun by a gang which broke open the armoury taking eighteen automatic weapons, twenty-nine rifles and a large quantity of ammunition as well as releasing 173 prisoners. That same night a number of gangs from the Kiambu reserve, acting on orders from the Central Committee in Nairobi, attacked and killed a loyal chief at Lari in the west of the district together with eighty-four of his followers, mainly women and children, thirty-one others being injured and hundreds of cattle maimed. This massacre, which received widespread publicity in England, at last woke people up to the gravity of the situation and the brutality of the Mau Mau. But by this time the government had already decided to send out a brigade of British troops and appoint a senior general as Commander-in-Chief, East Africa, directly responsible to London. As a result 39th Brigade, consisting of two battalions, 1st Buffs and 1st Devons, arrived in April. The general, Sir George Erskine, followed in June.

General Erskine had served as a subaltern in the First World War and later gained experience against insurgents in India. He had become well known as the commander of 7th Armoured Division in North Africa, Sicily, Italy and Normandy and he later became the military governor of Belgium. After the war he became Chief of Staff of the Control Commission for Germany, and then General Officer Commanding British Troops Egypt and Mediterranean Command. At the time of his appointment he was Commander-in-Chief Eastern Command. Personally selected by Churchill, Kenya now found itself with a top-class performer, and not before time.

Erskine arrived when the situation looked bleak. Whether in the reserve or on the farms or in Nairobi, the oath had poisoned the atmosphere completely. Many Kikuyu had been killed for resisting it and many others had taken it under duress and were fearful of the consequences. Nobody knew who to trust. In the settled area Europeans felt that they might be murdered by the very Africans with whom they had grown up. There were now between 11,000 and 15,000 in the forest gangs and nobody could even guess at the number of their passive wing supporters.

As if to compensate for the arrival of a full general, the Mau Mau chose this moment to issue ranks to their followers. Gang leaders became generals: below them brigadiers and corporals proliferated. Oddly enough there seemed to be a distinct shortage of men in the intervening ranks. Luckily the forest gangs were poorly armed with perhaps 1,500 precision weapons together with a large number of home-made guns which were only effective at close range.

Erskine's directive from London was to take the military measures required to end the emergency. Army units and a detachment of Harvard aircraft, soon to be joined by a squadron of Lincoln bombers, were under his direct command. Those elements of the Kenya Police concerned with operations against the Mau Mau were also placed under his command and fortified police posts were established at strategic points throughout the reserve, largely officered by members of the Kenya Regiment on secondment to the police. These posts proved invaluable as centres of communication and as a focus for security force operations. Realizing that he would need extra troops, Erskine asked for a further brigade of two battalions and an engineer regiment, as a result of which 49th Brigade arrived in September 1953. This brought the strength of the army to 10,000. At no time were there more than five British battalions in Kenya during the Emergency. Preparations to build up the intelligence organization by attaching army officers to the police Special Branch had already been made and these people started to arrive in August. Erskine himself became Director of Operations with Hinde as his deputy.

Erskine decided that his first priority must be to protect loyalists in the reserve since the purpose of the Mau Mau was to kill or subvert them. The reserve itself consisted of a patchwork of very small farms growing beans, maize and bananas, together with areas of scrub where goats, sheep and native cattle grazed. There were also patches of wattle, the whole being scattered along the sides of the steep valleys which separated the many streams running down from the forest. By deploying most of his forces in the reserve, from where the army made incursions into the forest, Erskine reduced the resources available for the defence of settlers' farms, although the expanding Kenya Police Reserve was affording some protection to these people. His apparent lack of concern for the settlers naturally made him unpopular with them.

By the end of 1953 three measures were beginning to bear fruit. First, after the Lari massacre the Kikuyu Guard started to receive firearms, despite the danger that some might find their way to the gangs. This boosted loyalist morale. Second, a start was made on concentrating the Kikuyu into protected villages, which made intimidation of loyalists more difficult and enabled the Kikuyu Guard to restrict the flow of food to the gangs. Third, army officers arriving to reinforce the police special branch in each district were given a number of Kenya Regiment sergeants to act as Field Intelligence Officers, who set up small posts throughout the reserve and settled area. They then collected a few loyalists for protection and to help with the initial interrogation of prisoners. At first they could do little more than collect overt information from anyone who had it and pass it on to those who might be able to make use of it, but as time went on they built up a network of informers capable of producing genuine intelligence.

As an example of the type of operations carried out by the Mau Mau it is worth looking at the doings of 'General' Kago between March 1953 and March 1954. During the first part of 1953 he carried out several successful raids, in one of which he captured a post manned by Kikuyu Guard, Tribal Police and a few Masai trackers. Having killed four of the defenders and captured seven others, he locked them into a hut and set it on fire before making off with four rifles, three shotguns, a pistol and some ammunition. To celebrate the Queen's coronation he burnt down one guard post, raided another unsuccessfully and destroyed several bridges in the reserve. In July he overran another post, killing all fourteen of the inmates and taking some more weapons. At the end of September he took most of his gang through the Fort Hall reserve into the Thika settled area where he made his camp in a wooded area, probably on the slopes of Ol Donyo Sabuk. From here they raided a police roadblock, capturing some more weapons. He then remained quiet until a detachment of his gang contacted an army patrol near the town of Thika on Christmas Eve. In the ensuing engagement, which lasted for some hours, the company commander, the District Commandant of the Kenya Police Reserve and two African policemen were killed and others wounded. Soon afterwards Kago crossed into the Kiambu reserve after which he ran out of luck and lost many men in a series of contacts with the security forces before getting back to the Fort Hall forest. After being wounded in a skirmish he lay up for some weeks before leading his whole gang out into the reserve where he overran another Kikuyu guard post, killing ten of the occupants. In the subsequent chase mounted by a large number of security force detachments he was killed together with some of his followers.[2] He was a daring commander whose death brought much relief and a certain sense of loss to his opponents.

During this period security force operations took the form of sweeps through the reserve searching for gangs together with the arrest and detention of passive wing supporters. When a large gang such as Kago's appeared, the nearest police post would contact the district operations room and whatever forces were available, whether army, police or Kikuyu Guard, would be directed into the area. They would then try to intercept and attack the gang, which would probably break up into several smaller groups in order to escape to the shelter of the forest, where they would be pursued by the army. Either the senior army commander or the police superintendent for the district would coordinate operations while the nearest brigade headquarters pumped in reinforcements from outside the district if necessary.

Using methods such as these the reserves became reasonably safe for loyalists by March 1954, by which time the Mau Mau leadership was showing signs of strain. A number of gang leaders had been eliminated, including 'General' China, who was captured after being wounded in December. Deciding to cooperate with his captors, China tried to organize a surrender of the terrorists in Mount Kenya, but this failed to materialize after several weeks of negotiation.

All operations had to be carried out within the law, which was the peacetime law of the colony reinforced by emergency regulations: together these gave wide powers to the security forces. For example, within prohibited areas such as the forest the enemy could be shot at on sight. Elsewhere they had to be challenged first. A number of offences such as possessing illegal arms or ammunition or consorting with an armed terrorist carried the death penalty and slightly over 1,000 were hanged after conviction by courts during the Emergency. Otherwise people could be detained without trial either on the orders of the governor or of a district commissioner.

Operating within the law was not always easy when faced by the horrors of Mau Mau. When Kago locked his prisoners into a hut and set fire to it, he told his men that anyone who did not sympathize with the Mau Mau cause could expect no pity. Another Mau Mau 'general' writing after the emergency pointed out that the slaughter of captives arose from the fact that the Mau Mau could not keep prisoners. He mentioned a number of ways in which they were despatched, such as chopping them up with pangas, using them for target practice, breaking their limbs and leaving them to die, strangling, drowning or burning them. As an alternative he said that some were castrated or otherwise mutilated and then sent back as an example to those opposing the movement.[3] General Erskine insisted that despite the way in which the Mau Mau behaved, the security forces should stick to the law, which the army and regular police did with few exceptions. This was not difficult because they were seldom in great danger themselves and had less of a stake in the country than local forces. For the settlers in the Kenya Police Reserve and the Kenya Regiment things were different. It was their country and it was often their workers, wives, children and animals that were being slaughtered. It is to their credit that lapses were few, but they did occur and where there was evidence, action was taken against them. It is also worth recording that many allegations were made against innocent men in an attempt to get rid of them, especially if they were proving effective in their jobs. The chiefs and the Kikuyu Guard who were in the forefront of the battle and in constant danger were the most likely to offend, particularly as their idea of justice was based on compensation rather than a court trial. When they did, it posed a problem for the district commissioners who could seldom afford to let the cornerstone of resistance in their area be removed for behaviour that most of the locals regarded as perfectly natural. Inevitably the Governor was left in the uncomfortable position of having to decide whether to back his attorney general or the officers of the administration, which sometimes obliged him to make a decision which ran counter to his strongly held feelings.

By the end of 1953 allegations of misconduct and enquiries were rife and were having an effect on morale in parts of the security forces. Furthermore these disputes reverberated around the colony, adding to the frustration of the settlers and to the unrest being displayed by their representatives in the legislative council and on the governor's (executive) council. Although the security situation had improved, this was not yet evident and cries of discontent were even making themselves heard in England.

In February 1954 the Colonial Secretary, Oliver Lyttleton, visited Kenya to work out a new constitution. Amongst other measures it was decided that a war council should be set up composed of the Governor, the Deputy Governor, General Erskine and a minister from the Governor's Council called Michael Blundell who was himself a settler and who was given direct access to the Colonial Secretary. This set the scene for more efficient management of the Emergency. At about this time Baring, who was suffering from ill health, returned to England on sick leave, his place being taken by his deputy, the robust and decisive Sir Frederick Crawford. Some thought that Baring would not return, although ultimately he did do so in June.

As the reserve became more dangerous for the gangs they found difficulty in getting enough food. Nairobi was now the main source of money, ammunition, medical supplies and recruits as well as being the political centre of Mau Mau. Erskine therefore decided that the city should be surrounded and searched in a large-scale operation called ANVIL. Detention camps were built and on 24 April a force of five battalions surrounded the city. For the next two weeks the troops and police carried out a series of cordon and search operations in which a very large number of Kikuyu were screened, some 16,500 of whom were detained under the emergency regulations: a further 2,500 were returned to the reserve to live under the supervision of their chief. The result was to disrupt the whole Mau Mau infrastructure in Nairobi and to separate Nairobi from Kiambu district. Although the Mau Mau were eventually able to rebuild a system for putting together small parties of recruits to join forest gangs, they never regained their political influence or their money raising capability, so that the gangs lost virtually all the support that they had been getting from this source.

Throughout 1954 the security forces kept up the pressure around the city and throughout the reserve. By this time the military intelligence organization within Special Branch was penetrating the passive wing in the reserve and settled area so that many of its members were being detained. Also in these months it developed a system for converting surrendered or captured terrorists, who together with a disguised Field Intelligence Officer would pass themselves off as a gang. The pseudo-gang, as it was called, by getting in touch with a real gang through the passive wing, was able to provide pinpoint information to the security forces which enabled them to bring the real gang to action: in certain circumstances the pseudo-gangs took action themselves. This was particularly useful for disposing of gangs resident in the reserve which had been killing loyalists and oathing. In the latter part of 1954 the system was adapted for use in the forest, where it proved equally effective.[4] From the start pseudo-gangs did much damage to the Mau Mau, who hated them.

While these operations were going on in the reserve and settled area, the gangs in the forest had been kept under pressure by the RAF using the Lincolns and Harvards and by deep patrols carried out by whatever military force could be spared from other tasks. By this time the army had greatly improved its technique for operating in the forest, trackers and specialized follow-up teams including Kenya Regiment NCOs being added to army companies. Opinions differed as to the effectiveness of bombing. So steep and densely forested were the ridges and valleys that a bomb passing within say thirty yards of an enemy group might easily go beyond a nearby ridge and explode at the bottom of the next valley unnoticed by its intended target. Interrogation of Mau Mau captured from areas in which bombing had taken place often showed that the prisoner was unaware that it had happened. On the other hand some Mau Mau writing after the end of the Emergency said that it was frightening, had caused some casualties and that it made large animals such as buffalo and elephants more dangerous, a circumstance also noticed by the army.

By January 1955 support for the forest gangs had virtually disappeared together with their entire logistic backing and Erskine decided that the time was ripe to go after them. This he did by mounting a large-scale operation called HAMMER in the northern part of the Aberdares, which was followed by a similar one in Mount Kenya called FIRST FLUTE. These operations, which were coordinated by General Hinde, involved dividing up the territories into battalion areas within which the troops carried out patrols and set ambushes. The Kikuyu Guard manned the great ditch that had earlier been dug along the forest edge and the strip behind it which had been cleared to mark the prohibited zone. The effect of these operations in terms of casualties was disappointing, but they resulted in the gangs breaking up into small groups, a trend that had already happened to some extent as a result of attrition and logistic difficulties. Indeed the forest Mau Mau had become so furtive and fragmented by this time that the troops taking part regarded their job as being more like shooting rabbits than fighting terrorists. But it was rabbiting under conditions of considerable discomfort as operations were taking place in rainforest or bamboo at an altitude of between 8,000 and 13,000 feet – roasting by day but literally freezing at night.

During 1954 Kimathi and Mathenge had grown apart. Kimathi, who had promoted himself to field marshal and had formed what he called a

Kenya Parliament, claimed to be the overall Mau Mau leader, but Mathenge and his followers did not recognize his claim. Eventually Kimathi gained the allegiance of the gangs in the northern half of the Nyeri forest and of most of the Fort Hall gangs while Mathenge, who was now based in the southern part of the Nyeri forest, retained the support of many of the Rift Valley gangs. At this time Kimathi made a determined attempt to gain the allegiance of the Kiambu gangs, which had become more numerous and active since the separation of Kiambu from Nairobi, but he was firmly rebuffed and his envoy killed by security forces. The Mount Kenya gangs, now under 'General' Tanganyka, who had taken over from China, also maintained their independence. In view of this disunity, and in response to an approach by one of Mathenge's 'generals', Erskine tried a further surrender offer early in 1955. Once again owing to misunderstandings and disagreements within the Mau Mau this did not succeed in producing a mass surrender, but it did result in numerous individuals giving up the struggle. It also made the rift between Kimathi and Mathenge and their respective adherents irreparable.

By April 1955, when General Erskine handed over to Lieutenant General Sir Gerald Lathbury, the numbers of terrorists remaining in the forest had dropped to an estimated 5,000 and the government's control of the reserve and Nairobi was assured. The concentration of Kikuyu into villages was well under way and by confiscating the land of Mau Mau adherents and giving it to loyalists, landholdings had increased to the extent that some Kikuyu were able to grow cash crops. This not only made for prosperity in the reserve but also built up a body of rich individuals within the tribe who were well disposed towards the government. At the same time the Mau Mau oath was beginning to lose its power, partly because people who had gone back on their undertaking found that the oath was not killing them and partly because the Mau Mau had gone on oathing and re-oathing as a way of raising money and people were getting tired of paying to join a movement to which they already belonged. Above all most members of the tribe could now see that Mau Mau was not going to win, which encouraged them to change sides. Thus the situation was much improved by comparison with that existing when Erskine arrived.

In July another large operation on the lines of HAMMER and FIRST FLUTE, called DANTE, was launched in the southern part of the Aberdare forest adjacent to Kiambu district. As before the number of terrorists killed was disappointing, but the gangs became fragmented. Thereafter they were gradually eliminated in a series of pseudo-gang operations and population sweeps organized by officers of the administration in which thousands of women interspersed with Kikuyu Guard hacked through areas of forest and scrub to expose and kill hiding terrorists.

By August 1955 Lathbury had decided against carrying out further major operations in the forest with the army. He intended to concentrate on using tracker combat teams and highly sophisticated pseudo-gangs there. The army would be based mainly outside the forest to destroy gangs as they emerged, the British troops operating from the settled areas. At this time Lathbury made a concerted effort to recover the good will of the settlers, which had been eroded by Erskine's policies.

As the months went by the last of the passive wing dissolved and the Mau Mau remaining in the forest became like wild animals in their ability to evade their pursuers. By the end of 1955 more than half of the original gang leaders had been killed although the leader of every tiny surviving group had promoted himself to general. Some, following the example of Kimathi, even gave themselves extravagant titles such as KCAE (Knight Commander of the African Empire).

Operations continued until October 1956 when a terrorist shot on the forest edge turned out to be Kimathi himself, fleeing from a number of pseudo-gangs that were pursuing him. After that military operations were deemed to be at an end and the army was withdrawn from the area. Mathenge alone of the major leaders remained unaccounted for. He had never made up his feud with Kimathi and in mid-1955 he disappeared from the forest with a sizeable number of his followers and was never heard of again. According to legend he took his men to Ethiopia or the Sudan. Stories were told of a ragged band of armed strangers seen passing through the far north of Kenya by the tribes resident there, but this has never been confirmed. It remains as the last mystery of the Mau Mau uprising.

Erskine's directive to take the military measures required to end the Emergency had now been fulfilled by his successor, but it would take a few more years before the administrative measures that were taking place in harness with them were complete. In particular there were still around 20,000 people in the detention camps out of the 80,000[5] who had been detained since the Emergency was declared. To the modern mind such figures appear unfortunate to say the least, but so widespread was the madness that had seized the Kikuyu as a result of the early oathing campaign that only a large-scale removal of this sort could give the chiefs and elders the chance to turn the tribe back into the paths of sanity and progress. Furthermore on occasions the power to detain people, often for quite short periods, provided an alternative to putting them in front of the courts where the penalties were more severe. On other occasions mass detention such as took place in Nairobi in April 1954 removed many who would have otherwise been recruited into the gangs where they would probably have been killed. As it was the bloodshed during the four years of military operations was bad enough. Around 10,500 Mau Mau were killed together with 2,500 of the Africans opposing them in the army, police, Kikuyu Guard or as loyal civilians. In addition 95 Europeans were killed and 29 Asians. It is unrealistic to try and distinguish between security forces and civilians because most of the security forces were civilians.

Undoubtedly General Erskine's experience and professional competence were responsible for the fact that there was a sound plan which was pushed through remorselessly despite criticism. Another major advantage arose from the fact that the Kenya Regiment supplied so many of the influential people at ground level, notably nearly all of the District Officers (Kikuyu Guard), a number of junior police officers, many of the platoon commanders and sergeants in the King's African Rifles, NCOs to work with the tracker combat teams in British battalions and all the field intelligence officers and some of the military intelligence officers in the police special branch. These men understood the Africans and could speak their language and for the most part they knew each other well, because they had nearly all been to the Prince of Wales School in Nairobi and they had mostly joined up within a few months of each other. The bond that existed between them ensured that the various branches of the security forces kept in close touch and worked together without friction or delay.

In conclusion it is worth considering whether Mau Mau forwarded the interests of the African community in Kenya. Although some praise it for having paved the way for Kenya's independence, this view was not shared by Kenyatta, who would not even allow participation by former Mau Mau fighters at the independence day celebrations. Some months earlier he had said: 'We shall not allow hooligans to rule Kenya. We must have no hatred toward one another. Mau Mau was a disease which has been eradicated and must never be remembered again.' But there is another side to the coin. In 1952 the colonial government was limited in the ways in which it could give advancement to Africans because of the political strength of the European settlers who wanted self-government within the Commonwealth on the lines of Southern Rhodesia, led by themselves. The regulations imposed during the Emergency gave rise to reforms which strengthened the Africans' position politically and economically so that afterwards the very idea of a settler run independent Kenya was unthinkable: this was the legacy of Sir Evelyn Baring, who was working for a multi-racial executive.[6] It can therefore be said that the uprising did, in addition to the frightful suffering involved, indirectly promote the African interest. If so, the dangers and terrible privations undergone by the Mau Mau in the forest, hunted by the security forces, harried by wild animals, half starved and ultimately without hope, were not entirely in vain. At least their endurance and courage dispelled the notion, widely held by the other tribes, that the Kikuyu lacked fighting spirit.

6

LAURIE MILNER

The Canal Zone and Suez, 1951–1956: Disputed Waterway

Laurie Milner joined the staff of the Imperial War Museum, London, in 1967 as a curator, and since 1984 he has been a Historian in the Museum's Research and Information Department. He has worked on many major exhibitions at the IWM and was principal historian on the Museum's 'Conflicts Since 1945' gallery. He has acted as consultant to military museums in Jordan, France, Germany and Egypt. He is author of two books, has contributed to a number of journals and periodicals, and has acted as technical adviser to several film and TV companies. He is a member of the International Institute for Strategic Studies and in February 2001 he was elected General Secretary of the British Commission for Military History.

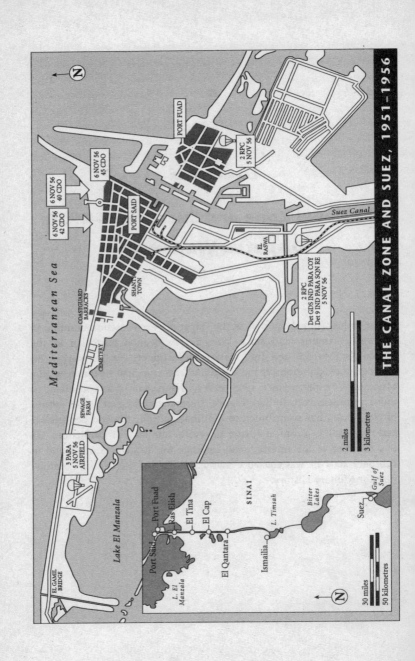

THE CANAL ZONE AND SUEZ, 1951–1956

In 1956 President Nasser of Egypt nationalized the Suez Canal. Anthony Eden, Britain's Prime Minister, decided on military action in an attempt to topple Nasser and restore Britain's dwindling influence in the Middle East. World opinion went against Eden and he resigned, leaving Britain's international reputation in tatters and Anglo-American relations at an all time low. The Suez Crisis, as it has become known, is all too often viewed in isolation; for Britain and indeed Anthony Eden were both carrying historical baggage when the crisis in Anglo-Egyptian affairs came to a head in 1956.

Much of Britain's involvement in the Middle East stems from the end of the First World War when Turkey was defeated and the former Ottoman Empire was divided between Britain and France. Soon after the end of the Second World War Britain started to give up its empire, beginning with India. It started to withdraw from Africa, and became involved in fighting the communists in Korea and Malaya. But the growing importance of oil prompted Britain to attempt to maintain its presence in the Middle East. By 1945 Britain's influence, including protectorates and mandated territories, extended from northern Iraq to the Gulf of Aden. Britain had dominated the region for nearly four decades, but its influence in Egypt had an even longer history.

Militarily Britain had been active in Egypt since the late eighteenth century. In 1798 Nelson destroyed Napoleon's Mediterranean fleet in the Battle of the Nile, and the French 'Army of the East' was defeated at Alexandria in 1801. In June 1882 the Royal Navy bombarded Alexandria and British forces invaded Egypt to put down a nationalist uprising which was threatening the Khedive's rule, and Britain's control of the Suez Canal. During the First World War the British army prevented the Turks from capturing the Canal, and in the Second World War Montgomery's Eighth Army ejected the Italians and the Afrika Korps from Egypt. Britain's main interest in Egypt lay in the strategically important Suez Canal, completed by a Franco-Egyptian consortium in 1869, in which Britain had held a major stake from the mid-1870s. At this time, financial mismanagement forced Ismail, Khedive of Egypt, to offer his country's 44 per cent shareholding in the new waterway for sale. This was snapped up by the British Prime Minister, Benjamin Disraeli, for £4 million firmly establishing Britain's influence in the running of this extremely important sea link with its empire.

From 1914 until 1922 Egypt was a British protectorate, but was given nominal independence when the protectorate was ended. It was not until 1936 that a real agreement was reached. The Anglo-Egyptian Treaty signed in London in 1936 proclaimed Egypt to be an independent sovereign state,[1] but allowed for British troops to continue to be stationed in the Suez Canal zone for the next twenty years, at the end of which time the need for their presence would be re-examined and, if necessary, renegotiated. British influence in much of the Middle East was maintained by treaties under which the Arab states achieved sovereign independent status and membership of the League of Nations. As one British journalist put it: 'under the treaties the Arab states were independent only so long as they did not want to act independently.'[2]

From October 1945 there had been Egyptian demands for an end to the British occupation and by 1951 anti-British riots had begun in the Canal Zone and Alexandria.

In an attempt to paper over the cracks in its relationship with the Egyptians, and to maintain its presence in the Canal Zone, Britain offered Egypt membership of a defence pact which would also include the United States, France and Turkey, but the Egyptians rejected this and the unrest continued.

Elsewhere in the Middle East Britain's influence had come under threat. Britain's promise of self-rule for the Arabs and pledged support for the establishment of a Jewish homeland caused conflict in Palestine. In 1947 the problem was referred to the United Nations, which decided on partition, and Britain's rule in Palestine ended on 14 May 1948. It was immediately followed by the first Arab–Israeli War. Among the Egyptian soldiers who took part in the attack on Israel was a thirty-year-old major named Gamal Abdel Nasser, of whom we shall hear more. The creation of Israel and the defeat of Israel's Arab neighbours in the 1948 War fuelled the post-war growth of nationalism in the Middle East. Britain's perceived support for the establishment of Israel therefore made its interests in the region an obvious target for nationalist attacks.

In May 1951 Dr Mossadeq, Prime Minister of Iran, nationalized the oil industry, then owned by the Anglo-Iranian Oil Company. Herbert Morrison, the British Foreign Secretary, favoured military action, but the US government urged restraint for fear of Soviet intervention. British forces were, however, sent to the Mediterranean. Clement Attlee, the British Prime Minister, whose Labour government was committed to the nationalization of British industry and utility companies, sent an emissary to talk to Dr Mossadeq, without success. But, with the support of the British cabinet, Attlee firmly rejected the use of military force unless British lives were threatened, which they were not. Unable to negotiate with Dr Mossadeq, whose policy was political rather than economic, Britain withdrew its workforce from Abadan on 4 October 1951. Britain's reluctance to take action in the face of a seizure of its assets gave an important message to the Arab nationalists, including those in Egypt.

At this time Attlee's narrow majority in the House of Commons had raised calls for a general election and on 27 October a Conservative government was elected with Winston Churchill as Prime Minister. Churchill's deputy, Sir Anthony Eden, who as Foreign Secretary had signed the 1936 Anglo-Egyptian Treaty on behalf of the British government, became Foreign Secretary once more.

On 3 January 1950 Nahas Pasha's nationalist Wafd party had been elected in Egypt and the anti-British demonstrations had escalated. In November that year Nahas announced his intention of abrogating the 1936 Treaty. On 26 August 1951, the fifteenth anniversary of its signing, there was a near riot when 500–600 Egyptians attempted to demonstrate outside the British Embassy in Cairo. Egyptian police retaliation resulted in two wounded demonstrators and some minor injuries caused in the scuffling. A contemporary account by the British Ambassador related how 'The crowd were able however to deposit at the gate of the Embassy the traditional "dead body" of a victim, who seems later to have made his own way from the scene'.[3] By noon the situation was under control.

The Foreign Office reviewed a number of possible responses including a propaganda campaign to be mounted in Egypt in order to secure a change of government if the 1936 Treaty was abrogated. It placed emphasis on the 'stick' rather than the 'carrot' by including the threat of a 'genuine military occupation of the Canal Zone'.

An alternative suggestion from the British Ambassador, however, was an attempt to bring down the nationalists by using Britain's influence on King Farouk, which proposed: 'it might be expected that the King would not have enough courage to get rid of the Government but this might be overcome by making his flesh creep with the danger of his own position if he continues to be associated with a government which is bringing Egypt to ruin and whose rule, if allowed to continue, is bound to end in internal unrest and probably revolution.'[4] Despite his prophecy at the end of this sentence, the Ambassador continued by outlining how public opinion in Egypt and even some members of the Wafd government might be persuaded to support, or even take part in, a new pro-British government.

On 8 October 1951 Nahas Pasha declared the Anglo-Egyptian Treaty of 1936 to be null and void. Furthermore he wanted to unite Egypt with the Sudan, which had been under Anglo-Egyptian control since 1899. What he was seeking was a total evacuation of British forces from Egyptian territory. It must be said that Britain was technically in breach of the 1936 Agreement because its forces in Egypt numbered over three times the agreed 10,000.

For the troops, life in the Canal Zone was monotonous: patrolling British installations in hot, dusty conditions while being plagued by flies was not exactly fulfilling. However, life was to become rather more eventful.

At 7.30 p.m. on 16 October 1951 Lieutenant General Sir George Erskine, then General Officer Commanding British Troops Egypt and Mediterranean Command, made a broadcast on British Forces Radio. He asserted the rights of the British forces under the 1936 Treaty and his intention to resist any attempt to force British troops out of the Canal Zone. He urged the servicemen to be ready to protect themselves and their families but reminded his command that they should 'treat this matter seriously and conduct ourselves with a full sense of responsibility, but with absolute determination.'[5] His forces' and their families' determination was soon tested when a large group of students from Cairo University, members of a nationalist organization known as the Moslem Brethren, ransacked and set fire to the NAAFI in Ismailia.

Doris Golder, the young wife of Warrant Officer Charles Golder of the Royal Engineers, living in a privately rented flat in the Rue Chemin de fer near the railway bridge in Arayshia, a suburb of Ismailia, witnessed the incident:

> In October, several hundred 'students' got off the train from Cairo at that railway bridge and scrambled down the embankment to run amok around the blocks of flats occupied by servicemen's families. The 'authorities' must have known they were coming and what they were up to as the train, which should have gone on to Ismailia, was stopped miles short of the station. These rioters broke into property wherever they could, looting and destroying. Our block was set on fire but the Sudanese ghaffir and residents put it out when the mob drifted elsewhere. Egyptian Police followed the crowd in its wake making no effort to control this lawlessness. Indeed they scavenged among the articles thrown out of doors and windows by their countrymen.[6]

Because the Egyptian police were unable or unwilling to disperse the crowd, soldiers from the 1st Battalion, The Lancashire Fusiliers were despatched from their garrison at Moascar by trucks and very quickly brought the situation in Ismailia under control. They drove the rioters back towards Arab Town at bayonet point and by discharging several rounds of ammunition in their general direction. They then erected a barbed wire cordon and posted armed guards on the street to keep the rioters away from British accommodation and installations. This prompted the *Egyptian Gazette* to accuse British forces of 'undiscriminating fire' on 'peaceful demonstrators who were expressing joy at the abrogation of the Treaty'. The British Ambassador in Cairo sent a note to the Egyptian Ministry of Foreign Affairs on 19 October. It reminded the Egyptian government of its responsibility for the protection of British lives and property, and protested about the attack on the NAAFI.

As the situation worsened the British forces and their families were moved into more secure accommodation and armed guards escorted the soldiers' wives on their shopping trips. Meanwhile plans were made to evacuate the women and children and to reinforce the British garrison. The reinforcements proved to be a real necessity because the Egyptian nationalists began intimidating the Egyptians and other foreign workers employed by the British, and the tasks formerly undertaken by the civilian workers now fell to the service personnel.

The attacks on the British forces were being orchestrated by an

Egyptian auxiliary police force known as the Bulak Nizam. They were recruited largely among the poorest sections of the population, who sympathized with the nationalist movement. Although they were supposed to carry only sticks as weapons, the auxiliary police in the Canal Zone carried firearms and it was not long before British soldiers were targeted. On 17 November the auxiliary police opened fire on a British patrol and on the 18th they joined in a terrorist attack in Ismailia which resulted in seven British soldiers being killed. Three days later, on the 21st, two British soldiers were found dead in the Sweetwater Canal in Ismailia by a British patrol. The two men, a lance corporal in the Royal Engineers and a bombardier in the Royal Artillery, had been missing from their units for forty-eight hours. They had been living in No. 211 Transit Camp following the evacuation of their families, but after spending an evening at a forces' cinema they had set out to revisit their former quarters to ensure that their personal effects were still secure. They were waylaid, beaten unconscious and thrown into the Canal. Early in December auxiliary police in Port Said opened fire and killed eleven British soldiers, and in another incident on 4 December 1951 a convoy led by a British major was ambushed. During the ensuing fight he was abducted from his vehicle, beaten and held down on the roadway while he was bayoneted to death. His mutilated corpse was delivered to the British Military Hospital by an Egyptian police officer later that morning. The autopsy report recorded that he had been forcibly held face down, fracturing his nose and lacerating his face, and was bayoneted in the back puncturing his lungs and breaking his spine. He died of suffocation, shock and wounds, especially to the spinal canal. Gravel from the road was discovered in his lungs.[7]

In the wake of the attacks British patrols were stepped up, a curfew was imposed and roadblocks were set up to control movement in the Canal Zone and prevent terrorist operations. The British water-filtration plants in the Canal Zone were, on the whole, well protected but one in particular, at Suez, which supplied the ships navigating the Canal with fresh water, was on the edge of the village of Kafr Abdu and was subject to frequent terrorist attack. The troops travelling to and fro were sniped at from the village and on 8 December members of 16th (Parachute) Brigade were sent to the village to move the population and to demolish some of the houses to allow for the construction of a new road between the British camp and the filtration plant which would be less vulnerable.

The British government had given notice of their intention to mount this operation and had offered compensation to the former inhabitants but this was refused and the demolition of part of the village provoked a furious response from the Egyptian government, which recalled its ambassador from London, passed laws permitting Egyptian civilians to carry firearms in the Canal Zone and introduced sanctions against anyone collaborating with the British.

On 31 December the Egyptian journal *Al Gamhour al Misri* offered a reward of £1,000 for the murder of the British Commander-in-Chief, General Erskine, and £100 for the murder of any other British officer. There followed another fierce exchange between the two governments, and an even fiercer protest from the officers in the Canal Zone who were incensed because they thought the offered reward was too low!

By the end of the year the total recorded incidents in the Canal Zone since abrogation was 391 including 18 murders. Early in January 1952 there was a clash between the Egyptian auxiliary police and the Coldstream Guards at Tel El Kebir.[8] This resulted in the arrest of a police major general, who was fairly rapidly freed when it was discovered that his task in the Canal Zone had only been to audit the local auxiliary police unit's books.

Despite the demolition of part of Kafr Abdu village and the diversion of the road, further attacks were carried out on British convoys en route to the filtration plant on 3 and 4 January. These were made from other nearby houses which had been evacuated on the orders of the police, although the local authorities had been assured that it was unnecessary. The empty houses had been promptly occupied by terrorists and it was from them that most of the firing was directed at the British troops. A report recorded that the soldiers behaved with customary restraint and only returned fire on recognizable targets. After the incident the Governor of Suez asked if the former inhabitants could return to their homes, but the request was refused and the area was wired off and put under armed guard.

Soon after the firing had ended a further incident occurred in Suez Town which was a clear indication of the escalating lawlessness. A rumour spread among the terrorists that they were being sniped at from behind by a Copt who lived in a nearby building. He was seized, stabbed and dragged through the streets with a meat-hook by a mob who poured petrol over him and set him alight. The mob then turned their attention to Copt and Christian places of worship. They were diverted from the main Roman Catholic church, but pillaged the Coptic church, piling up vestments, carpets and anything they could carry to make a funeral pyre in the centre of the church for the remains of their unfortunate victim. During this disturbance two other Copts were murdered and the attendant of the Coptic cemetery was badly burned.

Incidents continued on the main highway from Ismailia to Tel El Kebir, particularly at Abu Sueir. General Erskine considered another clearance operation but it was deferred because it would inflame the situation even further, and there might be an opportunity for a larger scale operation to greater effect. Villages were however searched, arms and ammunition seized and arrests made.

On 12 January a War Department train approaching Tel El Kebir railway station came under concentrated rifle and automatic fire from several directions. Troops and tanks were called out and crossed the Canal to El-Hammada village, the source of the firing. A sharp engagement ensued in which seven Egyptians were killed and thirty-two captured, of whom fifteen were wounded. Among the captives were five armed Fouad el Awal University students. A report of their interrogation sent to the Foreign Office revealed:

Of the 2000 university students who enrolled at the beginning of December only 300 actually turned up for their training. It had also transpired that these young students had expressed their resentment at having to associate with other gangs of lower social status. Although at present very contrite and tearful (they are accustomed to cry in bed at night), there is little doubt that they were caught with arms in their hands! The boys were all between the ages of 17 and 21 and came from respectable families. One of them was the son of a judge and another the son of a senior employee of Airwork Cairo. Their parents had known nothing of what they were doing or where they now were. The students were all from the faculties of Law and Science (Engineering). They had had about one month's training near Cairo and in the university itself and had then been sent to Faqus where they had been apparently given some more elementary platoon type training and exercises with small arms, light automatics and bomb-throwing. The boys under interrogation were all extremely frightened and very penitent, there was nothing of the Nationalist fanatic about any of them. They said that they thought that when they joined the liberation battalions that it was going to be something like the Boy Scouts or the Home guard and that their duties would be to protect houses in villages from marauding British soldiers.[9]

Further incidents took place in the same area on 13 and 14 January, and intimidation of foreign workers was stepped up. To this was added the threat of loss of residence rights under the new anti-collaboration law.

The British forces were, by this time, bringing in their own labourers. The first contingent of 1,022 members of the East African Pioneer Corps arrived in Suez on 5 January. Further contingents were expected to arrive weekly until the ceiling of 10,000 was reached. In addition some 250 Cypriots a week were arriving and by early January the total was in the region of 1,200. The British garrison meanwhile increased in number from 33,500 at the time of abrogation to 69,562 by the end of January 1952.

The trouble in the Canal Zone came to a head on 19 January when a bomb which had been concealed in a wheelbarrow was exploded at the YMCA Bridge, in Ismailia, killing two British soldiers and wounding five more. An eyewitness suspected that the Egyptian auxiliary police had advance information of the plot because traffic policemen left their positions about one hour before the explosion and were seen looking out of the windows as if waiting for something to happen. Meanwhile an English-speaking nun, Sister Anthony, was murdered in an attack on a French convent. The Mother Superior reported that the nun opened the door to a gang of toughs and had some conversation with them until one shot her in cold blood. British forces from 16th (Parachute) Brigade cordoned off an area including the Arab Quarter, the Convent and some of the Suez Canal Company's premises on 21 January and undertook a search operation which was completed without incident by 12.30 a.m. Three rifles and six pistols were recovered from the area. Another operation was mounted that afternoon when a cordon was put around the Catholic and Muslim cemeteries in Ismailia. The British troops carrying out the search were fired upon and during the gunfight one British officer was fatally wounded, one Egyptian killed, one wounded and thirteen captured. Four Sten guns and a rifle were seized and two tombs in the Muslim cemetery were found to contain 280 boxes of 40mm ammunition.

General Erskine had been authorized by the British government to

take strong measures if he thought it was necessary and he ordered
Brigadier Exham of 39th Brigade to mount an operation to disarm the
Bulak Nizam at their barracks at the Caracol and a former hospital,
the Bureau Sanitaire, in Ismailia.

Because proof had been obtained that the police had full knowledge of
the bomb incident on 19 January, I decided that the time had come to
expel the seven or eight hundred Bulak Nizam police that were now
present in Ismailia. So long as they remained there could be no security
against serious incidents resulting from trivial causes. My intention was
to expel the auxiliaries, leaving the regular police to carry on, provided
they showed themselves prepared to carry out their duties in a reasonable
manner. It would however not be practicable or wise to take action against
the auxiliaries without for the time being neutralizing the regulars, and so
it was necessary to disarm the whole force as a prelude to the expulsion
of the auxiliaries.

It was planned to surround both the Caracol and the Bureau Sanitaire
at first light on 25 January with an overwhelming show of force. At the
same time the sub-Governor was to be informed of our intentions, and
given the opportunity of preventing bloodshed by giving the necessary
orders for the police to lay down their arms. In the event the sub-
Governor insisted on first consulting Cairo, and the Minister of the
Interior, at a safe distance from the scene of the action, ordered maximum
resistance to be offered. Brigadier Exham then resorted to persuasion,
both through loudspeakers and by direct contact, but without success.
At the Bureau Sanitaire the Bulak Nizam had got completely out of
control, and possessed of a fanatical spirit worthy of a better cause were
lining the sandbagged roof of the building returning with vigour the fire
we were forced to open on them. Warning after warning was given, but
was ignored, and after each warning had failed heavier weapons were
employed. Eventually it was necessary to use the heavy armament of
our Centurion tanks to breach the building which was then stormed by
1 Lancashire Fusiliers.

Meantime at the Caracol an equally stubborn attitude was at first
shown, but reason prevailed and eventually the police filed out of the
building and laid down their arms. We lost three men killed and thirteen
wounded in this action, the Egyptians lost fifty police killed and thirteen wounded, nearly all Bulak Nizam, at the Bureau Sanitaire. Owing to
their violent resistance I decided to retain in custody the seven or eight
hundred Bulak Nizam now in my hands. Apart from other considerations

it was clearly impossible to let them return to the Delta in the tension now prevailing.[10]

As a result of his conduct during the operation one British soldier, Acting Sergeant Henry Foster, a platoon sergeant with the Lancashire Fusiliers, was awarded the George Medal for his leadership and gallantry. Despite being wounded three times he continued to lead and encourage his men until he was ordered by his platoon commander to seek medical treatment. As the Egyptians surrendered they were led away to nearby French Square, which was used as a temporary holding centre. They were eventually released on the understanding that they would no longer be able carry arms. A post-operation report recorded that 'Since the operation no British soldier has been killed or wounded in Ismailia', but the violence was far from over.

Riots in Cairo on an unprecedented scale followed, culminating in attacks on British property and the expatriate community on Saturday 26 January, thereafter known as Black Saturday. British threats to occupy Cairo prompted King Farouk to dismiss Nahas Pasha and to ensure that the auxiliary police remained unarmed.

In July 1952 King Farouk was overthrown in a military coup and General Mohammed Neguib seized power. There was much curiosity at the Foreign Office about the new Egyptian leader, and great interest in Colonel Gamal Abdel Nasser, who seemed to exercise considerable power in the new government. A confidential report, after Nasser had been a guest at a British diplomat's dinner party in September, described him as being shy and retiring. Nasser's views, it continued, which he expressed in good English, were sound and in no way extreme or fanatical. On the subject of Anglo-Egyptian relations he stressed the importance of first of all Britain showing confidence in Egypt. A new treaty would then follow which would meet the essential demands of both sides.[11] Eden had come to the conclusion that it would be better to negotiate with the new government to secure the best agreement possible, rather than insist on Britain's rights under the 1936 Treaty. Churchill did not however agree, and in a note to Eden on 9 March 1952 had expressed concern that the Suez Canal 'might be entrusted to a rearmed and strengthened Egyptian Army which may at any time come under the control of a Wafd or other hostile Egyptian Government'. He urged Eden to press for a Four Power Treaty, 'before we strip ourselves of power'. Eden, in reply, reminded Churchill that under the 1936 Treaty Britain was bound to get out of the Canal Zone in 1956. He continued,

> The present Egyptian Government is the best we can possibly hope for. Its position is precarious and its continuance in power depends on its ability to clip the wings of the Wafd. The plain fact is that we are no longer in a position to impose our will on Egypt, regardless of the cost in men, money, and international goodwill both throughout the Middle East and the rest of the world. If I cannot impose my will, I must negotiate. This is the best Government we have yet had with which to do so.[12]

Eden's negotiations with the new Egyptian government lasted for many months, during which there were frequent breakdowns. Eventually Eden accepted that the Egyptians would not join the proposed alliance, Egypt's claim to the Sudan was dropped, and talks focused on reaching an agreement about the British forces in Egypt.

During the period of negotiation, violence against the British forces was resumed, fortunately without fatalities. A review of the situation in 1953, from the beginning of the year up to 15 November, recorded 135 attacks, many of them involving knives, firearms or explosives. British casualties in the Canal Zone between the abrogation of the 1936 Treaty in October 1951 and the signing of the new treaty in October 1954 numbered 64 killed and 124 wounded by Egyptian police and terrorists,[13] more than the losses in many other post-war conflicts, yet the troops who had served in the Canal Zone were never given a medal, despite being 'on active service', for fear of upsetting President Nasser. The Egyptian government issued a Victory Medal to its forces to mark the evacuation of British troops from Egypt and even produced a commemorative postage stamp.

In March 1954 Nasser came to power in Egypt after General Neguib was dismissed by the young officers' Revolutionary Council, which had staged the military coup. On 19 October a treaty was signed by President Nasser and by Anthony Nutting, Minister of State for Foreign Affairs. It was to last for seven years. British troops were to be withdrawn from Egypt by June 1956, and the British bases were to be run jointly by British and Egyptian civilian technicians. Egypt agreed to respect the freedom of navigation through the Canal, which had been defined in the Constantinople Convention of 1888, and it was further agreed that

British troops would be permitted to return if the Suez Canal was threatened by an outside power.

In April 1955 Winston Churchill's health deteriorated and he retired. Eden succeeded him as Prime Minister and in a general election held a month later was elected with an increased majority. Eden was a very experienced politician and a particularly skilled negotiator, but Churchill was a difficult act to follow, and the British press was less than kind, accusing him of weakness. This was fuelled by a section of opinion within the Conservative Party known as the Suez Group which criticized the government for selling out British imperial interests by withdrawing troops from the Canal Zone. The protection of the Suez Canal by this time was in reality a political excuse, since the Canal was not threatened and Britain no longer had an empire. The British occupation of its base in the Canal Zone was therefore part of the strategy of the Cold War. As one soldier remarked, 'The troops are neither guarding the base nor the Canal, they are merely guarding each other.'

In February 1955 Anglo-Egyptian affairs had been strained by Britain's decision to deprive Nasser of British arms, thereby forcing him to seek his military hardware elsewhere. As the last British troops left Egypt, Nasser was completing the purchase of Soviet-made aircraft, tanks and arms from Czechoslovakia, which would perhaps help him to realize one of his goals, the destruction of Israel. But he still expected the United States and Britain to help finance the construction of a new High Dam at Aswan: despite anti-Western demonstrations in Egypt, in January 1956 the United States had pledged $54 million, and Britain £15 million, towards funding the Dam.

The United States was not entirely convinced that the Dam project would be a success and was under pressure to reduce expenditure on foreign aid. It was also concerned about Nasser's purchase of Soviet arms and, to a lesser extent, that increased production of Egyptian cotton made possible by the improved irrigation resulting from construction of the Dam might affect its own market.

On 19 July the United States Secretary of State, John Foster Dulles, informed the Egyptian Ambassador in Washington that the United States government had come to the conclusion that it would not be feasible for them in present circumstances to give any financial assistance towards the construction of the Aswan Dam. During Cabinet meetings at Downing Street on 17 and 20 July 1956 the British Foreign Secretary, Selwyn

Lloyd, said that the US government was likely to share our view that the offer of financial aid for the building of the High Dam at Aswan should now be withdrawn. He proposed to circulate a memorandum to the cabinet on the means of presenting this decision to the Egyptian government, and thought that it would probably be best to indicate to the Egyptians that, in view of their commitments for expenditure on armaments and military installations, the two governments had been forced to the conclusion that the financing of the Dam, even with the assistance which had been proposed, would be beyond Egypt's resources. He concluded that this might well lead to a deterioration in our relations with Egypt with possibly serious consequences for our trade. The cabinet agreed that the British government's announcement should be made in terms which would emphasize the economic considerations which had led to this decision and would give the Egyptian government no ground for assuming that it had been taken for political reasons. It authorized the Foreign Secretary to announce that the United Kingdom government would not provide any assistance towards the construction of the dam at Aswan in Egypt.[14] As a result of the withdrawal of the US and British loans, the World Bank refused to advance a promised $200 million. Nasser was humiliated, for the United States government had informed the world's press before telling the Egyptian Ambassador.

On 26 July 1956, President Nasser nationalized the Anglo-French Suez Canal Company, declaring that he would take the revenue from the Canal to finance his Dam.

Legally, the Suez Canal Company was registered as an Egyptian company under Egyptian law and Colonel Nasser had indicated that he intended to compensate the shareholders at ruling market prices. The ninety-nine-year concession granted by Said in 1854 to run from 1869, when the Canal was completed, was due to expire in 1968, at which time the Canal would legally revert to Egyptian ownership but could be re-negotiated. With this prospect on the horizon the Suez Canal Company had been adopting a policy of Egyptianization at all levels.

Britain's argument, however, was that although the Canal was Egyptian property it was an important international asset that Egypt could not be allowed to exploit for a purely internal purpose. It was also argued that the Egyptians had not the technical ability to manage the Canal effectively, and that their recent behaviour gave no confidence that they would recognize their international obligations in respect of it. It should therefore be managed as an international trust.

Eden, who recalled Britain's appeasement of Hitler in the 1930s, regarded Nasser's action as that of another dictator. He looked to military action which might result in Nasser's downfall and restore Britain's influence in the region. On 24 October 1956, in reply to the question: 'Was it not likely that a military operation to retake the Suez Canal would unite the Arab world in support of Egypt?' Eden replied, '... this is a serious risk; but against it must be set the greater risk that, unless early action could be taken to damage Colonel Nasser's prestige, his influence would be extended throughout the Middle East to a degree which would make it more difficult to overthrow him'. Eden continued that it was known that Nasser was already plotting coups in many of the other Arab countries; and Britain should never have a better pretext for intervention against him than it had as a result of the seizure of the Suez Canal. He correctly surmised that if a military operation were undertaken against Egypt, its effect in other Arab countries would be serious unless it led to the early collapse of Colonel Nasser's regime. He concluded, 'Both for this reason, and also because of international pressures which would develop against our continuation of the operation, it must be quick and successful.'[15] The United States however made it clear that unjustified military action would not be tolerated.

While Eden was considering his next move, a mission was sent to Cairo, headed by the Australian Prime Minister Sir Robert Menzies, to find a peaceful solution to the situation – but to no avail.

Enmeshed in conflict with Arab nationalists in its North African colonies, and with a financial stake in the Canal, France was, on this occasion, happy to support Britain. The French government had been meeting with Israel and invited Britain to join their secret negotiations. Israel was becoming concerned about Egypt's growing Soviet arsenal. An Israeli pre-emptive attack on Sinai would reduce the Egyptians' military strength. It would also provide justification for Britain and France to re-occupy the Canal zone. Stripped of his military might, unable to finance the Aswan Dam and with British forces once again in Suez, Nasser, it was thought, would surely lose his political credibility.

The agreement under which Israel was to attack Egypt, providing the justification of Anglo-French military intervention in Suez, was negotiated in a chateau at Sèvres just outside Paris. A secret accord was signed by representatives of the three governments on 24 October 1956. There were three copies, all drafted in French. The generally held opinion is that Eden had the British copy destroyed. This is supported by his well-recorded dismay on hearing that the agreement had been committed to paper. It is not known what happened to the French copy, but it now cannot be traced and was almost certainly destroyed. The Israeli copy was retained by the Israeli Prime Minister David Ben-Gurion, despite attempts by members of the British delegation to retrieve it, and was transferred to an archive in Israel, where it remains.[16]

As the weeks following nationalization of the Canal turned into months and as the political justification for military action by Britain slipped from Eden's grasp, plans for the invasion of Egypt became more and more contorted. Despite Britain's major role in the planning and execution of the greatest air- and seaborne landing in history, in 1944, and notwithstanding the conclusions of a White Paper on Defence published at the beginning of 1956 which emphasized the need for Britain's forces to be 'flexible, mobile and well trained', the preparations were at best chaotic. The airborne forces had not been trained for this type of operation and the RAF lacked the aircraft necessary to deliver them in strength. Indeed, 16th Parachute Brigade had been engaged on counter-insurgency work both in the Canal Zone and in Cyprus and had not undertaken parachute training for more than a year. The RAF had only enough troop-carrying aircraft to move a single parachute battalion, and the Champ, which had replaced the Jeep, one of the few new pieces of equipment to be brought into service since the end of the Second World War, could not be airlifted by the available aircraft. Meanwhile concern was expressed about the likely performance of the new Self-Loading Rifle in sandy conditions. The Parachute units were therefore reissued with Second World War vintage No. 4 rifles which had proved their worth in the Western Desert. The BAT recoilless anti-tank gun, the only air-portable weapon capable of knocking out the Soviet tanks in Nasser's arsenal, was also withdrawn because its ammunition had not been fully tested under tropical conditions. The amphibious forces too had their problems. Insufficient landing ships and landing craft had survived post-war cuts, and those that had been mothballed were found to be unserviceable. Eventually some that had been sold off for civilian use had to be commandeered back into service. The two Centurion tank units of the Royal Tank Regiment earmarked for service in Suez fared no better. Their personnel and equipment were spread all over Britain and they had to enlist the help of civilian transport companies to move their vehicles and stores to Southampton for the voyage east.

During the planning various options had been considered, including a landing at Alexandria, but only days before the British forces set sail from Southampton to Cyprus, Suez was confirmed as the objective. While Britain and France moved their forces into position for the invasion Nasser sank blockships closing the Canal to all shipping.

A joint operation with troops from more than one country is difficult to mount at the best of times, but because the cooperation with Israel could not be openly admitted, the likelihood of the timing of the operation being compromised was high. The original date for the Israeli attack was 7 November, but because the Israelis had announced their mobilization on 25 October and Eisenhower had immediately urged Ben-Gurion not to consider military action, D-Day was brought forward to 29 October in an attempt to seize the moment before an upsurge in world opinion could prevent the attack. The Israelis were victorious in less than a week. In order to keep ahead of the growing international resistance to British and French intervention it therefore became necessary to bring forward the Anglo-French assault on the Suez Canal. It was impossible, however, to advance the date of the seaborne landing but the initial airborne operation was brought forward by twenty-four hours, to 5 November. This was a risky decision because it meant that the British and French parachute units would be on their own except for air support until the seaborne landing came in on the following day, and the likely level of Egyptian resistance could not be determined.

The assault on Suez was preceded by five days of aerial bombardment which grounded and largely destroyed the Egyptian Air Force. Soon after dawn on 5 November, soldiers from 3rd Battalion, The Parachute Regiment (3 Para) dropped onto El Gamil airfield, while the French paratroops dropped south of the Raswa bridges and at Port Fuad. In contrast to the many problems faced during the planning, the airborne drop was very successful. Within forty-five minutes of landing the airborne troops had overcome all Egyptian resistance on the airfield, and helicopters from HMS *Ocean* and HMS *Theseus* were bringing in supplies. With El Gamil secured for the second lift, 3 Para moved eastwards towards Port Said. The only possible route took them through a sewage farm and a cemetery, where they met their first serious opposition. With air support they overwhelmed the Egyptian forces holding the area; ahead lay the beaches of Port Said. Because of shortage of ammunition, and because the beach area of Port Said was to be bombarded during the seaborne landing, Colonel Crook, commander of 3 Para, ordered his men to stop and dig in overnight.

On 6 November the sea- and helicopter-borne assault went in. Like the airborne plan, this too had been subject to last-minute changes. The original tasks of the seaborne 40 Commando RM were to capture the shipping basins around Navy House, the Customs Houses, and the Canal Company offices, while 42 Commando cleared the Rue Mohammed Ali and linked up with 45 Commando RM, who were to land by helicopter on the two bridges at Raswa. They would thus open the way for 6 Royal Tank Regiment (6 RTR) and 2 Para to drive south down the road to Port Suez. Instead the Raswa bridges were re-allocated to the French airborne force with a detachment from the Guards Independent Parachute Company supported by engineers from 9th Parachute Squadron Royal Engineers. 45 Commando RM became Brigade reserve, subsequently being landed behind the rest of the Commando Brigade, close to the de Lesseps statue. This was the first helicopter assault as part of an amphibious operation in history. Despite the helicopters being able to carry only tiny payloads (by today's standards), 415 men and twenty-three tons of equipment and ammunition were landed in eighty-three minutes. 45 Commando moved out to the right of 42 Commando's axis, the Rue Mohammed Ali, to link up with 3 Para advancing from Gamil airfield.

Shortly after midday on 6 November, 2 Para was brought in by the LST *Empire Parkeston* near the de Lesseps statue. The shipping basins captured by 40 Commando, specifically to allow 2 Para to land there, were found to be blocked with sunken vessels. 2 Para was not ready to move off until about 4 p.m. By this time the Royal Marine commandos had overwhelmed the Egyptian forces in the town and docks, capturing men, vehicles and many of the newly purchased Czech manufactured weapons.

At midnight on 6 November a ceasefire was called at the insistence of the UN Secretary-General. The Anglo-French forces had reached El Cap just south of Port Said but were not yet in control of the entire canal when they were stopped. British losses in the operation were twenty-two killed and ninety-seven wounded. Despite all the setbacks in planning and changes of timing, militarily the operation was well on its way to being a great success, the assault on El Gamil airfield was one of the most successful airborne landings ever attempted, and the use of helicopters to deliver a commando assault was an innovation, although their use as surrogate landing craft did not exploit their capacity for vertical envelopment.

Politically it was a disaster. President Eisenhower was incensed. World opinion, especially that of the United States, and the threat of Soviet intervention forced Britain, France and Israel to withdraw their troops from Egypt. In Britain too there had been widespread outrage. A UN force was sent in to supervise the ceasefire and to restore order. The Suez Canal was cleared and reopened, but Britain in particular found its standing with the US weakened and its influence east of Suez diminished by this operation. Accusations of collusion between Britain, France and Israel started in 1956, but were denied in Parliament by Eden who tried to avoid giving a clear and categorical answer. He was at last asked whether there was foreknowledge of the Israeli attack and on 20 December in his last address to the House of Commons, which has been recorded in Hansard, he replied: 'I want to say this on the question of foreknowledge, and to say it quite bluntly to the House, that there was not foreknowledge that Israel would attack Egypt. There was not.'[17] In January 1957, his health shattered, and his political credibility severely damaged, Sir Anthony Eden, the British Prime Minister, resigned.

Britain's strategic base in Egypt was lost and its bases in Cyprus, now of greater importance, were coming under threat.

7

ROBIN NEILLANDS

Cyprus, 1955–1959: EOKA

Robin Neillands served as a national service marine, and rose to the rank of corporal, serving in Cyprus during the EOKA campaign in 45 Commando RM. He subsequently became a member of the Royal Marines Reserve. After national service he became a journalist and travel writer, and now is best known as an author of popular military history, and has had some fourteen books published on this subject. His recent books have included *Voices from Normandy*; *The Conquest of the Reich: 1945*; *Fighting Retreat: The British Empire 1947–97* and *The Great War Generals*. His *The Bomber War: Arthur Harris and the Allied Bomber Offensive, 1939–1945* was published early in 2001.

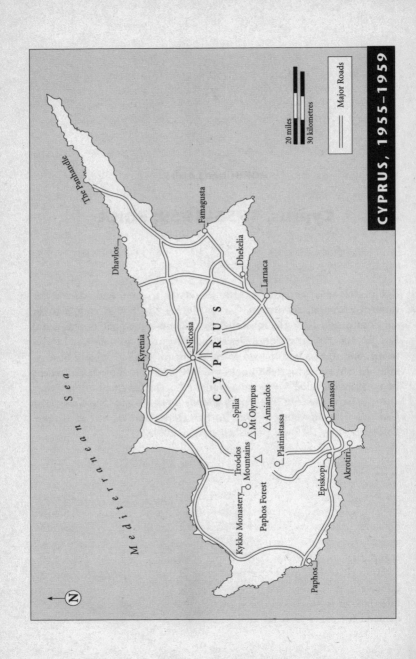

N

M e d i t e r r a n e a n   S e a

The Panhandle

Dhavlos

Famagusta

Dhekelia

Kyrenia

Nicosia

Larnaca

C Y P R U S

Spilia
△ Mt Olympus
△ Amiandos
△
○ Platinistassa

Troödos
Mountains
Kykko Monastery
Paphos Forest

Limassol

Episkopi
Akrotiri

Paphos

20 miles
30 kilometres

—— Major Roads

CYPRUS, 1955–1959

In April 1955 trouble broke out between the two local communities on the Mediterranean island of Cyprus. This trouble, basically an ethnic and political conflict, had been brewing for some time, but had been given a fresh lease of life in the 1950s by the continuing dismemberment of the British Empire. As a result, even while trouble was bubbling or brewing in other parts of that Empire, a fresh task was handed to Britain's long-suffering and sorely tried servicemen.

Cyprus, a large island in the eastern Mediterranean, lying fifty miles south of the Turkish coast, has had a long and chequered history and a variety of occupants. Over the centuries since the start of the Christian era, Cyprus has been ruled by the Lusignans, by the Venetian Republic and by the Ottoman Turks. From the 1880s Cyprus was run by the British, who acquired a lease on the island from the Sultan of Turkey after the Crimean War and annexed the island during the First World War, after Turkey joined forces with the Central Powers.

Between the wars Cyprus served as the northern guardpost for the Suez Canal, but until the end of the Second World War the island was a colonial backwater and played no major part in Britain's strategic plans. Cyprus lacked a deep-water port, so the Royal Navy remained in Malta, and British control of Egypt and the army bases in the Canal Zone provided sufficient security for that vital waterway. The Cyprus garrison remained small, and the only airfield, near Nicosia, handled civilian traffic rather than warplanes. Cyprus only started to figure in Britain's strategic calculations as pressure from the Egyptians mounted against the British garrisons in the Canal Zone, and the Empire crumbled.

Timing is often a factor in human affairs and Cyprus became important to Britain just at the moment the Greek Cypriots began their bid for independence and 'enosis' – union with Greece. It was the demand for enosis that lay at the heart of the Cyprus problem, for the population of Cyprus consisted of two distinct ethnic communities, the Greeks and the Turks – and the two communities detested each other.

Granting independence was less of a problem. By the middle of the 1950s, the intention of successive post-war British governments to turn the colonial Empire into a democratic Commonwealth was well underway and proceeding without undue difficulty. Trouble arose in places in various parts of the Empire – in Malaya, Kenya or Aden, for example – but these trouble spots were the exception rather than the rule. Most of the component parts of the British Empire that wanted independence from Westminster got it without strife or undue difficulty – their problems came later, after the British had left . . . but could be conveniently blamed on the departing British.

It has to be noticed that, in recorded history, Cyprus has never belonged to Greece. There may well have been Greek trading posts in Cyprus in the pre-Christian era but the modern Greeks arrived in Cyprus during the British occupation, in the late nineteenth and early twentieth centuries. The Greek population of Cyprus increased significantly after the Turkish–Greek War of 1920–21, when the British offered sanctuary to Greeks driven out of Smyrna (Izmir) and other places on the Turkish mainland, and by the 1930s the Greeks outnumbered the resident Turks, the descendants of families who had lived on Cyprus since the days of the Ottoman Empire, by a ratio of 70:30, but under firm British rule the two communities got along together well enough.

During the 1950s, however, the Greeks of Cyprus began to agitate for independence. At first, they were joined in this ambition by the Turkish community, which also wanted independence. Then it became apparent that the Greek Cypriots also wanted enosis, which understandably met with total opposition from the Turkish Cypriots, and dismayed the British. Once again, as in India, Palestine and Malaya, the British found themselves in the middle of a national and religious conflict which their previous occupation had been able to suppress. Nor was the difficulty confined to the Greek and Turkish Cypriots – the governments of Turkey and Greece were also interested in the future of Cyprus.

Turkish resistance to enosis was based on two factors, one historic, one geographic. The Ottoman Empire had included Greece from the fall of Constantinople in 1453 until the Greeks broke free in the early years of the nineteenth century. After centuries of warfare and racial strife between the two countries, there was no love lost between Greeks and Turks anywhere, or at any level, and the idea of handing the large Turkish minority in Cyprus over to the Greeks was anathema to the Turkish people and the Turkish government.

To understand the second objection it is only necessary to look at a map. Cyprus lies about fifty miles from the south coast of Turkey. Given the ever-delicate state of relations between the Greek and Turkish states, the Turkish government had no intention of allowing the Greeks to occupy a large island just off their southern shore.

The Greeks refused to accept the validity of these two points. Athens supported the majority community's desire for enosis as a democratic right, declaring that the Turkish community had nothing to fear from Greek rule – while clearly viewing the prospect of taking over Cyprus as a major strategic gain. Anxious to gain control of Cyprus, the Greek government offered not only to grant Britain sovereign bases on the island, but also bases on the Greek islands or mainland – adding that, since Britain, Greece and Turkey were all members of NATO, it was desirable to avoid conflict between them in the face of the Soviet menace. These were persuasive arguments – or thinly veiled threats – but the British were less than sure that the Greek Cypriots would treat their Turkish Cypriot neighbours as fellow-citizens, and felt a duty to protect the minority interest.

Britain was also motivated by a degree of self-interest. Since the British bases in the Canal Zone were due, by a treaty agreed in 1954, to be evacuated by June 1956, Cyprus was the only place from where Britain's strategic bombers could reach into Soviet Russia or her transport aircraft fly troops to aid the oil states in the Persian Gulf. Having lost Alexandria, the Royal Navy needed Cyprus as a base in the eastern Mediterranean. Though the island lacked a deep-water port, it had sheltered bays and anchorages and from airfields on Cyprus the RAF could provide the fleet with air cover. On balance, therefore, the British intended to keep Cyprus and develop it into a major strategic base and in 1954 Henry Hopkinson MP, a Minister at the Colonial Office, stated as much, saying: 'There are certain territories within the Commonwealth which, owing to their particular circumstances, can never be fully independent ... the question of the abrogation of British sovereignty cannot arise ...'

It can be argued that Britain could have accepted the Greek suggestion, built her military bases and radar stations, handed over power to Athens and departed, leaving the Greek Cypriots to deal with the Turkish Cypriots. Even without the benefits of hindsight, it is not hard to imagine what the outcome would have been, but apart from the fact that this scuttle would have been grossly unfair to the Turkish Cypriots, the mainland Turks would not have accepted the abandonment of their nationals to Greek control ... and the Turkish mainland and the formidable Turkish Army lay just fifty miles from the north coast of Cyprus. As elsewhere in the Empire, there were no easy answers to the Cyprus question.

In the 1950s Greek Cypriot desire for enosis found its leaders in two men, the Primate of the Orthodox Church of Cyprus, Archbishop Makarios III, and a Cypriot former soldier in the Greek army, Colonel George Grivas. Though their aims were the same, independence followed by enosis, their methods were different.

Makarios was more than a religious leader. He was also the *Ethnarch*, the leader of the Greek community in Cyprus, the spokesman for their political ambitions. In 1955 Makarios, though an imposing, heavily bearded figure and an astute politician, was still a young man, just forty-two years of age. He believed that by playing the anti-colonial card (and fudging the true reality of the situation with the Turks and Turkey), by applying diplomatic and political pressure, especially by inciting the vocal anticolonial lobby in London, among the non-aligned nations at the United Nations, and in Washington DC, he could get the British out of Cyprus. That this might then provoke a war in the eastern Mediterranean does not seem to have occurred to him or to Colonel Grivas, his confidant and muscleman, who believed in a more direct approach.

Grivas had spent most of the Second World War heading a guerrilla organization in the Greek Islands. When the war was over he took part in the struggle against the Greek Communist Party, and by 1950 he was looking for a fresh cause. He found it in enosis and spent the years from 1951 to 1955 setting up a clandestine terrorist organization, EOKA, a Greek acronym for the 'National Organization of the Cypriot Struggle'. Grivas's intentions and activities were well known to the Greek government and to Archbishop Makarios, though both remained on friendly terms with the British.

Grivas made reconnaissance visits to Cyprus quite openly in 1951 and 1952 but when he returned in early 1954 he was refused entry. He returned secretly in November in a small sailing caique filled with arms and explosives. A second caique, the *St George*, also carrying arms and munitions, was intercepted off the north coast of Cyprus by a Royal Navy frigate. It was this capture which alerted the British to the imminent start of a terrorist campaign.

Grivas believed that an independence campaign needed publicity and found plenty of examples in the terrorist campaigns that had been waged against the British in Palestine and elsewhere. The best way to attract the attention of the media was by creating incidents which would place the British government and army in a bad light. If he could present the British as oppressors, the true facts of the Cyprus situation and the interests of the Turks would all be drowned in the usual chorus of anti-British, anti-colonial outrage. Colonists – imperialists – were regarded as bad people in the 1950s and Britain and her troops would have few defenders against any allegation, however far-fetched.

Grivas's first intention was to run a terrorist campaign in Cyprus from bases in the Kyrenia and Troódos Mountains, and he set up five gangs to carry out the task. The original aim was not to cause much loss of life or drive out the British by military means; that was seen to be impossible. The purpose of terrorism was to draw attention to the Greek Cypriot cause, and he hoped that the response of the security forces would help the Archbishop to present Britain's rule in Cyprus as despotic. Grivas also set up killer squads in the main towns to kill any Greek Cypriot who found his actions distasteful or who declared enosis unnecessary.

Makarios was well aware of Grivas's plans and was not greatly concerned about the bloodshed that must follow; his concern was whether Grivas's campaign would prove counterproductive politically in Athens, where the Greek Prime Minister initially refused to support anything other than peaceful pressure for enosis. Makarios always refused to condemn terrorist violence – though he complained loudly about the reactions of the security forces – and gave his full support to Grivas's terrorist campaign.

The EOKA campaign began on 1 April 1955, with a series of bomb attacks throughout the island and the littering of streets with leaflets demanding enosis and signed 'Dighenis', Grivas's nom de guerre. These first attacks did little damage, caused no injuries and were soon discontinued, but throughout the summer of 1955 there was a great deal of unrest and some rioting in the main towns, especially by Greek students.

Otherwise, EOKA did not enjoy much support. The Turkish minority were pro-British and dead set against EOKA, and many Greeks were also against EOKA because they thought they were better off under British rule – though it was unwise to say so. The police force, which was managed by British officers seconded from the UK, soon became largely a Turkish force as the Greek constables were intimidated or afraid to serve.

The first pause in attacks gave Makarios time to assess the reaction in Cyprus, Athens and the UN. Cyprus was not some half-civilized, far-off country but a part of Europe, British rule was not tyrannical and the Greek and British people had been friends and allies for centuries. Few people could see any need for violence and most thought that a political solution was achievable. Violence, however, was Grivas's chosen path to enosis and his men were soon on the attack once more, concentrating now on British servicemen, who had to watch their backs and carry arms.

The main EOKA gangs were commanded by two men, George Afxentiou and Markos Drakos. One of Drakos's first attacks was an attempt on the life of the Governor, Sir Robert Armitage, by placing a bomb near his seat in a cinema in Nicosia. Fortunately the film ended early and when the bomb exploded the cinema was empty. In June 1955 there was serious intercommunal rioting in Nicosia, Larnaca and Limassol and a number of ambushes and attacks on police stations, by EOKA gangs trying to steal arms and ammunition.

Grivas relied for the bulk of his support on the Greek Cypriot students and schoolchildren and conflict between the students and troops also provided good copy for enosis propaganda. The sight of British troops and Cypriot police officers brawling with schoolchildren in the streets provided sympathetic footage for the television screens in Athens and in the USA. Riots were easy to film or report and tended to make the headlines. The growing number of EOKA murders, of British and Turkish men and women shot in the back by Grivas's killers, did not attract much attention or concern, but it did lead to a rapid increase in the Cyprus garrison.

In April 1955, at the start of the EOKA troubles, the British garrison consisted of just two infantry battalions, a regiment of the Royal Artillery, and sapper squadrons of the Royal Engineers engaged on the new British base at Episkopi. The first death of the EOKA campaign came on 19 June 1955, when a terrorist threw a grenade into the central police station in Nicosia. The explosion killed an innocent Greek bystander, injured a dozen Turks and infuriated the Turkish community but Grivas did not confine himself to random grenade attacks.

A Greek Cypriot policeman, Constable Pullanis, was murdered for allegedly being too eager to do his duty against terrorism, a grenade thrown into a bar injured a British soldier in Famagusta, and a bomb wrecked the home of the Commander-in-Chief, Middle East, General Sir Charles Keightley. The security forces hit back and in July 1955 a sweep picked up a number of EOKA leaders, including Drakos and Afxentiou, who were interned in Kyrenia Castle. A few days later another grenade attack killed the first British soldier to die in this campaign, a private of the Royal Scots – and more killings would follow.

These killing concentrated minds. The British Prime Minister, Anthony Eden, called a Tripartite Conference in London, a meeting between representatives of the Turkish, Greek and British governments – and the Cypriot community leaders – to consider the entire Cyprus issue. Eden's call confused Makarios, who told Grivas to stop the terror campaign but then flew to London to declare that the Conference was a snare for Greek Cypriot ambitions and that the Turkish government had no right to be consulted about Cypriot affairs at all – a view that did not extend to the government in Athens.

The Cyprus Conference went ahead on 29 August 1955, with the Foreign Secretary, Harold Macmillan, in the chair. Macmillan offered the Cypriots a constitution, granting internal self-government, with the participation of both Greece and Turkey in the island's affairs as interested parties, at which point the Conference collapsed. The Greek Cypriots were only interested if the constitution paved the way for a Greek takeover and enosis. The Turks would only agree to internal self-government if the Greeks stopped demanding self-determination which, given the Greek majority in Cyprus, would lead to *enosis*.

The first result of the Conference collapse was more intercommunal rioting in Nicosia, culminating in the burning of the British Institute by Greek students from the High School, and this led to the arrival of a major reinforcement for the garrison, the 3rd Commando Brigade, Royal

Marines – 40 and 45 Commandos RM, from Malta – together with two infantry battalions. They arrived just in time, for on the night they landed sixteen EOKA prisoners escaped from Kyrenia Castle, among them Markos Drakos and George Afxentiou. One prisoner, Michael Caraolis, the murderer of Constable Pullanis, did not escape; he was tried for the crime, found guilty and hanged.

Two weeks after the Commandos came ashore, Field Marshal Sir John Harding, recently retired as Chief of the Imperial General Staff, arrived as Governor and Commander-in-Chief, taking direct control of the anti-terrorist campaign. Brigadier George Baker became Director of Operations and the former Chief Constable of Warwickshire, Colonel Geoffrey White, became Commissioner of Police. Colonel White's first task was to send for 300 British 'bobbies', to back up the Turkish constables. The British police were deployed at stations throughout the island and guaranteed both communities impartial policing. British policemen continued to arrive throughout the Emergency, among them Constable Derek Snape from the Lancashire Constabulary:

> I was an ex-soldier, serving in the 2nd Bn., The Parachute Regiment, before coming out and joining the police service. I went to Cyprus in 1958 and was posted to a local police station to help the local police contain inter-communal riots and deal with EOKA. I have to say that some of the Army and security people were right bastards to the local people, but I have to add that the local people were always trying it on with the troops, especially during house searches, accusing the troops of deliberately breaking things or stealing. We then had to search the troops but we never found any evidence that they had taken anything. The ordinary squaddie was all right.

In spite of more troops arriving, in the autumn of 1955 and that winter the security situation deteriorated. Grivas had a dozen well-equipped gangs operating in the Troódos and Kyrenia Mountains and plenty of Greek Cypriot informers in the police and civil service to keep him informed about security operations. This leakage of information led to the failure of a massive sweep of the island's many monasteries, where the Cypriot Orthodox monks were in the habit of storing arms and giving food and shelter to the terrorists. At the end of October 1955 a British sergeant was shot in the back and killed while walking through Nicosia. In November 1955 the main Post Office in Nicosia was blown up and a week later a grenade was thrown on to the floor during the Caledonian Society's annual dance at the Ledra Palace Hotel. Five people were seriously wounded, including the young daughter of the Director of Intelligence.

The troops had a problem containing the violence, for the EOKA terrorist campaign was waged on a stop-and-start basis. Just when the troops felt they had a grip on the situation, Makarios would call for more discussions or Grivas would announce a ceasefire. With the world's media everywhere and world opinion anxiously waiting to brand the British as aggressors, the troops had no option but to relax their grip and the terrorists duly slipped away to regroup. A few weeks later Grivas would strike again; this on-off action was to bedevil security force operations throughout the entire Emergency.

Harding had declared a state of Emergency on the island in November 1955 and while terrorist attacks continued throughout the winter the search for a peaceful solution continued in London, Athens, Ankara and Washington. All attempts failed in the face of intransigence from Makarios, who flatly refused to condemn terrorist activity or the taking of lives or to recognize the valid Turkish interest.

The taking of lives came to involve the Archbishop's own family. In the early winter months of 1956 an EOKA gang ambushed a Champ containing a lance corporal and Captain Brian Coombe of the Royal Engineers and his driver Lance Corporal Morum. Captain Coombe's sappers had been working with 45 Commando in the Troódos Mountains, and had already lost two men in terrorist incidents. The first burst of fire hit the vehicle, killing Lance Corporal Morum. The Champ ran into the ditch, where Coombe abandoned it and, taking his Sten gun, climbed up the slope to find himself overlooking a group of terrorists in the ambush position. Captain cocked his weapon and shot it out with the group below until, having fired off both his magazines, and tried a few shots with his service revolver, he ran out of ammunition. He then went back to the vehicle and retrieved the dead corporal's weapon, returning to renew his private fight with the terrorists. After a few more bursts there came cries of surrender and three men came out of the gully below with their hands up.

This was a ruse. As Coombe stood up to take their surrender, a fourth man fired at him with a machine gun. In reply, Coombe promptly shot down the three men in the open and then emptied all his remaining magazines on the machine gunner. After a few moments, he too shouted, 'Don't shoot!' and came out with his hands up, before making a dash for cover and vanishing over the rim of the gully, hastened on his way by a further couple of shots from Coombe's revolver.

Coombe was now out of ammunition but the three wounded terrorists on the slope did not know that. He kept them covered and engaged them in conversation until after about half an hour a three-tonner arrived with British infantry from the Gordon Highlanders, who took charge of the prisoners and conveyed them to hospital and prison. It then transpired that the man who had fired on Coombe from cover was Markos Drakos and one of the wounded terrorists, who later died from his injuries, was Haralambos Mouskos, a cousin of Archbishop Makarios. His funeral procession was attended by thousands of people. Lance Corporal Morum was buried quietly by his regiment in the British Military Cemetery outside Nicosia.

In March 1956 a major tragedy was narrowly averted when a bomb was discovered on a civil airliner full of women and children about to take off for Britain, and this barely prevented atrocity proved the last straw for Harding. He had held many meetings with Archbishop Makarios in attempts to find a solution but to no avail. Whenever a solution seemed in reach the Archbishop came up with fresh and unacceptable demands – an amnesty for EOKA killers, Greek control of internal security. This time, however, EOKA had gone too far.

A week after the bomb was discovered on the aircraft, Archbishop Makarios and his henchman, the Bishop of Kyrenia, were arrested at Nicosia Airport as they were about to fly to Athens, and sent into exile in the Seychelles. The arrest of Makarios provoked riots in Cyprus and protests elsewhere, not least at the UN, protests which the British countered by releasing intelligence data showing the full extent of the Archbishop's involvement with the terrorist campaign. Inevitably, attempts were made to prove that the evidence of his terrorist involvement was forged but these all failed and the Archbishop's deportation was generally seen as completely justified, not least when Harding had a narrow escape from death a few weeks later; a bomb placed under his bed by a Greek Cypriot servant at Government House failed to explode.

The British now they turned their full attention to Colonel Grivas. During the winter of 1955–6 more British units arrived, including 16th Independent Parachute Brigade under Brigadier M. A. H. 'Tubby' Butler

17. Coldstream Guards search an Egyptian vehicle at a road block in the Canal Zone, November 1951.

18. Lieutenant General Sir George Erskine, General Officer Commanding British Troops Egypt and Mediterranean Command, examines a poster announcing the Egyptian journal *Al Gamhour al Misri*'s reward of £1,000 for his death.

19. The southernmost point reached after the Anglo-French assault on Port Said: soldiers of the 2nd Battalion The Parachute Regiment dig in by the Canal Road at kilometre 35, November 1956.

20. Murder mile, Nicosia, 1956: two British policemen lie dying on the pavement while the third, wounded and gun in hand, sits in the doorway after an EOKA ambush. Nikos Sampson, who seized power from Makarios in 1974, admitted to the murders in 1961, two years after he had been tried and acquitted.

21. Colonel George Grivas, leader of EOKA.

22. The end of Operation Black Mac, which resulted in two EOKA leaders killed and eighteen terrorists captured. A corporal of the 2nd Battalion the Parachute Regiment examines the entrance to a hide in which six terrorists were hiding. The hole was concealed under a fireplace in which a fire was burning.

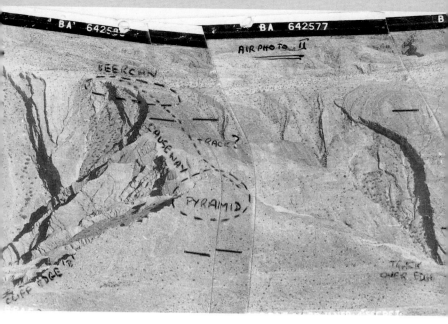

23. The original oblique perspective air photograph used by Lieutenant Colonel Deane-Drummond in the Jebel Akhdar operation. 'Beercan' is located approximately 1,000 feet higher than 'Pyramid'.

24. Lieutenant Colonel Tony Deane-Drummond and Syid Tarik on the Jebel Akhdar.

25. Lieutenant David Storrie RM, a Wessex helicopter pilot of 848 Naval Air Squadron, with a Dyak baby at Jambu, the base for C Company 1st/10th Gurkha Rifles. On his right is Captain Martin, OC C Company, and the baby's mother. On his left is Lieutenant Clarke RN, another helicopter pilot.

26. An Indonesian prisoner being interrogated by a Gurkha at Jambu, watched by two Dyaks.

27. A patrol of the 2nd Battalion The Green Jackets setting out. This was taken relatively early in the campaign; by the end the Stirling sub-machine guns and most Self-Loading Rifles (SLRs) had been replaced by Armalite AR15s, the forerunner of the US Armalite M16.

28. RN Wessex helicopter on a small jungle pad.

29. A Bren gunner of the 1st Battalion The Royal Sussex Regiment firing from a sangar in Wadi Taym area, South Arabia – a posed picture.

30. The Radfan from a helicopter – the camels on the escarpment give some idea of the scale of the country.

31. Soldiers of the Federal Regular Army near Mukeiras on an 8,000 foot plateau, some 120 miles east of Aden, in South Arabia.

32. A series of pictures showing a typical riot in Aden involving soldiers from the 1st Battalion The Royal Northumberland Fusiliers.

a) A bomb has already been thrown; Fusiliers follow up the thrower.

b) A second bomb is thrown, wounding the Fusilier. The thrower can be seen running away just to the left of the smoke.

c) Wounded Fusilier covered by his comrade.

d) Fusiliers withdraw, while a supporting armoured car enters the scene to come to their assistance.

and the armoured cars of the Royal Horse Guards. Harding and Brigadier Baker now had fifteen battalions on the island, enough troops to control the towns and mount major sweeps in the Troódos Mountains. Within weeks, as the winter snows melted, the army began to put relentless pressure on the mountain gangs, usually by cordon-and-sweep searches or house-to-house searches in remote villages. Like most of these post-colonial campaigns, Cyprus became a 'Corporals' War', where a great deal of the responsibility was placed on the junior and senior NCOs, often men in their late teens or early twenties. They led patrols, guarded police stations, laid ambushes, countered riots and demonstrations and put up with a great deal of hard work, discomfort and – certainly in the larger towns – a lot of verbal abuse and stone throwing. To this can be added long hours, little sleep and the constant possibility of ambush or bomb attacks . . . all this for a National Serviceman's pay of twenty-eight shillings a week.

In May 1956 Brigadier Baker began a series of cordon and search operations in the Troódos Mountains in an attempt to eliminate the terrorist gangs. The first sweep, Operation PEPPERPOT, concentrated on the Troódos Mountains and Kykko Monastery; the monks were fervent supporters of enosis and Colonel Grivas, so a good haul was anticipated and a quantity of arms and ammunition were found – and the search of the monastery was condemned by Athens Radio as desecration of a holy shrine. Operation PEPPERPOT lasted for eleven days and was highly successful. The troops made dozens of 'contacts', four gangs were dispersed and seventeen terrorists captured, most of them at once turning Queen's evidence to save their skins.

That done, the troops moved on to Operation LUCKY ALPHONSE, a major sweep in the Paphos Forest involving 40 and 45 Commando RM, the 1st and 3rd Battalions The Parachute Regiment, the King's Own Yorkshire Light Infantry, the Gordon Highlanders and the Royal Norfolk Regiment, under the tactical command of Brigadier Butler of 16th Independent Parachute Brigade.

Spike Hughes of Sp (Support) Troop, 45 Commando remembers this operation:

Lucky Alphonse was the largest anti-terrorist operation ever undertaken in Cyprus and the plan was to surround a large area of the Paphos Forest break it into sub-areas, like petals on a flower and the central area was called the 'Magic Circle' where Grivas and his gang were supposed to be. We brought up the heavy stuff, Vickers machine guns and 3 inch mortars to fire into areas which were too difficult to search on foot. Good fun for us: at last a chance to fire our three-inch mortars and we were firing away when suddenly we got the order. 'Cease Firing . . . We've dropped a bomb on 'A' Troop! Check ranges and bearings.' The radios were red hot. We were close to 'A' Troop so we went to their aid, the medics treated the wounded and four or five lads went out on stretchers. Our Sergeant, Vic Pegler, was adamant we had not caused the accident and pointed out that A Troop were firing 2 mortars at the same time. Whether a two-inch mortar bomb had hit an overhead branch or had exploded as it left the barrel . . . who knows?

We carried the stretchers up to the top of the mountain, where the casualties were taken to hospital by helicopter. We were left to pick up the unused bombs and dismantle the mortars and then we noted that the opposite hillside was alight. By following day the fire had spread, *Lucky Alphonse* began to collapse and some nineteen British troops died in the flames. Grivas and his men, if they were ever there, had all escaped. The reaction of the locals as we passed through their towns on patrol varied. Most of the Greeks ignored us. Some threw bricks and bottles. Some threw us fruit. Some, usually the older men, even saluted.

LUCKY ALPHONSE was less successful than PEPPERPOT. The troops broke up more gangs and scattered the terrorists across the mountains but lost the chance for major success when poor shooting enabled Colonel Grivas and a group of terrorists to escape unharmed from contact with a patrol of 3 Para near the village of Aya Arka. However, the patrol did find Grivas's personal diary, which gave full details of his meetings with Makarios and confirmed the Archbishop's involvement in the terror campaign.

Unfortunately, the 45 Commando mortar fire set light to the forest and started a blaze, which actually killed twenty-one soldiers, most of them from the Gordon Highlanders. One long-lasting effect of these two major sweeps was to chase Grivas and his main lieutenants out of the mountains: he withdrew to a safe house in Limassol and left the mountain fighting to other men. The riots in the towns and patrol skirmishes in the hills went on throughout the summer of 1956 as the attention of the world turned to the developing trouble with Egypt over the Suez Canal. In July the 3rd Commando Brigade was withdrawn to

Malta for amphibious training and in October the 16th Independent Parachute Brigade began parachute training.

With no solution in sight, political or military, the British government decided to ignore Makarios and proceed with plans for internal self-government in Cyprus, the first step towards independence. In July 1956, Lord Radcliffe, the man who had drawn up the partition plans for India and Pakistan in 1947, was asked to draw up a provisional constitution for Cyprus, which may have been why, in August, Grivas called another of his ceasefires. His forces had been written down and badly disorganized by PEPPERPOT and LUCKY ALPHONSE and he needed time to regroup, which the British authorities were ill-advised enough to give him.

Grivas revoked his ceasefire after two weeks and terrorism continued as more and more British – and French – troops arrived on the island in the build-up for the Suez operation. Markos Drakos was now leading a killer squad in Nicosia where a grenade thrown into a restaurant killed the American Vice-Consul in Cyprus, William Boteler.

Grivas hastily apologized for this attack, calling it 'a tragic error', but in November 1956 alone his men mounted more than 400 attacks – ambushes, shootings and bombings – against the British garrison. The casualty figures soared and forty people were killed, half of them British soldiers.

After the Suez debacle ended the odds again turned against Colonel Grivas. By January 1957 Harding had eighteen infantry battalions on the island and these were turned loose on the EOKA gangs until, by the spring of 1957, Grivas had to admit that his forces were on the run. Most of the EOKA leaders had either been killed or captured and the time seemed right for another 'ceasefire' and a further peace initiative. The Radcliffe proposals for a self-governing constitution met with approval in London and Ankara but the Greeks refused to discuss them as long as Makarios was detained in the Seychelles.

In a bid to force the British government's hand, Grivas offered yet another ceasefire – if his master, the Archbishop, was released. Anxious to be seen as conciliatory, and with the UN baying for a settlement, the British agreed. Makarios was allowed back into Cyprus in spring 1957, moving on from there to Athens where he renewed his campaign for enosis. By April the EOKA campaign had lasted two full years. The terrorists had set off more than 1,300 bombs and killed seventy-eight

British soldiers and nine British policemen, as well as sixteen British civilians, twelve Cypriot policemen and four Turks,.

In return the British had killed fifty-one EOKA terrorists and imprisoned a further twenty-seven; some 1,500 had been detained on suspicion of terrorist activity and many more injured in riots. The terrorists were now taking casualties, and among those killed in 1957 were Markos Drakos and George Afxentiou, the latter trapped in a mountain cave by British troops who killed him when he refused to surrender.

What these bleak figures do not tell is the vicious nature of the Cyprus Emergency; in this conflict, common humanity was often at a discount. For example, in April 1956 a Greek Cypriot police superintendent, Kyriakos Sristotelos, was killed when visiting his wife and new-born child in a maternity hospital. In May 1956, in response to the execution of two terrorists in Nicosia Gaol, Grivas hanged two captured British soldiers, Corporals Hill and Shilton. In 1955 a young English couple, Mr and Mrs Patrick Karberry, were ambushed when returning home from a day on the beach at Kyrenia, dragged from the vehicle and murdered. Mrs Karberry was heavily pregnant when she was shot down.

Such actions disgusted the British troops but although there were certainly incidents when rifle butts and entrenching tool handles were freely used in riots, their discipline held. This was true even in the village of Lefkoniko in October 1956, when a bomb hidden under a water tap exploded when soldiers from the Highland Light Infantry had gathered around it for a drink. There were a great many Highland soldiers in the village at the time and their search for the bomber did a lot of damage, but no villager was killed or even seriously injured. This did not prevent a visit from a British politician, Mrs Barbara Castle, who arrived on the island in 1957 and returned home to condemn the brutality of British troops.

In November 1957 Field Marshal Harding left the island and was replaced by Sir Hugh Foot, who brought with him high hopes for a diplomatic solution. At least the British need to retain Cyprus had been removed from the bargaining board, for it had now been decided that Britain's strategic interests in the eastern Mediterranean could be served in Cyprus by a good airfield and a couple of army bases. If a workable constitution could now be agreed by both communities the British could hand over responsibility to the local politicians and leave, but hopes of a constitutional settlement acceptable to Greeks and Turks were swiftly dashed and more violence broke out.

Colonel Grivas was still insistent on enosis and this caused rising concern among the Turkish community, which now began to express itself in demonstrations and more intercommunal violence, besides the setting up of their own terrorist organization, TMT, the Turkish Defence Organization. Grivas demonstrated that any compromise on sovereignty was impossible by attacking the British and stirring up trouble between the Greek and Turkish communities. He began by declaring a boycott of British goods but he had to terrorize the shopkeepers to make the boycott work. This move was followed by a series of bomb attacks on servicemen but the British were well used to these by now and they did little harm.

Grivas then called yet another of his ceasefires, which was accepted by Sir Hugh Foot in anticipation of a meeting with him. He had no intention of meeting the Governor and turned his attention to attacking the Turks. A number of Turks were murdered by the EOKA and several Greeks were murdered in reprisal by the TMT. On 17 July 1958 alone, five Turks were murdered by EOKA and there was more intercommunal violence but on 3 October 1958 Grivas demonstrated the impartiality of the struggle by sending his killers to shoot down two British women, who were shopping with their children at a supermarket near Famagusta when the gunmen moved in. Both women were shot in the back, one dying at once while her child stood by, the other being seriously injured.

Both women were married to British servicemen and this atrocity almost gave Grivas what he had been seeking for so long; an outbreak of violence against the local Greek population by British soldiers. Hundreds of British servicemen left camp and descended on Famagusta, where they beat up any Greek they could find, but their officers and NCOs were soon on hand to urge the troops back to barracks. No Greek lives were lost, and the fact that the troops of other armies in the world would have burned Famagusta to the ground went unrecognized. Athens Radio inevitably made a great play of the riot in Famagusta and scarcely mentioned the murders, but most people on the island, including the Greek community, were disgusted at these senseless and brutal killings of the British women.

Archbishop Makarios had begun to realize that enosis was not an option while the Turks were so set against it. If this demand were not renounced and the EOKA campaign against the Turks continued there was a likelihood that, sooner or later, the mainland Turks would invade Cyprus and enforce partition. Makarios therefore announced in September that he would accept the original British offer of an independent republic.

In this Makarios had the support of the Greek government but not of Colonel Grivas, and although the EOKA campaign was now seen as counterproductive, Grivas refused to call off the attacks. The next EOKA attempt placed bombs on British military aircraft at Nicosia airport and the bombers were suspected to be Greek Cypriots working for NAAFI, the servicemen's canteen organization. The Cypriots were dismissed and the NAAFI canteens closed but it is some indication of the public support enjoyed by the troops – as opposed to the scanty support they had from politicians – that no fewer than 20,000 British civilians promptly offered to come out from Britain and replace the canteen staff so that the troops could have their tea and buns.

At the end of 1958 a solution – the Zurich Agreement – was finally reached between the parties. Cyprus was to become independent in 1959 with a Greek Cypriot President and a Turkish Cypriot Vice-President. The government and administration was split on a 70:30 Greek–Turk basis and – a crucial proviso in view of what transpired later – Greece and Turkey were entitled to intervene in Cyprus on behalf of their nationals if these terms were violated. Britain was to have two sovereign base areas on Cyprus, but otherwise take no part in island affairs.

Colonel Grivas left the island in March 1959 after EOKA had handed in a token quantity of arms to indicate their surrender – a fact that the EOKA Museum in Nicosia chooses to ignore. Archbishop Makarios became the first president of an independent Cyprus, which was declared as a state within the Commonwealth on 16 August 1960, just over five years after the troubles began. The Cyprus Emergency cost the lives of 156 British soldiers. A further 238 civilians, mostly Greeks, were murdered by EOKA. Fifty-one EOKA terrorists were killed and some 1,500 imprisoned or detained and several were executed for murder. All this pain and bloodshed was for nothing since the agreement Archbishop Makarios settled for in 1959 had been on the table since he and his henchmen began the terror campaign in 1955.

As for the good intentions and pious resolutions that ended this violence, the post-independence history shows just how well they were kept. George Grivas, appointed to the rank of general in the Greek army, was back on the island within a few years and between 1963 and 1973 trouble flared up regularly between the Greek and Turkish communities. In 1974 the Greek Cypriots claimed that the 1960 constitution was unworkable and the arrival of Greek army units brought on civil war led by Nicos Sampson, a former EOKA terrorist, and the expulsion of President Makarios in an Athens-sponsored coup.

Then came UN intervention, which totally failed to prevent Greek and Greek Cypriot oppression of the Turkish Cypriot community. In 1976 the Turks invoked their rights of intervention agreed in the 1960 constitution and invaded, and the outcome of the subsequent fighting was the de facto partition of the island. Inevitably, the Greek Cypriots blamed the British for this state of affairs but by then the British had been gone for over a decade. President Makarios died in 1977 and in 1983 the northern part of the island declared itself independent as the Turkish Republic of North Cyprus. Cyprus is still partitioned and the problem has passed to the United Nations, where it remains, still unresolved, at the present time.

8

MAJOR GENERAL TONY DEANE-DRUMMOND

Muscat and Oman, 1958–1959:
Seize the Green Mountain

Major General Tony Deane-Drummond took part in the first ever British parachute operation, at the Tragino Aqueduct in Italy in February 1941. He was captured, but escaped in June 1942, and rejoined 1st Airborne Division which was then tasked for the Sicily invasion. Italy surrendered in September 1943; the division then took part in the great airborne operation at Arnhem in September 1944. Again he was captured, but escaped by hiding in a cupboard for thirteen days. After the Second World War he commanded 22 Special Air Service Regiment in Malaya, and, notably, on the operation to capture the Jebel Akhdar (the Green Mountain) in Oman in 1958, about which he writes in his chapter. He has had three books published.

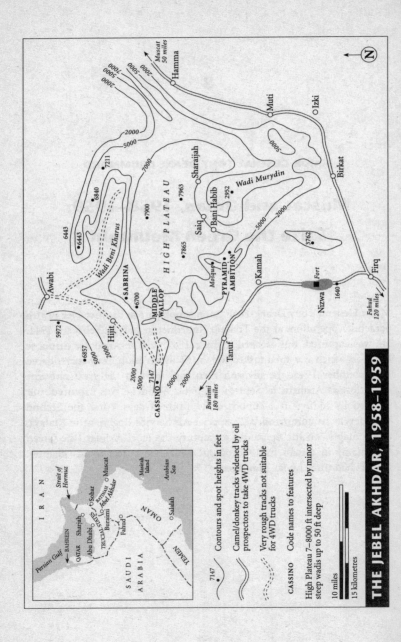

THE JEBEL AKHDAR, 1958–1959

Muscat 50 miles
Hamma
Muti
Izki
Birkat
Sharaijah
7211
6840
Wadi Murydin
6443
2952
7963
Beni Habib
Saiq
7900
HIGH PLATEAU
3762
7865
6700
Mojau
PYRAMID
Kamah
AMBITION
SABRINA
Awabi
Wadi Beni Kharus
5972
MIDDLE
WALLOP
Nizwa
1640
Fort
Firq
6857
Hijit
Fahud 120 miles
7147
CASSINO
Tanuf
Buraimi 180 miles

Contours and spot heights in feet

Camel/donkey tracks widened by oil
prospectors to take 4WD trucks

Very rough tracks not suitable
for 4WD trucks

CASSINO   Code names to features

7147   High Plateau 7–8000 ft intersected by minor
steep wadis up to 50 ft deep

10 miles
15 kilometres

IRAN
Strait of Hormuz
Sohar
Abu Dhabi Sharjah
Muscat
QATAR
BAHRAIN
TRUCIAL STATES
Buraimi Jebel Akhdar
Masirah Island
Fahud
OMAN
Arabian Sea
SAUDI ARABIA
Salalah
YEMEN
Persian Gulf

The operations that took place in Muscat and Oman in 1958 and 1959 brought stability to an area which had suffered many rebellious small wars for a very long time. To understand them, it is first necessary to set the scene and outline what took place in the recent past. Only then can the events be seen in perspective.

Even before the Second World War, Saudi Arabia wanted to revise her frontiers and extend her influence in south-eastern Arabia. After the war, under pressure from her own and American oil interests, her efforts redoubled and in 1952 she occupied the neighbouring Buraimi Oasis, a part of Oman that bordered Saudi Arabia and the Trucial Oman.[1] On being ejected in 1953 (after exposure of wide-spread bribery) by the Trucial Oman Scouts (TOS), she turned to intrigue against the Sultan of Muscat and Oman. On the death in 1954 of the elected Imam (the religious leader in Oman but with temporal powers in Central Oman), she supported the puppet Imam, Ghalib bin Ali, and on his removal from Buraimi provided refuge, training facilities and money for his ambitious brother, Talib bin Ali, so-called leader of the Omani Liberation Army. When Ghalib and Talib openly rebelled, with the support of Suleiman bin Himyar, Lord of the Jebel Akhdar (the Green Mountain), the Sultan turned to Britain for help.

In the past, the Sultan's Armed Forces (SAF),[2] paid by the Sultan's treasury which was usually broke, had been little more effective than an armed gendarmerie. Their weapons were usually second-hand war surplus and their ammunition was long past its sell-by date. Perhaps this was all that was needed up to that time. They had, after all, brought peace to most of the desert villages in Central Oman in 1957 without firing a shot. The TOS were quite different. They were a part of the British Army, were equipped accordingly and were run by a series of colourful commanding officers.

Colonel David Smiley, the new Commander SAF, rapidly came to the conclusion in late summer 1958 that the troops he had available were totally inadequate to guard the few tracks up the mountain let alone to defeat Suleiman, Ghalib and Talib by capturing the Jebel Akhdar. Major Frank Kitson MC,[3] who had recently returned from Malaya to take up a planning appointment in the War Office, proposed that about fifty volunteers from the SAS would form small killer squads to climb the mountain, find out where the three leaders were, and capture or kill them. He had employed similar tactics when combating the Mau Mau rebellion.[4] Kitson was regarded as an expert in situations of this sort and the operation could be conducted with little or no publicity. The Director of Military Operations in the War Office thought the idea was worth exploring and Kitson was sent out to Aden to explain his ideas to the C-in-C in Aden, Air Vice Marshal Maurice Heath and me, the Commanding Officer of 22 SAS. I had just arrived from Malaya where my regiment was operating, and we went straight into a conference with the C-in-C and his staff. The success of future operations, or even if they should start at all, would now be decided.

The C-in-C started by asking me how the SAS would tackle the problem, subject, of course, to a detailed inspection of the Jebel. I told him we would carry out fighting patrols and engage any pickets we found. This had been our normal procedure in Malaya. Actions of this sort would also show us the best way up the mountain and wear down the rebels to the point when negotiations might succeed in the short time frame of completion before the hot weather expected next April.

I could see across the table that Frank Kitson was not at all happy. He had expected to be asked for his opinion first. The C-in-C then asked him for his ideas.[5] He described what the War Office (and he himself) had in mind, but he did not persuade the C-in-C or anyone present. Frank Kitson was obviously disappointed that his scheme was unlikely to go ahead but he appreciated that the Commanding Officer of 22 SAS must have overriding influence on how his troops should be employed. Indeed, the CO's agreement, as he says in his book, would be essential to any plan he put forward to the War Office.

Next day we arrived in Muscat by air to meet Colonel Smiley and to hear his up-to-date description of what was happening on the Jebel Akhdar. He had only been there about six months and his story was worse than I expected:

In the period from January to October 1958, 198 trucks of all sorts have been blown up including all 30 Ferrets [light armoured cars] of the Life Guards Squadron. Other British casualties add up to 10 killed and 53 wounded. The small British contingent at Bait al Falaj have also suffered over 100 per cent medical casualties requiring evacuation in the same period. More than 120 tribesmen from the villages below the mountain have either been killed or carted up to the top in chains. Rebel morale is high and the SAF camps near Nizwa and Tanuf have been regularly sniped by day and by night using light machine guns, 81-mm mortars and rifles or all three.

Colonel David Smiley had a rather elderly but knowledgeable member of his staff called Colonel Colin Maxwell. He asked him to tell us more about what was happening.

The tribes of the Bani Hinna and Bani Riyam on the top are altogether far superior to the desert bedu in the villages below. The mountain tribes seem to accept more discipline, to operate in larger groups, to shoot straighter and to have more western type skills inherent in their make-up. They only have to be shown how to operate a mortar or a heavy machine gun to become experts, all this with an air of light hearted enthusiasm. So you can see that Talib has the right material ready to hand. He has become the commander on the mountain and is a master of tactics and intrigue. Cairo radio daily carries panegyrics on his efficiency in beating back 'thousands of British soldiers who are trying to oust him from his rightful home'. Our intelligence reports state that he visits all his pickets regularly and sees to it that they know what to do in an emergency, what alternative positions they should take up, that their food and ammunition supply is adequate and conducts regular reliefs from his central reserve of Saudi trained soldiers. The great man of the mountain is, however, still Suleiman bin Himyar, Paramount Sheikh of the Bani Riyam, whose word is law and on whose authority men can be flogged or even executed. He has always been noted for ruthlessness and only on one occasion has he submitted to the Sultan.

Frank Kitson and I were soon on our way the next morning, flying in a Single Pioneer to Nizwa.[6] We could see the Jebel Akhdar in the far distance as a pale blue and craggy mountain. Only when we came closer, flying at 8,000 feet, could we see how it was made up of an enormous plateau some twenty miles long by ten miles wide and 7,000 feet high. It was surrounded by near-vertical cliffs and steep-sided wadis, gouged

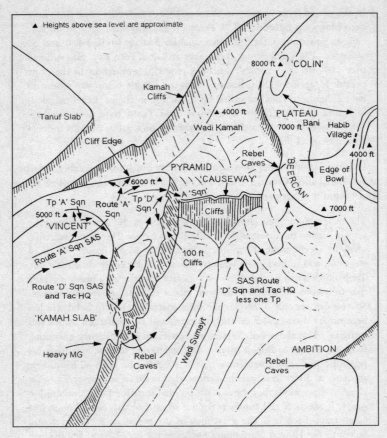

▲ Heights above sea level are approximate

8000 ft ▲ 'COLIN'

Kamah
Cliffs

'Tanuf Slab'

▲ 4000 ft

PLATEAU

7000 ft Bani   Habib
Village

Cliff Edge

Wadi Kamah

Rebel
Caves

▲ 4000 ft

PYRAMID

'CAUSEWAY'

'BEERCAN'

Edge of
Bowl

6000 ft ▲

A 'Sqn'

Cliffs

▲ 7000 ft

Tp 'A' Sqn   Route 'A'   Tp 'D'
Sqn   Sqn

5000 ft ▲

'VINCENT'

Route 'A' Sqn SAS

100 ft
Cliffs

Route 'D' Sqn SAS
and Tac HQ

SAS Route
'D' Sqn and Tac HQ
less one Tp

'KAMAH SLAB'

Wadi Sumayt

AMBITION

Heavy MG

Rebel
Caves

Rebel
Caves

Assault up the Jebel Akhdar

out of the mountain by floods of long ago. One very large wadi with a narrow entrance between 4,000 foot high cliffs was about ten miles long and ended in a giant amphitheatre about five miles across with stone and mud houses grouped in villages round the top edge. Below them were bright streaks of green, showing that cultivation was still taking place. We flew on, gradually losing height, and on our right we could see how the mountains had been formed from a series of sharp-pointed slabs in the shape of half-pyramids, leaning against each other like buttresses, with deep wadis in between, to keep up the solid plateau beyond.

We took off from Nizwa and flew north towards Tanuf to look down on one of the SAF camps next to a wadi with running water. We then started climbing steeply and after a little while we banked over to the right, high over the mountain as we threaded our way between occasional clouds. From our bird's-eye view we could see how the Wadi Tanuf cut the mountain range almost in two, ending with a cliff face, the top of which was a narrow bridge connecting the main high mountain on the left with the rebel-held plateau on the right. To clear the ridge we climbed to over 9,000 feet and suddenly, beyond, the mountain tumbled down into another very steep wadi which drove almost right through the mountain from the north. Down we came steeply, to land on a short strip adjacent to the Fort at Awabi, where we were met by a formidable-looking major with an enormous brown beard.

This was Jasper Coates, one-time Group Captain in charge of all RAF Operations in the Persian Gulf, and now commanding a platoon of the Muscat Regiment at the Fort. 'Come up and have some tea,' he said. 'I will try and tell you all I know about this side of the Jebel.' He continued: 'The wadi which leads up into the mountain from here is the Wadi Beni Kharus and about six miles up it divides. One part goes to the left up another wadi and a series of villages which are hostile to the Sultan. The branch to the right goes on to Hijir, which is friendly and from where guides might be obtained to get you to the top up a very steep track. This was also the way the Persians came nearly ten centuries ago and was thought to be the only way on to the plateau.'

Late on 2 November I arrived back in Malaya to find that authority had just been received from the War Office to deploy one squadron to Oman. Also authorized were two light helicopters for casualty evacuation and a field surgical team, to be in place at Nizwa by 25 November. Signals went out straight away recalling D Squadron as an 'emergency for another operation'. Helicopters brought everybody out by 4 November. John Watts,[7] the Squadron Commander, was astonished when he heard where he was going, as was my second-in-command, Bob Walker Brown.

A proportion of the squadron was married, with their families in Kuala Lumpur. The squadron was given forty-eight hours' leave followed by a week of intensive training for a complete change of role, change of theatre and change of visibility from 20–30 yards in the jungle to thousands in Arabia. Rifles had to be zeroed and two teams trained on 3in mortars – using individuals who had been mortarmen in their previous regiments. Everybody fired the 3.5in rocket launcher. Once again we practised fire and movement to remind everybody that this tactic might be essential. The squadron had never worked so hard in their lives. The day after their training they took off, changed planes twice and arrived in Oman on 18 November, kitted out to operate on the mountains and in the desert.

John Watts decided to split the squadron of four troops into two, with his second-in-command, Muir Walker, taking half to Awabi, whilst the remainder would operate under him from Tanuf. The journey from Bait al Falaj had been a nightmare with every truck breaking down at least once – they had all been supplied by Aden and were not in good shape.

The squadron camp was soon established upstream from the Northern Frontier Regiment (NFR) Company, whose fly-ridden burastis (plaited palm-leaf shelters) did not appeal. The company had two British officers, one of them a Royal Marines instructor on temporary loan. The night before the squadron arrived, the rebels had mortared the camp rather inaccurately and followed this up by firing several bursts of light machine gun fire into burastis where lights could be seen. NFR troops had tried going a short way up the shoulders of the wadi by day, but each time they were engaged by pickets and forced to fall back. They had lost three men a week previously from accurate rebel shooting.

The next day, 26 November, saw both SAS troops move out in small observation patrols by moonlight to cover both wadis and a wide area of hillside from Tanuf to Kamah. Their intention was to observe all day and come back at night. At about 1400 hours a hardcore tribesman climbed up towards the left-hand patrol, commanded by Corporal Smith. He was shot down, and his SMLE (Lee Enfield) rifle and forty-three rounds recovered. Sergeant Davidson, commanding the right-hand patrol, started to move over to give assistance. Corporal Swindells stood up on a crest and was shot dead by a rebel sniper from about 180 metres below. This was the first SAS casualty. The patrol immediately returned fire and dropped the wounded rebel, who was dragged off under cover. Both patrols came under heavy and quite accurate sniping and mortar fire for half an hour. They withdrew back to base that night carrying

Swindells, who was later buried with full military honours in the only Christian cemetery available on the coast south of Muscat, accessible only from the sea.

The right-hand patrol, under Peter de la Billière,[8] was highly successful. An extensive cave system and much rebel movement was spotted about 900 metres away. They withdrew that night and John Watts decided to mount a major operation using both his troops and air support to blast the cave area. This took place soon after first light on 1 December, supported by both squadron mortars and four Venoms from Sharjah. Peter led one troop by night into a position only 200 metres from the cave whilst John Watts, with the reserve troop and a radio to talk to the Venoms, moved up by night to get into a position on a cliff edge about 300 metres away from the caves well before dawn. Peter had with him a 3.5 in rocket launcher and his two LMGs. There were still two hours to wait until first light and no alarm had been given. Soon after dawn one man came out of the cave and stretched. He started a small fire to make coffee. Half an hour later three more came out and sat huddled around the fire. At 0725 another three came out and the time had come. Peter's troop gave the signal to open fire and all hell broke loose from both troops, with Brens, mortars and rifles all aiming at the rebels. This did not deter them. They started to fire back from behind stone sangars and a little later joined in with their own mortar. The rocket launcher had to be fired from a standing position and scored a direct hit into the cave mouth. The Venoms came in with accurate cannon fire and they not only shot up the cave but also obliterated the rebel mortar position. The RAF was delighted; never before had they had such targets. A total of eight rebels was thought to have been killed.

Muir Walker and the other two troops soon reached Awabi, and then up through Hijir to the highest point at over 7,000 feet, which was quickly named 'Cassino'. One of the difficulties of the position was administration, not only to provide rations but also ammunition and extra clothing and sleeping bags. The temperature varied from +30°C to −5°C, with a nearly continuous wind of up to gale force. This was the way the Persians had come ten centuries before and word soon spread round that we were now in position on the way in to the plateau. The narrow ridge from Cassino stretched out east for over a mile with near-vertical cliffs on each side of the Aqabat (pass), which was dominated by two small hills astride the ridge, which stuck up like tits, and were promptly named Sabrina. This was the obvious place for the rebels to hold with minimum force to seal off the entrance to the plateau and the villages some ten miles away, where the three leaders were said to be based. Muir protected his base on Cassino by putting Sergeant Hawkins with five men and an LMG about 1,500 metres away on the forward slope facing Sabrina.

Gales usually blew at 7,000 feet and an evening in December was no exception when the rebels attacked. It was not until Sergeant Hawkins and his men returned after dark at about 2000 hours that Muir even knew that a battle had taken place less than a mile away but downwind. Hawkins reported that he had seen forty to fifty rebels moving down the slope in front of Sabrina. The time was about 1630 and he lost sight of them as they dropped into a ravine. A rebel in a white turban appeared to do the controlling and when they had moved up to only about 200 metres from the patrol their LMGs opened up, using fire and movement in a classic infantry advance. Sergeant Hawkins held his fire until the rebels were within 150 metres and good targets presented themselves. He was certain that five had been killed and many more may have been wounded. This did not stop the rebel advance because they started to move round his flank and get on to another hill. By this time it was dark, which allowed the gallant Hawkins to pull out, with Corporal Cunningham manning his LMG in a quite brilliant manner.

There had been no casualties on our side behind stone sangars, except for cuts from bullets breaking off rocks nearby. About a week later there was confirmation that between nine and twelve rebels had died in this battle. After this, Muir decided to move his base up closer so that he could at least hear when a firefight was taking place.

Next morning before first light he sent out a strong patrol to check the position. The rebels had gone. They had been shattered by our fierce opposition. It had been a most savage and well-thought-out attack that might have come off had it not been for Hawkins' cool head. Smiley then gave orders for a platoon from the Muscat Regiment to come up to the Aqabat and help hold the base, allowing the SAS more freedom to move out on patrol. At the end of December one squadron of TOS also moved to Awabi and then to Hijir and from there maintained two troops on top of the Jebel, thus reinforcing the SAS base. Colonel Carter, who commanded the TOS and was a personality from the old school, very clearly stated that both his troops and the platoon from the Muscat

Regiment could only operate in support of the SAS; if the SAS were withdrawn his troops would have to go too. He did not want them to be in the front line and possibly risk any reverse.

The War Office now accepted that SAS operations in Oman took absolute priority over Malaya and we were free to take such reinforcements of men and equipment as was thought necessary. This was excellent. A Squadron was in the jungle and once again we had to get them out for another operation. The same procedure was then adopted with forty-eight hours' leave and only seven days' retraining for a complete change of role. In the meantime, we went ahead with the Tactical HQ and Captain John Spreull as operations officer, to reach Muscat by 1 January 1959. We now had to size up our operations and plan our assault on the Jebel.

David Smiley welcomed me on arrival and, after discussion, made me Deputy Field Commander of all forces in Oman with the authority to issue orders to any units deployed, whether British army, TOS or SAF. This enabled me to coordinate the action of ground troops and aircraft, and was the first step towards the defeat of the rebels on the Jebel. He wished me luck and hoped I would be successful.

Soon after arrival, we had to get up to date with operations and fill in the gaps in the signals I had received in Malaya. John Watts had decided to relieve Muir Walker and his two troops on Cassino by Peter de la Billière and his troop. There was now a whole squadron of TOS, plus the Life Guards on top to protect the base, but Peter had to be in position before Muir could be withdrawn.

Muir had arrived in Bait al Falaj the night before I arrived. He described what had happened.

My orders required both troops to carry forward a hell of a lot of ammunition for the Browning machine guns and LMGs. Their job would be to fire on Sabrina from good positions between 300 and 1000 metres away.

One troop and myself would have to get up the right tit by rope. Our patrols had already discovered it was much steeper than it looked from our base. Our job was to capture it, with the other troop giving fire support.

We started to move up just before last light at 1715, with the LMGs and Life Guards' Brownings giving covering fire whilst we moved up to the base of the right-hand tit. I put out a Troop on our left to cover us as we clambered in and out of a small wadi. The rebels knew the SAS were there and taunted us by calling out 'Come on Johnnie'. We then had to use ropes to get up the near vertical cliff, until we could see the astonished rebels only about ten metres away beyond and across a deep wadi. Once on top with the whole Troop we loosed off two magazines into the rebel sangar. We had captured the whole of the right hand tit.

As it was a raid, I gave orders to withdraw at 0200 and by 0800 we were back in the main ravine below the hill. Astonishing though it might seem, we had no casualties. We must have a charmed life.

We definitely hit four rebels whom we saw drop down. A few days later we heard that the rebels had lost nine killed.

We were back in the main base on Cassino by 1100 and handed over to Peter who had been watching the battle. The next day we dropped down the mountain and arrived back here yesterday.

John Watts had also just arrived back with his two troops. He looked nearly black from the sun and was now full of confidence when he heard about A Squadron. He too had had battles with rebels above Wadi Kamah and Wadi Sumayt. He had also just come in from a reconnaissance on one of the slabs of mountain, which later might be a possible way up the Jebel.

The next day we moved our tiny Tactical HQ to Nizwa and took the opportunity to meet Sayed (Prince) Tariq, the Sultan's half-brother. He had been invaluable in our link with the locals and spoke perfect English. He was an enormous man and carried a .303 rifle with a bandolier of ammunition and highly ornate curved Omani dagger or khunja in a decorated silver sheath stuck in his belt. Round the handle was strapped a gold Longines watch, it being thought effeminate to wear a watch on the wrist like a girl's bangle. We then took coffee in his house nearby and told him we hoped to get on top of the Jebel in the next few weeks, for which we hoped he would provide maximum support with his levies. Naturally he agreed and told me how delighted he was to hear about our many successes so far.

I spent the next three days based at Nizwa with our Tactical HQ. All the information produced by John Watts indicated that our main attack, with all the troops we could get hold of, would have to climb the mountain in one night. This would need moonlight to get us to the top by first light. Our Operation Order went out on 5 January for an attack due to start on 25 January.

Our detailed plan for assaulting the Jebel Akhdar took shape between 2 and 4 January 1959. Somehow we had to get Talib to move his pickets well away from the route up the mountain we had chosen, which was up the high ground on the face of the Jebel between Wadi Kamah and Wadi Sumayt. All our diversionary operations were designed to achieve surprise, which was the key to our plans.

D Squadron, now resting at Bait al Falaj and less its troop on the Aqabat, would move to Tanuf and operate offensively up the Jebel between 8 and 22 January, leaving three days spare before the full moon period starting on 25 January.

A Squadron was due to arrive in Oman on 12 January and would need a few days' rest and retraining to sort themselves out. Their first task would be to move on 17 January to Awabi and then to the SAS base 'Middle Wallop', halfway between Cassino and Sabrina. On arrival they would take over from the troop of D Squadron, who would return to their squadron at Tanuf. A Squadron would carry out detailed reconnaissances every night and capture the Sabrina feature by 22 January. This would acquaint them with the problems of mountain warfare and act as a training operation for later on. They would have to leave a troop on 'Middle Wallop' (with the two troops of the TOS and the platoon of the NFR) and find a way down the 5,000 foot descent to Tanuf.

Administrative problems were considerable and the success of the operation depended on pre-stocking containers with the right loads on the airfields and also arranging the different loads for the donkeys.

*

We were determined that our coming assault up the Jebel had to be planned in meticulous detail. The RAF had provided us with excellent vertical and oblique air photographs. The objectives for all troops including the Life Guards, the TOS and the NFR had to be decided, including their start times, so as not to interfere with the SAS higher up the mountain. Objectives for each SAS squadron and troop had to be planned, so that if battles took place on the way up the whole operation could be mutually supporting. Every single trooper knew exactly what was required and the part he had to play.

Back down at Nizwa we had to put our deception plan into operation. Provided security was tight, we were confident it would work. The rebels had become jumpy and had been turned from a self-confident and aggressive enemy into something a lot less daunting. Our own forceful patrols were beginning to pay off. We had to keep Talib on the hop and with a little luck we could do the job without suffering too many casualties ourselves.

Between 15 and 22 January we had violent storms and all the dry wadis became rushing, roaring torrents of water. The heavens opened and down came buckets of water, which on top of the Aqabat was driven by a sixty-mile-an-hour gale. Cloud enveloped the upper part of the mountain on the 22nd, so all our attacks had to be postponed by twenty-four hours. The forecast for the following few days was good and so it turned out to be.

The next day by 1100 hours the storms in Arabia moved out over the Indian Ocean and left a bright blue sky, which was soon studded with cumulus from horizon to horizon. The air smelt clean and our spirits went right up.

D Squadron in Tanuf had been pushing up the Jebel in aggressive patrols from a forward base on the first false crest about 1,000 feet up. From here, smaller patrols of half-troop size were sent further up the main mountain. Rebel mortars had been active and the men had become champion sangar-builders in the shortest possible time after reaching a new position. They had scored three more rebel kills in a chance contact.

Johnnie Cooper, commanding A Squadron, and an original member of Stirling's SAS in the Western Desert in the Second World War, described his attack on Sabrina.

We started out at 0200 hours on the 24th. We were supported by our own mortars together with two LMGs from The Muscat Regiment now back at 'Middle Wallop'. Further forward and just behind our start line just below Sabrina we had our own LMGs together with a section of the Trucial Oman Scouts. My plan was to creep up the left tit and when that was firm to take on the right.

It took forty minutes for Tony Jeapes and his Troop to get to the top whilst the Troop on his left unfortunately took twice as long. It was much steeper than we thought. The rebels did not wake up until we had been on top for five minutes. They were now in their sangars behind the hill and started shooting back at us, from only 50 metres. We cleared them out with hand grenades and energa bombs [shaped charges] fired at point-blank range. Three rebels were dropped. The remainder stuck to their positions and fired back. It was here that a rebel hand grenade badly wounded Trooper Wright with a splinter.

At first light we moved forward and found only one rebel dead in a sangar, but there was plenty of blood scattered around in at least five other places.

We stayed on Sabrina until 1100 when we withdrew to Cassino. Our one casualty was evacuated by helicopter but I have heard that his wounds are not too bad. He should be fit again in a few weeks. The next day we had a mighty tough scramble down to Tanuf which we reached last night.

I was even more confident that Talib would now be drawn back to Sabrina. The next day I spoke to all the soldiers at Tanuf, which included the assault troop commander from the Life Guards and a British officer from the NFR.

This afternoon we are getting hold of the four principal donkey drovers and, in deadly secrecy and on pain of death, we will ask them about conditions for watering the animals up the Wadi Tanuf. As you know, all the donkeys are concentrated at Kamah but we wanted to indicate we were not going up Wadi Kamah at all, but really up Wadi Tanuf. We rather expect that the rebels will hear about this 'secret' briefing a few hours after it has been given. The object is to get Talib to withdraw his pickets from where they cover our climb up and reinforce his positions on Sabrina or Tanuf.

D Squadron will start at 2030 hours tonight and get three of its four Troops to the plateau by first light. The fourth Troop will be back on the cliff edge of Pyramid prepared to give fire support to the rest of the Squadron climbing up the final slope. I will be at Tac HQ together with John Spreull and an RAF pilot with a radio to talk to the planes and we will climb up to the plateau as soon as we can. A Squadron will seize the cliff edge to the west of Pyramid having passed Vincent.

Soon after first light, the RAF are going to drop nine Valetta loads of ammunition, water and food on the top during the first day.

Good luck to all of us.

*

The time had come to start our climb at 2030. I was delighted to see David Smiley, who had just come up from Bait. He wished us good luck as we started to move up the lower slopes. There were no tracks to follow, but we all wound our way in and out of enormous boulders, always going upwards at about forty-five degrees. By midnight we had reached the edge of Vincent, which ended in fifty-foot rough cliffs as the slab rested on the equally steep slope of Pyramid which went on up another 1,000 feet. We had just passed two groups of empty rebel sangars, which was encouraging.

In the distance we could hear the troop of A Squadron at Sabrina putting in their diversionary attack. It was good to hear them doing their stuff.

A Squadron soon reached their objectives, but D Squadron followed by the HQ had to find a way down the hundred-foot rough cliffs on the edge of Pyramid, before crossing the head of Wadi Sumayt for the final climb up to the edge of the plateau. A Troop of D Squadron was dropped off on the edge of Pyramid to cover us as we crossed the Wadi. We did not believe we would get up to the top without any rebel opposition.

Tac HQ was moving right behind John Watts, when Peter de la Billière and his troop sent back word that they had discovered an unmanned heavy machine gun mounted on a tripod in the rocks. Peter and his troop soon had a short fixed rope in place (our detailed planning had revealed that there might be a problem getting up or down cliffs and both squadrons had them), and dropped down about 500 feet to the Wadi to be followed by the 1,500 foot climb to the plateau. Tac HQ and two troops from D Squadron were about to use Peter's fixed rope, when we could just see diagonally and below us the two-man MG crew coming to life outside their cave and boiling up coffee. They had not heard us and they disappeared into their cave. They were quickly eliminated with hand grenades lobbed into the cave mouth.

As we crossed Wadi Sumayt we were reassured by the knowledge that the troop on Pyramid was in position on the cliffs right behind us. We could see, in front and above, SAS troops spread out as they moved up the final shoulder, leading to the plateau. The sky was lightening in the east as D Squadron pressed on upwards in a race against time. We could hear the sweet music of aircraft engines and there off to the right were the three Valettas circling for their run-in to drop supplies. The higher-pitched whine of jet aircraft could be heard as they also circled over the area where the drop was to take place. D Squadron was tired all right, but they set to and built sangars round some minor features on top whilst others collected the air-drop packs and distributed ammunition, rations and water.

Tac HQ reached the top at 0700 carrying bergens (rucksacks) and the radio to talk to the aircraft. We had arrived on the unguarded plateau absolutely shattered by our climb up and had to advance and consolidate what was still a tenuous hold on the top.

Following up behind the SAS came the assault troop of the Life Guards, who reached Vincent cliff edge to relieve A Squadron at 1500 hours, some fourteen hours after they had started. A Squadron then moved up to the plateau along the top of 'Causeway'. A small rebel position near the plateau was overrun and one scared rebel took a death leap over a fifty-foot cliff. The squadron then took up positions on the plateau. Also behind the Life Guards came a company of the NFR, whose task was to man the cliff edge of Pyramid looking down on the Wadi Kamah which they had reached by 0830. Most unfortunately, A Squadron came under rebel sniper fire as they were climbing up and one bullet exploded an energa grenade being carried by Trooper Carter. This also wounded Troopers Bembridge and Hamer. All three wounded were evacuated successfully by helicopter but tragically both Carter and Bembridge died later of wounds. They too were later buried in the British Military Cemetery near Muscat.

The sun was just tipping the mountains on the horizon, bathing us in brilliant yellow light, in contrast to the rest of the troops who were in the shadow and still sweating their way up. Now we had our supplies nothing should stop us expanding the area we held, providing the rest of the SAS could close up quickly behind us.

From our position we could see an occasional rebel dart quickly between low hills and an infrequent bullet from a sniper's rifle winged its way towards our men, who were fast building up their sangars. The RAF pilot with me was talking to the Venoms as they came sweeping in from shallow dives to shoot their rockets at rebels also building sangars on a hill about 1,000 metres away and out of range.

When the patrols all returned and made their reports, it looked as though the rebels had pulled right back and the rebellion might even be over. We had all been scaling cliffs and marching nearly continuously for forty-eight hours, but we knew that Suleiman had his cave near Saiq and one last effort was needed before resting our weary legs.

Just before the squadron started off we were joined by Major John Clark, a contract officer, with fifteen of the fifty 'tribal levies', with whom he had started. When they came to the fixed rope down Pyramid, all but fifteen had turned back. He and his merry men then joined up with A Squadron for the advance to Bani Habib. Their presence was essential to show that they too had taken part in the capture of the Jebel, as had troops from the SAF.

We now had SAS troops in the main villages and had also occupied the features overlooking them. The three leaders decided then and there to get out quick leaving their men behind. Never again could they come back as sheikhs – they had all lost face. We never caught up with them. They had plenty of money from Saudi Arabia and were able to bribe their way out past guards placed at the mouth of the Wadi Muaydin for that very purpose. They then went by camel to the coast road and, so the story goes, by taxi to Abu Dhabi and dhow to Dammam in Saudi Arabia.

A few days later we heard that our plans to divert pickets from our way up had worked perfectly. Talib had concentrated over a hundred extra men on Sabrina and the top end of Tanuf was reinforced by pickets from Wadi Kamah and Wadi Sumayt. This was all very satisfactory. We had taken big risks but it had paid off.

Next day, 30 January, David Smiley and Sayed Tariq arrived near Bani Habib by helicopter. One of John Clark's 'tribals' who spoke English knew where Suleiman's cave was located further up the wadi. We soon came across a high wall of stones protecting the entrance to a cave. This was stacked with chests and trunks, and another low entrance inside, which had to be crawled through, led into yet another cave with carpets on the floor. Some of the boxes held rather smelly clothes, others were piled high with weapons. Old swords were lying around, as were brass trays, blackened bulbous coffee pots and round cauldrons. He must have left in a hurry, leaving all his personal letters and documents behind. From the thousand-odd that were later translated much valuable intelligence was gleaned on the rebel organization, arms suppliers and those who were rebel helpers or sympathizers.

Air Marshal Heath had arrived by helicopter. He asked to speak to a few of our men nearby and asked me to pass on his comments to everyone.

> I want to congratulate you all most sincerely for the excellent work you have done. You have taken part in what is really an epic battle and you are now standing on soil last conquered by the Persians ten centuries ago.

I can now see that your easy passage to the top was the result of a really excellent plan, which could not have been carried out without two months of aggressive patrolling you put in to prepare the way. Now all the Sheikhs round the Gulf can breathe more freely. For me, the most astonishing feature is your small numbers and once again I congratulate every one of you.

The War Office decided that, on balance, our success should be given publicity and authorized *The Times* to publish a main feature article on 9 April 1959 describing the action. It ended with the following:

It had been victory at the first attempt by a numerically inferior force against an able enemy with geography on his side. The mountain itself was conquered by the astonishing physical fitness of the British troops. Within a few days of their arrival from the swamps of Malaya, the SAS troopers were operating with their usual efficiency seven thousand feet above sea level in totally novel conditions, and the dismounted troop of the Life Guards had turned themselves into first-class infantry. As for the enemy, they were conquered by surprise not slaughter, a brilliant example of economy in the use of force.

A few weeks later the weapons handed in to our patrols added up to no less than twelve LMGs, nine 81mm mortars, four heavy machine guns, twenty .303 rifles, thirty-nine mines and grenades, seven pistols and several thousand rounds of ammunition of all calibres. Undoubtedly there were as much more concealed in the thousands of caves on the Jebel. The temptation to hang on to a real .303 rifle instead of the usual Martini-Henry carried by all Omanis was probably too strong.

Between November 1958 and January 1959, the SAS had killed fifty-two rebels confirmed, although many more must have died of wounds, with virtually no medical attention available. We had lost three killed and two wounded, which was probably much less than we deserved.

The oil company was delighted. They restarted prospecting and were rewarded with a large find near Fahud three years later. This was so promising that a thirty-six-inch pipeline was put in to carry the oil two hundred miles to Muscat. The economy of Oman was transformed in the process, although it was a few years before the funds would start rolling in.

David Smiley was fulsome in his thanks for what we had done. He was now convinced that no other unit of our size could have done the job. We at least had ensured that from a military and political point of view the long-term future of the SAS was reasonably assured. Much later, Frank Kitson pointed out in his book *Bunch of Five* that although his own method of employment had been rejected, it was his initiative that had provided a case for the use of the SAS in Oman. He confirmed that 'the most important effect of the campaign was that it ensured the continued existence of the SAS'.[9]

The politicians were gratified and relieved. We had succeeded when all the senior military had said that a brigade operation might have been needed, but with unacceptable publicity.

David Smiley put in recommendations for our success. Deane-Drummond received the DSO, John Watts, Muir Walker, Peter de la Billière and Tony Jeapes all received MCs, Sergeant Hawkins a well-deserved DCM and Corporal Cunningham an MM. In addition there were six individuals including Johnnie Cooper who were mentioned in despatches. The Life Guards, the TOS and the SAF were all recommended for suitable awards.

9

GENERAL SIR WALTER WALKER

Brunei and Borneo, 1962–1966: An Efficient Use of Military Force

General Sir Walter Walker served in Burma in the Second World War and Malaya post-war. He took part in the retreat in Burma in 1942, and in the campaign to liberate Burma in 1944–5 where he commanded 4th/8th Gurkha Rifles. He formed and commanded the Jungle Warfare School in Malaya. He subsequently commanded 1/6th Gurkha Rifles for three years and the 99th Gurkha Brigade in Malaya. He was appointed Director of Borneo Operations after the outbreak of the Brunei revolt in late 1962, where he was the instigator of the tactics that eventually brought the Indonesians to the conference table in 1966. He was subsequently Deputy Chief of Staff of Allied Forces Central Europe, and ended his army career as Commander-in-Chief Allied Forces Northern Europe when the Cold War was at its height.

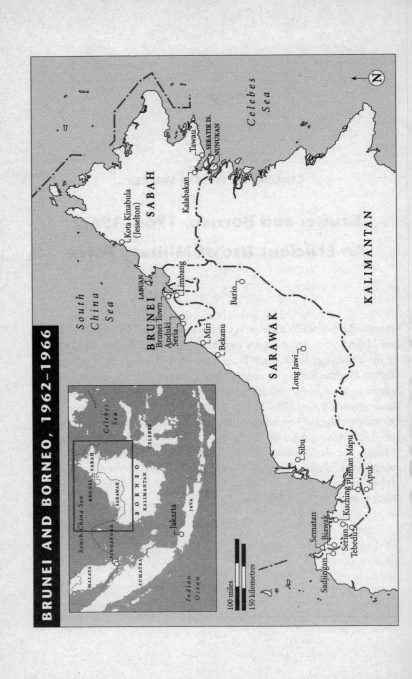

BRUNEI AND BORNEO, 1962–1966

The future of Brunei and Borneo in the early 1960s was in the hands of three key players. The first was Tunku Abdul Rahman, the Prime Minister of the Federation of Malaya, who in May 1961 had first proposed the formation of Malaysia, an economic and political union of Malaya, Singapore, North Borneo, Brunei and Sarawak. Although this appealed to the British government, wishing to divest itself of its colonies, it was anathema to the second key player, President Sukarno of Indonesia. His grandiose schemes included forming a large pan-Indonesian Confederation of States which would include Malaya, Singapore, North Borneo (later to be called Sabah) and Sarawak. Sandwiched in between North Borneo and Sarawak was Brunei, which, as far as Sukarno was concerned, would join with, or without, the consent of the Sultan.

The third player in this power game was the Sultan of Brunei. His aim was to preserve the old autocratic regime in this small but oil-rich state, while giving it the outward appearance of a parliamentary democracy.

When the Brunei Revolt broke out on 8 December 1962, General Walker was commanding 17th Gurkha Infantry Division and was also Major General, Brigade of Gurkhas. The troops to be sent immediately were those who could get there 'the fastest, with the mostest', the 1/2nd Goorkha Rifles (1/2 GR) from Singapore, because the stand-by battalion, the Queen's Own Highlanders, were on a training exercise, while the Commonwealth Brigade had numerous political procedures to undergo at a time when speed was the essence of success. By the late afternoon on 8 December two rifle companies of 1/2 GR and a small headquarters were on their way to Brunei by air with the remainder of the battalion due to follow the next day.

Armed rebels under their leader, Yassin Affandi, had already made attacks in several different places, including the Shell oil field at Seria some seventy miles away from Brunei town. (It was not until five months later that Affandi was the last rebel to be captured, putting the final end to the rebellion.)

The situation was somewhat chaotic and the two Gurkha Rifle companies, with maps only of the town and expecting to be engaged in riot control rather than armed insurrection much further afield, had to adjust quickly to the new reality. The troops fought through the night; the remainder of the battalion joined them the next day. By this stage 1/2 GR's battle bag exceeded 800 prisoners.

The battalion then drove through the night in commandeered vehicles to recapture Seria, where Shell workers were being held hostage, but were delayed by a series of ambushes. The next morning the Queen's Own Highlanders landed at Anduki airfield and began to clear Seria town, where they linked up with 1/2 GR. Meanwhile L Company from 42 Commando RM landed under fire at Limbang on the border with Sarawak, where it was thought that about seven hostages were being held, including the British Resident, Mr Morris. L Company accounted for fifteen dead and fifty wounded rebels out of a total force of around 350, and suffered five dead and seven wounded themselves. They released fourteen hostages, learning from Mr Morris that the rebels had planned to hang him that day. The pace and potency of the actions in Brunei town, at Seria and Limbang broke the revolt, but many weeks were to pass before all the rebels were rounded up. The remainder of 42 Commando RM arrived in Brunei soon after the Limbang action, and took Bangar, where six hostages had been beheaded. The next battalion to arrive, the 3rd Green Jackets, landed from the cruiser HMS *Tiger* which had transported them from Singapore, and cleared the oil towns of Miri and Bekanu. A few days later HMS *Albion*, the helicopter carrier (LPH), arrived off Brunei, hot foot from exercising off Aden, with 40 Commando RM, and the helicopters of 845 and 848 Naval Air Squadrons (NAS) embarked. The two helicopter squadrons and 40 Commando immediately began operating ashore.

On 19 December, General Walker was appointed Commander British Forces, Borneo. On his departure from Singapore he was seen off by the Commander Far East Land Forces, General Sir Nigel Poett, who said to him, 'I will see you in three months' time.'

Walker replied, 'I have told my wife to expect me back in two to three years.'

He arrived by RAF bomber aircraft at Brunei on 19 December and was met by the High Commissioner for Brunei, Sir Denis White, who said that on the following day he would chair a secret meeting to be attended by the Governors of North Borneo and Sarawak respectively. He asked General Walker to join them.

Sir Denis White told General Walker that the Commander Far East Land Forces had just visited Brunei, met the two Governors, and told them that he was sending General Walker as Commander of British Forces, Borneo. He had added that there was no general in the British army who had so much experience of fighting either guerrillas or a first-class enemy in the jungles of South-East Asia, starting in the Second World War in Burma, followed by the twelve-year Malayan Emergency when he rose from battalion commander to brigade commander, and finally commander of the 17th Gurkha Division.

At the meeting with the Governors, General Walker explained the three key players in the region and said that he intended to keep a wary eye on Indonesia, for unless the rebellion in Brunei was dealt with successfully and as quickly as possible, President Sukarno might well decide to cause trouble in Sarawak. The General recalled that when he was commanding the Jungle Warfare School in Malaya 1948–9, he had pointed out to his superiors that the number of students from Indonesia exceeded those from any other country in South-East Asia, not just officers but also senior NCOs. Therefore they had been taught the jungle warfare doctrine devised by him.

Walker said he was convinced that the trouble which flared up in Brunei earlier in the month was fomented by the secret and militant wing of the People's Party, which had strong Indonesian links and backing. This being so he made it clear that he intended to clear the rebels out of Brunei well before Malaysia was established in August 1963. In the event he achieved this task by April 1963, with some months to spare. By this time cross-border raids all along the Indonesian border with the former British colonies confirmed General Walker's strong conviction – not shared by Whitehall, let alone Far East Land Forces, Singapore – was that the Brunei revolt was not a one-off event but the prelude to a larger and far more serious conflagration.

In the event Malaysia did not come into being until 16 September 1963, and by then Brunei had opted out, preferring independence under British protection. Two years later the predominately Chinese Singapore also pulled out.

Finally, the General spelt out to the two Governors and to the High Commissioner for Brunei his directive, which he intended to issue that very day. He said it was based on his experience of the Malayan Emergency. In this directive, the ingredients of success would be sixfold.

First and foremost was winning the local people's trust, confidence and respect, in other words winning the hearts and minds of the people and especially the indigenous people. This was absolutely vital to success, because in this way he would succeed in isolating the enemy from supplies, shelter and intelligence.

The second principle was unified command of the civil administration, the police (particularly Special Branch), the army, the navy and the Royal Air Force. Thirdly, timely and accurate information, which required a first-class intelligence organization. Fourth, speed, mobility and flexibility of operations. Fifth, security of all military and civilian bases wherever they were and whatever they might be (airfield, patrol bases etc.), and sixth, total domination of the jungle.

He ended by reminding the Governors that limited war had been going on continuously in South-East Asia, in varying degrees of intensity, for the past twenty-one years. There had been four important conflicts: eight years of war in French Indo-China, Indonesia's fight for freedom against the Dutch, the Malayan Emergency, and the current large-scale fighting in Vietnam.

He ended by saying that his appreciation of the situation might not be in line with opinion in Far East Land Forces or Whitehall. But if he had learnt anything from his battle experience it was that the British had underestimated the enemy in the Second World War, particularly the Japanese, which had led to the loss of Malaya, Singapore and Burma. This had been followed by our unpreparedness when the Malayan Emergency broke out, which had taken twelve years to quell. Now, if we were not careful, we would make the same mistake in Borneo.

None of the Governors asked him any questions and all seemed somewhat stunned by the firmness of his views, and his emphasis on the danger ahead posed by Indonesia.

The final act of the Brunei revolt took place in May 1963 near Limbang, when B Company 2/7 GR, who had taken over from 1/2 GR, captured the overall leader of the rebels, Yassin Affandi, with Saleh Bin Sambas, who had commanded the insurrection at Limbang. The signals officer of 2/7 GR donated blood to keep the wounded Bin Sambas alive, imagining that he was being preserved to stand trial for his life. In the event he was sentenced to twenty years' imprisonment.

Just before this, in April 1963, Walker was recalled to Singapore, for in the eyes of his superiors not only had the rebellion been crushed but there was no longer any danger ahead. On the very day that he was due to fly to Singapore the Indonesians crossed the border and annihilated the police station at Tebedu, uncomfortably close to Kuching, the capital of Sarawak. This confirmed his strong conviction from the very outbreak of the Borneo Revolt that the rebellion was not a one-off event, but the prelude to a larger and far more serious conflagration with Indonesia. Until this incursion, Walker had several times been accused of crying wolf by his superiors and by the two Governors. The enemy force consisted of around a hundred insurgents and almost as many porters, commanded by a Major Mujono. The career of this dedicated guerrilla had begun during the Japanese occupation of Borneo and continued with the return of the Dutch. Now he confronted the British, whose Jungle Warfare School in Malaya (only one of several he had attended) was where he had learned Walker's jungle warfare techniques. Now these were about to be put into practice by the Indonesian insurgents and their fighting professional army.

Soon after his arrival, Walker was appointed Director of Borneo Operations. He had already established a Joint Headquarters for he was determined to conduct his operations on a tri-service basis. The forces available to him in April 1963 to cover the thousand-mile frontier, a considerably longer coast and the air space above, consisted of only one brigade of three battalions, six naval coastal minesweepers, and some fifteen naval and air force helicopters. By the time he handed over to Major General George Lea in March 1965, he commanded a combined multi-national force consisting of:

a. Coastal minesweepers and naval and maritime police fast armed patrol boats, for both inshore and up-river patrolling.
b. Eighty helicopters (originally seventy, this was still about forty short of what was required).
c. About forty fixed-wing aircraft.
d. Four regular infantry brigades, totalling thirteen infantry battalions – British (including RM Commandos), Gurkha, Malay, Australian and New Zealand.

e. The equivalent of one battalion of SAS (Special Air Service Regiment), the squadrons being British, Gurkha, Australian and New Zealand.

f. The equivalent of about two battalions worth of police field force or police jungle companies.

g. About 1,500 Border Scouts, recruited from the indigenous tribes.

h. Two regiments of armoured cars – British and Malay.

i. The equivalent of two regiments of artillery – British, Malay and Australian.

j. Two regiments of engineers – British, Gurkha, Malay, Australian and New Zealand.

k. An excellent joint communications system, which gave him rapid inter-communication with the troops in the jungle, the aircraft in the air and on the airfields, the ships at sea, the four joint army, naval, air and police headquarters, and the headquarters of the National Operations Committee in Kuala Lumpur, as well as the Commander-in-Chief's headquarters in Singapore.

Claret Operations

After a year of operations in Borneo, the end of 1963 brought an uneasy truce. Walker issued an Order of Day, saying that it was:

> A year which began with the end of a revolution and ended with the beginning of an undeclared war. No one knows where this exercise in brinkmanship will end. We are sure only of one thing: we have set our faces to the enemy and until more reasonable counsels prevail we shall not look back.

The Indonesians held the initiative because they could attack from safe bases in Kalimantan (the Indonesian part of the island of Borneo), the majority of which were conveniently close to the border. They knew that their bases were safe from attack because there had been no official declaration of war and, not unnaturally, the British government was anxious to avoid taking any steps that would be presented to the Third World element in the United Nations Assembly as being 'imperialist aggression'. Thus, with one arm tied behind his back, Walker had little chance of forcing the Indonesians to go on to the defensive, unless he could go on the offensive.

Hitherto British and Malay forces were only allowed to cross the border in hot pursuit following an Indonesian incursion for a distance of up to 3,000 yards. All this changed when as a result of abortive Indonesian sea and parachute landings on the mainland of Malaya (now Malaysia) in August and September 1964 the Malaysian government in Kuala Lumpur, thoroughly alarmed at Sukarno's latest aggression, supported Walker's continual requests that cross-border operations, as deliberate raids, should be approved up to a depth of 5,000 yards inside Kalimantan. Faced with this request from its Commonwealth ally, the British government gave its approval, stressing that there was to be no public announcement of this change of policy, and that the operations were to be carried out under conditions of maximum secrecy.

The wheels had already been oiled to bring about this change of policy, because Walker had convinced Mr Fred Mulley, Army Minister and Deputy Secretary of Sate for Defence to Mr Healey, during a visit to Borneo, of the vital necessity of limited and secret cross-border operations. Mulley had come via Singapore, where he had been briefed by Admiral Begg, who sent Walker a secret message saying: 'It only requires a push from you to convince Mulley of the vital necessity for cross-border operations.'

It was essential that the first troops to cross the border should be from the SAS, because it was then and still is one of its roles to probe deeper into enemy territory than the conventional forces, reconnoitring and disrupting potentially dangerous enemy deployments and positions. This would be done in its normal clandestine manner, with four-man patrols searching for the tracks of raiding parties, and watching rivers which were the main highways on both sides of the rugged and mostly undefined border.

In addition to watching and reporting, the SAS patrols would begin interdiction operations, such as ambushing tracks and rivers and setting booby traps where it was known that only Indonesian raiders would pass. On occasions, their ambushes would be sophisticated affairs using the electronically detonated Claymore mines at both ends of prepared ambush positions while in the middle the troopers raked the killing ground with automatic fire. Such activities suited the SAS well, and with typical wry humour they called such groups the 'Tiptoe Boys', because after a sudden sharp little action by the ambush parties they vanished leaving behind them an apparently empty jungle.

Shortly afterwards the General decided that infantry attacks could be launched in order to pre-empt any suspected or anticipated Indonesian attack. These operations were given by the General the code name of CLARET and all were graded Top Secret, to be handled with the greatest care by the minimum number of officers, on a 'need to know' basis. CLARET operations changed the fortunes of war for both the Indonesians and their Commonwealth opponents. No longer could the Indonesians feel secure in their border bases and camps even if they were within Kalimantan territory, nor would the security forces ever feel as frustrated as they had been earlier in the campaign.

There was a set of definite, clear and detailed orders governing CLARET operations, which Walker called the 'Golden Rules'. In time these were amended as the situation changed but, initially, his guidelines were as follows:

1. All raids had to be personally authorised by the General as the Director of Operations.
2. Only tried and tested troops were to be used – in other words, no soldiers were to be sent across into Kalimantan during their first tour in Borneo. This meant that only Gurkha battalions were used initially, apart from the SAS, but this was changed after British infantry battalions and commandos had gained the requisite experience in jungle fighting.
3. All raids were to be made with the definite aim of deterring and thwarting aggression by the Indonesians. No attacks were to be mounted in retribution with the sole aim of inflicting casualties on the foe. Civilian lives must not be risked.
4. Close air support could not be given except in an extreme emergency and then only authorised by the General.
5. The depth of penetration had to be carefully controlled, initially up to 5,000 yards, eventually reaching a maximum of 20,000 yards but only for one or two special operations.
6. Every operation had to be meticulously planned with the aid of a sand-table and thoroughly rehearsed for at least two weeks. The General always went to the battalion headquarters and the headquarters of the company that was actually going to carry out the raid. He visited the company first, listened to the company commander's briefing, watched him do the rehearsal on a sand-table or cloth model, and so was thoroughly in the picture on what was being planned, and how it would be executed right from the beginning.
7. Each operation had to be planned and executed with maximum

security. Every man taking part must be sworn to secrecy; full cover plans must be made and the operations to be given code names and never discussed in detail on telephone or radio. Identity discs must be left behind before departure and no traces – such as cartridge cases, paper, ration packs etc. – was to be left in Kalimantan.

8. On no account must any soldier taking part be captured by the enemy – alive or dead.

The control and power of veto remained with the Director of Operations; by holding the reins tightly in his hand, he was able to diminish the possibility of escalation. Minimum force was to be the principle used, rather than large-scale attacks which would have invited retaliation and risked turning the border situation into something very different, costly in lives and fraught with international problems.

An American general commented that only the British could have conceived CLARET operations and devised the masterly 'Golden Rules' that governed them. Later he was generous enough to add that only well-disciplined troops such as the SAS and Gurkhas [and British infantry battalions and RM Commandos], under their experienced, capable leaders, could have won the successes that were obtained.

Perhaps the most remarkable aspect of CLARET operations was the security and secrecy that was maintained at all levels. It is doubtful whether the Indonesians realized that they were seeing the beginnings of a new Commonwealth strategy. This was partly because the new series of actions took place so near to the border, which was in any case badly defined, and partly because their communications and administration with Kalimantan could not cope with the flow of reports and assess them quickly and accurately – as was happening in Walker's headquarters. British Intelligence at the time considered that there might be some 24,000 Chinese sympathizers giving moral support to the 2,000 Chinese Communist Organization (CCO) terrorists within Sarawak, while dotted along the border were over 22,000 troops of the Indonesian army (Tentera Nasional Indonesia, or TNI), supported by an unspecified number of volunteers.

To meet these threats, the forces available within Borneo under Walker were still pathetically small; the total number of soldiers within the Borneo territories was little more than 10,000. Eventually his strong protests did produce three more infantry battalions, bringing the total up to thirteen, but his urgent plea for helicopters only produced another twelve Whirlwinds for the whole theatre. By January 1965, as a result of these reinforcements, the British and Commonwealth forces in Borneo had risen to some 14,000 soldiers supported by twenty-nine guns, two squadrons of armoured cars and four field squadrons of engineers, with less than sixty troop-carrying helicopters to help him deploy and switch his troops over an area the size of England and Scotland together. Walker was convinced that the only way he could throw the Indonesians off balance was to increase the number of preventative, cross-border operations, and the Labour government in London showed its trust in him by allowing more CLARET raids and authorizing the depth of penetration first to 10,000, and later to 20,000 yards. In addition, Royal Marine Special Boat Sections were authorized to make small-scale amphibious raids round either flank on the coast.

Walker's soldiers were hampered by the heavy loads they were forced to carry, caused by equipment designed for troops transported to battle in armoured personnel carriers, in Europe against the Warsaw Pact. Weapons such as the Self-Loading Rifle (SLR) and General Purpose Machine Gun (GPMG) were heavy and unwieldy. Manpack radios were cumbersome, and often incapable of working among trees and over the long ranges required. Rations were unsuitable and far too heavy and bulky for the climate, terrain and role in which the infantrymen operated. The plea for lightweight equipment, radios and rations did not meet with a quick response in Whitehall, which failed to appreciate that victory in guerrilla warfare goes to the tougher, more resourceful soldier, the one who can remain for longer periods than his opponent at peak physical condition in the jungle – which, among other things, means that the load he has to carry on his back must be cut down to the minimum. This important lesson was heeded only in the latter stages of the campaign, and better equipment provided, thanks to Lord Mountbatten and his Chief Scientific Adviser, Sir Solly Zuckerman, when they visited Walker and listened to what the troops operating in the jungle had to say.

The 'undeclared war' was in many respects an unknown one because the fighting was not reported and few pictures of any significance reached the television screens in the United Kingdom or elsewhere in the world. Walker could mount CLARET cross-border raids without news-hungry journalists breathing down his neck, and in a rush to 'scoop' their fellows, breaking security. In contrast, the Falklands and Gulf Wars were often fought in a glare of publicity (in the Falklands less so than in the Gulf),[1] and as a result government ministers and senior officers were constantly having to tread a difficult path to ensure the necessary security for operational reasons, while satisfying the desire of everyone in the UK to know what was going on. Although the 'undeclared war' never hit the headlines, certainly it was a campaign that, in the words of Denis Healey, 'witnessed one of the most efficient uses of military force in the history of the world'.

Strange War

It was a strange, undeclared, and unknown war, but a most successful one. It showed that the British army, and the British Gurkha infantry in particular, could fight as well as anyone else in the jungle providing they had time to adjust to the conditions. The British soldier especially had to dispense with the habits of comfortable peacetime European soldiering, and learn to live and fight in the jungle. Confrontation lasted three years and nine months, and at its height it involved some 17,000 British and Commonwealth soldiers, sailors and airmen, with another 10,000 in support. This force suffered 114 killed and 200 wounded. Indonesian casualties are difficult to assess. It is known that they lost at least 600 killed and 700 captured, but towards the end of the confrontation, when CLARET raids across the border broke their logistic chain, there were indications that hundreds more died of malnutrition and starvation.

Walker realized that he was a very controversial character and in fact got on far better with his Royal Air Force and Royal Navy comrades than he did with his immediate Army Commander in Singapore. The blurb of Tom Pocock's book *Fighting General* quotes him as saying, 'I fought many wars and I also fought my superiors.' Unlike his superiors in Singapore, he believed profoundly in the unified system of command (land, sea and air), introduced in the Far East Command by Lord Mountbatten (then the Chief of the Defence Staff) in November 1962. As Director of Operations in Borneo, Walker insisted on dealing direct with the overall Commander-in-Chief Far East in Singapore, Admiral Sir Varyl Begg, thereby bypassing the single-service land, navy and air force commanders, all of whom outranked him. It is hardly surprising that they took grave exception to this. When military and civilian potentates came to Singapore to discuss the Borneo situation with the single-service commanders, they were told rather ruefully that Walker's 'bamboo curtain' effectively kept them out of Borneo, and that they would be obliged to discuss the situation with the Commander-in-Chief Far East.

SAS

It was Lieutenant Colonel John Woodhouse, the highly professional commanding officer of 22 SAS, who recommended to Walker that if he wanted to dominate the jungle along such a long frontier, in addition to cross-border raiding, the SAS should be used in four-man patrols, which would befriend the local tribal villagers, whose land extended across the frontier, and thereby obtain early warning of the movements of the Indonesians. Thus the tribal people, carefully briefed and protected by the SAS, would become Walker's eyes and ears.

Walker had no hesitation in agreeing with Woodhouse's proposal, for it fulfilled four of the six ingredients of success that he had already promulgated, namely: unified operations; timely and accurate information, which meant a first-class intelligence machine; speed, mobility and flexibility; and hearts and minds, or winning the local people's trust, confidence and respect.

He was not worried about launching the SAS deep into the jungle on such a wide front to undertake this task, because he could judge a professional commander when he met one, and John Woodhouse was such a soldier to his fingertips. When one squadron returned to base, Walker addressed them saying:

> I should like to congratulate you on your excellent performance. You have been deployed in your classic role over a 900-mile front to provide me with my eyes and ears. Above all the work of your signallers and medical orderlies has been quite outstanding and they have made a significant contribution both to our Intelligence sources and to our efforts to win the support and loyalty of the tribes.

He regarded seventy troopers of the SAS (one squadron) as being as valuable to him as seven hundred infantry in the roles of hearts and minds, border surveillance, early warning, stay behind, and eyes and ears with a sting. Eventually both A and D Squadron of 22 SAS were deployed.

Walker continued to press strongly for a third squadron. Realizing that this would take time to implement, and that the long Borneo frontier could absorb more SAS, or SAS-type soldiers, than would ever be available, he decided to train the Guards Independent Parachute Company in the SAS jungle role. Later, the Gurkha Independent Parachute Company was retrained and added to the strength. Both these units proved their worth and became worthy inheritors of the SAS way of warfare in the jungle. Both drew blood on their very first cross-border operation.

Border Scouts

One of the problems facing the screen of SAS, and later the Guards and Gurkha paratroopers, was the inaccuracy of the maps and imprecise demarcation of the frontier with Indonesia. Walker decided that he must have friendly eyes and ears watching, listening and reporting on, or near, every likely incursion route. In the face of opposition from some senior police officers he obtained permission to raise a new type of auxiliary police, which he called the Border Scouts. They consisted of Borneo tribesmen and were given a modicum of training by the SAS and the Gurkha Parachute Company. Their role was to watch and report, based in their villages, wearing their normal clothes and carrying on with their original occupations. They were unarmed and their job was to pass on any reports or rumours of Indonesian activity to the security forces. Many of them had land across the border and they and their relatives regularly crossed. Walker summoned from the UK a British officer of a Gurkha regiment, Major Cross, a talented linguist, and gave him command of 1,500 Border Scouts, impressing upon him that he and his Border Scouts were his 'eyes and ears, without a sting'.

Royal Navy

A few years earlier two light fleet carriers, *Bulwark* and *Albion*, had been converted to commando ships (LPHs) to carry RM commandos, helicopters and landing craft. As related earlier, the arrival of HMS *Albion*, with the helicopters of 845 and 846 NAS early in the Brunei revolt, had added a new dimension to operations. For example, no longer was it necessary for battalions to make dangerous air-assault landings in transport aircraft, as the Queen's Own Highlanders and the 1/2 GR had been forced to do at the outbreak of the insurrection in Brunei.

The effective use of British sea power played a vital part in preventing confrontation with Indonesia from escalating to all-out war. Apart from the abortive raids mentioned earlier, and the occasional landing of a tiny handful of intruders, the mainland of West Malaysia remained inviolate because Sukarno did not dare risk large parties on forays, which – he soon learnt – would have ended in disaster. In Borneo waters the Royal Navy exerted maritime power quietly and efficiently so that help from outside for the CCO and the indigenous Indonesians was minimal.

The part played by the Navy is one of the lesser known facets of confrontation, and its operations, often out of sight, were almost certainly out of mind as far as the troops in the jungle were concerned. The soldiers saw the Whirlwind and Wessex helicopters from the Fleet Air Arm operating in their support, and understandably, in their eyes, this was the most important part of the Royal Navy's effort. The pilots, aircrew, and even ground crews were in the thick of it with the soldiers and SAS, operating from bases well inside the interior of Sarawak in order to ensure that helicopter support was always available at the drop of a hat, and also to avoid wasting flying hours returning to their ship. Walker insisted on this despite opposition from on high, but not from Admiral Sir Varyl Begg, who never failed to support him.

In addition, throughout the Confrontation *Albion* and *Bulwark* took turns to operate off the coast of Borneo, often in the trooping role, bringing in units to relieve those who had completed their six-month tour, and taking the relieved unit back to its base in Singapore, Malaya or Hong Kong. This turn around, *roulement* in the jargon of the day, was often carried out by helicopter, flying new units straight from the ship into their company bases, and extracting the tour-expired troops on return. For example in 1964–65 HMS *Bulwark* operated with twenty battalions and commandos and six sub-units in this role.

During the peak period of the Confrontation Royal Naval ships were on patrol continuously for over 700 days and nights and intercepted 90 per cent of the known attempts to infiltrate into West Malaysia by sea. Between 1963 and 1966 Britannia ruled the waters around East and West Malaysia thanks to the Royal Navy.

The Use of Air Power

The helicopter proved to be a real battle winner. Operationally, Walker reckoned that one minute in a helicopter equalled a day's march in the jungle; that one hour equalled five days; and that one battalion with six helicopters in direct support was equal to a whole brigade. The RAF, the Royal Navy and the Australian, New Zealand and Malaysian air forces all contributed in full measure, ensuring that helicopters played a dominant role in the campaign both tactically and logistically. The high serviceability rate was a credit to the maintenance crews who worked long hours under hot humid conditions to ensure the maximum number of aircraft were available on any given day.

It was a unique war as far as the opposing air forces were concerned. Numerically strong, Sukarno's air force consisted of 550 aircraft, but they were of mixed national origin and of varying vintage. As the Confrontation went on it became clear that the Indonesian pilots had a wholesome respect for their RAF opponents; once it was known that RAF fighters had been scrambled. Although from sheer weight of numbers the RAF's opponents in the Indonesian Air Force should have been capable of exerting a considerable influence on the campaign, a deep fear of retaliation from the Royal Air Force grounded them for most of the time. That there were no casualties from enemy air action is proof enough of how Sukarno's pilots regarded their British, Australian, New Zealand and Malaysian opponents. In addition, the Indonesian Air Force, due to chronic maintenance problems as well as indifferent administration, did not use its machines to the best advantage in support of their army, especially when units were in isolated camps near the border. Unchallenged air superiority resulting from Indonesian timidity gave immense strategic, tactical and logistical advantages to the security forces during all phases of the campaign.

British and Commonwealth airmen faced one aggravation in that known and clearly identified Indonesian bases, sometimes a matter of yards on the other side of the border, were inviolable. For political reasons camps or supply routes were off limits, however obvious they might be to everyone who flew along the border. It must have been frustrating, but in forbearance lay the seed of final victory because the Confrontation never escalated into a full-scale war.

For the Royal Air Force the main opponents were the inhospitable terrain and the climate, which could deteriorate dramatically without any warning, rather than the Indonesian pilots. In most parts of the interior a thick mist remained until about 1000 hours, followed by a period of good flying weather, which lasted for four to five hours. Thereafter there was a gradual build-up of cloud, which in the mountainous regions meant there could be hours of violent turbulence and severe down-draughts, testing the skills of even the most experienced of pilots. As a consequence tactical air operations were usually confined to a few hours in the middle of the day, while to operate at night, especially among the mountains and hills, was impracticable even if it had proved possible to locate targets.

To add to the meteorological problems, accurate mapping and surveying of most parts of the country was virtually non-existent and consequently the few small-scale maps available were of little value when tactical flying had to be carried out. Pilots and navigators were compelled to resort to contour navigation to a target area, and had to rely almost entirely on their personal knowledge of the main features, such as prominent ridges, large rivers, and distinctive valleys. It soon became clear that experience in the theatre of operations counted for everything and that there was no merit in rotating aircrews too quickly; continuity was all-important.

As the tempo of ground fighting increased, single- and twin-engined Pioneers and the lumbering, box-fuselage Beverleys were used to lift troops, ammunition and stores to the rough and ready airstrips that had been established in the forward locations close to the border. Where supplies could not be air landed they were dropped by parachute. The workhorses of the campaign, helicopters, supplemented the fixed-wing supply aircraft.

Helicopters were able to increase the mobility, flexibility and range of the 105mm pack howitzers and 81mm mortars located in the forward positions. One helicopter would pick up a 105mm gun while the second carried its equipment, ammunition and gun crews to a temporary gun position or convenient base. In this way cross-border operations were provided with fire support 'on call', while the moving of guns from one infantry company base to another led the Indonesians into thinking that there were many more guns opposed to them than there actually were in the forward positions. The tempo of air and ground operations rose sharply until by December 1964 one million pounds of supplies were dropped in that month alone, and the total continued to rise thereafter.

Two important lessons in the use of air power were learned during the Borneo Confrontation. The first was that the Joint Headquarters under the one Director of Operations worked extremely well. Second, and equally important, the use of helicopters in support of operations enabled the British and Commonwealth forces to adhere to the Director of Operations' fourth principle: speed, mobility and flexibility of operations.

Conclusion

In his book *Defeat into Victory* Field Marshal Lord Slim says: 'I believe that jungle fighting is today, strange as it may seem, the best training for nuclear war.' He goes on to explain this by saying that formations will be compelled to disperse and that dispersed fighting will require skilled and determined junior leaders, and self-reliant, physically hard, well-disciplined troops. He ends with these words: 'In nuclear war, after the first shock of mutual devastation has been survived, victory will go, as it does in jungle fighting, to the tougher, more resourceful infantry soldier ... The easier and more gadget-filled our daily life becomes, the harder will it be to produce him.'

In Borneo we did produce him, and victory was ours, with a loss of life that was less, over three years, than the slaughter on the roads in Britain in a single year.

On 27 November 1967, Denis Healey, the Secretary of State for Defence, speaking in the House of Commons, paid this tribute to our Forces:

When the House thinks of the tragedy that could have fallen on a whole corner of a Continent if we had not been able to hold the situation and bring it to a successful termination, it will appreciate that in the history books it will be recorded as one of the most efficient uses of military force in the history of the world.

10

STEPHEN HARPER

South Arabia and Aden, 1964–1967: Tribesmen and Terrorists

Stephen Harper followed two brothers into the RAF in 1943, became redundant for further pilot training in 1944 and transferred to the Royal Navy as coder aboard the destroyer HMS *Petard* in the East Indies Fleet. During nearly twenty-five years as foreign correspondent of the broadsheet *Daily Express*, from bases in nine capitals, he reported on the first UN mission to the Congo; the Cuban missile crisis from Moscow; three Arab–Israeli wars; two wars between India and Pakistan; wars in Laos, Cambodia and most major clashes in Vietnam from 1960 to the fall of Saigon in 1975; revolutions in Baghdad, Libya and Ethiopia; many Middle East coups; and the last one in South Korea. He ended his newspaper career as chief foreign correspondent. He has published two novels and three non-fiction books.

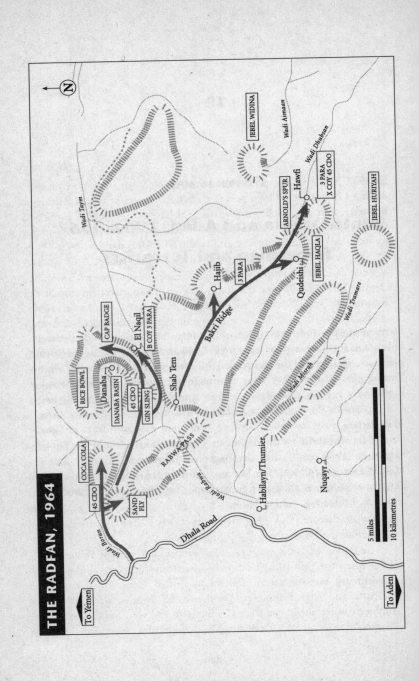

THE RADFAN, 1964

In 1967 British forces withdrew from Aden in 'an operation of war', ending 128 years of British rule. Throughout that time it was a strategic keystone, first as a coaling replenishment base on the way to India and the Far East, and then, after the loss of the Suez Canal Zone, a major military base and headquarters of Middle East Command.

Aden was a fishing village on the edge of a shoreside extinct volcano when it came into the possession of the East India Company's Bombay Council in 1839 following the plunder of an Indian merchant ship forced aground nearby. Commander Stafford Haines, of the Indian navy, obtained 8,000 Maria Theresa dollars (still currency in the area today) in 'reparation' from the local ruler, the Sultan of Lahej, who also agreed to sell Aden for annual payments of 8,700 dollars. Haines returned with settlers to find his landing opposed by the Sultan's eldest son with 150 tribesmen supported by Egyptian gunners manning fourteen cannon. After a naval bombardment landings by sepoy troops met little resistance. The few inhabitants had taken refuge in Aidrus Mosque under a white flag.

It was the dawn of the steam age and Aden's natural harbour quickly became a key coaling and watering port. Haines established a duty-free port, and settlers from the Yemen, Somalia and India as well as Arabs from neighbouring sheikhdoms soon increased its population to about 20,000. Haines recorded, 'The tribes in the neighbourhood of Aden are more treacherous and false than any other. They are incapable of estimating the value of good government.'

The Sultan of Lahej was granted a Perpetual Treaty of Protection in 1858 when the East India Company's territories were put under British government administration, known as British India, ruled first from Calcutta and later from New Delhi. Similar treaties were granted to nineteen other sheiks, emirs and sultans in the wild hinterland known as the Aden Protectorate. With India approaching independence Aden was made a crown colony in 1937, the only British colony in the Arab world. In 1963 it was merged with the Federation of South Arabia, into which the earlier protectorate states had been formed.

Inland from Aden, beyond the lush oasis of neighbouring Lahej, desert stretched to a huge massif rising to 6,000 feet surrounding narrow fertile wadis where tribesmen lived in fortified villages. They were known as 'Red Wolves of Radfan' because they painted their faces red when they raided caravans on a road linking Aden with Yemen, an ancient pilgrim and spice trade route. British troops and Arab levies clashed with them occasionally to keep the road open, but no European was known to have entered the remote mountain valleys since a missionary disappeared there before the First World War.

After the collapse of the Ottoman Empire the Yemenis refused to accept borders agreed between the British and their former Turkish rulers, and frequent tribal incursions were bombed by planes from the RAF's 8 Squadron based in Aden. In January 1964 the Federal Army attempted to impose authority, briefly controlling the Wadi Taym before withdrawing to their normal frontier holding positions.

The formation of a federation by autocratic rulers of the protectorate states was seen in Yemen and Cairo as a British attempt to form a puppet state that would enable them to keep a base in Aden after independence. The presence of 40,000 Egyptian troops in Yemen and British failure at Suez increased the sniping and ambushes that Royal Marines in a frontier strongpoint at Dhala called a 'Pot-shot War'.

In Aden, home for more than 200,000 people by this time, serious terrorism began on 10 December 1963 when a grenade was thrown at the High Commissioner, Sir Kennedy Trevaskis, as he and ministers of the South Arabian Federal government gathered at Khormaksar airport to fly to London for constitutional talks. Trevaskis was saved by his aide, George Henderson, who pushed him aside, took the full blast and died. An Indian woman was also killed and fifty-three people, including Trevaskis and several federal ministers, were wounded.

Terrorism and incursions on the Yemen frontier mounted after the publication of a Conservative government's 1964 Defence White Paper declaring that South Arabia would be granted independence 'not later than 1968', but that Britain would maintain a military base there. A military housing development costing £8 million at Bir Fuqum near the Little Aden oil refinery reflected British determination to stay. It had an airstrip close by. Deep-water jetties already existed in the oil refinery dockyard. Sitting on a headland across the bay from Aden town and twenty-eight miles distant by road, it lay just outside Aden territory in the sheikhdom of Akrabi, the smallest state in the Federation.

President Nasser visited Yemen in 1964 and boasted that Egypt would 'kick the British right out of the Arab world'. Soon afterwards, encouraged by Egyptian agents with arms, cash and promises, militiamen of the National Liberation Front (NLF) joined the Radfan tribes and closed the main road passing close by the Radfan to the Yemen frontier town of Dhala.

Radfan was home to six small tribes, normally feuding among themselves, with a total population estimated at only 3,000. Natural defences of naked granite rock rising fold after fold around their lair were strengthened when dissidents trained in Yemen planted landmines, some stolen from British stores in Aden, some Czech-made provided by Egypt, in the narrow wadis that gave access by camel or donkey to their villages.

The Federal government decided that a major show of force and occupation was necessary to prevent rebellion spreading to other tribes, and asked Britain for help under the treaties of protection. British commanders assembled 2,500 troops backed by armoured car squadrons, field artillery batteries, sapper units, helicopters, jet aircraft and four-engine Shackleton bombers for a punitive campaign. Troop reinforcements came from Britain and Kenya for what was to be Britain's last colonial campaign, echoing the imperial past on India's North-West Frontier.

Force HQ was set up beside a desert air strip overlooked by a cliff-top building known as Fort Thumeir. RAF twin-engined Pioneer transport planes shuttled in supplies while Hunter fighters strafed ridges 500 yards away, and 105mm howitzers fired shells onto likely targets. The temperature at midday reached 110° Fahrenheit in the shade and 130° in the sun.

The first major objective was to be a 6,000-foot peak named 'Cap Badge' dominating the Radfan heartland, opening the way to the relatively fertile valleys of the interior. B company of 3rd Battalion The Parachute Regiment (3 Para), brought in from Bahrein, were to drop into a drop zone (DZ) in Wadi Taym and take Cap Badge by first light. The DZ was to be marked and secured by 3 Troop of A Squadron, 22 SAS, just arrived in Aden for a month's exercises.

At first light on 29 April 1964, covered by artillery barrages, three Scout helicopters lifted the nine-man SAS troop into Wadi Thaym to secure the DZ. By daylight they lay up close to the village of Shab Tem listening to radio chatter from a house that was clearly used as headquarters. They counted twenty-two Arabs in khaki uniform jackets, shorts and turbans, all carrying rifles. At 11 a.m. they were spotted by a goat-herdsman and came under accurate fire from village houses and rock spurs on all sides.

Captain Robert Edwards of the Somerset and Cornwall Light Infantry[1] radioed field headquarters, seven miles away, for air and artillery support. RAF Hunters made repeated pinpoint rocket strikes causing enemy casualties, but artillery had to cease fire because shells were falling too close to the British position. Sniping continued all day as more tribesmen gathered. Captain Edwards and two others were wounded, and a breakout was to be made at dusk. The radio operator, Sapper John Warburton, was shot dead by a sniper, and Force HQ heard nothing more from them until seven survivors reached Thumair camp soon after dawn on 1 May.

They told how some ninety tribesmen had rushed them as they began the breakout. Captain Edwards was hit again, this time fatally, and he ordered Sergeant Reg Lingham to take over command and try to reach camp. Trooper Bill Hamilton, wounded in the shoulder, and Lance Corporal John Baker, wounded in the shoulder and both legs, were flown to the RAF Hospital in Aden. Four other members of the patrol had been grazed by bullets, but were soon back on duty.

Sergeant Lingham told the writer:

> The Arabs rushed us and extremely fierce hand-to-hand engagements took place with the enemy reaching our positions. Trooper Nicholas Warburton was killed and others wounded. We then made a run for it firing as we went. Captain Edwards was hit in the stomach from a burst of automatic fire, and had to be left. After the break out we were shadowed by only about three tribesmen, and we killed one of them.

Two Army Air Corps Scout helicopters tried to drop another SAS patrol to mark the DZ, but were forced back damaged by heavy ground fire. B Company 3 Para volunteered to drop into the unmarked DZ, but the drop was cancelled because intelligence revealed that a larger enemy force was in Wadi Thaym than had been supposed.

At his Thumeir headquarters the Field Force Commander, Brigadier

Louis Hargroves, was outraged at intelligence reports that the heads of two British soldiers had been sent for public display in the Yemen city of Taiz. He invited the writer to attend his briefing on the offensive beginning later that afternoon. (One officer, wary of my presence, paused outside the tent to tear an SAS flash from his shoulder. He later became famous as Lieutenant General Sir Peter de la Billière, commander of British forces in the Gulf War.)

Paras and 500 men of 45 Commando RM had occupied two towering mile-long ridges beyond the Wadi Rabwa the previous night. The ridges ran parallel on each side of a deep gorge called the Wadi Boran. The nearest one was codenamed 'Sand Fly' and the further higher one was 'Coca-Cola'. Scorching funnels of air from rock surfaces buffeted helicopters as they dropped water in forty-gallon drums and lowered ammunition by rope.

That afternoon the main element of the East Anglian Regiment was to take over Coca-Cola ridge, and 45 Commando and the Paras were to make a ten-hour night march to secure heights, dubbed 'Gin Sling' and 'Cap Badge', which dominated the Danaba Basin and the broad Wadi Thaym, the fertile tribal heartland of the Radfan.

A large fortified house sat squat on top of a ridge five miles away labelled 'enemy OP' on operational maps. From there the enemy could observe every move made on the plain below. Brigadier Hargroves had asked the RAF to 'take out' this enemy position before final dispositions were made for the major push into the Radfan next day, but the air strike was vetoed from Aden. The rules of minimum force, laid down for the conduct of the military in aiding the civil power, forbade firing on habitations unless hostile fire from them was confirmed beyond doubt.

Brigadier Hargroves shrugged this off, although a crucial part of his plan was a surprise outflanking of tribal positions by taking all the main heights by stealth while a single company of the Anglians made a noisy frontal attack up the Wadi Rabwa, the direct camel route into the Radfan heartland. The Anglians made a deceptive detour before doubling back to scale Coca-Cola ridge to take over positions vacated by the commandos.

By then batteries of 105mm howitzers had begun firing the opening bars of a rowdy night-long symphony, primarily to distract attention from columns of troops snaking through the pitch black depths of deep gorges. Sappers of 12 Squadron, Royal Engineers, working in the blackness of the Wadi Boran, tried to blast a way for Saracen armoured cars of the Royal Tank Regiment to reach the upper Danaba Basin. A droning Shackleton bomber circled all night ready to drop flares if the Paras or Commandos called for light.

The Paras were making the long march to the further side of Cap Badge while RM commandos of X Company, led by Everest expedition climber Major Mike Banks, took a direct frontal route, and Y Company climbed Gin Sling. At dawn both Commando companies were on top of their objectives, meeting no opposition, but B Company 3 Para, overladen and following a longer route, were still on low ground dominated by the village of El Naqil, below Cap Badge.

To aid them Lieutenant Colonel 'Paddy' Stevens of 45 Commando called in an RAF twin-rotor Belvedere helicopter to lower the leading troop of his reserve Zebra Company by rope to positions below the summit from where they could give X Company covering fire. The remainder of Zebra Company followed in Wessex helicopters of 815 Squadron and were landed under fire. They moved down the mountain to clear tribesmen from sangars on the slopes.

In a fierce four-hour battle that ended with a bayonet charge the Paras captured El Naquil. They were besieged by tribesmen among surrounding rocks. It was out of range of artillery, and armoured cars could not reach them. RAF Hunters made low-level strikes while Belvedere helicopters dropped water and ammunition. Covered by fire from British positions on surrounding peaks the Paras later broke out to join them.

Two Paras were killed, and they were buried in shallow graves as a padre read brief burial words and an officer made notes on the location for later recovery of the bodies (when recovered the heads were missing). Ten wounded were lifted out by helicopter.

Flocks of vultures gathered over the scene as RAF Shackletons returned at low level to drop leaflets warning that anyone failing to leave the area was liable to attack, and that the area was under proscription, which meant crop burning, removal of livestock and demolition of fortified buildings. The hilltop observation post, spared before the attack, had become fair game because fire at passing aircraft came from it. Two Hunters made twelve runs, four with rockets, eight with cannon, blowing it to pieces.

News of beheadings caused uproar in Parliament. But the American Consul-General in Taiz, who looked after British interests in the absence of diplomatic relations, reported that no heads were displayed there. The Soviet leader, Nikita Khrushchev, visiting Cairo, told cheering Egyptian MPs of his 'sympathy and understanding for demands to liquidate foreign military bases in Aden, Libya and Cyprus'. He went on, 'We also support demands to abolish the slave treaties imposed by Britain on countries of this area, which provides an excuse to introduce British troops into these countries.'

The Radfan campaign continued through May, and on 8 June the tribes made a final stand as a column of the East Anglian Regiment and Federal infantry, supported by armoured cars of the Royal Tank Regiment and guns of the Royal Horse Artillery, advanced towards the highest peak, Jebel Huriyah. For the first time they made a prime target for strike planes and artillery. When British and Federal troops took the peak on 10 June they found a scene of butchery. That was the end of the insurrection. The campaign closed with what was laconically termed 'Intense application of air control' and constant patrolling.

By August most of the Radfan tribal leaders agreed to keep the peace that this last show of imperial firmness imposed on the Radfan. A motor road into the Radfan, providing easy access to the outside world, was its memorial. In costing the campaign at £1 million, half for the use of helicopters and planes, the chief RAF scientist noted that the use of 53,000 rounds of 30 mm cannon shell had been costly and wasteful.[2]

The Radfan success meant that Britain could stay in the area as long as she chose, but a change of government in London soon afterwards brought a totally revised policy. In 1966 the Labour government announced withdrawal from East of Suez in a Defence White Paper, saying that all British forces would leave Aden within two years.

The Federal rulers saw this as a gross betrayal of their trust in British promises of protection, and rivalry intensified between the main terrorist organizations, the National Liberation Front (NLF) and the Front for the Liberation of South Yemen (FLOSY). Both aimed at claiming they had driven the British into the sea.

Frequent strikes cut movement in the bunkering harbour, and closed the civil airport and most shops; and in the mainly Arab Crater district, sited in the mouth of the long extinct volcano, teenage mobs rampaged, piled up barricades, burned old tyres at road junctions, wrecked and burned cars and set fire to offices. Outside Crater grenades were tossed from passing cars at British soldiers, and unarmed Europeans became

targets of opportunity. An early victim of a serial Steamer Point assassin
was a woman liner passenger, and liner passengers ceased to make
shopping trips ashore.

A huge cache of Czech and Belgian rifles and ammunition, Belgian
bazookas and anti-tank missiles was found along with a stack of
explosives and bomb-making materials. Roadblocks became permanent,
and internal security duty in Aden became a tedious, nasty, brutalizing
round of patrols, searches and shots in the night.

The Federal government pleaded with London for postponement of
independence for two years, a military guarantee against external attack,
for British troops to stay until the Federal Army had been doubled to
ten battalions and help in establishing an air force. Foreign Office
Minister George Thomson flew to Aden to reject all these requests.[3]
Instead he offered carrier-borne air support against external aggression
for six months in place of protectorate treaties that would lapse. He also
asked the sultans to agree to naming independence day the following
November or no later than the second or third week of January 1968,
and urged them to share government with the terrorists of NLF and
FLOSY, or to hold a general election under United Nations supervision
for the formation of a provisional government to negotiate independence.

The arrival of a three-man mission from the UN Committee on
Colonialism brought a week of sustained rioting with over seventy
grenade attacks and heavy sniper fire. At least twenty-two Arabs died
during the mission's stay, and eight British soldiers and ten Arabs were
wounded. When the UN mission visited detainees in Mansoura prison
near Sheikh Othman, grenade attacks, machine gun and rifle fire raged
more furiously than Aden had seen before. The UN mission was futile
from the start. They boycotted the Federal government and the terrorist
prisoners boycotted them.

A general strike ended when the mission departed, but the terrorist
organizations announced that the armed struggle would go on until the
British government dealt with them instead of with the government of
sultans and sheikhs. To meet mounting violence Britain was fielding
two brigades – one of four battalions – in Aden itself and two more up
country along with five battalions of the South Arabian Army, as the
Federal Army was newly named.

Tension was heightened by news of Israel's swift defeat of Egypt in

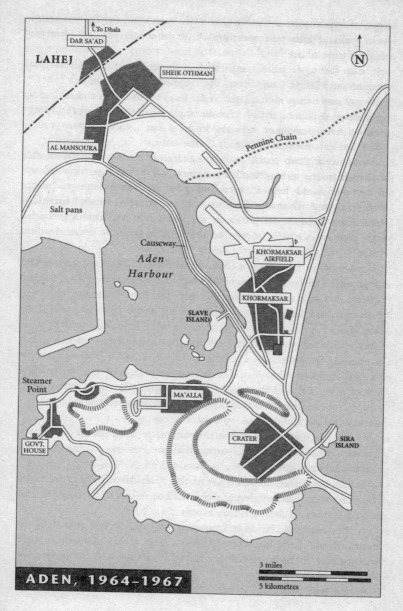

To Dhala

DAR SA'AD

LAHEJ

SHEIK OTHMAN

AL MANSOURA

Pennine Chain

Salt pans

KHORMAKSAR
AIRFIELD

Causeway

*Aden
Harbour*

KHORMAKSAR

SLAVE
ISLAND

Steamer
Point

MA'ALLA

CRATER

SIRA
ISLAND

GOVT.
HOUSE

ADEN, 1964–1967

3 miles

5 kilometres

N

what became known as the Six-Day War. As at Suez, Britain was seen as Israel's ally. During the morning of 20 June a 3-ton lorry carrying nineteen men of the Royal Corps of Transport came under machine gun and rifle fire as it turned into Radfan camp inside the Khormaksar cantonment. Firing came from the neighbouring Champion Lines, a Federal Army camp, killing eight of the lorry's passengers and wounding eight more. A passing British civilian employee of the Ministry of Works and two Aden policemen were also killed. A Lancashire Regiment officer was killed in subsequent firing on Radfan camp.

Earlier four Arab battalion commanders had been suspended after objecting to the promotion of members of the Aulaqi tribe from a distant part of the federal states, and tribal rivalries brought exchanges of fire in the Arab army's Champion Lines barracks. Federal Guards, a tribal force recently merged with the Federal Army, had then turned their guns on the RCT lorry, the first British target that came within range.

A company of the King's Own Royal Border Regiment surrounded Champion Lines, backed by armoured cars of the Queen's Dragoon Guards. Loudspeakers announced that the four colonels had been reinstated, and the entire misunderstanding would be overlooked if the Arab soldiers put down their weapons at once. The Arab soldiers were said to have become so frightened that they surrendered without a shot being fired. However, Sir Humphrey Trevelyan, who had replaced Sir Richard Turnbull, the High Commissioner, and used the old colonial title of governor, told the London government in a secret report dated 5 July, closed until 1999, that 'the machine gunner in the minaret of a mosque had been shot dead' by British troops.[4]

Word spread quickly that British soldiers had attacked the Arab army barracks. A routine patrol of Northumberland Fusiliers passing along the Crater dual carriageway in an armoured lorry known as a 'pig' noticed a Bren gun positioned on the roof of the Arab Armed Police barracks. Their radio was not working and they had to return to headquarters for Second Lieutenant John Davis to report.

In the meantime, the Aden garrison was put on red alert, and the Northumberland Fusiliers moved into Crater to set up their forward headquarters at the Armed Police barracks as they had routinely done during many alerts before.

As the first two Land Rovers, carrying ten soldiers, turned off the

Queen Arwa dual carriageway into the Armed Police barracks they came under fire from the Bren gun on the roof and from the upper windows of flats on the other side of the dual carriageway.

Mobs celebrated the ousting of British authority from Crater by burning down the Legislative Council building, the British Bank of the Middle East and a secondary school. When daylight broke next morning British troops on surrounding ridges looked down on buildings flying NLF flags and armed Arabs walking the streets.

A total of twenty-two Britons were killed and thirty-one wounded, seventeen of them seriously. Nine of these were killed in the Crater ambush, among them three men of the Argyll and Sutherland Highlanders, the regiment due to take over security in Crater when the Fusiliers went home. The only known Arab casualties were eleven dead and fifteen wounded.

The only survivor of the Crater ambush was Fusilier John Storey, aged twenty, who was in the back of the second Land Rover. Sitting up in hospital, he told the writer

Heavy firing began as we came level with the police barracks. The leading Landrover crashed against the barrack wall, and we rammed the centre island of the dual carriageway and rolled out into the road. I tried to get as low as I could in the gutter beside the centre island. The major was firing from under the Landrover which was starting to burn. Just afterwards the major was lying still and his batman was lying in the road with his clothes on fire. I was hit in the back and ribs and then in the arm as I made a run for it, zig-zagging across the road to a block of flats where I ran upstairs. There was nobody on the roof. All my mates seemed to be dead in the road below. Four of the bodies were burning.

Shooting suddenly stopped, and I tied a hanky around my arm to try to stop the bleeding. Firing began again and I saw two Arabs on the next roof. I fired at them. One put his hands on his head and fell backwards, the other ran away. Then I realised I was out of ammo, having left my spare clip in the Landrover. You see, we hadn't been as alert as we should have been with the police barracks between us and the streets where sniper fire and grenades were normal. I went downstairs and saw a policeman with a rifle across the road. I thought they were still on our side and shouted to him 'John, come here'. He raised his rifle and fired at me. I ran back upstairs. Heavy machine guns opened up outside and armoured cars went by at full speed. I thought the whole battalion would be coming soon.

An Arab resident warned me that police had started searching the flats, so I ran downstairs and hid in an alcove. Then I found a window on to a side road. I pushed my rifle out and clambered after it. Police spotted me and soon caught up because of my injured leg. They put me into a three-tonner and drove me into the barracks. Then they drove me back to the dual carriageway, where they piled the bodies of my mates into the truck with me. A crowd gathered around shouting for me to be killed. One man tried to make me say 'Nasser tamam' (Nasser is best), but I just stared into space. Police and the crowd were shouting at each other. I think I was only saved by a new burst of firing that scattered the mob and allowed the police to drive back to the barracks. The police were okay after that. An officer looked after me and gave me coffee and cigarettes. After about three hours an RAF ambulance with a British doctor and two medics, escorted by a police Landrover, arrived to collect me. As the ambulance drove back up the dual carriageway it came under sniper fire.

After reporting personally about the gun on the roof of the police barracks Second Lieutenant Davis returned to the lower pass in the armoured pig and took position on the roof of a garage at the bottom of the dual carriageway to give covering fire to any ambush survivors. It was this firing that broke up the mobs demanding Fusilier Storey's death. Again he was bothered by radio failure and sent armoured cars back for reinforcements. He and two men remaining with him were never seen again.

Second Lieutenant Nigel Stephens, of the Queen's Dragoon Guards, drove up the dual carriageway looking for them. He told me:

Fire was so intense my Browning machine gun was knocked out and I couldn't close my turret lid. Without cover from another Ferret we were pretty helpless. I asked permission to use my 76 to knock out the Bren gun on the police roof, and waited for it to be cleared with High Command. Permission was refused and we were forced to retire even though we thought three British soldiers might still be alive in nearby flats.

The Crater rebels had also taken over an old Turkish fort at the top of Main Pass, commanding the only road from Aden to the airport and the rest of South Arabia. A Saracen armoured car was authorized to fire a single '120 pounder' shell to destroy it and Northumberland Fusiliers reoccupied Main Pass while RM commandos used ladders to establish positions on heights above the pass.

Sir Humphrey Trevelyan insisted on a policy of maintaining the usual internal security doctrine of minimum force. He reported to London that this was necessary to avoid total mutiny by the Arab army and police, which would lead to massacre of British citizens still up-country, a fighting withdrawal with many British and Arab casualties and repercussions throughout the Middle East.[5]

An emergency evacuation began of all remaining British women and children, civilian families as well as the 2,300 service wives and children. There were about 1,500 wives and children of Britons employed in government, shipping, oil companies, banks and commercial offices. Planes bringing in troop reinforcements from the Strategic Reserve flew back with evacuees.

All British troops on the Yemen frontier and stationed in federal states were withdrawn to Aden leaving security to the South Arabian Army. Some traditional rulers were abroad and stayed in exile, some were flown to exile by Britain, all were overthrown.

Meanwhile civil war raged inside 'liberated' Crater, and Crater residents sought shelter in areas still under British control. Some 650 left with cars laden with personal possessions, and poorer people left on foot with goods loaded on bicycles or weighed down with what they could carry. Children drove family goats and poultry.

Voice of the Arabs Radio from Cairo jeered at 'the toothless British Lion', and the Argylls became increasingly angry at meek acceptance of the humiliating position. The battalion commander, Lieutenant Colonel Colin Mitchell, put in a formal request for his soldiers to re-enter Crater, claiming they could reoccupy it without heavy loss of life. His soldiers felt they knew every foot of Crater. In their barracks at Plymouth they had trained in street fighting among buildings and streets named to match those in Crater, and since arriving had made several night reconnaissances. Permission for a nibbling reoccupation was given after discussions with senior officers of the mutinous police.

At the Marine Drive entrance to Crater in the sweltering dusk of 3 July a single piper broke into 'Moneymusk', the regimental air, as two Argyll companies, supported by armoured cars of the Queen's Dragoon Guards, advanced into the rebel-held district. The operation was supposedly limited to recovering control of the area around the Chartered Bank, tallest building in the commercial core of Crater, commanding a key road junction at the lower end of the Queen Arwa dual carriageway.

Orders were to avoid close approach to the Armed Police barracks halfway up the dual carriageway towards Main Pass. Lieutenant Colonel Mitchell was authorized to use the 76mm guns of the armoured cars if necessary, the first time such discretion was delegated below command level.

The bagpipe music was joined by the rattle of heavy machine guns in a routine dusk exchange of fire with Arab guns on Sira Island, just off Crater's shingle beach. Soldiers hugged the walls of villas below sheer cliffs and the beach. Bullets pinged off rock faces, and tracer poured across a small sea inlet into houses in terrorist territory along the Esplanade. Flashes lit up rooms of villas from which snipers were firing. Soon the firing slackened to odd bouts of sniping.

The burnt-out shell of a school loomed through the shadows on the left, then the ruins of the Legislative Council building stood against the night sky on a rocky escarpment to the right. The corner of the Chartered Bank jutted out like a ship's prow into the junction facing Queen Arwa road, a deadly place to be caught in cross-fire from many points overlooking it. The main doors into the building were around that corner, and Mitchell pondered whether to blow a hole in the bank wall. All was quiet.

A flare fired from the area of the Armed Police barracks lit up the scene, but no bullets came out of the surrounding darkness. As the flare sputtered out the Scots found a back door and battered it in. The main objective was taken. Armoured cars, with red and white hackles of the Northumberland Fusiliers on their radio masts, swung around that exposed corner and raced down the Esplanade and along a causeway to link up with an Argyll company coming from Ras Marshag where they had earlier been dropped by helicopter. The gun positions on Sira Island were silenced. Lorries began unloading pre-filled sandbags and oil drums, raw material of new roadblocks and strongpoints.

Brigadier Charles Dunbar, deputy to the General Officer Command-ing, General Philip Tower, authorized Colonel Mitchell to advance beyond the first stop line and the Argylls fanned out through the small commercial area and occupied all the bank buildings. They established observation posts overlooking the market square in the heart of the town, and on rooftops across the Queen Arwa road from the Armed Police barracks.

The Argylls had captured half of Crater, from which they could dominate the rest, in ninety minutes and without the predicted blood-bath. They had done it without a single British casualty, and with only two Arabs killed. At dawn the battalion's twelve pipers and four drummers played a 'Long Reveille' on the bank roof, fifteen minutes of it. The *Daily Express* headlined the 'Mad Mitch' nickname over an account of Mitchell leaving his bodyguard in the Land Rover to swagger through the market stalls and along narrow alleys greeting astonished Arabs with smiles and hand-shakes. It made him famous.

Strict orders to avoid clashes with the Armed Police did not deter Mitchell from warning Chief Superintendent Mohammed Ibrahim, commander of the police barracks, that if he had any trouble he was prepared to wipe out the Armed Police to the last man. More diplomatically General Tower reached agreement with Ibrahim and told reporters, 'We shall be back to a working relationship. There is no question of recriminations.'

A few days later General Tower took the salute at a ceremonial march past of the Arab Armed Police in their barrack square. On the surface this parade was a splendid colonial occasion. A Union Jack hung limply from a flag pole, but bitter distrust soured the humid atmosphere. Arab and British eyes were equally wary. Guns of armoured cars and rifles of Scots soldiers covered every rooftop around. Police sepoys in flared scarlet turbans, officers with swords at the salute, looked tense and angry. Officers of the Argylls stood behind the general dour-faced. The police pipe and drum band – a legacy of British cultural imperialism – played 'Scotland the Brave'. The Argylls wore kilts so that battalion riflemen in surrounding rooftop OPs could more easily tell friend from foe in the event of renewed treachery.

General Tower carried it off with the smooth aplomb becoming a former director of army public relations. He managed to conceal whatever discomfort he felt at returning the salute of a parade of men responsible for the treacherous murders beyond the boundary wall just seventeen days earlier. In staging this public rehabilitation of the Arab Armed Police the general saw his duty as safeguarding the lives of his soldiers since they had no cause but a lost one. Neither the Governor nor the Commander-in-Chief, Admiral Sir Michael Le Fanu, was advised that the parade was being held.

Sir Humphrey Trevelyan was busy writing the report to London that remained secret until 1999. He passed the ambush off as mainly an NLF action in which 200 Arab Armed Police took part, noting that twenty-two had since gone missing. He wrote that the military agreed that dismissal of the men concerned (about 120) would result in the instant disintegration of the Armed Police and have repercussions on South Arabian forces. He added, 'I do not intend to disband Aden police, useless as they are in relation to terrorism, as it would swell the ranks of those actively against us.'[6]

Under its no-nonsense Scottish chieftain, Crater became the most peaceful part of Aden. For nearly eight peaceful days, while gun battles, grenade attacks and murders raged in every other district there was not one incident in Crater. On the eighth day of reoccupation two Argylls were wounded when a grenade was thrown at a working party, and three days later five others were wounded in two simultaneous grenade attacks. An Arab was shot dead when running away after an order to halt. Several hundred suspects were held in unshaded wire cages through the afternoon heat before being screened and released. The only no-go areas for Argyll patrols were the township's fifteen mosques, and a pattern of incidents showed that every grenade attack was made within fifteen yards' running distance of a mosque. In following weeks four Argylls were killed and six wounded and nine Arabs were shot dead.

During August and September forty-two days passed without a single incident, making Crater an oasis of peace as the NLF and FLOSY fought out their bloody civil war elsewhere.

As senior officers prepared for a fighting withdrawal, troops in Aden were at last classified as being on active service. A last-ditch perimeter around Khormaksar airfield was formed to secure the runway from mortar and machine-gun attack until the last plane got away.

Adjacent to the airport perimeter the 1st Battalion The Parachute Regiment (1 Para) and the Lancashire Regiment defeated all efforts to turn the Sheikh Othman district into a no-go area, regaining a strong presence in the town and along the border with Lahej.

The hitherto faceless men of the NLF had meanwhile agreed to come to the negotiating table, a breakthrough for Governor Trevelyan's policy of firmness combined with flexibility. He had lifted a ban on the NLF as a political organization. Like the never legally banned FLOSY, the NLF had been encouraged and trained by the Egyptian intelligence service in Yemen, but its leaders had grown away from Cairo as the Egyptian presence in Yemen became less popular.

Meanwhile the first fighting at Steamer Point had erupted on 14 June when the NLF called a public holiday to celebrate what they termed their 'four years of struggle to throw the British into the sea'. It began with the thin crack of a Russian Kalashnikov that kicked up dust on the football field in front of the Crescent Hotel. As firing increased marines of 42 Commando crawled in the dust to the slender cover of circular concrete tubs around young trees. Fire came from rooftops behind the shopping crescent facing shoreside Canute Barracks across the only road connecting military headquarters and Government House with the rest of the colony. British troops cleared the shopping crescent of NLF gunmen and established a holding line on rooftops overlooking the crowded Arab streets behind them.

A serious attack on these British positions came on Saturday 14 October when two men of the Prince of Wales's Own, due to leave for home next day, were wounded in an observation post called Imphal (after the battle on the Indian frontier with Burma), 300 yards behind the shopping crescent. Their evacuation to hospital was delayed ninety minutes because the use of armoured cars in the Steamer Point area had to be sanctioned. Then the wounded were carried at a run into an armoured lorry, and others carrying weapons and equipment clambered hastily into a second armoured car and Aden's Imphal was abandoned. Troops withdrew to the rooftops of the Crescent itself, their backs to the harbour 300 yards away, from where they watched fighting between FLOSY and the NLF in the back streets, under orders not to intervene unless fired on.

On Sunday 5 November the words 'The Navy's here' flashed around the tiny British community as the strike carrier HMS *Eagle* appeared off the port heading twenty-four ships of a naval task force. Its arrival brought fresh outbreaks of firing across Steamer Point the next day which lasted into the afternoon when seven Hunters appeared overhead in a farewell fly-past by the RAF's 8 Squadron, stationed in Aden since its formation. Buccaneer strike bombers, Sea Vixens and Gannets from HMS *Eagle*, steaming off Aden with the task force, took over the support role.

Army engineers were removing British monuments and plaques, to head off any rude sport that might be made of them. The biggest of these was Queen Victoria's eight-foot bronze statue, too expensive to send back to Britain to join many more of its kind. It was moved within the walls of a small fortress built against a rock face on Tarshyne Bay that was to be a British Embassy. Most of the items removed were regimental memorials taken from rock faces in Crater where the British first landed after its capture in 1839. The Union Jack planted then was sent to the Maritime Museum at Greenwich. South Arabia was the first British colony not to be offered membership of the Commonwealth.

On 20 October the High Command of FLOSY, eleven senior officers of the Aden Civil Police and twenty-four officers of the South Arabian Army, including seven lieutenant colonels and senior CID officers, gathered together for a press conference, jointly to charge Britain with 'fomenting civil war and bloodshed, with attempting to keep FLOSY out of power in favour of stooge elements of the NLF.'

A short period of comparative calm ended with grenade attacks and gun battles in all parts of Aden. Five Arabs were shot dead in Crater, a sixth was shot dead in Maalla. All British forces were put on general alert while the Argylls took over the strategic rooftops the Armed Police had reoccupied. Mitchell advised the police that the only place their personal safety could be guaranteed was within their own compound across the dual carriageway from the rooftops, and they withdrew.

Gun battles raged furiously in Steamer Point. Arab gunmen poured concentrated fire into every British position along a 400-yard front. Military headquarters moved from Flagstaff Hill in the hitherto most secure British perimeter to a command post within the airport perimeter.

Five days after the FLOSY press conference the NLF spokesman Seif al Dhali, a British-trained agriculturalist, gave one in Zingabar thirty miles along the east coast. He introduced a chubby man, who slipped off sandals to hold his feet in manicured hands, as chief of military operations. He was Qushtan Al-Shaabi, soon to occupy Government House as first President of a People's Republic of South Yemen.

An off-duty soldier of the Royal Corps of Transport became the ninth victim of a Steamer Point assassin, killed by a bullet from a 7.65mm pistol while shopping in Steamer Point. The assassin, who always fired at point-blank range, had claimed fourteen deaths by the end.

In the first week of November, assassinations and factional gun battles grew into full-scale civil war with anti-tank rockets, mortar bombs and heavy machine guns. Taxis, crammed with frightened women and children, streamed into areas still controlled by British troops.

The soldiers had grandstand seats in sandbagged observation posts as fighting flared up between rival factions in Steamer Point, Maalla and Khormaksar, areas still nominally under British control. New orders banned them from intervening unless fired upon.

The Arab army joined in the civil war on the side of the NLF on 5 November, and four days later the last pockets of FLOSY resistance outside Crater were wiped out. The army used heavy weapons without regard for civilian casualties and damage to property, and the death toll, including many non-combatants, women and children, numbered hundreds with many thousands wounded.

When the pro-Nasser regime of Marshal Sallal in the neighbouring Yemen Arab Republic was ousted in an army coup, the South Arabian army chiefs, suddenly rid of fear of Egyptian intervention to install a FLOSY government, declared themselves with a statement calling on the NLF to open negotiations to take over total power from Britain. They warned that the Arab Army of South Yemen, as they newly styled themselves, would oppose 'any other front or party that stood against the will of the people'.

Next day Aden's streets were festooned with NLF flags, filled with exuberant crowds and honking motorcades. British soldiers were confronted with hundreds of Arabs brandishing Kalashnikovs and pistols and clutching hand grenades as though they were sporting trophies. After a tense ten minutes when the first crowd was held at a roadblock in Maalla, troops withdrew to fortified positions and let the crowds pass.

From then on Aden was in fiesta. An exuberant second head waiter of the Crescent Hotel invited the writer to meet the NLF commander in Steamer Point, Abdullah Farhan, a twenty-nine-year-old school teacher and father of three. He claimed total victory over FLOSY in the tiny rock-walled area of narrow streets and squatter camps behind the Crescent shopping arcade. 'We killed six and arrested three hundred and fifty,' he boasted, but promised, 'No more British civilians will be executed if the soldiers leave soon.'

There were no NLF flags in Crater under the firm grip of the Argylls. An Arab seen with a gun or a grenade was certain to be shot. The last FLOSY redoubt was there, a few alleys covered with their slogans hemmed in by rock walls and an Argyll roadblock. But the Pax Scotia was broken when a grenade was thrown over the wall of the Armed Police barracks as Colonel Mitchell passed, wounding three of his escort. The same evening the Argylls shot five Arabs dead.

On Sunday 8 November, as the carrier *Eagle* and a task force appeared
on the horizon, the writer was invited to a house in Sheikh Othman
where the NLF spokesman, Seif al Dhali, had a message for Sir Humphrey Trevelyan. He said, 'Britain must publicly accept the NLF as sole
representative of the people before we will agree to negotiations for a
handover of power.' Sir Humphrey asked George Brown, the Foreign
Secretary, to agree to him inviting NLF leaders to immediate negotiations
for a transfer of sovereignty to them.

The underlying British worry was that the Arab army might join NLF
attacks and use heavy weapons against British positions. Senior Arab
army and police officers led by Colonel Mohammed Al Aulaqui, designated to take over command of the Federal Army, had an hour-long
meeting with Sir Humphrey and all the British senior officers at
Government House. Afterwards Brigadier Dunbar told me, 'The situation
is more tense than it's ever been – more dangerous than at the time of
the mutiny in June.'

Negotiations with the NLF began in Geneva on 21 November. Lord
Shackleton, leader of the British delegation, wrote to Harold Wilson,
the Prime Minister, saying it was vital to offer the NLF £12 million
'conditional on good behaviour'.[7] The NLF demanded £60 million but
accepted the British offer after a week of haggling.

As the end neared Sir Humphrey reviewed the twenty-four ships of
the Task Force, including two aircraft carriers, an assault ship (LPD) and
a commando carrier (LPH), the first fleet review since the Spithead
Coronation Review of 1953. They were anchored in four lines off Aden
harbour and a seventeen-gun salute reverberated around the rock faces
of Aden. This ceremonial display backed a warning to the NLF and the
Arab army that British forces would hit back hard if any attempt was
made to interfere with withdrawal. It was made clear that Arab military
headquarters and barracks would be primary targets. The military had
the measure of the Arab mentality.

The first part of a three-phase final withdrawal organized 'as an
operation of war', was completed by dawn on 26 November, a full
twenty-four hours ahead of schedule. In Crater the skirl of a single
Scottish bagpipe played 'The Barren Rocks of Aden' as the Argylls'
regimental flag was lowered, signalling the rearguard to stay for just
fifteen minutes more. At the same time marines of 42 Commando and
soldiers of C Company of the King's Own Borderers, covered by

armoured cars of the Queen's Own Hussars, abandoned positions in Steamer Point and in the high-rise apartments of Maalla. The evacuation airlift to Bahrein and flights onward to Britain was fully under way, lifting out 1,000 soldiers a day.

Arab soldiers took over the abandoned positions, and their British commander, Brigadier Jack Dye, who had led the Anglians in Radfan, took the salute of a march past of eight camels of a desert patrol, before formally handing over command to Colonel Ahmed Aulaqi. Then Brigadier Dye boarded one of forty airliners which left the airport that day, protected by patrolling naval aircraft and helicopters.

Just before sunset 1 Para, young veterans of 800 terrorist assaults with rockets, mortars, grenades and machine guns in Sheikh Othman, came out of Saltpan positions, cut the perimeter wire, formed ranks of eight abreast and marched straight down the runway as a patrolling helicopter dipped in salute. General Tower, himself a para, saluted them as they marched past. 1 Para had captured 128 terrorists, and lost three killed and twenty-five wounded.

On the morning of 28 November Sir Humphrey Trevelyan boarded an RAF Britannia as a Royal Marine band played 'Fings Ain't What They Used To Be'. The British Forces Radio, broadcasting from the airport, went off the air after playing the National Anthem, three verses including the pointed words, 'confound their politics, frustrate their knavish tricks'.

As the last transport plane disappeared a cloud of helicopters moved in from the task force, splitting out of formation towards different objectives. Commandos climbed dangling drop ladders to board them from lonely picquet posts on Aden's peaks, while other marines moved back from sandbagged positions on the perimeter wire.

A reduced perimeter was held by 110 men of the King's Own Borderers until they scrambled to helicopters to be lifted out. Marines of 42 Commando pulled back on the last redoubt, the clubhouse of the Aden Golf and Polo Club, massively sandbagged and called Fort Alamo. The flagpole had been cut down from the exposed roof and re-erected where men lowering the flag for the last time would have better protection and a quick sprint to the helicopter.

At 11.20 GMT the flag of 42 Commando was hauled down and General Tower, the men holding Fort Alamo and a few pressmen sprinted for Sioux helicopters hovering a few inches above the sand.

As a last Wasp helicopter, carrying the rear-guard commander,

Lieutenant Colonel 'Dai' Morgan, of the Royal Marines, rose above the runway the red, white and black NLF flag was broken over Fort Alamo, and Arab officers were seen gesticulating around the military vehicles left parked, ignition keys in place, around the last British redoubt. It seemed they were already quarrelling over the spoils.

The final statistics: terrorist incidents increased from 36 in 1964 to over 3,000 in 1967. During that period 57 British soldiers were killed, 44 of them in the last year, and 651 wounded, 325 in the last eleven months. Eighteen British civilians were killed and 83 wounded.[8] Most British dead were left behind in the Silent Valley military cemetery near Little Aden.

The naval task force remained off Aden for two months, and elements of it were on standby till April 1968 in case the 350 Britons working at the Little Aden oil refinery and the British Ambassador and his staff needed rescue.

Tribal rivalries within the NLF broke out within six months of independence, and for years Aden became a refuge for airliner hijackers and terrorists and a base for the Soviet navy.

11

GENERAL SIR JOHN AKEHURST

Dhofar, 1965–1975: The Unknown War

General Sir John Akehurst served throughout the Cold War and in many of the British army's campaigns in the withdrawal from Empire. He commanded the Dhofar Brigade in 1974–75, and was responsible for the operations that resulted in the successful conclusion of that bloody but almost unknown war. He published *We Won a War*, the narrative of this war. Following other appointments he rose to be commander of the UK Field Army, and finally Deputy Supreme Commander Europe. He has recently published his autobiography, *Generally Speaking: Then Hurrah for the life of a Soldier*.

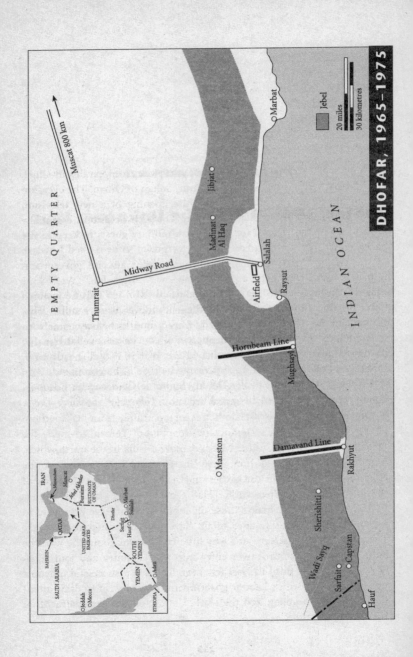

DHOFAR, 1965–1975

Jebel

20 miles
30 kilometres

Muscat 800 km

EMPTY QUARTER

Thumrait

Midway Road

Madinat Al Haq

Jibjat

Salalah

Airfield

Raysut

INDIAN OCEAN

Marbat

Hornbeam Line

Mughsayl

Manston

Damavand Line

Rakhyut

Wadi Sayq

Sherishitti

Sarfait

Capstan

Hauf

SAUDI ARABIA

IRAN

Muscat

Jebel Akhdar

Buraimi

QATAR

BAHRAIN

Jeddah

Mecca

UNITED ARAB EMIRATES

SULTANATE OF OMAN

Dhofar

Sarfait

Hauf

Marbat

Salalah

YEMEN

SOUTH YEMEN

Aden

ETHIOPIA

'So how is the war going, Brigadier?' asked the Commander-in-Chief, His Majesty, Qaboos bin Said bin Taimur, Sultan of Oman. The occasion was an afternoon reception to mark the opening of a new television station in Salalah, the capital of Dhofar. On such occasions, essentially Omani, it was the custom for any British military guests to keep in the background and the brigadier was very surprised to be invited forward, to the envious stares of many important diplomats and government ministers present, to share a chaise longue with the Sultan. 'Well, Your Majesty,' he replied, 'in my opinion you have won it.' This he justified by saying that although a few diehard enemy terrorists were still at large the mission he had given the brigade fifteen months before, namely 'to secure Dhofar for civil development', had now been achieved. Later that day he confirmed his opinion to the Sultan in writing and shortly after, in December 1975, the Sultan announced to the world that the war had indeed been won, thus bringing to an end the rebellion which had been raging for ten years and had at one time come very close to success.

Oman has about 1,600 kilometres of coastline, from its southern border with the People's Democratic Republic of Yemen, formerly the British colony of Aden, to the Musandam peninsula in the north which, only fifty kilometres from Iran, forms the Hormuz Strait entrance to the Gulf through which, in the sixties and seventies, passed two-thirds of the oil needs of the free world.[1] Had Oman lost its war with Soviet-backed communist guerrillas those oil supplies might have been held to ransom and other Gulf states might have fallen like a pack of cards. There were three main reasons why little was known about the war: the Sultans had total control over entry into their country and journalists were denied visits until the last few months when a successful outcome was certain; the British Labour government did not wish to draw attention to its involvement; and the world's attention was concentrated on Vietnam at the time.

Oman in the sixties was ripe for rebellion. Said bin Taimur, the Sultan, was a repressive autocrat who, Canute-like, tried to hold back the march of progress by withholding development of any kind, and this included health, education, pluralism and communications. When he ousted his father in 1932 his country was bankrupt but for nearly forty years he just managed to balance his budgets and keep the country narrowly in the black. Though personally gentle and cultured he was a stubborn and thrifty procrastinator by nature and abhorred debt in any form. He despised as irreligious and garish the excesses of his newly oil-rich Gulf neighbours and was seriously repressive, denying his people fuel, modern clothes, transistor radios, cameras, indeed any form of technology or development, and all manner of petty restrictions were brutally enforced. He allowed no secondary education because he felt it would teach aspirations which he could not afford to meet and any who escaped the country to receive it were simply not allowed back. Although he maintained an efficient internal information system for himself he seldom met his people. His second wife was a Dhofari woman and apart from one expedition to the north he lived permanently in his palace in Dhofar, as had his own father most of the time. The province had often sought independence over the centuries. Indeed, for a short time in the nineteenth century, it achieved it. Sultan Said and his father made one of their reasons for living there the need to ensure its continuance as an integral part of their sultanate.

Dhofar, roughly the size of Wales, is a geographical phenomenon. Separated from arid and mountainous northern Oman by 600 kilometres of desert it is uniquely affected by a monsoon bubbling up from the Indian Ocean from late May to early October every year. This forms a dense fog and sheds up to 762 millimetres of mostly gentle precipitation to a depth of never more than fifty kilometres from the coast and, in some parts, much less. Salalah is at the centre of a coastal plain fifty kilometres long and up to eleven kilometres deep on which once grew the vegetables for the British campaign in Mesopotamia in the Great War. Behind this and running parallel to the sea is the jebel. For more than 160 kilometres, sometimes falling sheer to the sea, it rises 600 to 1,200 metres. The monsoon has carved deep valleys, or wadis, everywhere, craggy heights dominating the surrounding country particularly in the west, and, in the east, open rolling country not unlike Salisbury

Plain but gashed by deep wadis. Where the monsoon reaches, and this is a line that seldom varies, the wadis are full of lush vegetation; in the west below the treeline is thick bush and, in the east, fertile grassland. North, beyond the monsoon line, is jagged moon country gradually flattening out into the deserts of the Empty Quarter. In tactical summary, where there is vegetation there is concealment and guerrillas can be effective out of all proportion to their numbers, but in the open desert control of the air can obstruct enemy movement. Similarly control of the sea can prevent any form of logistic supply. The war was therefore confined to the jebel.

Few of the Dhofar people were ethnically Omani. The Salalah plain was largely populated by descendants of Zanzibaris originally imported as slaves, and mostly despised by the jebel people (jebalis) who themselves are thought to have migrated from the Horn of Africa. They have their own language and culture, and are Islamic. Socially they are essentially tribal, with clear tribal areas, mostly determined by grazing, for they are cattle people, and these areas may be quite small, for there are many tribes. North of the monsoon line are the Mahra, whose nomadic style has been forced upon them by the constant search for food for their camels. The jebalis have fine, angular features and are supremely fit. Tribal disputes through the ages have made fighting a constant companion and they are courageous and tactically skilful.

Britain's association with Oman began in the late seventeenth century, with the East India Company protecting its Gulf trade. It continued into the early twentieth century with various treaties by which Britain pledged naval and military forces to help the Sultan to stamp out piracy, dissident tribesmen and slavery: major insurrections in 1915 and 1957 were put down with British help, and in the mid-fifties British-led Trucial Oman Scouts had cooperated with Sultanate forces to put an end to the Saudi occupation of the Buraimi Oasis and defeat tribesmen trying to seize control of the interior. Arrangements were made more formal by the Amery Agreement in 1958, during the Jebel Akhdar emergency, by the creation of the Sultan's Armed Forces (SAF), in which there was to be a framework for the secondment of a commander and other seconded officers. For the next fifteen years, until Omanization got fully under way, almost all captains and above were either seconded or contract, mostly of British, and all of Commonwealth origin. An annual subsidy of £1 million was awarded, rising to £2 million by 1967 when it was stopped, to Sultan Said's fury, because the British government felt that burgeoning oil revenues made it unnecessary.

In 1962 a small group Dhofari tribesmen, some of them former Trucial Oman Scouts soldiers, who were seeking to overthrow Sultan Said and win independence went to Iraq, and Saudi Arabia, for training and returned in 1965. On 9 June they formed the Dhofar Liberation Front (DLF) and began a campaign of ambush, mining sabotage and minor attacks on isolated locations. At that time there was one infantry battalion in Dhofar but though ill-equipped, poorly armed and seriously short of logistic support it was able to pursue and subdue the rebels. There are those who feel that if miserly old Sultan Said had spent some money on his forces and made a few concessions to development at that time the rebellion could have been quashed completely, but it was not to be. In November 1967 the British left Aden and both Russia and China leapt in to fill the vacuum. Both nations recognized the potential of bringing Oman into the communist camp and both set about training, financing, arming and supplying the Dhofari dissidents. The Chinese pulled out in 1970 but the Soviets continued throughout the war. A training base was established at Hauf, near the Omani border, and to this were brought not only tribesmen for training, but also children forcibly taken from their families for education and indoctrination.

In the next three years, while SAF continued to be starved of resources the DLF, later aggrandized to the People's Front for the Liberation of the Arabian Gulf, and later still, under pressure, to The People's Front for the Liberation of Oman, went from strength to strength. The hard core, originally thirty-two, was multiplied to over 800 and some 3,000 militia were recruited or coerced by terror or by tribal or family loyalty. The insurrection was not universally popular on the jebel, particularly when communist atheism was forcibly imposed, but fearsome punishments were inflicted for dissidence, such as execution by hideous means, burning out of eyes, cutting off of noses and forcing of daughters to provide sexual favours to the young fighters – although this last seems unlikely and may only be a propaganda claim.

During this time the Commander SAF was Brigadier Corran Purdon, who fought a continuous battle with the Sultan and with London for expansion of his forces to counter the growing insurrection. The single battalion in Dhofar was reinforced with another, but despite remarkable courage, efficiency and all possible aggressive action the soldiers were ill-shod and clothed, their support weapons were little short of primitive and, worst of all, they lacked the means to remain on the jebel for more than a few days at a time. Probably the most serious deficiency was in helicopters, which could have moved troops quickly in the difficult terrain, resupplied them with food, water and ammunition, and speedily evacuated casualties, but no order was placed for these until October 1969. The effect of these constraints was that when essential defensive tasks had taken up soldiers there was simply not the strength for sustained offensive action on the jebel to reduce enemy power and provide security for the oppressed jebalis. Commanders at the time recognized the potential value of cutting the enemy supply line as far west as possible but simply lacked the numbers to do it. The essential 'Hearts and Minds' campaign was simply not possible while the enemy held total sway on the jebel and tactics tended more towards the punitive for giving support to the enemy rather than persuasion and reward for not doing so. SAF's total strength when Brigadier John Graham took over as Commander SAF in 1970 was less than 4,000.

The most significant milestone in the campaign came in 1970 when in a nearly bloodless coup Qaboos took over from his father as Sultan. Qaboos had had a closely sheltered private upbringing and education. Not until he was nearly twenty was he sent to the Royal Military Academy, Sandhurst, and, on commissioning, to serve briefly in the Cameronians (a Lowland Scottish regiment disbanded in 1968). Qaboos still regards this period as the most essential preparation for ruling his country. Some years later he endowed Sandhurst with a magnificent swimming pool and gymnasium complex to show his gratitude for motivating him and teaching him about hard work, responsibility and service. On his return to Oman, however, his father confined him to a small house, outside the Salalah Palace, and isolated him from the politics and personalities of his country. Nevertheless, by mid-1970 his own assessment of the military position in Dhofar and the worsening situation elsewhere in Oman convinced him that if the Al Bu Said dynasty and the Sultanate were to be saved, his father's rule would have to be terminated.

A small group of British officers serving in SAF had become aware of Qaboos's intentions. They welcomed them, for they, too, realized that the salvation of the Sultanate and the continuing loyalty of the hard-pressed Arab soldiers in SAF lay in Qaboos's enlightened hands. Among these officers was Brigadier Graham himself, who knew Oman from earlier tours in the Gulf with British parachute troops. He foresaw that a clash between Qaboos's supporters and the numerous and well-armed Palace guards might be a bloody affair which could result in the death of either the Sultan or Qaboos or both of them. Such an outcome would be for the Sultanate a calamity. Graham therefore resolved that the best contribution that SAF could make would be to ensure that the transfer of power should be as smooth and bloodless as possible.

On 23 July Captain Tim Landon, a former regular officer on contract to SAF, brought to Headquarters The Desert Regiment, which was then serving in Dhofar, a letter signed by Qaboos stating that he had decided to take over from his father that very day and appealing to Lieutenant Colonel Teddy Turnill, the commanding officer, to rally swiftly to his side 'in order to minimise bloodshed and to maintain law and order'. Brigadier Graham told Turnill to comply without delay and a party of Omani soldiers led by Lieutenant Said Salem al Wahaibi moved into Salalah and entered the Palace complex. There a fierce gun battle had already broken out between the Sultan himself and Qaboos's supporters who were led by two sheikhs, Buraik, the son of the Wali (province governor), and Hilal bin Sultan al Husni. During this shooting both Buraik and the Sultan were wounded, but the early arrival of Said Salem and his men put an end to the shooting, disarmed the Palace guards and saved the life of the Sultan. The wounded were taken to the medical centre in the nearby RAF station for treatment. On the following day the Sultan formally abdicated and was flown to London where he lived in the Dorchester Hotel until his death there in 1972. Qaboos was acclaimed as Sultan amid scenes of prolonged nationwide rejoicing and shortly afterwards he changed the name of his country (from Muscat and Oman) and his title to His Majesty the Sultan of Oman.

The new young Sultan got to work quickly, announcing the relaxation of many of his father's unpopular restrictions, plans for rapid and large-scale civil development (thus demolishing at a stroke the raison d'être of the rebellion) and for a substantial expansion of SAF. He also declared an amnesty for any enemy who deserted their communist masters and came down from the jebel to support him. They were to be welcomed and rewarded for any weapons they brought with them. This amnesty at first brought down a mere trickle but they provided important intelligence and gradually over the next five years the trickle increased to a steady flow; by the end of 1972 to over 1,000 and by 1975 to three times that number.

Another important event in 1970 was a visit by Lieutenant Colonel Johnny Watts, commanding officer of 22 Special Air Service Regiment (SAS). He was sent by Britain to look into the situation, decide whether there might be a role for the SAS and recommend ideas for the future development of the campaign. His assessment completed, he suggested that there was indeed a role for the SAS, and a minimal involvement was increased to two squadrons for a limited period. Watts, acutely aware of the need to make progress with the jebel people, also recommended the establishment, initially under SAS management, of an intelligence cell, an information team, a roving medical officer supported by SAS medical men, a veterinary officer for the cattle which were so important to the jebalis and the raising of local units of Dhofari tribesmen ready to fight for the Sultan.

All of these were hurriedly put into effect on the understanding that the measures were to be temporary until the Omani government could undertake the tasks. The last one was the origin of the Firqa forces. These were recruited from surrendered enemy personnel and the only initial mistake was to believe that they could be multi-tribal. This took away one of their key motivations, which was to return to their tribal areas and dominate them as tribal leaders. After a sticky start this was recognized and all subsequent Firqa units were essentially tribal. Meanwhile Brigadier Graham saw clearly that for these policies to be put into effect it would be necessary to establish a permanent presence on the jebel. Setting this up would take a powerful attack followed by building defences capable of withstanding all enemy attacks, especially during the monsoon when air and artillery support were so much less effective. It would also be important to bring the SAS and SAF into close cooperation and break down the mutual suspicion that inevitably arose. All of this was at a time when apart from occasional aggressive but brief forays SAF was confined to the Salalah plain and the RAF station itself suffered occasional rocket and mortar fire. The airfield at Salalah was operated, maintained and defended under treaty arrangements by Britain, who provided the necessary RAF personnel, a Field Surgical Team, an RAF Regiment squadron and a battery of guns known as Cracker.

In 1971 SAF had four battalions and these were rotating between nine months of operations in Dhofar followed by a similar period of rest, recruiting and training in the north, which was home to virtually all Omani soldiers. These soldiers did not really consider Dhofar to be part of Oman and it was a credit to good leadership that they fought so well there when they felt themselves only to be mercenaries. Two battalions permanently in Dhofar together with associated support units and logistics, and the placing under command of all Sultan of Oman's Air Force (SOAF) and Sultan of Oman's Navy (SON) deployed there, justified the establishment of a brigade headquarters and this, Dhofar Brigade, was set up and commanded by Colonel Mike Harvey, who had earlier experienced a tough fighting time in the province commanding The Northern Frontier Regiment. SOAF now had Strikemaster fighters, a few helicopters and some short-take-off-and-landing supply aircraft, and SON already having armed dhows was getting fast patrol boats, which ensured that the coastline was denied to enemy shipping.

In October 1971, directly after the monsoon, a major operation, JAGUAR, was mounted, including two SAS squadrons, Firqa forces and all of Dhofar Brigade which was not involved in guarding and defensive tasks. The objective was to capture a position on the jebel with a view to remaining there permanently, and the site chosen initially was an airstrip west of Jibjat at the far end of the eastern area. The initial approach achieved total surprise and it was decided to reinforce success by moving some ten kilometres westwards to 'White City' or Madinat al Haq. This was an inspired choice because it was central to the tribal area of one of the Firqa units involved, it was well populated and it offered the best grazing and waterholes. The enemy soon recognized the threat and there was hard fighting, especially in November, but they were outgunned and the base was firmly established, never to be left.

With JAGUAR complete some forces were now available to undertake two other milestone tasks before the 1972 monsoon season. They were aimed at the enemy supply line, both for the long-term effect and to reduce the mortar and rocket ammunition supplying the weapons harassing Madinat al Haq and other positions. The first, called LEOPARD, set up positions in a line north from Mughsayl astride the routes which had to be taken by enemy camel convoys. Only three positions could be held in a line some fifty kilometres long and they could not be leak-proof, but by vigilance and frequent patrolling they made enemy movement increasingly difficult and certainly reduced the flow of supplies.

The other operation was SIMBA, a daring airborne attack at Sarfait, a bare mountainous position, 1,200 metres high, close to the Yemen border, which offered views out to Hauf and down the escarpment to the sea. From this position the jebel falls to the shore in a series of steps. Unless the steps are also held camel convoys can still move safely by night in dead ground but their flow can be interrupted by mortar and artillery fire. The *coup de main* assault, by The Desert Regiment under Lieutenant Colonel Nigel Knocker, was completely successful and the position was firmly established, but unfortunately, although the enemy were taken completely by surprise, they reacted quickly and prevented the development of the position down to the first step 600 metres below and soon had the descents well covered and mined. Sarfait was an important position, especially for its psychological effect, and it was never left, but it became a heavy drain on resources because there were no overland approaches to it and there was no water there. Every soldier, every weapon and all ammunition, food and water had to be delivered by air, frequently harassed by small-arms fire, onto a runway subject to mortar and rocket attack.

After the 1972 monsoon brought active campaigning to a halt the enemy, desperate for a success to raise their status with the jebalis and having lost the military initiative, mounted their biggest single attack of their war on 19 July. The target was Marbat, held at that time by a Firqa, a few askar (locally recruited) guards, and an SAS team of eight commanded by Captain Mike Kealey, who won a richly deserved DSO for his actions that day. The enemy aim was to capture the town and hold it for a few days, execute the Wali and any other government sympathizers and then withdraw, having ensured that no one else in Marbat would dare to support the Sultan again. The attack was well conceived and more than 250 hard-core fighters were assembled for the task, together with plenty of mortars and recoilless artillery. The plan was simple. Take out the Jebel Ali piquets a kilometre north of the town, and then, after an opening barrage and curtain of small-arms fire, launch the whole force in an infantry attack concentrated mostly on the Beau Geste-type fort on a hill immediately to the north-east of the town. Once taken, this fort would dominate the town and most of the

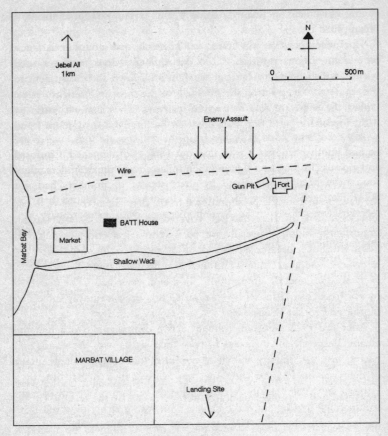

Marbat, 19 July 1972

approaches to it. Monsoon-time was chosen because the low cloud would negate SOAF jet firepower and helicopter reinforcement. It could have been a master-stroke and ruin months of government progress. It very nearly succeeded.

The assault began at 0530. At that time almost all of the Firqa were out to the north on patrol. About a platoon of wali's askars and Dhofar Gendarmerie armed with aged rifles held the fort, and the SAS team was in the building allotted to them at the north edge of Marbat and known as the BATT (British Army Training Team) house. One of the men, a Fijian called Labalaba, ran the 1,100 metres along a very shallow wadi to the fort where an Omani gunner was manning a 25-pounder in a gun pit nearby. Together they serviced this gun until both were seriously wounded, Labalaba mortally; another Fijian trooper ran to their aid but was also soon wounded, although he continued to fight. Meanwhile the remaining SAS men were providing heavy machine-gun and rifle fire from the BATT house and attracting much fire in return. At this point Kealey became worried at silence from the gun pit and under fierce fire he and another trooper ran to find out what had happened. Confused and vicious close-quarter fighting then followed and the defenders might soon have been overwhelmed by sheer weight of numbers had not SOAF managed to intervene. Under a cloudbase never higher than 150 feet Strikemaster jets from Salalah managed with extraordinary skill and courage to give the closest possible support with guns, rockets and bombs until the enemy were forced to call off their assault and begin to retire. Three SOAF helicopters approaching at wave height now managed to fly in SAS reinforcements from a new squadron (G Squadron) which, by happy coincidence, had only arrived in Dhofar as reliefs the day before. These men, low in numbers (only twenty-three strong) but high in firepower, landed just south-east of the town and skirmished forward, mopping up and ensuring that the enemy could not continue the action.

Thanks to the bravery and skill of the defenders and of the SOAF pilots, and to the lucky chance that a second squadron of SAS had just arrived, the Battle of Marbat was won. Thirty-eight bodies were recovered and a number of others were retrieved by the enemy. Up on the jebel in the next few weeks kangaroo courts were held to identify scapegoats and there were some executions, followed by a sudden increase in the numbers of defectors. This was the last significant attack mounted by the enemy and it was thus a turning point in the war.

During the 1972 monsoon there were command changes. Oil revenues were now on stream and very substantial resources were being poured into defence with a view to bringing the war to an end as quickly as possible. The forces involved were now judged to be a major general's command and Brigadier Graham was succeeded by Major General Tim Creasey, an officer of commanding presence and personality. General Creasey's first step was to organize a National Defence Council, headed by the Sultan, which included himself and cabinet ministers. This

Council provided central, coordinated direction of the war and ensured that the development programme, which had been lagging behind the military effort, was accorded appropriate priority. A similar arrangement was established in Dhofar, where the brigade was now commanded by Brigadier Jack Fletcher, and a Dhofar Development Committee was set up, chaired by the Wali and including military, civil, Development Department and intelligence membership. Simultaneously a diplomatic offensive was mounted with the aim of enlisting moral and material support for the campaign, especially among Muslim states.

General Creasey's next step was to establish a military command and control system which could handle the substantial array of forces now involved, nearly double that of a year before and still expanding. A steadily increasing flow of defections from the enemy into Firqa forces justified creating a new headquarters to administer them.

Until this time SAF infantry battalions included native Omanis and mercenary Baluch soldiers in almost equal proportions. Baluchistan was desperately poor and there was no shortage of recruits to join the well-paid Sultan's forces. The mix of Omanis and Baluch was not always comfortable and it was decided to create two new battalions entirely of Baluch soldiers, The Frontier Force and The Southern Regiment, both of which would contain the customary proportion of seconded and contract officers and serve permanently in Dhofar.

The 1972–3 campaign season was one of hard graft: maintaining the Sarfait position, ensuring the security of the Salalah plain, harrying the enemy in the open eastern area and establishing permanent positions there, and interrupting his supply line wherever possible. The LEOPARD line north from Mughsayl had been relinquished the previous year for lack of troops but it was now re-established and the positions were maintained during the 1973 monsoon. Until this time the enemy had been able to fire recoilless artillery missiles into the RAF Salalah base from the safety of the jebel so four platoon-strength picquets were permanently established in the area of their former firing positions, thus bringing that threat to an end.

After the monsoon it was clear that although enemy supply lines were interrupted they were still capable of infiltration by night so it was decided to develop the LEOPARD positions into a manned physical barrier on the lines of the French Morice Barrage in Algeria. The fifty-three-kilometre-long Hornbeam Line, as it was called, was built in six months. It demanded huge engineer effort in ferocious terrain and broiling heat mainly by a British engineer squadron on loan, a Jordanian squadron similarly loaned and a newly created Omani squadron. Providing Oman with military support was a brave and wise decision by King Hussein of Jordan which few members of the Arab League would then risk. 15,000 coils of barbed wire, 12,000 pickets, 12,000 reels of wire and 4,000 anti-personnel mines went into its construction. The enemy quickly recognized the threat and there were fierce battles but construction was never interrupted for long.

In December 1973, at the Sultan's request and in support of his need for non-communist stability on the southern side of the Gulf, the Shah of Iran provided a battle group with a number of helicopters and lavish administration. The task allotted was to open and hold permanently the 'Midway Road'. The only land route to Salalah from the north was the long road adjacent to the Empty Quarter and finally across the jebel from north to south from Midway, an old airstrip at Thumrait. The road over the jebel had seen much action, ambushes and mining, and each move along it had demanded a slow picqueting operation on the lines learned on the North-West Frontier of India. It was now decided to turn the graded track into a tarmac road but first it had to be opened and held. A simultaneous assault by the Iranians from the north and SAF from the south went well and the Iranians then occupied a series of positions along the road. Having been trained for more general warfare by the Americans, they lacked the subtlety and tactical skill to cope with the highly mobile enemy and they worshipped at the shrine of firepower. From their new positions they drenched the surrounding countryside with fire, sometimes aimed at each other, and the road was rarely crossed by the enemy except in small parties by night.

During August 1974 Brigadier Jack Fletcher handed over to the author. It was now clear that the Sultan would eventually win his war and the only question was how long would it take. Forecasts generally were of the order of five years. General Creasey gave a clear directive: maintain Sarfait, secure the plain, maintain Hornbeam and pacify the east and centre to free up troops for mobile operations in the west.

Firqa forces were now about 1,500 strong. They were notoriously unruly and choosy about what they were prepared to do. Each unit had an SAS team of four men who exercised their management with quite remarkable skill and courage as they responded to the incessant cry of '*ureed*', the Arabic for 'I want'. Many times a day the BATTs had to decide whether what was wanted was reasonable or not. Usually it was not and they then had to deal with the consequent frustration and anger of these potentially dangerous tribesmen.

The Firqa were the key to pacifying the eastern and central jebel and their leaders wanted nothing more than to return to their tribal areas. If this could be arranged they could provide their own defence under the government's threat of evicting them if anything went wrong. This eviction might be carried out by force or by cutting off water supplies, two very potent methods. The policy was formalized. First the Firqa leader would be invited to select a suitably defensible spot in his area. This he could do well with his natural tactical skill. A battalion operation would then be mounted to capture that area and a track graded to it. The position would be fortified and along the track would come a drill. Under the limestone of the jebel were countless aquifers and, with suitable equipment, wells could be drilled almost anywhere. The water would then be stored in tanks and distributed to human supply points and cattle troughs. The time was now ripe for the Development Department to send in a Civil Action Team to set up a mosque, a shop, a school and a clinic and from this beginning the tribe could create its own new village. This would attract people from throughout the tribal area, who, in turn, would provide intelligence and be told to advise their enemy friends and relations that this was all a good thing and they were on no account to upset the applecart. By the 1975 monsoon this operation had been carried out successfully twenty times and as early as January enemy activity had effectively been confined to the west of Hornbeam.

The Shah now provided further Iranian support. The battle group on Midway Road was withdrawn and joined by another at a new Iranian Brigade base at Manston, roughly halfway between Hornbeam and the border. It was replaced on the Midway Road, now tarmac, by a Special Forces battalion from Jordan, some of the best troops in the Jordanian army. King Hussein was keen for them to be used more aggressively than had been the practice of the Iranians but they were not accustomed to the very close country in the wadis below the road and took some casualties before getting the measure of the enemy.

The task given to the Iranian Brigade was to establish a line, codenamed Damavand, similar to Hornbeam from Manston south to the sea at Rakhyut. The terrain was mountainous and clothed in bush offering very short visibility, thus largely negating the Iranian dependence on firepower. A large number of casualties were suffered and it was decided in January that the Dhofar Brigade should mount an operation against the Sherishitti caves in order to take the heat off the Iranians. This operation began well but two serious mistakes were made. The Firqa, in some strength, were detailed to lead the advance but were clearly nervous and created all manner of delays, thus losing the important element of surprise. The caves were to be assaulted on the first day but this had to be postponed until the second. By this time the enemy had redeployed in some strength and a navigational error in close country brought an SAF company onto a forward slope in full view of the waiting ambushers. In a short, ferocious battle the SAF company suffered thirteen killed and twenty-three wounded, and had to withdraw. It was decided that to risk a similar debacle later might seriously demoralize the Omani soldiers but the operation was not called off for three weeks. From their positions on a hill that dominated the caves SAF artillery and armoured cars were able to make them uninhabitable and inflicted a number of casualties before freak bad weather forced them to pull out.

Happily for the SAF this setback was soon countered by a success. Operating west from the Hornbeam Line, the Frontier Force under Lieutenant Colonel Jonathan Salusbury-Trelawny made brilliant use of helicopter-borne operations. Enemy communications were poor and they were too slow to react to these fast-moving mobile attacks. Their 9th June Regiment, which had been bombarding Hornbeam for months, was wiped out and quantities of arms, ammunition and other stores were captured.

The Damavand Line was eventually completed and by the 1975 monsoon effective enemy operations were now confined to the area between there and the border. Planning began for Operation HADAF which would, it was hoped, end the war by establishing a new line just out of gun-range from the border and not far from Sarfait. The Dhofar Brigade was now 10,000 strong, and this was to be a brigade operation preceded by diversions towards Sherishitti, by the Iranians, and by the Muscat Regiment at Sarfait. The approach to the site for the new line had to be across the deep and precipitous Wadi Saiq and this was simply impossible on foot. A helicopter-borne assault on the south side of the wadi was therefore envisaged, covered by heavy air and fire support.

With the lifting of the monsoon and allowing for a further delay until the Ramadan month ended it was decided to launch HADAF on 21 October, with the diversions seven days beforehand. These were all successfully launched, one of them spectacularly so. But before this the enemy unveiled, prematurely, a new weapon, the surface-to-air missile system SAM7. The first firing brought down a Strikemaster. The pilot ejected into enemy territory and was rescued by the skin of his teeth by a passing helicopter full of soldiers. All aircraft were warned not to fly over enemy territory below 6,000 feet but soon a second aircraft, this time a helicopter, was brought down from 10,000 feet, which meant that the system was a new version of SAM7. Rather like the wasting of the tank in its first use in the First World War the enemy would have achieved much greater effect by deploying its new weapon in numbers at a critical moment during the coming operations.

A year earlier the Desert Regiment under Lieutenant Colonel Christopher Dale had tried to get down from the Sarfait position to the plateau sixty metres below, known from an unusual rock formation there as Capstan. Sadly the descent ran into anti-personnel mines which caused casualties and cost surprise, and it had to be called off. Now the Muscat Regiment under Lieutenant Colonel Ian Christie attempted a similar operation by a slightly different route. To the delight of everyone and a degree of surprise, some very careful preparations paid off and, after a tense night, the dawn saw Muscat Regiment in full possession of the Capstan plateau and almost unopposed. The enemy had been caught completely napping. Looking down at Capstan the author asked Colonel Christie if, given reinforcements, he thought he could carry on down the further 600 metres to the sea and, if he did, whether he could hold that line despite it being in artillery range from the guns at Hauf. He was confidently affirmative so authority was immediately sought from Major General Ken Perkins, who had succeeded General Creasey as Commander SAF in February. The general not only agreed, he decided, with the Sultan's authority, to use Hunter aircraft given to Oman by King Hussein to bomb the guns at Hauf and thus reduce their effectiveness. It was also decided to use a Chinook helicopter borrowed from the Iranians to lift a troop of 5.5in medium guns to Sarfait. With their greater range and weight of shell they would provide effective counter-battery fire to the Hauf guns.

The plans for the helicopter assault were scrapped, to the considerable relief of the helicopter pilots, and the troops allotted to it diverted at once to Sarfait. The new operation was quickly put into effect and by nightfall the next day the enemy supply line was effectively cut close to the border and the rebellion could only wither on the vine. Further operations to mop up were necessary during the next month and it was particularly gratifying to capture the Sherishitti cave complex, for so long the enemy's main storehouse.

The Dhofar War must be one of the most successful counter-insurgency campaigns in recent history. It certainly helped to put paid to the theory that communism was eventually inevitable. The first five years were very difficult and the rebellion was only held at bay by the bravery and vigorous aggression of the ill-equipped, under-resourced forces, who were simply not strong enough to win. The turning point came with the accession of Sultan Qaboos. From that time the outcome was seldom in doubt, although there was a time in 1973 when a shortage of helicopters put the retention of the Sarfait position in danger and its loss would have extended the war considerably if not fatally. Fresh helicopters provided by the Shah saved the day.

From 1970 onwards the main ingredients of success were:

1. Sultan Qaboos's policy of putting the new oil revenues to best effect by promising development and by expanding and equipping his forces.
2. The joint approach from top to bottom to military operations and civil development.
3. Air power, the greatest single advantage enjoyed by the Sultan's forces.
4. The enemy's mistake in trying to supplant deeply held religious views with atheistic communism, and trying to break down tribalism.
5. Exploiting the enemy's cumbersome command system by mobile operations and by targeting his single, narrow supply line.
6. The ever-increasing use of local people and forces, especially the Firqa.
7. Recognition of the paramount need for intelligence.
8. Superior firepower.
9. The parts played by British seconded and contract officers, and the SAS, which were out of all proportion to their numbers.

12

MICHAEL DEWAR

Northern Ireland, 1969–2001: Unfinished Business

Michael Dewar was commissioned into the Rifle Brigade in 1961, and served in Cyprus, Borneo and Northern Ireland. He now comments on defence matters on radio and TV, and runs his own public relations company. He has published several books of popular military history, including one on Northern Ireland.

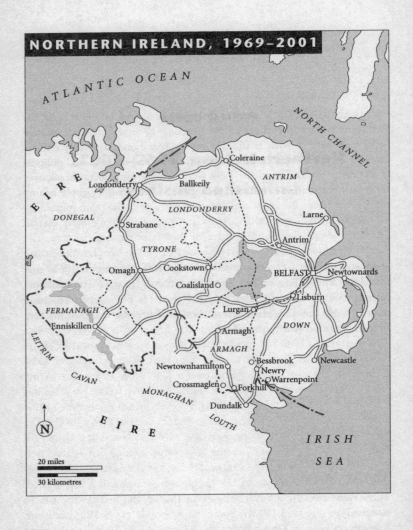

NORTHERN IRELAND, 1969–2001

Clearly any attempt to chronicle the undeclared war in Ulster over the past thirty years in one short chapter can only be superficial and selective in its treatment of what is still a complex, tragic and seemingly endless struggle – for despite a ceasefire of sorts and a tenuous political settlement culminating in the 1998 Good Friday Agreement, breakaway terrorist organizations continue to impose violence on a people aching for a peaceful Ireland. This chapter can only outline the main milestones of the campaign against terrorism in Ireland and highlight certain incidents which may be illustrative of the wider strategic picture. The war in Northern Ireland has always essentially been between the British army and the IRA. A number of Loyalist paramilitary organizations – in particular the Ulster Defence Association (UDA), the Ulster Volunteer Force (UVF) and the Ulster Freedom Fighters (UFF) – have been, and still are, involved in inter-sectarian violence, and in the 'marching season' they have taken on the security forces. This narrative, however, will focus on the strategically and politically more important war against the IRA.

Éire's relations with the United Kingdom both before and since Independence have always been stormy. The Irish Republican Army (IRA) emerged as the military arm of Sinn Féin (Ourselves Alone) following the 1918 elections; its initial guerrilla tactics against the British army turned into civil war when some Sinn Féiners refused to accept the Anglo-Irish Treaty of 6 December 1921, which created the Irish Free State in a divided Ireland. In the south the installations of the new Free State government were attacked and in the north there was a bitter Protestant backlash in which 232 people were killed and 1,000 injured. There were sporadic insurrections in the thirties and in 1939 the attacks switched to England, where some nasty bomb explosions occurred. Soldiers on leave in Ulster during the Second World War thought twice about walking down the Falls Road in Belfast in uniform. Following a period of relative inactivity immediately after the end of the Second

World War another IRA campaign in 1956–62 never got off the ground properly because it failed to generate sufficient public support.

In February 1967, however, the Northern Ireland Civil Rights Association was formed to protest against gerrymandering and plural voting to the disadvantage of the Catholic minority and against the undoubted discrimination in matters of housing and jobs. It organized a series of marches and demonstrations throughout Northern Ireland during 1968, with the marching slogan of 'One man, one vote'.

Few disagree that the Catholic minority in Ulster had been discriminated against for years, but the problem went deeper than that. Irishmen have given to the terms Catholic and Protestant a meaning which would not be understood anywhere else in the Christian world. The terms do not necessarily in themselves have any intrinsic religious significance. In Ulster, whatever else one is, one is born a Catholic or a Protestant and this divide is encouraged and perpetuated by a segregated system of religious education. It was for these reasons and against this background that the civil rights movement gained momentum throughout 1968.

On 5 October a major civil rights parade took place in Londonderry at which rioting broke out. During a similar march the following January from Belfast to Londonderry the marchers were set upon in the village of Burntollet by Protestant thugs, who beat up and severely injured many marchers. As the year progressed the rioting became more serious. During the weekend of 20 and 21 April over 200 members of the Royal Ulster Constabulary (RUC) and seventy-nine civilians were injured in Londonderry, and various acts of sabotage took place in country areas against water mains and electricity substations. The IRA was beginning to climb on the bandwagon.

It was then that the violent action of some of its members prompted a split in the organization's ranks. The nationalist wing became the Provisional Army Council and sought direct confrontation with the traditional enemy at the end of which they hoped a republic of thirty-two counties would emerge. The Provisional Army Council thus created the Provisional IRA, usually referred to as PIRA or the Provisionals. The Official IRA, or Officials, which was a Marxist organization, took a longer-term view and aimed to create without violence a United Ireland in which the working classes of both religious persuasions would co-exist. Thirty years later the Official IRA is effectively extinct.

In August 1969 there was serious rioting in Belfast. This reached a climax on the 14th when eight people were killed, 170 houses were destroyed and the cost of damage to life and property totalled some £8 million. On 13 August, when the RUC had clearly lost control, the government took the fateful step of dispatching troop reinforcements to Ulster for deployment on the streets. Garrison troops had been used earlier in the year to guard key installations but the August decision meant that British troops had been deployed to quell riots in a British city. The soldiers were welcomed as saviours by the bulk of the Catholic population. Although the IRA was not slow to make political capital out of the genuine sense of grievance felt by the civil rights movement, the violence had been hitherto almost entirely sectarian and not aimed at the army. However, it was not long before PIRA gunmen started to shoot at soldiers struggling to keep Catholic and Protestant crowds apart. On 17 August PIRA officially announced in Dublin that their northern units had been defending Catholic areas which had been 'attacked by deliberately fomented sectarian forces . . . with the aim of destroying the natural solidarity and unity of working-class people.'

Serious rioting during which men of the 3rd Battalion the Light Infantry came under sniper fire occurred in the Shankill area of Belfast in October 1969. Fortunately on this occasion no soldiers were killed though some thirteen were wounded. There followed a brief lull until the IRA bombing campaign started in January 1970. Ominously the first Catholic riot against British troops occurred on 3 March. The welcome given to the soldiers the previous summer by the Catholic population was beginning to turn sour. PIRA propaganda had been remarkably successful. In April troop reinforcements were sent to the Province and the GOC, General Sir Ian Freeland, announced that anyone seen carrying or throwing a petrol bomb was liable to be shot. The bombing campaign continued throughout April and into May, however. In June serious rioting resulted in five civilian deaths and many injuries but this was only a foretaste of the riots in the Lower Falls area of Belfast between 3 and 5 July. The disturbances were sparked off after a successful search by men of the Royal Scots of a house in Balkan Street in the Lower Falls in which fifteen pistols, a rifle and a sub-machine gun and a quantity of ammunition were found. For three days the Royal Scots, the 2nd Battalion the Queen's Regiment and the Devon and Dorset Regiment battled with rioters who hijacked city buses to form barricades across the streets and who threw nail and petrol bombs indiscriminately at them.

Several gunmen engaged the troops with extremely accurate sniper fire. At the end of the three days thirteen soldiers were admitted to hospital suffering from gunshot wounds and a further five from grenade-splinter wounds. Four civilians died from gunshot wounds and well over 300 people were injured. Vast quantities of weapons, ammunition and explosives were found in houses in the Lower Falls.

It seems in retrospect that the senseless orgy of violence that the people of the Lower Falls engaged in that July made them perhaps question – if only temporarily – the course they were set on. In August a ban on all parades and marches was imposed by the Northern Ireland government for six months. Terrorism continued in a small way but by and large people seemed to be taking stock.

The storm broke again the following February. Again it was anger resulting from a successful search for arms that brought the crowds on to the streets again. This time the violence spread all over the Province. On 8 February Lance Bombardier Laurie of 32 Heavy Regiment Royal Artillery received gunshot wounds in the head when his Land Rover was ambushed in Belfast's Crumlin Road. He died a few days later. On 10 February five BBC employees were killed in County Fermanagh while on their way to check a faulty transmitter by a landmine that had been intended for a military patrol. On 11 March three young Scottish soldiers, two of whom were under the age of eighteen, were abducted from a pub, where they had been drinking, and murdered. Their bodies were found in a ditch in Ligoniel on the outskirts of Belfast. The subsequent furore in the press forced the Ministry of Defence to announce that henceforward soldiers under the age of eighteen would not be permitted to serve in the Province.

On 20 March Major James Chichester-Clark resigned as Prime Minister of Northern Ireland. Chichester-Clark, an honest country gentleman of limited shrewdness and political acumen, had replaced the dilettante Captain Terence O'Neill in April 1969. Whereas O'Neill had unashamedly upheld the Protestant Supremacy while at the same time managing to utter soothing platitudes about equal rights for all Ulstermen, Chichester-Clark had genuinely tried to remove some of the more glaring inequalities. He had for instance approved the setting up of the Hunt Commission which recommended in October 1969 that the hated so-called 'B-Specials' (an armed Volunteer Police Reserve which had recruited exclusively from the Protestant community) should be disbanded. Chichester-Clark was replaced on 23 March by Brian Faulkner, an able middle-class businessman of Presbyterian values who was prepared to go to almost any lengths to preserve the British connection.

Faulkner inherited a rapidly worsening situation. PIRA was now engaged in open war and it was a terrorist campaign rather than the continuing communal violence which had by the summer of 1971 become the main preoccupation of the security forces. From the start of 1971 the incidence of terrorism had been showing an alarming increase: by early August twelve British soldiers, two policemen and sixteen civilians had died as a result of the growing violence in the Province. Bomb explosions had long since become a daily occurrence. On 9 August a soldier was shot in the head in Belfast and died instantly. Throughout that day mobs roamed the streets burning and looting. There was now no doubt that the Provisionals had launched a full-scale terrorist campaign against the civilian population of Northern Ireland. The police had lost control in many Catholic areas; witnesses, intimidated by the IRA, would not give evidence; even juries were in danger when convicting. In a situation where terrorist intimidation exists, together with some degree of sympathy with the terrorists among a large section of the community, the successful arrest and conviction of terrorist criminals becomes virtually impossible; in such circumstances some alternative must be found for the normal procedures of criminal justice. In Ireland, both North and South, this has traditionally been detention and internment without trial. In the inter-war and post-war years it had been accepted that the use of internment was necessary to public order. Neither Whitehall nor the army was particularly keen on the idea. Reluctantly, in the face of the increasing violence in August and under pressure from Faulkner, Reginald Maudling, the Home Secretary, gave his consent. The arrest operation began on 0430 hours on 9 August and predictably caused a violent reaction throughout the Province. The net was cast fairly wide and internees varied from known terrorists to comparatively harmless pamphleteers.

On 6 October Faulkner announced that three more battalions would be deployed in Ulster, bringing the troop level to 13,600. Most of these additional troops were deployed in the border areas where troops cratering border crossing points regularly came under fire from terrorist groups inside Éire. During 1971 forty-three British soldiers were killed. The newly formed Ulster Defence Regiment (UDR), composed mainly of part-time soldiers, had five men killed, the RUC another eleven. In addition sixty-one civilians died in the violence during the year. Fifty-two Republican terrorists were killed by the security forces.

On 30 January 1972 occurred in Londonderry what has since become known as Bloody Sunday. A Sunday afternoon protest march was infiltrated by hooligans determined to provoke a confrontation with the troops policing the march. The Brigade Commander decided to mount an operation to attempt to arrest some of the hooligans who by 3.30 p.m. were hurling stones, bricks and even CS grenades at his soldiers. Although shots had been fired at soldiers as early as 4 p.m., at 5.55 p.m. a shot was fired at soldiers of the 1st Battalion The Parachute Regiment (1 Para) who were in occupation of a house in William Street. Immediately following this incident two soldiers from 1 Para shot dead a man lighting a nail bomb. Minutes later 1 Para went into the area of the Rossville Flats from three directions in an attempt to cut off as many of the hooligans as possible. As they dismounted from their Pigs (wheeled armoured personnel carriers) they came under fire. A burst from what was probably a Thompson sub-machine gun struck the ground around them. It seemed to come from the Rossville Flats. Simultaneously one or more gunmen opened up from the direction of Rossville Street. Then several nail bombs were thrown at the Para soldiers. What looked like three armed men were seen running across the open ground in front of the flats and were engaged. It was at this stage and during the minutes that followed that thirteen civilians died of gunshot wounds. Their deaths attracted great publicity and 1 Para were accused of sheer unadulterated murder by the Londonderry City Coroner. The controversy has raged ever since and has been given new impetus by the British government's decision in spring 2000 to allow a second inquiry to take place. Certainly the original Widgery Report published on 10 April 1972 appeared to be pretty clear in its findings. Quite what purpose a second inquiry will serve is not easy to discern. Conclusion 1 of the Widgery Report read: 'There would have been no deaths in Londonderry on 30 January if those who organised the illegal march had not thereby created a highly dangerous situation in which a clash between demonstrators and the security forces was almost inevitable.' Conclusion 3 read: 'If the Army had persisted in its "low key" attitude and had not launched a large scale operation to arrest hooligans the day might have passed off without serious incident.' Conclusion 7 read: 'When the vehicles and soldiers of Support Company [of 1 Para] appeared in Rossville Street they came under fire. Arrests were made; but in a very short time the arrest operation took second place and the soldiers turned to engage their assailants. There is no reason to suppose that the soldiers would have opened fire if they had not been fired upon first.' Conclusion 8 read: 'Soldiers who identified armed gunmen fired upon them in accordance with the standing orders in the Yellow Card [which regulated the use of firearms in such situations]. Each soldier was his own judge of whether he had identified a gunman. Their training made them aggressive and quick in decision and some showed more restraint in opening fire than others. At one end of the scale some soldiers showed a high degree of responsibility; at the other, notably in Glenfada Park, firing bordered on the reckless. These distinctions reflect differences in the character and temperament of the soldiers concerned.' Finally Conclusion 11 read: 'There was no general breakdown in discipline. For the most part the soldiers acted as they did because they thought their orders required it. No order and no training can ensure that a soldier will always act wisely, as well as bravely and with initiative. The individual soldier ought not to have to bear the burden of deciding whether to open fire in confusion such as prevailed on 30 January. In the conditions prevailing in Northern Ireland, however, this is often inescapable.'[1]

These paragraphs really say it all. There must be an inherent danger in using troops who are trained for war and to be aggressive in a situation such as so often prevailed in Ulster. Much later in the 1980s the IRA accused the security forces of a so-called shoot to kill policy. In fact there was never such a policy, but of course there were circumstances when British troops took every opportunity given to them providing the Rules of Engagement applied to shoot dead gunmen or bombers engaged in a terrorist act. As attrition of the IRA by the security forces increased in the 1980s, resulting directly from increasingly accurate intelligence, it suited IRA propaganda purposes to allege a shoot to kill policy. Mistakes were undoubtedly made, as will always be the case in split-second life or death decisions, but there is no evidence whatsoever that a shoot to kill policy ever pertained. Similarly on Bloody Sunday, whilst the evidence suggests some soldiers were more robust in their reaction than others, the Paras did not set out to murder unarmed civilians, as is alleged by some republican elements. In the untidy business of warfare, unfortunately such incidents occur.

An open verdict was recorded on the victims of Bloody Sunday at the inquest in Londonderry. As a military operation the Para sortie into the Bogside was highly successful; the political consequences though were catastrophic.

The bombing campaign reached its height in 1972. There were 1,853 bomb incidents, among the most horrific of which were the Aldershot Officers' Mess bomb in February, which killed seven people; the Abercorn Restaurant explosion in March, which killed two girls and injured many more; the many bombs of Bloody Friday, 21 July, which killed seven people in Belfast; the virtual destruction of the village of Claudy on 31 July by three enormous car bombs, which killed six people; and the 500lb bomb which exploded on 10 September under a Saracen armoured personnel carrier on patrol in County Tyrone, which was large enough to throw the vehicle and its occupants off the road and over a hedge, killing three soldiers. 1972 saw more violence than any other year in the campaign. There were more bombings, more shootings, more soldiers killed, more terrorists killed and more civilian casualties. Many Irishmen could not believe that it had come to this. The despair of the majority of the people was pitiful to behold.

The army, despite the enormous pressure it was now under, managed to keep up the pressure on the IRA. Perhaps the greatest success of 1972 was Operation MOTORMAN, which took place on 31 July. For months the Provisionals had controlled the Creggan and Bogside areas of Londonderry as well as parts of Belfast. These areas had become so-called no-go areas for the security forces. Intelligence indicated that an attempt to take the no-go areas, in which gunmen openly patrolled and manned roadblocks, would result in massive civilian casualties. The political decision was therefore taken not to interfere, thus permitting gun law to rule for a time in parts of two cities of the United Kingdom. Finally, however, it was decided enough was enough. Among the armoured vehicles that went into the Bogside were four Royal Engineer Centurion bulldozer tanks, specially brought into the Province for the operation, which quickly removed the barricades. A parallel operation in Belfast involving eleven battalions went off equally smoothly. There was in fact little resistance in either Londonderry or Belfast though two snipers were shot dead by security forces. Most importantly a military presence was re-established in the no-go areas.

The incidence of terrorism in the area of the border with the Republic increased in 1971 and 1972. By 1973 regiments deployed in Fermanagh, Tyrone and Armagh were having a particularly busy time. It was in the rural areas that the regiments of the Royal Armoured Corps came into their own. Their Saracens, Ferrets and Saladins were proof against small-arms fire but vulnerable to the culvert and milk-churn bombs that the IRA were now beginning to use with increasing regularity. South Armagh, usually referred to as bandit country by the press, became in the years 1973–9 probably the most dangerous area in Northern Ireland. Cross-border gun battles regularly took place and army bases such as Crossmaglen could only be supplied by helicopter. The part played by the Puma and Wessex helicopters of the RAF and the smaller Sioux, Scout, Gazelle and Lynx helicopters of the Army Air Corps was vital.

There were, of course, any number of gun battles fought between the IRA and the security forces during the thirty-year war against the IRA. One of these took place on 31 August 1973. On the morning of that day a corporal from the 3rd Battalion The Royal Green Jackets accompanied by a rifleman climbed stealthily into the attic of a flat directly overlooking a circle of open ground surrounded by council houses known as the Bullring. A hole in the roof, caused by some missing tiles, afforded them a good view of the Bullring and the roads leading off it. This was part of a pattern of three or four Observation Posts or OPs that were maintained to collect tactical intelligence and maintain general surveillance over the area. Soldiers would stay in the OPs for several days on end then, if the position had not been compromised, they would be relieved by another team.

At 1830 hours that evening it was the corporal's turn on duty. He was bored and had seen nothing of interest all day. He noticed an olive-green Hillman Hunter approaching the Bullring. Suddenly to his astonishment he saw three rifles sticking out of the window. Before he could do much the car drove off out of sight. He reported on his radio to Company HQ all he had seen. Moments later another OP reported on the radio net that the car was continuing to cruise around the area followed by a red van. It subsequently transpired that what in fact was happening was that Jim Bryson, a notorious IRA terrorist responsible for the murders of a number of British soldiers and who had recently escaped from custody, was driving round Ballymurphy accompanied by three leading PIRA terrorists, Paddy Mulvenna, ex-adjutant and commander of the Ballymurphy Company, Bimbo O'Rawe and Frank Duffy, partly to demonstrate disregard for the army and partly to humiliate the Officials.

The Hillman followed by the red van reappeared in the Bullring, motored slowly around it and then stopped at a junction some forty metres beyond. The occupants got out and Bryson began to direct them to ambush positions. The corporal carefully moved one of the tiles in front of him to one side to get a better view and to create a cramped fire position for himself. As he did so he inadvertently dislodged a tile which clattered down onto the ground, alerting the ambush party to his presence, one of whom fired in the general direction of the OP. The corporal immediately fired four rounds although he could scarcely aim in his cramped position. He was forced to pull his rifle in when it developed a stoppage. In the interval which followed Bryson and his gang made good their escape in the cars as, when the corporal looked again, the road was empty. Their position now compromised, the corporal and the rifleman set about enlarging the hole by kicking more tiles out. The corporal stuck his head out to try and get a better view and withdrew it sharply as two rounds hit the roof. He fired three quick rounds at a gunman he glimpsed but missed.

Thinking that the gunmen were now making good their escape both soldiers hurriedly prepared to leave their OP. As they were doing so, the corporal was amazed to see the Hillman returning to the same junction. Ironically Bryson had become confused by the problem that had faced so many British soldiers in Belfast, that of determining where the fire had come from. In built-up areas it is virtually impossible to tell from which direction a shot is fired, the crack and thump of a high-velocity round echoing and re-echoing off the walls of the tightly knit Belfast streets. Bryson, thinking he was driving into danger, had thrown his car into a wild U-turn. As they came back into view the corporal fired at the accelerating Hillman, trying to incapacitate it before it reached the corner. The first rounds hit O'Rawe in the shoulder and catapulted him from the back seat into the front of the car. Then a 7.62mm round entered the back of Bryson's neck. As he slumped forward the car careered into the small front garden of 99 Ballymurphy Road. The corporal and rifleman watched the car crash some 180 metres away and took the opportunity to jump down from the OP in the attic to the flat below where they took up fire positions to cover the car.

Mulvenna was the first to recover; he flung open the door of the car

33. Former Dhofari rebels, who declared for the Sultan, and joined the Firqa. The two men on the left are equipped with US M203 40mm grenade launchers attached to their M16A2 rifles. The man on the right has a British Self-loading Rifle.

34. The fort at Marbat, scene of the battle in July 1972.

35. The view down from Sarfait on 'Capstan', the next plateau down the 4,000 foot escarpment during the monsoon, showing typical sangars and positions with overhead protection.

36. A parachute soldier making an arrest, March 1971.

37. Soldiers in riot gear with a 'pig' armoured one-ton truck.

38. Lieutenant Colonel 'Big' John Mottram, the CO of 40 Commando Royal Marines, being interviewed by the media after removing barricades in the New Lodge area of Belfast during Operation Motorman in July 1972. Interviewing servicemen in Northern Ireland, commonplace in the 1970s, is almost unheard of now.

39. A soldier of the Black Watch in a covering position while on border patrol in 1987.

40. An Argentine Mirage Dagger overflies the LSL *Sir Bedivere* in San Carlos Water. The *Sir Bedivere* survived a bomb which skipped off the head of her crane and passed through a bulwark forward without exploding.

41. A member of HMS *Cardiff*'s deck party sitting on a Sea Skua fitted to a Lynx helicopter. Sea Skua is an anti-surface vessel missile with a range of 15 kilometres.

42. Two marines of 45 Commando Royal Marines brewing up in their slit trench somewhere on East Falkland.

43. Men of 45 Commando Royal Marines walk into Stanley, having marched all the way across from San Carlos Water.

44. A Tornado F3 flies over an Iraqi airfield, showing bomb damage to hardened hangars.

45. A Type 42 destroyer and a *Hunt*-class minesweeper in the Gulf.

6. A British Gazelle helicopter hovers over scenes of death and destruction on the Basra Road.

47. A Warrior armoured infantry fighting vehicle of 1st Battalion the Cheshire Regiment crossing a bridge in Bosnia. Part of the United Nations Protection Force (UNPROFOR), the Cheshires and their successors had the unenviable task of securing safe routes for aid convoys, in a high-profile political operation obfuscated by the often conflicting and unreasonable demands of a burgeoning number of self-important Non-Governmental [Aid] Organisations (NGOs).

48. A Bosnian sniper with a 7.92mm Yugoslavian Crvena Zastava M-76. This is a posed photograph which plays to the macho-poseur streak in most of the Balkan soldiers irrespective of which side they are on. The position adopted is very unprofessional, being far too close to the window with his rifle barrel protruding through.

49. A Serb T-72 tank destroyed by air attack in Kosovo. Most of the Serb army got away unscathed.

50. A KFOR armoured personnel carrier outside a Serb Greek Orthodox church near Istok, May 2000.

and rolled onto the ground from where he engaged the OP with his Armalite. Duffy also began to fire from the back of the car with an M1 carbine. Mulvenna then decided to make a run for it. As he did so the corporal fired three shots, two of which hit, and Mulvenna died instantly. The next to go was Bimbo O'Rawe who, though wounded, was still clutching a Garand as he ran towards the front door of 99 Ballymurphy Road. Again the corporal fired three shots hitting O'Rawe as he pitched forward inside the house. He then turned his attention to Duffy, who was firing wildly as he sprinted away down the road. The corporal fired but missed.[2]

When reinforcements arrived they found Mulvenna dead, Bryson unconscious and O'Rawe badly wounded. Bryson died three weeks later. In the follow-up thirteen rifles and pistols and large quantities of ammunition and explosives were found. The perseverance, alertness and good shooting of the two soldiers in the OP had rid Ulster of three heartless murderers. That August six gunmen were killed in all, bringing the total number of terrorists put out of action in one way or another to 2,265 including 195 Protestants. In Belfast the three Provisional battalions ceased to exist. In their place the Provisionals created small Active Service Units (ASUs) based on the communist cell system whereby members would be known only to others in the same unit, and whose commanders would be directly responsible to the Belfast Commander, Ivor Bell. Ironically the Provisionals were convinced that Bryson had been eliminated by the Officials; no one had of course seen from where the shots had come. Soldiers only appeared on the scene after the event. It suited the army to perpetuate the myth.

The experiment in Direct Rule from Westminster ended on 31 December 1973, having been imposed in March the previous year. The Sunningdale Agreement of 9 December 1973 produced a power-sharing formula that would involve representatives of all sections of the community in a new Executive to replace the old Assembly. On 23 January 1974 the Loyalists walked out of Stormont. The political in-fighting worsened until on 15 May the Ulster Workers' Council called a general strike with the purpose of forcing the British government to shelve the Sunningdale Agreement and the power-sharing Executive. The strike was chillingly effective and demonstrated clearly that, without the support of the majority, the power-sharing Executive could not get off the ground. Direct rule was resumed in June.

Meanwhile the process of slowly handing over control to the RUC was starting. At the time of Operation MOTORMAN there were 21,000 British troops in Ulster; by July 1974 this had been reduced to 15,000. The pace did not lessen, however, in South Armagh which became known in the press as the Murder Triangle. Fortunately, at an early stage in the campaign the army had set up bases at Crossmaglen, Newtownhamilton, Forkhill, Bessbrook and other border towns. South Armagh had always been a republican stronghold and it was easy for the Provisionals to operate from such towns as Dundalk across the border. The border itself meanders through fields and hedgerows. It is difficult to know precisely where it runs, let alone guard it or block it in any way. The army has always been the first to admit that the IRA can cross the border almost at will. It soon became far too dangerous for the army to operate in vehicles in the border area; the distinctive whine of an armoured vehicle could be heard kilometres away and made an easy target for a remotely detonated mine in the narrow winding lanes. Instead soldiers moved stealthily on foot or by helicopter. The base at Crossmaglen was exclusively supplied by helicopter except for occasional heavily escorted and picqueted convoys bringing in heavy plant and equipment.

The authorities felt strong enough to end Internment without Trial on 5 December 1975. Its long-term utility was doubtful, though it may have served its purpose as short-term palliative in the worst years of 1970–75. Throughout 1976 and 1977 the security forces changed their tactics towards more targeted operations with the introduction of the SAS into Northern Ireland on 8 June 1977.

In August 1979 a command-detonated mine killed eighteen mostly Parachute Regiment soldiers who were travelling in the back of a four-ton truck along a main road adjacent to the border and close to the village of Warrenpoint. As the incident had occurred in his area of responsibility Lieutenant Colonel David Blair, Commanding Officer of the Queen's Own Highlanders, landed by helicopter to assess the situation. He ran from the helicopter towards the side of the road whereupon the terrorists watching the scene from across the border detonated a second device which immediately killed him. So close was he to the explosion that his remains have never been found. In the same week Earl Mountbatten of Burma was killed in Éire while on a fishing trip in his boat with members of his family. His death and the holocaust at Warrenpoint stunned the nation and the world.

The IRA, meanwhile, started to prepare for what they called a long war. This marked a realization on their part that they could not defeat the British army. At the same time British military commanders acknowledged that there was a limit to what could be achieved by military means alone. The army strategy was to contain the IRA by disrupting their operations, by causing as many casualties as possible in their ranks and by keeping the level of violence as low as possible to allow both influences to work.

Whilst the IRA had initiated bomb atrocities on the British mainland before, in particular for instance in the Birmingham pub bombings on 21 November 1974 which killed nineteen and injured 182, it was not until much later that they launched a wider war in earnest. Already in 1980 they had targeted British troops in Germany but in October and November 1981 they initiated a bombing campaign in London: on 20 July 1982 a bomb explosion in Regents Park killed six bandsmen of The Royal Green Jackets giving an afternoon concert to the public and on the same day a second bomb killed men and horses of the Household Cavalry in Hyde Park.

In October 1984, during the Conservative Party Conference at the Grand Hotel, Brighton, the most audacious attack of the entire IRA campaign took place, against the Prime Minister, Margaret Thatcher. A bomb, secreted weeks beforehand by an IRA team, demolished the centre of the hotel, killing two and nearly killing the Prime Minister. This event gave added impetus to the political process and a year later, in November 1985, the Anglo-Irish Agreement was concluded. The war, however, continued with the adoption by the army of new tactics, employing the SAS to act on more precise intelligence provided by an increasingly successful intelligence network penetrating deeper and deeper into the terrorist infrastructure: on 8 May 1987 the SAS ambushed and killed eight known PIRA terrorists as they attacked a police station at Loughgall. The IRA hit back the following November with the perpetration of an appalling atrocity when they planted a bomb at the Remembrance Day service at Enniskillen killing eleven civilians and injuring sixty-one.

With many more seizures of illegal weapons and bomb-making equipment and arrests by the security forces, in 1988 the IRA again sought to take the war abroad. After a highly successful intelligence and surveillance operation, the SAS confronted and killed three IRA terrorists in Gibraltar who were planning to plant a bomb. But despite these SAS successes, the IRA remained an effective terrorist organization: in the spring and summer of 1988 alone, two British army corporals were dragged from their car and murdered in Belfast in March, six soldiers taking part in a charity run were murdered by a bomb detonated under their van in June, and eight soldiers of the Light Infantry were killed by a remotely detonated bomb while travelling in a bus near Omagh in August.

In the middle of the Gulf War, in February 1991, the IRA managed to park a flat-bed truck in Whitehall and lob a number of mortar bombs into the back garden of 10 Downing Street. This, of course, was a brilliant publicity stunt by the IRA, but it was in the midst of a relentless and increasingly successful campaign against the IRA by the security forces in Northern Ireland. In February 1992 four more terrorists were shot dead by the SAS at Dernagh and in September there were more large finds of weapons, munitions and explosives by security forces at Strabane and Castlewellan.

By this stage informal talks between Gerry Adams, the President of Sinn Féin, and John Hume, the leader of the Social Democratic and Labour Party (SDLP), had been going on for four years. The first meeting took place on 11 January 1988 and was probably the start of the process which led to the IRA's announcement of its cessation of military action on 31 August 1994. It seems that the IRA had by late 1992 probably accepted that they were not going to beat the British army and indeed that they were increasingly getting the worst of the military confrontation in Northern Ireland itself. They therefore decided on a last bombing campaign on the mainland as a demonstration of their power and as a negotiating tactic prior to any peace talks. The campaign started in November 1992 with a series of bomb attacks in London as well as in Warrington and North Shields. The Bishopsgate bomb caused massive damage in the City of London on 24 April 1993. The British police brought the campaign to an end by July by making a number of arrests and uncovering several bomb factories.

In August the following year, therefore, the IRA called its ceasefire and the British government reciprocated with a series of troop reductions. But the progress in negotiations achieved by Sinn Féin was rejected by the IRA when they exploded a 1,000lb bomb in London's Docklands on 9 February 1996. A series of other bombs in London culminated in the IRA detonating another 1,000lb bomb in Manchester on 15 June, injuring over 200. This was the last bomb exploded by PIRA on the British mainland. Since then breakaway factions of the IRA, the so-called Continuity IRA and the Real IRA, have exploded a number of devices on both the British mainland and in Northern Ireland, the most notorious of which was the bombing in Omagh High Street on 15 August 1998. This caused such horror worldwide that even the Continuity IRA called a ceasefire.

After two years of talks, which were never truly inclusive of all political parties in Northern Ireland, an agreement was reached on Good Friday, 10 April 1998. The agreement was endorsed in two separate referenda, in Northern Ireland and the Republic of Ireland, on the same day, 22 May 1998. There were delays in fully implementing the agreement as Unionists refused to establish the various institutions of devolved government until there was movement on the issue of decommissioning paramilitary weapons. Following a review of the working of the agreement Unionists were persuaded to enter into an Executive with Sinn Féin and devolution of powers from Westminster to Stormont occurred on 2 December 1999.

At the beginning of February 2000 Unionists remained unhappy at the lack of progress on decommissioning and indicated that they would resign from the Executive. On 3 February 2000 the British government announced that it would introduce legislation to suspend the Executive and the institutions of government in Northern Ireland and reintroduce direct rule from Westminster.

The reimposition of direct rule was not to last long. With the IRA initiative to allow the inspection of their arms dumps by neutral observers to confirm that they had been put beyond use, the Unionists agreed by a small majority in early summer 2000 that the Executive be reinstated.

In August 2000 an uneasy peace prevailed. On the 11th the RUC intercepted a 500lb car bomb no doubt intended to attack the Londonderry Orange marches on the 12th. There are still those who would destroy the peace process. But it would seem the corner has been turned.

The vast majority both north and south of the border desperately want peace. The infrastructure of war is being slowly dismantled. This time, just perhaps, peace may come to Northern Ireland.

The British army has been transformed by its thirty-year experience in Northern Ireland. It has had to learn – often painfully – the complications and subtleties of operating in support of the civil power, with relatively limited powers itself in what has at times amounted to a state of war. Keeping two bitterly opposed communities apart has often been, particularly during the 'marching season', their unfortunate task. This acquired expertise has stood the British army in good stead in Bosnia and Kosovo. During the Northern Ireland Emergency, the security forces reduced violence and the potential of the IRA to achieve damage, disruption and destruction to a degree that in the dark days of the early 1970s often seemed impossible. Within the current constraints of the law, it would have been difficult for the army and the RUC to have reduced the level of violence much further. Unless the conditions of a police state are imposed – unthinkable in the context of British Parliamentary democracy – the terrorist can always operate with relative ease. And there is a limit to what can be achieved by military means alone. The security forces' role in Northern Ireland always had to be, to a certain extent, reactive, though as intelligence gathering improved over the years it was possible to wrest the initiative from the gunman and the bomber more often. A purely military victory in Northern Ireland therefore has never really been on the cards. The security forces' task has been to keep the level of violence as low as possible in order that other influences can work. The only permanent solution to the Irish problem must be a political one. It remains to be seen whether politicians both north and south of the border have the imagination and courage to grasp the opportunity which now faces them. One thing is certain, however: the opportunity would not have been there without the sacrifice of the British army and the RUC, who held the ring for thirty years.

13

JULIAN THOMPSON

The Falklands, 1982:
War in the South Atlantic

Julian Thompson joined the Royal Marines a month after his eighteenth birthday and served for thirty-four years, retiring as a major general. His service, mainly in Royal Marines Commandos, took him to seven continents. He commanded the 3rd Commando Brigade, which carried out the initial landings to repossess the Falkland Islands in 1982 and fought most of the subsequent land battles. He is now a visiting professor in the Department of War Studies at King's College, London, and has published seven books on military historical subjects.

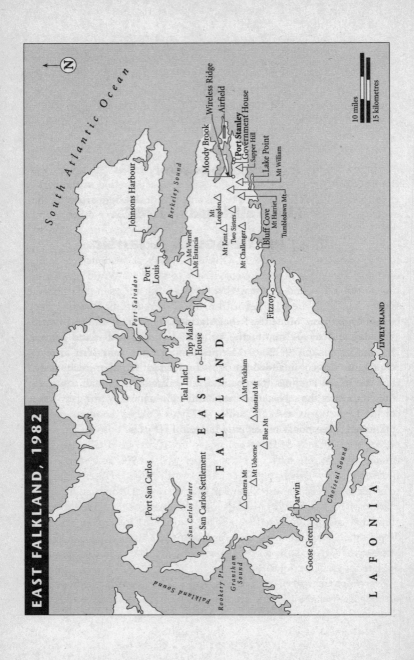

EAST FALKLAND, 1982

South Atlantic Ocean

Johnsons Harbour

Berkeley Sound

Port Salvador

Port Louis

△ Mt Vernet
△ Mt Estancia

Top Malo House

Teal Inlet

EAST

FALKLAND

△ Mt Wickham

△ Mustard Mt

Port San Carlos

San Carlos Water

San Carlos Settlement

△ Cantera Mt

△ Mt Usborne

△ Blue Mt

Grantham Sound

Rookery Pt.

Falkland Sound

Darwin

Goose Green

LAFONIA

Choiseul Sound

Fitzroy

Moody Brook   Wireless Ridge
                    Airfield
                Port Stanley
                Government House

Mt
Longdon △   Sapper Hill
Mt Kent △   Two Sisters △   Lake Point
        Mt Challenger △   Mt William

Bluff Cove
Mt Harriet
Tumbledown Mt.

LIVELY ISLAND

N

10 miles
15 kilometres

At around 9 p.m. local time on 14 June 1982, Brigadier Thompson, the Commander of the 3rd Commando Brigade, was standing in the darkened room of a house occupied by his small tactical headquarters on the outskirts of Port Stanley in the Falkland Islands. In every other room, the soldiers of B Company the 2nd Battalion The Parachute Regiment (2 Para) slept in heaps on the floor, having been marching and fighting for the past seventy-two hours. One of the tactical headquarters radio operators tuned his high-frequency radio to the BBC World Service in time to catch the announcement that the Argentine forces in the Falkland Islands had surrendered. The instrument of surrender had been signed by Major General Menendez, the Argentine Governor of the Islands, and Major General Moore, the commander of British Land Forces Falkland Islands (CLFFI), about an hour before in the Secretariat, around 800 metres from where Thompson was standing. A few minutes later, Captain Bell, the Royal Marines interpreter on Moore's staff, came in and confirmed that what had just been announced by the BBC was correct.

The next morning, the Governor's Union Flag was raised once more on the flagstaff outside Government House. It had been taken back to Britain by the Marines of Naval Party (NP) 8901 following their surrender to overwhelming force on 2 April. Many of these Marines returned to the Falklands as part of J Company, 42 Commando Royal Marines. The flag had been down for just seventy-four days. An operation that many considered impossible had ended in dazzling success, despite the many doubters, who included the US Navy, many in the Ministry of Defence, the Army Department, the RAF and the Secretary of State for Defence, John Knott.

Ever since the end of the Second World War, Argentina had claimed sovereignty over the Falkland Islands (the Malvinas to them), and South Georgia. The political situation had blown hot and cold over the years while the islands remained a British colony inhabited by people of entirely British stock, as they had been without a break since 1833, and intermittently for decades before that. Matters were brought to a head with the accession in November 1981 of a new Argentine junta, headed by General Galtieri, who immediately gave orders to the relevant head-quarters to prepare plans to seize the islands and South Georgia, 1,300 kilometres to the south-east of the Falklands.

The catalyst for the Argentine invasion was the arrival in South Georgia in mid-March 1982 of Argentine scrap-metal workers and a party of marines, landed from a naval transport, followed by the raising of the Argentine flag. The ice patrol ship HMS *Endurance* (Captain Barker) was ordered to return to South Georgia from the Falkland Islands and keep the scrap-metal workers under observation. She left behind in Port Stanley some of her hydrographers and their berths were taken by members of NP 8901 to augment the ship's small detachment.

On 2 April 1982 an Argentine Marine battalion group in armoured tracked amphibians (Amphibious Assault Vehicles or AAVs) landed at Port Stanley.[1] The seventy-strong NP 8901 had no effective means of dealing with these swimming, armoured personnel carriers, equipped with heavy machine guns, and were outnumbered over sixfold. After seeing off part of the Argentine Amphibious Commando Company tasked with seizing the Governor, Rex Hunt, the Royal Marines of NP 8901 were ordered by him to surrender to this overwhelming force which was backed by naval gunfire, artillery and fighter-bombers from the carrier *Veintecinco de Mayo*. In fact the force was even more overwhelming than was apparent at the time, because the Argentines had already started to fly in the 25th Infantry Regiment by C-130s to Stanley Airport.

In South Georgia, *Endurance* had landed the twenty-two-man Royal Marine detachment under the command of Lieutenant Mills RM at King Edward Point. Here, on 3 April, they put up a gallant fight against the Argentine corvette *Guerrico*, damaging her with two anti-tank rounds from a Carl Gustav 84mm recoilless weapon, and some 1,275 hits by GPMG, as well as downing her Puma helicopter by machine-gun fire and forcing her Alouette helicopter to land. Mills surrendered only when *Guerrico* stood off and engaged him with her 3.9in gun, to which he had no answer. The latter part of this action was observed by Lieutenant Commander Ellerbeck in *Endurance*'s Wasp helicopter from a concealed position on the Barff Peninsula. An opportunity to further damage or even sink *Guerrico* was lost when his request to engage her with AS 12 missiles (wire-guided anti-ship missiles fired from helicopters) was refused after orders were received from Whitehall that *Endurance* was to retire to safety among the icebergs south of the island.

For some days before the invasion, intelligence had been building up in Whitehall that the Argentines were up to something, but nothing was done to deter them. However, the Royal Navy had quietly been making some preliminary moves. On 30 March, Rear Admiral Woodward, off Gibraltar with a flotilla on exercise SPRINGTRAIN, was briefed on the deteriorating situation by Admiral Sir John Fieldhouse, the C-in-C Fleet, who was visiting the exercise. On 31 March, the First Sea Lord, Admiral Sir Henry Leach, persuaded the Prime Minister to give approval for a task force to be readied to retake the Falklands should the Argentines invade. Nobody, however, bothered to inform the 3rd Commando Brigade (still at seven days' notice), who would have to play a leading part in the retaking. Early on 1 April some ships were brought to forty-eight hours' notice for sea, but Commodore Clapp, who would command the amphibious group, was not told, and, curiously, neither was the key landing ship HMS *Fearless* (Captain Larken). Eventually, as a result of a late evening cabinet meeting that day, all the available ships had their notice shortened to four hours, and the 3rd Commando Brigade to seventy-two hours. It was the small hours of Friday 2 April before these orders trickled down to many of the ships and units concerned. Rear Admiral Woodward was ordered to sail covertly for Ascension Island with seven of his thirteen Springtrain Group. Having topped up with stores from the six northbounders, the following headed south: HM Ships *Antrim* (Captain Young), *Glamorgan* (Captain Barrow), *Glasgow* (Captain Hoddinot), *Sheffield* (Captain Salt), *Coventry* (Captain Hart-Dyke), *Brilliant* (Captain Coward), *Arrow* (Captain Bootherstone) and *Plymouth* (Captain Pentreath), and Royal Fleet Auxiliaries (RFA) *Appleleaf* (Captain MacDougall) and *Tidespring* (Captain Redmond). Three nuclear-powered submarines were also on their way south, *Spartan* (Commander Taylor), *Conqueror* (Commander Wreford-Brown) – with number 6 Section of the Special Boat Service (SBS) embarked, and *Splendid* (Commander Lane-Nott).

Starting on 6 April, a greatly expanded 3rd Commando Brigade sailed south. The intervening days were spent in planning, briefings, and loading of the Brigade's men, ammunition and other warlike stores into a variety of ships, including merchant ships taken up from trade (or STUFT for short). Units were to be added to the Brigade as the days went by, and on arrival in the theatre of operations it consisted of the three Royal Marines Commandos (40, 42, and 45), 2 and 3 Para, a reinforced artillery regiment, a Rapier air defence battery, two troops of the Blues and Royals, a reinforced engineer squadron, a reinforced light helicopter squadron, most of the Special Boat Squadron and two squadrons of 22 SAS, as well as logistic support and other sub-units. The commander of the Amphibious Task Group, Commodore Clapp, and Thompson, commanding the Landing Force Task Group (3rd Commando Brigade reinforced), travelled south in the Headquarters and landing ship HMS *Fearless*.

By now many more ships were steaming south; as well as the carriers HMS *Hermes* (Captain Middleton) and *Invincible* (Captain Black), each with Sea Harriers (SHARs) and anti-submarine helicopters embarked, there were more escorts, RFAs and merchantmen. The latter included the liner *Canberra* (Captain Scott-Masson), carrying 3 Para (Lieutenant Colonel Pike), 40 Commando (Lieutenant Colonel Hunt), and 42 Commando (Lieutenant Colonel Vaux). Most of 45 Commando (Lieutenant Colonel Whitehead) were in RFA *Stromness* (Captain Dickinson). Eventually the 3rd Commando Brigade was distributed in fifteen ships.

On 17 April a council of war was chaired at Ascension Island by Admiral Fieldhouse, who had flown out. By this time the command arrangements 'down south' were settled. All three task group commanders (Woodward commanding the carriers, Clapp and Thompson), were responsible direct to the Commander Task Force (CTF) 317, Admiral Fieldhouse, located in Northwood. A number of matters were raised at this meeting including the requirement for more troops, eventually necessitating the despatch south of the 5th Infantry Brigade, and a divisional headquarters to command the two brigades. Major General Moore would command the division with the somewhat unwieldy title Commander Land Forces Falkland Islands (CLFFI). A key issue emerged at this meeting; by the end of June the overall number of ships available for operations down south would start to diminish from battle damage, and because machinery and equipment would deteriorate through lack of maintenance and rough weather in the southern hemisphere winter. It was consequently necessary to finish the job by that date.

Following the meeting, Woodward continued south with the Carrier Battle Group to start winning sea and air control of the area around the Falkland Islands, and to land Special Forces reconnaissance teams, all necessary before any landings by the 3rd Commando Brigade. The Amphibious Group with 3rd Commando Brigade embarked remained at Ascension to restow the ships into which stores and vehicles had been piled with such haste in Britain that they were not combat-loaded (i.e. stowed so that equipment and stores can be offloaded in the beachhead in the right order). A pause at Ascension would also allow other ships and units of the Amphibious and Landing Force Task Groups that had left Britain after the first wave, or had yet to sail, to catch up.

The outline order of battle of the Argentines on the islands became clearer from intercepts and other intelligence as the days went by. Deployed round Port Stanley was a reinforced infantry brigade of six infantry regiments (each battalion-sized) and a comprehensive gun and surface-to-air (SAM) air-defence system (the numerous 35mm and 30mm air-defence guns were also extremely effective in the ground role). The artillery consisted of thirty-eight 105mm pack howitzers, and three towed 155mm guns. Assessments of enemy strengths at Darwin and Goose Green varied, but eventually proved to be a weak battalion of three companies, each from a different regiment, three 105mm guns and some 30mm air-defence guns. In addition there were nearly 1,000 airmen, because Goose Green was one of the two the major alternative air bases to Stanley (the other was Pebble Island). A brigade of two infantry regiments (battalions) with artillery and air defence garrisoned West Falkland.

From the start the enemy force at Port Stanley alone outnumbered the 3rd Commando Brigade, had more guns, more helicopters, and the added bonus of T34C Mentors, Pucarás, Aermacchi M339s and Augusta Bell 109A attack helicopters positioned in the islands. All these posed a threat to ground forces, and – far more serious – to helicopters. The British declared a sea and air blockade. The former was tightly imposed once the Carrier Battle Group arrived, but not the latter: during the day Argentine fighters were able to penetrate to the islands and carry out attacks up to the last day of the war, and on most nights right up to the end Argentine C-130s landed at Stanley to bring in urgently needed equipment and evacuate casualties. Canberra bombers carried out sporadic raids by night, and the threat posed especially by the Pucarás to helicopters transiting the bare terrain, often with heavy underslung loads, was a constant concern throughout. The efforts of the Carrier Battle Group to keep the skies clear of enemy aircraft cannot be faulted. Without airborne early warning, which had long gone from the British armoury, without considerably more fighters, including night fighters, and possibly another carrier deck, to enable more extensive and continuous Combat Air Patrols (CAP) throughout the day to keep the enemy at arm's length, or grounded, total control of the air was a pipe dream.

South Georgia was retaken on 25 April by a Task Group under command of Captain Young of HMS Antrim, and consisting of HMS Plymouth, HMS Endurance and RFA Tidespring, plus M Company group of 42 Commando, an SBS section and D Squadron 22 SAS. First it was necessary to locate the Argentine garrison. Their strength and locations were not known for sure, but almost certainly they were in Leith and Grytviken. The operation, codenamed PARAQUET, got off to a bad start when an SAS patrol was landed on the Fortuna Glacier with the aim of conducting a reconnaissance of Leith, against the advice of the landing force commander, Major Sheridan RM, an experienced mountaineer. After twenty-four hours they asked to be extracted. This was only achieved after some brilliant flying by Lieutenant Commander Stanley, Antrim's Wessex Mk 3 pilot, but in the process two valuable Wessex Mk 5 helicopters crashed, although their crews were rescued. Further reconnaissance by both the SBS and SAS was frustrated by a combination of high winds and ice in the fjords. At this stage the bulk of M Company was carted miles out to sea in Tidespring following reports of an Argentine submarine in the area, leading to the comment by Captain Barker, 'in military terms the whole operation had become a monumental cock-up'.[2] By now HMS Brilliant had joined the Task Group.

At dawn the following day the submarine Santa Fé was sighted on the surface, on course to attack the Task Group, and was attacked by helicopters with depth charges and missiles. Badly damaged, she fled, under attack all the way, to the pier at King Edward Point, where she remained listing and sinking. Sheridan pressed Young to allow him to land an ad-hoc force of SAS, M Company HQ, the reconnaissance section, and Antrim's Royal Marine detachment in Brilliant's two Lynx and Antrim's Wessex. A Naval Gunfire Forward Observer (NGFO) was landed by Endurance's Wasp who spotted for Antrim's, Brilliant's and

Plymouth's 4.5 in guns, 'walking in' the fall of shot to within a few metres of the Argentines, who hoisted a white flag. The surrender at Leith followed soon after *Plymouth* and *Endurance* appeared in the offing.

The first shot fired, or rather bomb dropped, on the Argentine garrison of the Falkland Islands was delivered by an RAF Vulcan which had flown a 12,650-kilometre round trip from Ascension, to bomb Port Stanley airfield. The aim was to drop at least one bomb on the runway to deny it as a staging field for mainland-based Argentine fast jets. The Vulcan carrying twenty-one 1,000lb bombs required five air-to-air refuelling rendezvous with Victor tankers just to get it to the target, and the same number of refuellings to return to Ascension. It was a heroic task, and admirably carried out. One bomb landed plumb in the centre of the runway, the others did considerable damage around the airfield. It signalled to the Argentines and the Islanders that the British were coming.

Woodward followed up the Vulcan attack with twelve Sea Harriers (SHARs) in three waves, two to attack Port Stanley airfield again, the third to hit Goose Green. In case of Argentine reaction, the CAP (Combat Air Patrol, the aircraft over the Carrier Battle Group that would see off enemy aircraft or attack ground targets in support of ground forces) would be provided by a further six SHARs. He wanted to keep the Argentines guessing as to the eventual landing place by the Amphibious Group, while hinting that it would be near Port Stanley. He aimed to draw out the enemy air and surface forces, to achieve sea and air control. He realized that he risked losing large numbers of the all too few SHARs, but as he said, 'You don't win the lottery unless you buy a ticket.'[3] In the event the raid was successful, and no SHARs were lost. The remainder of that first day of action was full of incident. *Glamorgan*, *Arrow* and *Alacrity* (Commander Craig) bombarded Stanley airfield, while *Brilliant* and *Yarmouth* (Commander Morton) carried out an anti-submarine offensive to the north-east of Stanley. Four Mentors were sent from Stanley to attack *Brilliant* and *Yarmouth* but were driven off by SHARs. Later in the day, the Argentine air force mounted a concerted attack consisting of forty aircraft against the Carrier Battle Group, but although there were some near misses on the ships on the gun line, none got through to the carriers. Several Argentine aircraft were shot down and two key airfields were damaged, for no losses on the British side.

Never again did the Argentine air force attempt to engage the SHARs in air-to-air combat. However, the Argentine navy was now shaping up for a pincer attack on the Carrier Battle Group.

The northern pincer consisted of the carrier *Veintecinco de Mayo* carrying ten A-4 Skyhawks, and three escorts armed with Exocet missiles. The cruiser *Belgrano* and her two Exocet-equipped escorts constituted the southern pincer. Woodward anticipated a thirty-bomb attack from the Skyhawks on his two carriers, possibly thickened up by a salvo of surface-launched Exocets from the *Veintecinco de Mayo* group, and while he was dealing with that, the *Belgrano* group could swing in from the south, and launch yet more Exocets. Both groups could close during the long southern hemisphere winter night. *Belgrano* may have been old, but she was armoured, and with fifteen 6in guns and eight 5in, all bigger than any in the British Task Group, she would be difficult to sink by gunfire or Exocet, and could also 'dish it out'. The *Belgrano* group was being shadowed by *Conqueror*, but neither of the nuclear powered attack submarines (SSNs) in the north were in contact with the *Veintecinco de Mayo*, so for the moment there was nothing Woodward could do about the enemy carrier, except stand by to be attacked. He decided to attack the southern pincer. To do so he had to obtain a change in the Rules of Engagement (ROE) so that *Conqueror* could attack *Belgrano* outside the Total Exclusion Zone, although she was still inside the General Warning Area announced in April (that all enemy warships outside the Argentine twelve-mile territorial limit were liable to be attacked without warning). The necessary change to the ROE having been approved by the Prime Minister, *Conqueror* duly attacked and sank *Belgrano*. Later much was made by the tiny anti-war faction in Britain of the fact that *Belgrano* was heading away, but Woodward was not to know that she might not reverse course, and at the stage she was sunk the Argentine carrier group still posed a threat as far as he knew. The notion that the Prime Minister deliberately ordered the sinking of the *Belgrano* to 'torpedo' peace moves in the UN is nonsense. The high casualties among her crew were the fault of her captain: *Belgrano* was not zigzagging, and the ship was at the lowest state of damage control, with all water-tight doors and hatches open.

It later transpired that because conditions in the South Atlantic that day were unusually windless, the *Veintecinco de Mayo*, whose catapult was defective, could not launch her Skyhawks, so she turned away. After

Belgrano was sunk, the Argentine navy remained in port for the rest of the war; which could have done little for the ego of Admiral Anaya, the arrogant C-in-C of the Argentine navy, the most hawkish member of the junta, and moving spirit behind the invasion of the Falkland Islands.

Sea control was won, the battle for air control continued. Two days later the Argentine naval air arm struck back with air-launched Exocets from Super Étendards, hit HMS *Sheffield* and damaged her so badly she was eventually abandoned and sank. Twenty sailors were killed and twenty-four wounded.

Most nights, and once more by day, ships closed the coast to bombard the enemy, while Special Forces patrols from the SAS and SBS were landed by night to prepare the way for the landing by the 3rd Commando Brigade. The daylight bombardment of Port Stanley on 12 May saw a concerted attack by three waves of A-4s on *Glasgow* and *Brilliant*. Two A-4s in the first wave were shot down by *Brilliant*, one crashed into the sea trying to evade and the fourth dropped two bombs, both of which just missed *Glasgow*, whose Sea Dart and gun had chosen that moment to jam. *Glasgow*'s gun (but not her Sea Dart) was fixed in time to receive the second wave, but *Brilliant* asked *Glasgow* to cease firing with her gun because the shells were producing confusing tracks on the radar. Except for GPMG gunners on her upper deck, *Glasgow* was defenceless as the fighter-bombers came barrelling in, weaving and confusing *Brilliant*'s missile radar. Two bombs skipped over *Brilliant* like ducks and drakes, one hit *Glasgow* just above the waterline, passing through to leave two gaping holes through which tons of water poured. Miraculously, no one was even injured, and the damage control parties had the situation sorted out within thirty minutes. The next wave of four A-4s decided to call it a day, perhaps put off by what had happened to their predecessors, or possibly because the A-4 which had hit *Glasgow* and had suffered damage from her GPMG gunners in return was shot down by his own side as he headed for home over Goose Green, which could not have been good for morale. *Glasgow* was patched up and back on line within three days.

The runways at Stanley and Goose Green were also attacked several times during this period. The second Vulcan sortie on 4 May was unsuccessful, but the SHARs persisted, without, however, managing to land any bombs on the Stanley runway. Nevertheless considerable damage was caused to parked aircraft and stores on both airfields.

On the night of 14/15 May forty-five men of D Squadron 22 SAS and an NGFO party carried out a highly successful raid on Pebble Island. Having landed some distance away from the airstrip, in four Sea Kings from *Hermes*, the SAS destroyed six Pucarás, one Skyvan and four Mentors, plus ammunition dumps, for one soldier wounded. *Glamorgan* provided supporting fire to cover the party's withdrawal. The position of this airstrip off the northern entrance of Falkland Sound posed a threat to the landings which were planned for San Carlos Water on East Falkland just inside the Sound.

Meanwhile the Amphibious Task Group had left Ascension in two waves, the slower Landing Ships Logistic (LSLs) sailing on 30 April, followed by the main body on 7 May. Both groups rendezvoused with the Carrier Battle Group on 18 May, a total of thirty-two ships in company, a brave sight to those who were there. Less encouraging was the news that the Argentines now knew that a landing was imminent thanks to a BBC World Service announcement, which can only have been cleared by someone senior in the MOD. This was neither the first nor last indiscretion by Whitehall. Earlier, Clapp had taken pains to conceal the departure of the Amphibious Group from Ascension by means of an electronic deception plan, only to hear the Secretary of State for Defence announce it on the BBC.

Approval for the planned landing on three beaches at San Carlos Water had been given only on 12 May. This plan, devised by Clapp and Thompson and their staffs, working jointly, was sent to the Task Force Headquarters at Northwood before the amphibs sailed from Ascension. Two other potential beachheads had been included in the proposal which General Moore took back personally after he had visited Clapp and Thompson to be briefed on the plan and the rationale behind it. With hindsight there was no other place that provided all the advantages of San Carlos Water for a landing that, for lack of sufficient helicopters, relied almost totally on landing craft. The only disadvantage from Thompson's point of view was the distance to Port Stanley, the operational objective, eighty kilometres as the crow flies. The upside was that the Argentines would have to move guns and troops this same distance if they were to attack the beachhead. The downside was the similar effort that would have to be made by the British moving in the reverse direction, with, initially, fewer helicopters than the enemy. There were no roads in the Falklands outside Port Stanley and a rough track from

Fitzroy to Stanley. The terrain was all peat bog and moorland hills crowned with huge rocky spinebacks. Rivers of boulders, aptly named stone runs, proliferated; some were kilometres long and hundreds of metres wide. Wheeled vehicles carrying a load or towing guns could get nowhere. The Commando Brigade had taken south seventy-six tracked BV 202 oversnow vehicles (Bandwagons), on the premise, correct as it transpired, that with the same ground pressure as a man on skis, they could traverse the peat. They were not designed as load-carriers, and the majority were allocated to brigade and unit headquarters to carry the heavier radios, and for carrying essential ammunition and heavier equipment required right forward. Once ashore, guns, ammunition, rations and most heavy equipment would have to be moved by helicopter. Pending the arrival in the beachhead of five Chinooks carried in the container ship *Atlantic Conveyor* (Captain North), the helicopter lift available was pitifully small. Until *Atlantic Conveyor* arrived, tactical troop lift would have to come a long way second to logistics, and, above all, the guns and their ammunition.

At 2215 local on 20 May, HMS *Yarmouth* preceded the Amphibious Group towards Falkland Sound to take up her anti-submarine station across the northern entrance. She was followed by a ghostly file of eighteen ships which

> slid quietly and darkly through the northern entrance to Falkland Sound. Certainly no navigation lights gave the game away and not one candle power of light shone out from behind the blackout screens. Yet behind those screens five battalions of men, plus their support, were completing last-minute preparations: large breakfasts, blackening of faces, the umpteenth checking of magazines and bayonets.[4]

As the two LPDs, *Fearless* and *Intrepid* (Captain Dingemans), came to their anchorages off Chancho Point, the flashes of bursting 4.5in shells could be seen on Fannings Head, at the northern entrance to San Carlos Water. Here a half-company of Argentines with a 105mm recoilless anti-tank gun were being engaged by *Antrim*, whose fire was being directed by an NGFO landed by helicopter earlier that night, with a strong SBS party, commanded by the OC, Major Thomson. On the other side of East Falkland, *Glamorgan* was shelling the beaches in the vicinity of Berkeley Sound to divert the enemy's attention in that direction. General Menendez, the Argentine Governor, was woken to be told of her activity, but so far the rattling of anchor cables and the sound of landing craft engines in Falkland Sound had gone unremarked. Meanwhile D Squadron 22 SAS, supported by *Ardent* (Commander West), was attacking Darwin to keep the Argentines there pinned down and prevent them from interfering with the landings.

Despite a number of snags, by breakfast time on 21 May all beaches were secure, and the troops were digging in. The amphibs steamed into San Carlos Water, and disposed themselves according to Clapp's plan. The only enemy encountered on land was on Green Beach, consisting of the other half of the company on Fannings Head, who fled east when confronted by 3 Para. They subsequently shot down two Gazelles of 3rd Commando Brigade Air Squadron, the only losses sustained by the Brigade that day. The main threat was from the air. The enemy still had thirty-eight A-4s, two dozen Daggers and six Canberras, as well as seven Naval A-4s landed from *Veintecinco de Mayo* available from the mainland, plus the Pucarás, Mentors and Aermacchis already deployed in the islands.

The sailors suffered the most dead and wounded on 21 May and the six subsequent days, as the Battle of San Carlos Water – which included the whole of the Amphibious Objective Area (AOA) – roared into life, starting with a Pucará attacking *Canberra* at 0845 local. By the end of D-Day, *Ardent* had been sunk with one third of her ship's company killed or wounded, *Antrim* and *Argonaut* (Captain Layman) were badly damaged (*Argonaut* with an unexploded bomb aboard) and *Brilliant* and *Broadsword* (Captain Canning) had been strafed by cannon fire and taken casualties; of all the escorts, by nightfall only *Plymouth* and *Yarmouth* were unscathed. On 24 May, *Antelope* (Commander Tobin) sank after a massive explosion caused by a bomb detonating while it was being cleared. Also that day, a morning of heavy air attacks on the AOA resulted in three LSLs being hit, but the bombs did not detonate. The Argentine National Day, 25 May, saw air attacks all day, both in the AOA and further out to sea, during which *Coventry* was sunk and *Broadsword* was damaged, and, critically for the Commando Brigade, *Atlantic Conveyor* was hit by an air-launched Exocet and sank taking all but one Chinook to the bottom.

Before this Thompson had been ordered by the CTF at Northwood to move out of the beachhead. This conflicted with the directive issued by General Moore on 12 May, which both Clapp and Thompson understood to mean that movement out of the beachhead was restricted to attacks on nearby enemy positions and to preparing the way for an advance to Port Stanley until after the General's arrival with the 5th Infantry Brigade. However, Thompson was not able to speak to Moore, now coming south in the liner *Queen Elizabeth II*, because of communications problems. So he was unable to inform him that the plans had changed, for lack of information to the contrary assuming that they had been changed after discussion with CTF. Finishing touches were being made to the plans to move the brigade by Chinooks forward to the Mount Kent area when the news of the loss of *Atlantic Conveyor* arrived. Notwithstanding the loss of these vital helicopters, the order to move out was repeated by the CTF on the morning of 26 May.

The move out of the beachhead was to include the capture of Darwin and Goose Green. A raid on these two had been planned earlier, but cancelled by Thompson as helicopter assets would have to be diverted from what he judged was more important, the insertion of an SAS Squadron on Mount Kent, the highest feature, and vital ground, overlooking the series of mountains to the west of Port Stanley. Accordingly 45 Commando and 3 Para were ordered to march to Douglas Station and Teal Inlet, while 2 Para (Lieutenant Colonel Jones) was despatched to Darwin and Goose Green. 42 Commando was warned for a helicopter move to Mount Kent using the one Chinook, and 40 Commando remained to protect the beachhead.

While 2 Para were making final preparations for their battle, lying up in a very exposed location north of the Darwin and Goose Green isthmus, the BBC World Service announced that the attack was about to begin. The BBC had gained this information thanks to an indiscretion by a member of the government; the third, but not the last, example of such crassness. Fortunately the Argentines treated it as a ruse. At 0230 local on 28 May the leading company of 2 Para crossed the start line, and after fourteen hours of fighting the battalion was on the outskirts of Goose Green. By now the garrison had been reinforced twice by helicopter. The Commanding Officer, Lieutenant Colonel 'H' Jones, and nineteen others were dead, and forty wounded. The attack had hung in the balance when the battalion was held up by anti-aircraft guns at Goose Green firing in the ground role. Fortunately, the mist at sea, which hitherto had prevented the Harriers from supporting the battalion, cleared, and three RAF GR 3s, which by now had joined the Carrier

Battle Group, attacked the guns. Although the guns themselves were not hit, the shock effect of cluster bombs and cannon silenced them and the garrison. After a bitter night out in the peat, surrounded by largely unmarked minefields, Major Keeble, the second-in-command, negotiated a surrender of the garrison. It was a brilliant victory by the outnumbered battalion. The CO was awarded a Victoria Cross posthumously.

On 30 May, General Moore arrived at San Carlos, approved the moves that had been made so far, and ordered the 5th Infantry Brigade to move to Goose Green, and from there on the southern axis to the Fitzroy area. The 3rd Commando Brigade was to continue on the northern route. The following night part of 42 Commando was flown to Mount Kent, an attempt the previous night having been aborted due to snow blizzards; the remainder of the Commando were flown forward on subsequent nights. They were joined in the Mount Kent area by 3 Para on 1 June, and by 45 Commando on 4 June. The way for these moves had been made safe by a brilliant little action by the Brigade Reconnaissance Troop (Captain Boswell), eliminating enemy special forces overlooking the Brigade's route. The SBS had also secured Teal Inlet before the arrival of 3 Para. 40 Commando, much to their chagrin, were charged by Moore with defence of the beachhead, following intelligence that the enemy were planning an airborne assault there. Numerous efforts by Thompson to extricate the Commando from their exile at San Carlos failed.

In a bold move 2 Para, temporarily under command of the 5th Infantry Brigade, flew forward to Fitzroy in the surviving Chinook, having first ascertained that the enemy had left. Failure by 5th Brigade to inform Divisional Headquarters of this move nearly led to the biggest 'blue on blue' of the war. 3rd Commando Brigade's Reconnaissance Troop Observation Posts (OPs) reported what appeared to be enemy moving to Fitzroy, and artillery fire was about to be brought down, when a final check with Divisional HQ by a staff officer at 3rd Commando Brigade HQ elicited the information that the 'enemy' was 2 Para.

Some eleven days of patrolling by the 3rd Commando Brigade now followed, to fix and dominate the enemy, while guns and ammunition were laboriously flown forward in ever worsening weather. The move of 5th Brigade to Fitzroy and Bluff Cove was slow and attended by numerous glitches, including the major incident involving the air attack on the LSLs *Sir Galahad* (Captain Roberts) and *Sir Tristram* (Captain

Green) in Port Pleasant, resulting in considerable casualties, mainly Welsh Guardsmen.

On the night of 11/12 June the 3rd Commando Brigade attacked three objectives: from left to right, 3 Para Mount Longdon, 45 Commando Two Sisters, and 42 Commando Mount Harriet. 2 Para (now commanded by Lieutenant Colonel Chaundler) and 1st Welsh Guards (Lieutenant Colonel Rickett) were in brigade reserve, the Welsh Guards having had two of their rifle companies, who had lost all their equipment in the bombing of *Sir Galahad*, replaced by two of 40 Commando's. By first light on 12 June, all three objectives were secure.

3 Para's fight for Mount Longdon was long and bloody, lasting most of the night. At times the outcome hung in the balance. At a key moment of the battle, Sergeant McKay's platoon commander was wounded, and the platoon was stalled in front of a heavy machine gun, with which all Argentine positions were liberally equipped. McKay charged on alone as those with him were either killed or wounded. He despatched the enemy with grenades, before falling dead into the sangar. He was awarded the Victoria Cross posthumously.

In the centre, the excellent plan by the CO of 45 Commando to attack Two Sisters looked like unravelling, when X Company, through no fault of its own, took six hours to reach its start line instead of the three that had been estimated. Initially having relied on this company to distract the enemy while his main attack came in, Whitehead swiftly rejigged the plan, and carried on. At one stage Z Company was pinned down by heavy machine-gun fire, when the leading troop commander, shouting the company battle cry, 'Zulu, Zulu!', charged forward, and soon had his men skirmishing up the slope and sweeping on to the crest. Two Sisters was a very strong natural position, and Whitehead commented that if he had been given the task of holding it he would have died of old age before it was taken.

Least known of all the three battles, even by the pundits, is 42 Commando's attack on Mount Harriet. Thanks to exceptionally good patrolling, especially by Sergeant Collins, Vaux was able to devise a bold plan, which involved a long outflanking march and attack on the enemy rear, while their attention was directed 180 degrees in the wrong direction by a feint attack. For the loss of two killed and twenty wounded, 42 Commando captured a position held by what amounted to a weak battalion, capturing over 300 men, and numerous weapons. As an example of inflicting the maximum damage on the enemy, with the minimum loss to own troops, it is hard to beat. Again there were deeds of individual courage, such as Corporal Newland's single-handedly wiping out a position occupied by about half a platoon.

In all three battles the Commando gunners of 29 Commando Regiment Royal Artillery provided magnificent support, on occasions bringing down fire well within the safety distance of their own troops. The fire from *Avenger*, *Glamorgan* and *Yarmouth* on the gun line also played a major part in success. The Captain of *Glamorgan* gallantly remained just too long, and while cutting a corner, at 0635 local, as dawn was breaking, came within range of a land-based Exocet in Port Stanley. *Glamorgan*'s hangar area was devastated, but she managed to regain the Carrier Battle Group under her own power.

When the dawn came, so did the Argentine artillery fire on positions they had just lost. Most daunting were the 155mm shells, and many of these were directed on to 3 Para on Mount Longdon, under direct observation from Mount Tumbledown.

A forty-eight-hour pause was now necessary to replenish artillery ammunition – the guns had fired nearly 480 rounds per gun during the long night battle – and to move some of the guns forward.[5] Both brigades were now engaged on the night of 13/14 June. On Mount Tumbledown the 2nd Scots Guards (Lieutenant Colonel Scott), supported by *Active* (Commander Canter) and *Avenger*, had a tough fight against the best the Argentines had, the 5th Marine Regiment. At one stage the attack looked like stalling, until Major Kiszley, commanding Left Flank Company, led two platoons into the attack, supported by the third. He personally bayoneted two enemy before he and six men of the leading platoon reached the end of the company objective.

On Wireless Ridge, Chaundler fought a model all-arms battle. The terrain allowed full use of the light tanks (Combat Vehicle Reconnaissance Tracked – CVRT), impossible elsewhere, and he put them to good use. With two batteries, and *Yarmouth* and *Ambuscade* (Commander Mosse) in support, he had plenty of firepower. By first light the battalion went firm, and Chaundler moved up onto Wireless Ridge in time to see large numbers of Argentine troops streaming back into Port Stanley.

The 1st/7th Gurkhas (Lieutenant Colonel Morgan), passing through

2nd Scots Guards to attack Mount William, found the enemy gone – to their intense disappointment, as the Gurkhas already had their kukris out in anticipation. The last shots of the war were fired by 7 Troop C Company 40 Commando, which with A Company was flown forward as part of a two-company lift to secure a forming-up position for 1st Welsh Guards to move onto Sapper Hill. The helicopter pilot carrying 7 Troop misread his map, and deposited the troop on Sapper Hill by mistake. The enemy opened fire, wounding two marines. In the subsequent battle several Argentines were killed before the remainder surrendered.

At this stage General Menendez requested a ceasefire, so the attack prepared by 3rd Commando Brigade for the next night would not be necessary. The Commando Brigade was led into Stanley by 2 Para, closely followed by 3 Para and 42 Commando. Sapper Hill was secured by 45 Commando and 1st Welsh Guards. The Scots Guards spent a freezing night on Mount Tumbledown surrounded by the debris of battle.

The Carrier Battle Group remained fully alert, until the surrender of land forces signed later that night was accompanied by a South Atlantic-wide cessation of hostilities.[6] As the surrender was being signed, the weather was deteriorating sharply. A force 10 storm and confused seas reduced ships' speeds to 11 knots. By early on 15 June, the Carrier Battle Group had to abandon replenishment, and withdraw the Sea Kings from the anti-submarine screen, for the first time for over a month.[7]

Although it may sound trite to repeat the Duke of Wellington's remark after the Battle of Waterloo, the Falklands War really was a very 'close run thing', especially from the point of view of the Carrier Battle Group. The ship serviceability problem alluded to earlier was beginning to bite. Destroyers and frigates were not being replaced as fast as they were being hit. Only 50 per cent of the original SHARs were airworthy. Only one submarine was available to replace the three on station. The helicopter situation ashore had been improved only by dint of Woodward lending some of his helicopters, at the expense of drastically reduced anti-submarine protection for the carriers. Finally, the ships were running out of 4.5in ammunition, so essential for shore bombardment.

Nevertheless, despite all these problems, and many more that have not been enumerated, the British succeeded, and the Falkland Islands were returned to the form of government desired by their inhabitants. An additional, and unforeseen, bonus resulted from British victory, of whom the main beneficiaries were the Argentine people: the military junta was eventually replaced by a democratically elected government.

14

AIR MARSHAL IAN MACFADYEN

The Gulf, 1990–1991: Desert Storm

Air Marshal Ian Macfadyen is an RAF fighter pilot who flew Lightnings and Phantoms in the UK and Germany. He has been a member of a formation aerobatic team and a solo Phantom aerobatic display pilot. After a mix of staff and command appointments, he was selected as the Chief of Staff to Lieutenant General Sir Peter de la Billière at HQ British Forces Middle East for the duration of the Gulf War against Saddam Hussein. On completion of the war he took over the post of Commander of British Forces Middle East. He spent his last four years in the RAF based in Saudi Arabia, in charge of the Saudi Armed Forces Project. He is now Her Majesty's Lieutenant Governor in the Isle of Man.

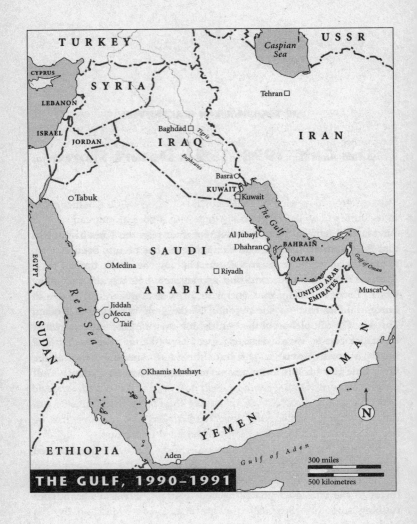

THE GULF, 1990–1991

This brief narrative concentrates largely on the planning and execution of the air war in the Gulf, to the deliberate exclusion of the war at sea and on land, other than a reference, for completeness, to some aspects of each because, despite a popular impression otherwise, it was very largely an air battle.

The background to what became known as the 1991 Gulf Conflict could in itself fill a book. Suffice it to say that, with hindsight, one can see that Saddam Hussein had long-standing ambitions on the Kuwaiti oilfields that he intended to fulfil. That he might have gone on into Saudi Arabia, if unchecked, remains interesting speculation. His attack timing, on 2 August 1990, was precise, with the long summer holidays already underway in Europe and America, and with many key figures in Kuwait and Saudi Arabia having sought the cooler climate in more northern latitudes. The result was a near complete surprise attack, and the rapid overrun of Kuwaiti forces by a vastly larger force. It may be that Saddam's initial success surprised even himself, but the fact remains there was, at the time, little to stop him from advancing further down the Arabian Gulf coast to capture both the Saudi Arabian port of Al Jubail and the strategic airfield at Dhahran, whilst also engulfing important Saudi oilfields and isolating Bahrain at the same time. His problem was, however, that he had outstripped his logistic support and needed to regroup.

Whatever Saddam's subsequent intentions, he had not reckoned properly on some key factors. Firstly, the resolve by the West, firmly led by George Bush and Margaret Thatcher, to prevent, at any cost, the threat to the vital oil that was needed to keep the world's economies running smoothly. Secondly, the brave and astute decision by His Majesty King Fahd of Saudi Arabia to allow, for the first time in his kingdom's ninety-year history, foreign troops on what the Muslim world regards as holy soil. Once that key decision was made, the final outcome of a secure Saudi Arabia was perhaps inevitable and only a matter of time. But Saddam nevertheless posed a real threat, possessing a known chemical weapon capability and an embryonic nuclear weapons programme. These two facts alone were sufficient to cause the West some alarm, but when combined with a developing ballistic missile inventory they were sufficient to be of real concern.

The political will being readily forged at a meeting between George Bush and Margaret Thatcher in early August at Boulder, Colorado, and with Saudi agreement, the United States looked to its Central Command (CENTCOM) to take the lead in carrying out the task. This major unified command (one of seven in the US covering the globe) was responsible for Gulf security. The Command was fortunate to have two strong leaders: General Norman Schwarzkopf of the US Army, a bear of a man with a growl to match, whose headquarters was in Florida, and Lieutenant General Chuck Horner of the USAF (the CENTAF Commander), whose other peacetime role was Commander of the USAF 17th Air Force at Shaw Air Force Base, South Carolina. Chuck Horner was the ideal man to get the necessary air power into place and organized for full-scale war. He was a great air commander – tough, pragmatic, quick of mind and with a great sense of humour. Horner quickly drew together a top team of those whom he knew well to set about the huge task of planning for what was inevitably to become, at least initially, an air campaign. Brigadier General Buster Glosson (later Lieutenant General) was another key player: an all American star and fighter pilot with the looks to match, he was to execute Horner's orders in near perfect fashion.

Turning to the British contribution, the Royal Navy had been operating in Gulf waters since the early days of the Iran–Iraq War and was well versed with the area. The RAF, on the other hand, had no recent experience of Gulf operations following the strategic withdrawal from the Middle East some twenty years earlier. It had been organized and committed to the European Central Region with its very different climatic conditions. RAF tactics were based almost entirely on the needs and demands of war on the northern European plains: poor weather, layered defence, backed up with the need to provide for a nuclear deterrent. The dramatic changes in world affairs of 1989 had barely begun to be felt by 1990, although a strategic defence review was already underway to reassess Britain's military needs in a new world order.

The air build-up was rapid and effective. Amongst the first to arrive in Saudi Arabia was a squadron of RAF Tornado F3 fighters; they immediately set up combat air patrols to intercept any possible Iraqi incursion. These patrols continued round the clock until after the conflict was over. Over 200 US and RAF aircraft, with increasing numbers from France and other coalition partners, were in place by the end of August. The airlift to support this, and the subsequent build-up, was on a scale never seen before; more tonnage was delivered by air in the first six weeks of the crisis than in the whole of the fifteen-month-long Berlin airlift, and over a vastly greater distance. This feat was repeated again and again up until March 1991.

As the autumn of 1990 moved on Schwarzkopf's plans developed and he asked for more forces. Britain, having committed 7th Armoured Brigade (Brigadier Patrick Cordingley) in September, decided to reinforce this with 4th Armoured Brigade (Brigadier Christopher Hammerbeck) to form 1st Armoured Division (Major General Rupert Smith), as well as add more aircraft and ships. Thus what had begun for the UK as an air build-up soon became a large-scale multi-service operation. Margaret Thatcher wanted a well-recognized military leader with Gulf experience, and found the ideal man in Lieutenant General Sir Peter de la Billière, a highly decorated officer with much operational experience in Oman. Air Vice-Marshal Sandy Wilson, the initial overall commander, was about to assume command of RAF Germany, and was replaced as the senior airman in theatre by Air Vice-Marshal Bill Wratten, who had a reputation for firmness, clarity of thought and fairness. The UK headquarters of what was known in Britain as Operation GRANBY was at RAF High Wycombe. The large underground bunker there grew into a large joint service headquarters led most ably by Air Chief Marshal Sir Patrick Hine, Commander in Chief of RAF Strike Command at High Wycombe, a greatly respected commander and the ideal man to lead the British end of the operation.

On 29 November 1990 the United Nations passed Resolution 678, which authorized the use of force to expel Iraq from Kuwait if it did not withdraw by 15 January 1991. The build-up now had UN backing.

The initial British HQ was on one floor of a requisitioned building in Riyadh; the other ten floors was the Gulf HQ of the US Marine Corps. This puts the relative scale of effort into some perspective, although the British HQ was eventually to rise to nearly 1,000 personnel, requiring a new headquarters. However, this was not found until the end of December and, after fitting out, was not actually occupied until nearly a week after the air war had begun. Fortunately, the main RAF element, set up nearly six months previously at the Royal Saudi Air Force HQ, was already well established alongside its USAF counterpart.

Coalition warfare was new, and its proper integration was key to success. CENTCOM, located within the vast Saudi Ministry of Defence and Aviation (MODA) headquarters, led the effort. With, eventually, thirty-six nations taking part, some with almost all-Russian equipment (Syria, for example), there was a real need for firm leadership to bring things together. A joint Coalition HQ was set up in MODA: there were weekly meetings of the Coalition leadership in the lead-up to the outbreak of war, and daily ones thereafter. It was a new experience for all to sit around a table with such a diverse group from the seven leading nations. A particularly strong grip was needed to ensure a full understanding of the conduct and safety of any air campaign, and a key part of this was air–land coordination, a field in which Britain took a lead by briefing the Coalition partners. It was clearly essential that Russian-made SAMs and AAA, an integral part of Syrian and Egyptian forces, were kept under a tight rein if unfortunate mistakes were not to be made. The idea that constraints would be put on the use of such weapons was new to their doctrine and some persuasion was necessary. To smooth the process, the Americans decided, wisely, to have a liaison group in each Coalition Divisional and Brigade HQ. As may be imagined, communications were generally difficult if not impossible between adjacent ground units unless common (US) communications were used. In the event, the process worked well.

Planning for an offensive air campaign had begun during August 1990, but because of political and other constraints, only the US and Britain were initially formally involved. The strong bonds between the USAF and RAF led to close cooperation in planning. Buster Glosson formed what became known as the Black Hole, a highly secret planning group that worked on the overall strategic and tactical approach to the air war. Wing Commander Mick Richardson of the RAF was chosen as the only non-US officer on this planning team, and became a respected member of the group. General Horner's headquarters was known as the JFACC (after the Joint Forces Air Component Commander), and was located underground in the RSAF headquarters. By the start of the air campaign it had grown to around 1,000 people with representatives from all twelve Coalition air forces. This group planned and executed the air campaign in accordance with the Master Attack Plan that had initially been drawn up by the Black Hole planning team.

On the ground, the British division, under the command of Major General Rupert Smith, was by December beginning to settle down well. However, there was some disquiet by armoured corps officers (Rupert Smith was a former Para) that we were not making the best use of the division. Thus it was that around mid-December the question of moving the 1st British Division away from working with the US Marines came to a head. We felt the best employment of a division, equipped specifically for manoeuvre warfare, was the main thrust into southern Iraq, which became known as the long left hook. The plan was that this should move rapidly forward to engage the Iraqi Republican Guard divisions being held to the rear in and around Kuwait. The whole matter of resubordination to the US VII Corps, the corps tasked to undertake this role, was a sensitive matter to both the UK and the US. The UK wanted the change but had no real wish to upset US plans, and the US Marines wanted to keep things as they were. General Schwarzkopf backed the US Marines but was eventually won over by the arguments put forward by us that the UK Division, not only tailor-made for manoeuvre warfare, could be properly supported despite the long lines of supply. In the event the British army excelled itself in every way, thus further enhancing its already fine international reputation.

Two further topics dominated the planning for the land and sea campaigns: the question of an amphibious landing and the thorny question of casualties. The US Marine Corps were keen to prove their expertise in amphibious operations, but two largely unknown factors were the strength of shore defences and the degree to which Iraq had laid sea mines in the northern Gulf. The Royal Navy, who had the best ships to tackle mine warfare, were rightly cautious in their approach to the problem. Commodore Chris Craig, Senior Naval Officer Middle East and another fine leader, was firm in his view that the coalition should prepare for the worst and thus expect delays whilst mines were cleared. At a key meeting in December 1990, it was accepted that the risks were too high and no amphibious operation should take place.

The fear of casualties was very real. Brigadier Patrick Cordingley, commander of the 7th Armoured Brigade, unwittingly touched a nerve when he let it be known to the press that he expected heavy casualties, partly because of the strength of numbers of Iraqi defences, and partly because of the very clear nuclear, biological and chemical threat. General Norman Schwarzkopf was particularly sensitive to casualties both because of his experience in Vietnam and because the whole idea of large-scale repatriation of body bags to the United States was highly charged politically. It was, in any case, right and appropriate to keep casualties to a minimum and it was recognized from the start that an extensive air campaign would precede the ground phase.

As the British HQ in Riyadh settled down, thoughts turned to some of the 'what ifs' of the likely forthcoming hostilities. With the possibility of casualties in some numbers, a major concern for all members of the Coalition was the need for proper field hospitals and an effective casualty evacuation system. Whilst there were a number of Army Field Hospitals, more were considered necessary and so the use of Reservists became a necessity. Typical of these was the deployment of No. 205 Field Hospital TAVR, whose home was in Glasgow. Comprising some of the UK's best surgeons, nurses and accompanying staff, they did not arrive until the war was underway – indeed, within a few hours of arriving at King Khaled Airport in Riyadh, where they were to be housed on the site of the RAF airhead, they were subjected to Scud attack. They soon set up a 700-bed hospital in the basement of a never used part of the magnificent civil air terminal there. In the event the need for the hospital was thankfully never really tested, with most of the casualties brought in being Iraqi POWs.

Although the UK clearly needed primarily to look after its own troops, it went further and was the first to consider how Iraqi casualties might be treated. As a consequence, a message went out from London seeking assistance from any country that wanted to help. A number of nations responded, with the biggest contributions coming from New Zealand and Sweden. New Zealand provided elements for a field hospital as well as Hercules transport aircraft; Sweden provided a full field hospital, which was set up on the outskirts of Riyadh. Hungary, very recently a member of the Warsaw Pact, provided an NBC warning station as well as a small field hospital. Coordinating these disparate elements became a major in-theatre task, with Colonel (later Brigadier) Bill Strong, Assistant Chief of Staff for Logistics (J5) and the Command

Secretary, Norman Abbott, doing marvellous work. To add to their burden it was necessary, for the first time since the Korean War, to set up major POW camps. Setting them up for the 25,000 people who would come within the British sphere of operations was a major undertaking and one that was expensive on manpower. The question of numbers of British forces in the Gulf obsessed ministers from the start and each new request for more people became a tortuous and tedious process. Perseverance and a lot of extra hard work paid off. Fortunately, Saddam Hussein did not give the coalition too many surprises, and the build-up of forces proceeded at the planned pace. One surprise did come late in November 1990 when the Iraqis test-launched a Scud missile from eastern Iraq to a target near the Jordanian border. An American infrared satellite detected the launch and set alarm bells ringing. As a result of this episode, the detection of a Scud launch was subsequently flashed upon British computer screens to give a valuable warning period of potential attack. This was to become a part of the routine during the conflict itself.

As the mid-January UN deadline approached, CENTAF preparations for the air campaign were nearing completion. The training had been intensive and realistic with low flying authorized down to very low level. Flying over sand can be dangerous as it is often difficult to judge one's height. Even the all-weather Tornados, on automatic terrain following, were having occasional difficulty with their radar, which sometimes 'saw through' sand dunes. Modification solved many of the difficulties, but other modifications were vital to provide full operational effectiveness, and many Urgent Operational Requirements (UORs) were pushed through in minimal time. Without some changes, such as to the IFF systems, which identify friend or foe, the RAF could not have worked with the Americans. The new satellite navigation system, GPS, was just becoming available and many aircraft were fitted with relatively crude stand-alone systems, which made the task easier than it might otherwise have been. The army, too, had to make many changes to bring equipment up to a full operational standard, and altogether £75 million was spent on upgrading the British contribution.

There was much debate on the likely effectiveness of the forthcoming air campaign. Some were convinced it could all be done from the air but that was never realistic, if only because the Coalition ground forces of over 500,000 deployed to the theatre were simply not just going to watch it all happen and then go home. With real cuts in Western armed forces in prospect, as a result of the end of the Cold War, there was too much at stake for that. In any case, no sensible military commander would want to enter a campaign without a balance of forces, and it should not be forgotten that Saddam Hussein had a 500,000-strong army, and with worries about such a large force and his unpredictability there was a clear need for a considerable 'softening up' of his armies, especially the elite Republican Guard divisions, before any ground war.

By mid-January the RAF had a mixed fleet of over seventy Tornados and Jaguars in-theatre, backed up by tanker, maritime patrol and transport elements, and forty-three Chinook and Puma helicopters largely to support the 1st Division. The Royal Navy had a number of ships in the Arabian Gulf, including two Type 42 destroyers which provided both a key element in the air defence of the northernmost element of Coalition forces as well as an attack capability using Lynx helicopters armed with what was to prove the highly effective Sea Skua missile. The British 1st Armoured Division, with its large logistic back-up, was still training south of Kuwait for the ground war and had deliberately yet to move to its forward location with the US Seventh Army because such a move needed to be in great secrecy, and certainly after the air war had begun.

One aspect that had very much been foreseen was how to create surprise in any attack on Iraq. Coalition flying patterns had been increasingly intensive as more and more aircraft moved into theatre and peaked at around 1,500 training sorties per day; this was in marked contrast to Saddam's air force which rarely flew more than 100 sorties, and sometimes very much less. Thus, whereas Coalition air forces were ready to fight, it seemed Iraq was either uninterested or did not believe any attack would be launched against its territory. The preferred time of attack was when there was no moon, and so it was that 17 January, the start of the darkest period in the month, became the highly secret date for the first attack. This date was known by only a very few people until a matter of hours before the event. Elaborate deception plans had therefore been made to give no hint at all to the Iraqis of imminent attack. Just before the start of hostilities the tactical control of all British Forces in theatre was passed to the United States which, along with Saudi Arabia, was to be in overall command.

Even in Riyadh, the start of the air war was dramatic. At about 11 p.m.

on 16 January the first of over 300 tanker aircraft in theatre began to get airborne. Many of these were based either at Riyadh Air Base near the centre of the city or the nearby King Khaled International Airport, which had so many tankers on site that they were either parked against the airport terminal like airliners or filled taxiways in long lines. It was an extraordinary sight that will probably not be seen again. For over one hour these aircraft continued to take off. An eerie silence followed.

The scene early morning in the British headquarters was of quiet activity; few had any idea what was about to happen and CNN was on the TV quietly in one corner. By 3 a.m. things were beginning to happen and CNN reported the first raid on Baghdad. One of the more dramatic moments of the night was the sudden termination of a CNN live broadcast from Baghdad; clearly early attacks on communications sites were going according to plan. The first waves of RAF Tornados were in action during the night and by daylight news was coming in that one aircraft was missing. This was one of six Tornado losses during the war, in which some five gallant aircrew died and seven were made prisoners of war.

A typical Coalition night attack on an Iraqi airfield in the opening three days of the war consisted of a package of aircraft made up from USAF and US Navy fighters and fighter-bombers, USAF F-111 and B-52 bombers and F-4G Wild Weasels, and RAF Tornados, all backed up by AWACs command and control aircraft and a small armada of US and RAF aerial fuel tankers: in total perhaps fifty aircraft. The fighter aircraft would roam ahead at medium altitude to sweep the skies of any Iraqi air opposition. The Wild Weasel aircraft then fired their anti-radar Harm missiles, backed up by RAF Tornados using their brand-new Alarm missiles, to suppress enemy radar activity and effectively blind the opposition. Each bomber aircraft, using a combination of weapons, some precision guided, had a specific target to attack, timed to the second; if the RAF Tornados, running at high speed at very low level, were only a matter of ten seconds out in their timing they would have been dropping bombs at the same time as B-52s flying only a very few feet above them. It was an awesome amount of firepower to deploy in less than two minutes. Repeated several times over each night, at different air bases, it is no wonder air opposition was quickly eliminated. The only surprise was that on 26 January the Iraqi air force began a mass exodus to Iran. Over 120 aircraft were eventually to defect.

The RAF had some worrying moments in the early days of the war, as it seemed to be taking more than its share of aircraft losses. Whilst these were of great concern, it was well recognized that the task of attacking targets by night from very low level with conventional bombs and the anti-airfield JP233 weapon was a hazardous one, especially in an environment where the ground defences were several times denser than those that had been expected of the Warsaw Pact nations.

The decision to move attacks away from low to medium level, however, was completely unrelated to losses. The business of gaining air superiority, in which the JP233 weapon played an important part, had first to be done. When it was, it was time to review tactics. The fact was that within a very few days, perhaps rather more quickly than had been anticipated, the Coalition had achieved total domination of the skies over Iraq. The Iraqi air force, thoroughly beaten in the air by superior training, tactics and equipment, was either destroyed or no longer had the stomach to come out and fight. A joke at the time was that the five most feared words in Iraq were: 'You are cleared for take-off.' The only Iraqi air defence now therefore became the ground-based SAM and AAA. Avoidance of these threats was best achieved by flying well above the area of coverage of small-calibre guns and into a regime where tactics could better defeat SAM and the larger AAA. There was therefore no longer any justification for remaining at low level, and consequently Tornado JP233 operations ceased, despite ideas from some quarters, away from the theatre of operations, that the weapon ought to be used against much less well defended targets such as oil installations. The arguments against these ideas, based on risk and need, quickly won the day.

A few words about the JP233 are perhaps needed for the reader to understand why it was regarded as a key weapon in the initial Coalition offensive. It had originally been designed to close an airfield for a period of time through a combination of runway-cratering submunitions and minelets. Each Tornado carried two JP233s and in just one pass one aircraft could drop sixty runway-cratering devices and no less than 430 minelets. A typical force of six Tornados could therefore drop a considerable number of disruptive munitions, many of which had a built-in delayed action or would explode if disturbed. The evidence is that operations well nigh ceased for some hours following JP233 attacks even though the sheer size of an Iraqi airfield, very much larger than

Heathrow, forced RAF planners to think in terms of harassment rather than airfield closure. One myth about JP233 operations has continued to this day: that aircraft losses resulted from the need to drop the weapon in a straight pass over very heavily defended airfields. No losses were recorded as a result of using JP233, despite the five seconds or so that it took to release all the submunitions. Of the six RAF Tornados lost in the campaign, only one had been armed with JP233, and even this aircraft was destroyed several minutes after attacking an airfield, which points towards a post-attack problem as the most likely cause. The element of surprise, combined with the 550-knot delivery speed and 30-metre release altitude, all on the darkest nights of the month, combined to make such attacks relatively safe. It was, nevertheless, an alarming experience for aircrew just to deliver the weapon (which had never been done prior to the war) not only because, once initial surprise had been lost, the sky was filled with AAA tracer gunfire (however inaccurate), but also because the whole aircraft shuddered during the lengthy weapon release. One can only but admire the courageous manner in which these attacks were carried out with very great accuracy.

The problem for the RAF of moving bombing to medium level was that of how best to carry out the new task when they lacked the ability, experience and even the weapons to do this with precision. Initially, therefore, new bombing techniques, using onboard computers, were tried out on actual operations. Various tactics were used, including dive-bombing from high altitude, but none were giving sufficiently accurate results and consequently were largely ineffective. A better method of medium-level bombing was clearly needed, but it was not immediately to hand. Lieutenant General Horner had agreed, prior to the war, to provide USAF aircraft for the task, but in conflict the tactical situation soon dictated otherwise. The priority for the Coalition, following the achievement of air superiority, was that of countering Scud missile attacks, particularly those launched on Israel; these became of overriding political importance, and the USAF laser-equipped aircraft were needed for such small targets. Consequently, the offer of help had to be withdrawn.

It would be wrong to say medium-level bombing had not been foreseen, because the question had been considered several months previously, but dismissed at the time, partly because of the US offer of help but also on the grounds that large numbers of aircraft on any one base would offer too great a potential target. With Coalition dominance of the skies the situation was now different. Twelve of the RAF's Buccaneer bombers, equipped with the US-made Pave Spike laser designator system, were brought rapidly into theatre and the first of these were put to work operationally on 28 January, just a day after the decision to deploy them had been taken. This was in itself a remarkable achievement that reflected very well on all concerned. Now the Tornado force had a daylight means of precision bombing from medium level but not by night.

The only other laser designation pods in Britain were the new Ferranti all-weather pods, called TIALD, capable of day and night operations; these two pods were heavily involved in trials work before being ordered into production for the RAF. However, again due to some remarkable work by British industry, these were brought out to theatre in early February to the Saudi airbase of Tabuk in the north-west of the kingdom, where they were fitted to two of the RAF Tornados based there. Thereafter, these pods did an excellent job for the remainder of the conflict. One Tornado, equipped with TIALD, would designate targets for several others carrying the Paveway Two laser-guided 1,000lb bomb; in this way the whole of the Tabuk force could be properly employed on accurate medium-level operations both by day and by night. The Buccaneers were based in Bahrain, from which island they could look after the Tornados from two bases in that region again by marking targets for them. Later in February the Buccaneer added weight to the RAF's offensive attack capability by both designating targets for Tornados and carrying its own bombs.

The RAF had one other unique capability to bring to the Coalition, and that was a low-level twenty-four-hour reconnaissance capability using a version of the Tornado adapted for the purpose. Six aircraft were deployed to Dhahran and were in constant use by night, especially in the quest to detect mobile Scud missile launchers. They brought back valuable evidence of Iraqi movements and deployments well behind the front lines as they flew alone at around 100 feet at very high speed throughout the forty-four-day conflict without loss, proving that night low flying in hostile territory could be done without loss.

The RAF's twelve-strong Jaguar force, based at Muharraq in Bahrain, had been in theatre since the very beginning, and had been training hard to fly down to fifty feet and below at their maximum economical low-level speed of 450 knots. With a daylight only capability there were concerns about this approach, especially as the Americans were only planning to fly at medium level by day. The new Jaguar force commanding officer, Wing Commander Bill Pixton, began to look at the medium-level alternative late in 1990. A few days before the outbreak of war, he had obtained agreement to change to medium-level operations, where the best tactic was dive-bombing. This switch was not nearly as difficult as might be perceived, and was a far different and easier problem than suddenly moving to low level, where flying skills are tested to the full. It proved a very wise move as, on the first day of the fighting, four French Air Force Jaguars attempted a low-level attack on an airfield in Kuwait, only to suffer from ground fire so badly that three of them never flew again. RAF Jaguars were used chiefly for attacking artillery and missile sites using 1,000lb bombs. Later, in February, the force began dropping the US-made CBU-87 anti-armour weapon, since it was much more accurate at medium level than the RAFs own BL755 weapon, designed for very low level release. The Canadian CRV-7 rocket also proved highly accurate and effective when it came into use late in the war, even on dive attacks with weapon release at 10,000 feet altitude. Not one RAF Jaguar was lost on operations, a great tribute to their skill and tactics.

All RAF Tornado, Buccaneer and Jaguar operations used either Victor or VC-10 tankers in support, and missions were frequently over five hours in duration. The Victors alone flew 300 sorties during the air campaign, and along with their VC-10 counterpart refuelled US Navy, Canadian and French aircraft. The by-word was that 'anything fitted with a probe was refuelled by the RAF'. With the large number of USAF tankers also around, the skies to the south of the Iraqi border were full indeed, with tankers often stacked five deep at 150 metre intervals, along with their attending chicks. Another important RAF element in the region was a small detachment of two Nimrod maritime patrol aircraft that operated out of Seeb in Oman. In the period before mid-January, they were heavily committed to providing a complete surface plot of all merchant shipping in the Gulfs of Arabia and Oman and were instrumental in imitating ship-search operations in support of the UN embargo on Iraq. During the conflict they flew daily in support of the US carrier groups in the Gulf of Arabia, where their task was chiefly to locate and identify Iraqi naval vessels and subsequently direct aircraft and RN Lynx helicopters onto their targets. The latter operations were carried out with considerable success.

The scale of effort in the air campaign provided by the Americans was very different from that of the RAF. In general, the US had ten times the force size of anyone else in the Coalition, and it is no wonder they dominated events. They fielded a formidable and varied force of nearly 75 per cent of the 2,430 fixed-wing aircraft in theatre, including those based on six large aircraft carriers in the Red Sea and Arabian Gulf. A number of additional aircraft were based in Turkey, where they attacked northern Iraq, and a further 350 aircraft had arrived in Saudi Arabia by the start of the ground war. Many aircraft were relatively new in service, but even the aged B-52 bomber performed remarkably well with its huge bomb load of fifty-one 750lb bombs. Three of these aircraft took off from their base in Louisiana sixteen hours before the start of the air war and flew to Saudi Arabia where they launched a number of cruise missiles before returning home after thirty-five hours in the air, and after setting a new record for long-distance bombing. These giants went on to drop 26,000 tons of bombs, about 40 per cent of the total Allied tonnage.

Key to early dominance in the war were the F-117A Stealth fighters, whose very existence had been publicly known for less than two years in 1991. Flying by night out of Khamis Mushayt in south-west Saudi Arabia, the forty-two aircraft involved were employed against the most heavily defended targets using their 2,000lb GBU-27 laser-guided bombs. Between them, these fighters attacked 30 per cent of the key heavily defended strategic targets whilst flying less than 3 per cent of the total sorties, all with no losses; the baptism of stealth technology had indeed been revolutionary. Such was the effect of general air strikes on airfields that by the end of the campaign 375 of the 594 available aircraft shelters had been destroyed. It is therefore perhaps no wonder that over eighty Iraqi aircraft defected to Iran at the end of January where they have since remained.

Phase III of the campaign plan, the attack of ground forces, was aided by the setting up of what were known as kill boxes in Kuwait and southern Iraq. These were 2,300 square kilometres in area and helped to focus firepower by day on where it was most needed. Initially, however, the idea was not as successful as had been hoped and tactics had to be changed. The idea of killer scouts was born, based on Vietnam experience. The idea was that the killer scouts (USAF F-16 fighters with 500lb bombs) would validate targets and then help to coordinate attacks to inbound fighters. A typical Scout mission would last over five hours, mostly in Iraqi airspace; in this time a scout aircraft might coordinate attacks for twenty or thirty others. Scouts would respond to the tactical situation; for example, a SAM launch would immediately draw an attack on the launch site. The result was that, after a short time, daylight missile launches virtually ceased. Scout pilots used binoculars to identify whether targets were occupying revetments, and whether they were real or decoys. Pilots would get used to their kill box area and this helped further to find real targets. It was estimated that the attack success rate went up at least threefold using these tactics.

As the air campaign drew on, the number of daily air combat sorties increased from 1,500 to over 3,000. To put such a complex force safely together required a large Coalition air force planning team in Riyadh and an effective computer program: the Air Task Order, or ATO, was the result. It was a two-part document. The first gave details of the targets to be attacked and the forces allocated; the second contained special instructions such as communications, tanker and reconnaissance support, the airborne command AWACs dispositions, the routes to be flown in and out of Iraq and how combat search and rescue would be undertaken. It was a remarkable document that sometimes ran to over 700 pages; what is more, it was issued each day of the war to all units concerned including ships, ground forces and of course flying bases. Such a complex document took time to put together even with computers, and was initially prepared two days before the ATO was to be executed and then gradually refined until ready for release about twelve hours before execution was due to begin. Distribution of such a large document was a major problem as, in many cases, the necessary secure communications simply did not exist. For example, the US Navy had to employ aircraft to fly a hard copy of the ATO directly on board the aircraft carriers.

One other aircraft is worth a special mention because of its diversity of use in the conflict. Built as a tactical transport aircraft and used extensively by nearly all coalition air forces in this way, the C-130 was also used in a variety of specialized roles. Vietnam experience had demonstrated its value as an airborne gunship platform. These highly specialist machines were equipped with a 105mm howitzer backed up by 20mm and 40mm cannons that could lay down withering firepower from around 15,000 feet. Several were used most effectively against the surprise Iraqi attack on the Saudi town of Khafji at the end of January when one aircraft alone knocked out twenty-eight Iraqi vehicles. Another specialist C-130 was modified to carry an entire tactical air command post into the air: known as the ABCCC (A-B-tripleC), it carried a battle staff fitted with fifteen operator consoles and twenty-three secure speech radios. The ABCCCs were employed in the tactical direction of aircraft, particularly when target priorities changed at short notice. Another special operations C-130 dropped two colossal 15,000lb bombs, parachuted out of the back of the aircraft onto Iraqi minefields. Little real damage seems to have been done other than to the eardrums of anyone close by the resulting explosion, which could be heard over 160 kilometres away. Yet another modification of the C-130 was to employ it on electronic and psychological warfare operations. The latter were involved in broadcasting propaganda through onboard radio transmitters and known as the 'Voice of the Gulf'. Psyops in general played a larger part in the war than is generally recognized. Besides the airborne broadcasts, nearly 30 million leaflets were dropped over Iraqi dispositions. A US Psyops battalion, aided by British army language specialists, had prepared these and the airborne broadcasts, and also set up ground-based loudspeaker systems. Even before the start of the ground war this carefully planned programme led to the direct surrender of over 1,000 Iraqi troops, besides an unknown number who had deserted their post under the pressure of this and the constant aerial harassment.

Much has already been written about the work of the British Special Forces, and only a brief mention need be made here. General Schwarzkopf needed much persuasion that Special Forces (SF) could be of any use at all; his experience of US operations had made him profoundly sceptical of their value. General de la Billière was just the man to persuade him otherwise, but it took time. Consequently the air war was about to begin when the Americans finally agreed to allow the deployment of SF teams. The real value of such operations was to become apparent as time went on, and in an unexpected way. It had always been recognized that the Scud threat was a very real one, but what had not been appreciated was the problem of mobile Scuds, of which only a few were thought to exist in Iraqi service. The fixed Scud bases in western Iraq were heavily attacked on the first night of the war and quickly rendered useless. The surprise was the difficulty Coalition forces had in tracking and attacking the mobile Scud launchers, as the Iraqis proved very adept in operating them. Thus it was that the main SF task became that of tracking Scud launchers; the weakness was the lack of the right equipment and training to do the job. US Special Forces soon began to arrive to assist with the work, but since neither US nor UK air or ground forces were trained in anti-Scud operations the tactics had to be developed as best as was possible. They were never as effective as had been hoped but were instrumental in reducing the number of launches.

By the start of the ground war, Phase IV of Operation DESERT STORM, on 24 February, little Iraqi traffic was moving in or out of the Kuwait theatre without being attacked by day or night. Iraqi ground forces neither got supplies nor, with communications cut, knew what was going on, and troops were consequently left shaken and demoralized. Furthermore, the air campaign had so blinded Saddam Hussein that he had no real idea of where he would be attacked on the ground. Thus ground forces, with their considerable logistic support, were able to be redeployed with impunity prior to the ground operation, something that could never have been achieved in a hostile air environment.

The US XVIII Corps, on the western flank of the Coalition armies, was tasked to rapidly penetrate north to the River Euphrates, about 400 kilometres away, to cut off any retreating Iraqi forces. Over 300 helicopter sorties ferried troops and equipment into the objective area in the largest heliborne operation in military history, and by the end of the first day the corps had cut the first road leading up the Euphrates to Baghdad. The US Marines, meanwhile, attacked across the Kuwaiti border in the east and began a swift advance towards Kuwait City. The Egyptians, Saudis and Syrians also crossed into Kuwait and began moving north. All this was planned to mask the real punch coming from the US VII Corps with its British 1st Armoured Division. They next entered Iraq just to the west of Kuwait. Despite appalling weather at times, with rain and winds gusting to 40 knots, attacks on all fronts continued well. The superior technology and training of the Coalition gave them such a clear advantage that Iraqi tanks could be spotted and attacked from over 3,500 metres, long before the Iraqis even saw them. A good plan, boldly executed, found Coalition forces spread across Iraq from the banks of the Euphrates to Kuwait in just four days, with the best units of the Iraqi army heavily defeated, and all with just forty-four Allied troops killed.

Over 80,000 Iraqi POWs were taken and many more had died in the severity of the fighting.

The war thus ended as suddenly as it had started and a flood of congratulatory messages came in. Sir Peter de la Billière, struggling to cope with another kind of mountain, was heard to say: 'I wonder how Saddam Hussein is getting on with his signals?'

This brief history would be incomplete without a mention of Saudi Arabia. The eyes of the world were on a kingdom that had never been so exposed to media and other outside pressures. For a nation used to privacy, this, combined with an invasion of foreign troops, was a major shock and a real test. Despite this, the kingdom had from the beginning generously agreed to pay for the infrastructure, fuel and daily ration support of all foreign forces; this remarkable and costly support continued even when their number had grown to over 700,000. Finally, when the test of war came, its armed forces, led by the example of the Royal Saudi Air Force, gave a good account of themselves. A new spirit of nationhood and confidence emerged.

With such dominance of the air, and with so few casualties on the ground, it may be that future historians really will say the Gulf War was 'the end of the beginning' in air power terms. It is worth reflecting that since 1991 the balance of precision-guided air-delivered weapons and their non-precision counterpart has changed dramatically; this has more than offset a halving in aircraft numbers amongst the world's leading air forces. In 1991 the USAF had eighteen laser targeting pods on F-15 and F-16 fighters: today that figure is over 400. To match this, whereas in the Gulf War only around 10 per cent of air-delivered munitions were precision-guided, the figure today is greater than 80 per cent. Additionally, there are now thousands of GPS-guided weapons in the US inventory that can be dropped inside 4.5 metres anywhere on earth in any weather. It is no wonder that in the twenty-first century air power has become the weapon of political choice.

15

ROBERT FOX

Bosnia and Kosovo, 1992–2000:
Balkan Stew

Robert Fox graduated from Magdalen College, Oxford, and became a journalist reporting on BBC radio on major terrorist cases in Italy and Northern Ireland from the late 1960s to the early 1980s. He was a BBC Radio war correspondent in the Falklands War. He saw the Battle of Goose Green at first hand with 2nd Battalion The Parachute Regiment, and assisted in negotiating the surrender of the Argentine garrison of Goose Green after over twenty-four hours of fighting. He took part in the Battle of Two Sisters with 45 Commando RM, and entered Port Stanley with Tactical Headquarters 3rd Commando Brigade. He subsequently became defence correspondent of the *Daily Telegraph*, and was war correspondent attached to Headquarters British 1st Armoured Division in the Gulf War. He carried out numerous assignments in Bosnia, and was one of the first correspondents into Kosovo. His publications include *Eyewitness Falkland Islands* and *The Inner Sea: The Mediterranean and its People*, and he is now a freelance writer and journalist.

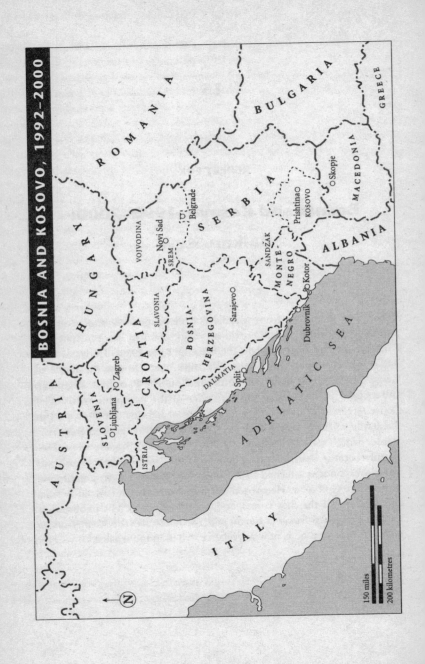

BOSNIA AND KOSOVO, 1992–2000

AUSTRIA

HUNGARY

ROMANIA

SLOVENIA
○Ljubljana ○Zagreb

CROATIA

ISTRIA

SLAVONIA

VOJVODINA

Novi Sad
○
SREM

BOSNIA-
HERZEGOVINA

Sarajevo○

DALMATIA
Split○

Belgrade

SERBIA

SANDŽAK

MONTE-
NEGRO

Dubrovnik○

Kotor○

ALBANIA

Prishtina○

KOSOVO

Skopje○

MACEDONIA

BULGARIA

GREECE

ADRIATIC SEA

ITALY

150 miles

200 kilometres

N

British Forces in the Balkans – Keeping the Peace in Bosnia and Kosovo

In the winter of 1992 a retired major general wrote to his son, commanding a squadron in his old regiment, the 9th/12th Lancers, in the UN contingent in Bosnia. He warned him of an old adage of war: 'Don't march on Moscow, don't eat yellow snow, and avoid involvement in the Balkans.'

The advice had apparently come too late. British forces were becoming involved in the Balkans by November 1992, and stayed there, primarily in Bosnia and Kosovo, into the new century. The Balkans peace mission became the single most sustained deployment of British troops at the close of the twentieth century outside Northern Ireland. Specialist arms, Signals, REME and Royal Engineers endured continuous postings. The Royal Navy and Royal Air Force also made their contribution in the front line. Eighteen servicemen died in the service of UNPROFOR (the UN Protection Force) in Bosnia, and forty-six died on active duty there. Three more died in the first year of deployment in Kosovo from June 1999.

Britain was the second largest contributor of troops to the UN force in Bosnia, after the French. The British won healthy respect from friend and foe; in Bosnia they were nicknamed GUNPROFOR instead of UNPROFOR.

The international community appeared to drift into the Yugoslav crisis in the summer of 1991, for trouble had been brewing for some time. The alliance of Slovenes, Croats and Serbs forged into Yugoslavia at the Versailles Conference of 1919 had always been an unhappy coalition of like-minded and like-cultured but suspicious and vengeful nationalities. After the Second World War it was only the muscular communist rule of Marshal Tito that kept them together. He had given the six republics and two autonomies of the Yugoslav federation a degree of latitude, but the arrangement was creaking at the time of his death in 1980.

By 1989 it was becoming evident that the break-up of the old federation was likely to prove violent. On 28 June President Slobodan Milošević of Serbia, who had risen to power through the Communist Party Tito had forged, raised the battle cry of a new Serbia. He did so at the site of the Battle of Kosovo Polje, where 600 years earlier the forces of Prince Lazar had been defeated by the Ottoman Turks – in what was to be the symbolic martyrdom of the Serb nation. 'Six centuries later again,' he told a crowd of an estimated 1 million Serbs, 'we are in battles and quarrels. They are not yet armed battles – though such things should not yet be excluded.' He proclaimed that the Serbs should seek solidarity in one nation and in one land, portrayed by the four Cyrillic 's' symbols in the modern Serbian monogram.

Milošević and the Serbian government were, on paper, in the best position for the ensuing struggle in the break-up of Yugoslavia. His party had the backing of trained nationalist paramilitaries – such as the White Eagles, the new Chetniks, and the Tiger Commando of the notorious Captain Arkan. He also had the backing of the Yugoslav Federal Army, the JNA, where Serbian officers were still the majority. In the summer of 1989 communities in Serb enclaves, like Knin in the Krajina border regions of Croatia, erected barriers and roadblocks and talked of self-rule.

The big break came two summers later, on 25 June 1991, when Slovenia and Croatia, after some forewarning, declared independence. This led to ten days of skirmishing between the JNA and the Slovene territorial defence forces, before a truce was declared on 7 July. From late July the fighting in Croatia grew into an all-out war. In that time nearly a third of all Croatian territory was lost. Vukovar on the Danube and the port of Dubrovnik came under siege. Vukovar fell in mid-November and hundreds of civilians were killed; the bodies of many have not been found. Hundreds of mortar bombs and shells fell on Dubrovnik each day in November, but by the end of the year the attacking Serbs and Montenegrins withdrew.

The accusations of atrocities at the fall of Vukovar, the once sleepy Danube town, brought greater involvement by international agencies such as the Red Cross and the UN. When a ceasefire was signed in

January 1992, it was decided to deploy a UN force, UNPROFOR, in the Serb-occupied areas. The force was to work in four UN Protected Areas (UNPAs). The first British units to be deployed with the UN in the Balkans were to be a Field Ambulance and a field hospital under the command of Lieutenant Colonel Lois Lodge. Its prime role was to support the UN forces, though it helped in emergencies dealing with the displaced from the war – by this time over a quarter of the population of Croatia were refugees.

The War in Bosnia, April 1992 to December 1995

The contingents of UNPROFOR had not fully deployed along the disputed areas of Croatia before the war had broken out in neighbouring Bosnia, which brought a much longer and deeper commitment of British forces. Curiously, Sarajevo, the Bosnian capital, had been designated as headquarters for the UN forces – on the grounds that it was in 'neutral' territory. Bosnia-Herzegovina declared independence on 6 April 1992, and the war was already under way.

The origins of the war in Bosnia are complex. Independence had been voted by a referendum called at the end of February – but it was a vote which the Serb community, roughly one-third of the population, boycotted. For many Serbs, Bosnia was a birthright of which they had been cheated repeatedly: when it was annexed by Austria in 1908, in the Balkan Wars of 1912–13 leading to the First World War, and finally in the last constitution of Tito's Yugoslavia in 1974 when the Bosnian Muslims were fully recognized as a separate nationality. This sense of betrayal by history has been compounded by the twists and turns of demography. For the early part of the century, the Serbs were in the majority in Bosnia, but by the last Yugoslav Federation census, the Muslims were just over 44 per cent of the population, the Croats 17 per cent and the Serbs somewhere in the region of 33 per cent. Nationalist Serbs dispute these figures, and they also claim title to more than 60 per cent of the land of Bosnia.

The dispute between the Bosnian minorities was compounded by the deep personal dislikes and rivalries of the local leaders. There was a strong suspicion that President Franjo Tudjman of Croatia had cooked up a deal with Slobodan Milošević of Serbia to carve up most of Bosnia between them, and evidence from the Tudjman tape archive goes some way to support this. President Alija Izetbegovic, leader of the Bosnian nationalist Muslim party the SDA, has been accused in turn of trying to set up Europe's first Islamic republic. This was based on his treatise on Muslim political economy, 'the Islamic Declaration', for which he was jailed.

At first the powers of northern Europe and America tried to keep away from the collapse of Bosnia. The remark attributed to Chancellor Bismarck at the Congress of Berlin in 1878, that 'the Balkans are not worth the healthy bones of a single Pomeranian grenadier', was oft repeated. (It appears at the time to have been a ruse to direct the Austrians away from central and northern Europe.) But the powers were to learn in the late twentieth century how close the lands of the southern Slavs were to the rest of Europe, as the flow of hundreds of thousands of refugees was to prove.

Militarily the Serbs had the advantage in the late spring of 1992, but it was one they appeared to do their best to squander. Earlier in the year Belgrade had arranged that Bosnian Serbs in the Federal Army would be posted to Bosnia to prepare for the coming fight; it was a veiled coup. Even so, the JNA units inside Sarajevo became virtual hostages in the first weeks of fighting.

Superiority elsewhere allowed the Serbs to seize almost 70 per cent of all Bosnia in the first few months of war, putting to flight nearly 1 million refugees. The Bosnian Muslims, on the other hand, found they had a war, a new country, but no army. They formed a scratch defence in the capital from the old Territorial Reserve units and about nine highly successful criminal gangs. Nationalist Croats, sensing the weakness of the Muslims, tried to carve out their own statelet of Herceg-Bosna; this would generate a war within a war between Muslim and Croat from 1993 to 1994.

The fighting in Sarajevo, the flight of refugees, reports of killings in remote towns, roads blocked and villages under continuous bombardment, brought the extension of the UNPROFOR mission to Bosnia. As the battle for the airport in the capital worsened, the UN appointed its own commander for Bosnia, Major General Lewis MacKenzie of Canada. He brought the famous French Canadian Vingt Douze Infantry Regiment across from Croatia to bring calm to Sarajevo. But, following a conference in London that July, it was decided a separate peace force was needed for Bosnia. No single UN Security Council resolution defines the mission of UNPROFOR, and this was to be much of the trouble: it grew from a steady accretion of mandates and resolutions, on an arms embargo, banning hostile military flights, sanctions on the rump Yugoslavia. Security Council Resolution 776, passed on 14 September 1992, declared that four or five battalion battle groups should be sent to Bosnia to assist refugees, help feed the displaced, and obtain the release of detainees. This was always something of a half measure: the UN troops could fight in self-defence, but not take the battle to the aggressors. This sense of the pitcher half full or half empty was to be a familiar story for international agencies in Bosnia for the next three years.

Britain agreed to send a battalion group. For all the reluctance of some of those who sent, the British troops took to their mission with resource, a degree of cunning, and courage. The deployments in Northern Ireland had made British soldiers familiar with political and social confusion. The doctrine of mission command meant that responsibility was devolved to those in charge of subunits – corporals and sergeants commanding sections and platoons.

The first battle group, the 1st Cheshires (Lieutenant Colonel Bob Stewart), soon knew that they had to write the script as they went along. Their main task was to secure safe routes for aid convoys to central Bosnia and the industrial town of Tuzla, which was in danger of being cut off by the Serbs. They set up their base at a school in Vitez near Travnik in the Lasva valley in a freezing November; it was the base of the main British presence for nearly three years.

Running convoys was tricky from the first. The route to Tuzla was over rugged mountain tracks and along roads frequently raked by heavy anti-aircraft machine guns and mortar fire. No sooner was the battalion set up in Vitez than it had to cope with a wave of refugees from northern Bosnia. In early November the Muslim and Croat forces defending the fortress town of Jajce broke amid recriminations about fuel supplies. Some 30,000 refugees fled on carts, wheelbarrows, lorries and anything with wheels that would move. The Cheshires helped prepare reception centres in Travnik, the former seat of Ottoman viziers, whose minarets and coloured mosque were to survive the war – despite being on the front line.

The dispute between the Bosnian Muslims and Croats edged towards all-out war by the end of 1992, and the Cheshires were caught in the middle. Muslim and Croat militias fought for the town of Gornji Vakuf, which controlled the valley of the River Vrbas, and was a vital junction on the aid convoy route. The Cheshires had established a base for their B Company in a factory on the edge of town. On 13 January 1993 fighting in the town itself, round the main café, had brought casualties. A British patrol of two Warrior Armoured Fighting Vehicles and a wheeled ambulance set out to help. Driving the leading Warrior was Lance Corporal Wayne Edwards, on loan from the Royal Welch Fusiliers. As he came to the crossroads by the cafe, he prepared to shut down his canopy. As he reached for the lever he was struck in the cheek by a sniper's bullet. He died within minutes, the first British casualty in UNPROFOR service.

That winter convoys of aid were regularly sniped at as they made the run up the road from Gornji Vakuf. On mountain tracks desperate families tried to slash the canopies of the trucks to get food. The road from Vitez to the main UN base at Kiseljak, under the headmasterly rule of Brigadier Roddy Cordy-Simpson as Chief of Staff, was a regular practice ground for snipers.

The Muslim–Croat feud took an uglier turn at Easter that year. Fighting had spread from Travnik as the Croats tried to stake out new territory. At dawn on 19 April militiamen of the Croat HVO (Defence Council) entered the Muslim part of the village of Ahmici and murdered 104 civilians, decapitating some, and burning women and children trapped in their homes. Colonel Bob Stewart later recalled, 'What struck me was what a normal neighbourhood it must have been and how awful it was now ... the mosque had been burnt and its minaret toppled like a rocket ready to be fired into the sky.' The Cheshires helped clear the village and prepare the burials. A huge trench was ripped open beneath the blossoming apple trees beside the mosque in Old Vitez. The Royal Engineers helped burial parties lay the victims in the improvised grave. Many of the victims had only old carpets for shrouds; a plastic bag held the heads of three little girls.

Later the local HVO commander Tihomir Blaskic was given a life sentence and the local warlord Dario Kordic, who had a direct link to the Tudjman regime in Zagreb, was similarly charged at the War Crimes Tribunal in the Hague for the massacre.

As the Cheshires were replaced by the 1st Battalion The Prince of Wales's Own Regiment of Yorkshire, Lieutenant Colonel Alastair Duncan commanding, the fighting round Vitez hotted up. Croat militiamen opened fire on a convoy of buses, inappropriately called the 'convoy of joy' bringing Muslims back from Germany to join their families. The much respected interpreter for Bob Stewart, Dobrila Kolaba, was deliberately singled out and shot by a Croat sniper as she stood in the garden of a house by the Vitez base.

At Gornji Vakuf the base came under regular attack. 'A round hit the liaison officer's bedside light', ran an account in the PWO regimental journal, 'A mortar shell came through the roof of 4 PI's accommodation, shrapnel destroyed our water purification unit ... Sgt Williamson was shot in the chest whilst on patrol.' The OC B Company, Major Graham Binns, was determined to keep the road open. If his men were fired on, they fired back, and no questions were asked, and they kept the convoys moving. Major Binns received the MC for his efforts. Colonel Duncan and Colonel Stewart were both awarded the DSO.

The PWO were unshowy, highly successful and very popular with the increasingly large corps of international journalists who came to Vitez, drawn by the thoroughness of their regular briefings. They had to content with the novel and growing threat of imported Muslim militants ('Mujahadin') from Gulf countries and Afghanistan.

In early June the Mujahadin attacked the monastery at Guci Gora, where the C Company PWO had taken Croat refugees on the night of 7/8 June 1993. The next day 'dawn broke and the dead were laid to rest by the padre in a moving service,' wrote Lieutenant J. C. Medley in the regimental magazine. 'Heavy machinegun fire penetrated the cloister. Some 200 rounds of chain gun were returned while the Commanding Officer negotiated safe passage. Covered by our Warriors a stream of 28 armoured vehicles brought by OC C Coy moved the civilians to safety. The compassion and determination of our soldiers had saved 186 lives.'

A hard winter followed, and by Christmas the unit that followed the PWO, the 1st Battalion the Coldstream Guards, were almost frozen into their camp at Vitez. Snow, ice and continuing fighting between the Croats and Muslims made roads dangerous; few aid agencies would risk convoys to central Bosnia. The worst of the fighting between Croat and Muslim had shifted to Mostar, where nearly 60,000 Muslims were crowded into a ghetto on the east side of the River Neretva, under continuous shelling and rocket fire. In a calculated action of psychological spite and vandalism the Croats deliberately shot down the beautiful sixteenth-century single-span bridge of Hairudin, perhaps the greatest Ottoman monument in Europe.

The warring between Croats and Muslims was brought to an end by skilful diplomacy led from Washington, and powerful efforts on the ground from local commanders – particularly the new British force commander, Brigadier John Reith, who had moved his HQ to Gornji Vakuf.

At the beginning of the year Lieutenant General Sir Michael Rose took over as the UNPROFOR Commander in Bosnia. A highly charismatic figure, he had been commissioned into the Coldstream Guards but then saw distinguished service with the Special Air Service Regiment, which he commanded in the Falklands in 1982 and at the daring breaking of a terrorist siege of the Iranian Embassy in the heart of London the year before.

Rose was determined to sort things out. His catchphrase was, 'I am going to put them right about this.' He issued a mission statement based on three things: the need for a unified command, a clear concept of operation, and a single plan. He also insisted that UNPROFOR was a peace mission, and should not make war on any of the parties in Bosnia. In his words, that would be 'to cross the Mogadishu Line' – an expression coined from the behaviour of American peacekeepers in Somalia the year before when they changed their mission from peace-keeping and declared war on the chieftain Mohammed Aideed, at the cost of the lives of their own marines and, ultimately, the mission itself.

On 5 February 1994, a few weeks after General Rose's arrival, a mortar bomb hit the Markele market place in the heart of Sarajevo. The scenes of the slaughter, in which sixty-eight died and more than a hundred were injured, were shown on television, particularly CNN. Rose seized the opportunity and under threat of strikes from Nato aircraft persuaded the leaders of the Serbs and Muslims to sign a ceasefire and agree to withdraw heavy weapons to UN-guarded dumps round Sarajevo.

Weapons were dumped, though their guards were set up to be hostages in any future trouble, and peace came to Sarajevo with the spring. To enforce the truce the CO of the Coldstreams, the scholarly Lieutenant Colonel Peter Williams, moved a company of his battalion to Sarajevo. As they moved onto Mount Igman overlooking the capital a patrol of Warrior vehicles came under heavy machine-gun fire. The leader, Lance Sergeant Darren Waterhouse, was on the ground reconnoitring the terrain. He quickly organized a fighting withdrawal, engaging seven different firing points, believed to be Bosnian Serb Army positions. For this he was the first NCO to receive the Military Cross, hitherto reserved for officers and warrant officers.

As the weather began to heat up towards summer, crowds returned to the streets of Sarajevo. Cafes opened. Trams began to run again. General Rose organized a concert by the band of the Coldstream Guards and a series of sports events to celebrate. His watch as commander was to bring more peace than war to Bosnia; it ended with a four-month Cessation of Hostilities Agreement (COHA) in December. But a real peace was far away. That summer the snipers started firing on the trams once again, sending shoppers scurrying for cover.

Rose confessed himself depressed at the perfidy on all sides among the combatants and their political backers, known in UN parlance as the Warring Factions (WF). The biggest difficulty for the UN peacekeepers was the six zones designated by the UN as 'safe areas' in 1993, the enclaves of Srebrenica, Goražde and Zepa in the east, Bihac in the north, and Tuzla and Sarajevo. The UN had given the peace forces a lot of responsibility for these areas, where more than 100,000 people were trapped in the eastern enclaves alone, but little real power.

The position was clearly understood by the senior UN official for Yugoslavia, Yasushi Akashi, a professional diplomat who was appointed Special Representative for the Secretary General for Yugoslavia in the spring of 1994. He has been accused of being to emollient to the combatants – but for him another day of peace in Bosnia was a day gained, and he had to keep the mission going. He understood better than any that all the UN cards in Bosnia were low ones.

Later he would reflect: 'With a consensus absent in the Security Council, lacking a strategy, and burdened by an unclear mandate, UNPROFOR was forced to chart its own course. There was only limited support for a "robust" enforcement policy by UNPROFOR. Consequently UNPROFOR chose to pursue a policy of relatively passive enforcement, the lowest common denominator on which all the Council more or less agreed.'

The Safe Areas

The eastern enclave of Srebrenica first came under heavy attack by Serb forces in spring 1993. The UNPROFOR commander of the day, Lieutenant General Philippe Morillon of France, went personally to witness the shelling and carnage, and British escorts of the 9th/12th Lancers went with him. His Military Assistant, Major Piers Tucker of the Royal Artillery, won an MC for his efforts. Already some of the wounded had been got out, but the Muslim regime in Sarajevo refused safe passage offered by the Serbs for most of the 40,000 now trapped in the enclave.

Morillon made a brave pledge by megaphone from the post office in the town of Srebrenica that he would stand by the people of the enclave, and so would the UN. But it was largely bluff. The Security Council passed three resolutions, 819, 824 and 836, setting up the safe areas – but there was less to this than met the eye. Few of the fifteen member countries of the Council were prepared to contribute to the 11,000 extra troops needed; accordingly the resolutions said the UN forces should not defend the enclaves but merely 'deter' threats to them. National agendas at the UN came first, second and last once more.

This was the position facing General Rose when fighting intensified round Goražde in spring 1994. He had special reconnaissance teams, Joint Commission Officers (JCO), with a contribution from special forces, in the area. On 15 April 1994 the Muslim command in Goražde asked a JCO team to investigate ceasefire violations on the north of the town. As the team went forward, the Muslim defenders ran back, and Corporal Rennie of the Parachute Regiment was killed. Rose was furious.

Rose decided to call in air strikes from Nato. One of the first in was by Sea Harriers of the Royal Navy. A JCO witnessed one make five passes to try to hit a tank in murky weather. 'The aircraft has been hit and is on fire. It's going down ... the pilot has ejected,' he reported. 'I can see a parachute.' The pilot was picked up by Muslim forces and smuggled to safety; the plane had been hit by a simple shoulder-launched rocket.

That summer General Rose had persuaded the British to send a second battalion to UNPROFOR to bolster the safe areas. By the end of April two companies and the battalion HQ of the 1st Battalion the Duke of Wellington's Regiment had reached Goražde. The CO, Lieutenant

Colonel David Santa Ollala, immediately tried to get the lie of the land. One of the first patrols, led by Corporal Wayne Mills on 29 April 1994, came under heavy fire from Serb positions as it moved through the wooded hills above the town. The patrol opened fire and killed two Serbs. As the men of the Dukes pulled back they were fired on again. Mills set up a firing position in a clearing to delay the attackers. As they came into sight, he shot the leader and scattered those with him, thus allowing his men to get away from the clearing safely. For this he won the first Conspicuous Gallantry Cross, a new bravery award next only to the Victoria Cross; the citation said he killed two Serbs, drove off the attackers and saved all those under his command. The JCO commander, Captain Andreas Carlton Smith, Royal Green Jackets, and Captain Paul Russell, Royal Engineers, won MCs. Later Colonel Santa Ollala was awarded the DSO.

The Dukes were followed into Goražde in the autumn by the newly amalgamated Royal Gloucestershire, Berkshire and Wiltshire Regiment. They were harassed frequently but had a quieter time on the whole, though they lost five men in two accidents with Saxon personnel carriers.

1995: The Road to Dayton

In January 1995 General Rose was succeeded by Lieutenant General Rupert Smith, a paratrooper who had led the British 1st Armoured Division in Operation DESERT STORM in the Gulf in 1991. In style he was very different from Rose; he hated appearing before the media, but was a subtle negotiator behind the scenes. Like his civilian UN boss in Zagreb, Yasushi Akashi, he knew the options for UNPROFOR were limited, and very soon came to wonder if UNPROFOR had a credible future at all.

He thought that the Bosnian Serbs commanded by Ratko Mladic would try to end the war soon. They would do so by moving against the UN areas. In this he proved right, for the Serbs in the summer of 1995 attacked all six including a devastating air-fuel rocket fired on Tuzla which killed some eighty young people in street cafes. By March 1995 Smith warned the UN that they must prepare to thwart the Serbs otherwise the Serbs would draw the UN into the fight on their own terms. Akashi and the UNPROFOR Commander Lieutenant General

Bernard Janvier acknowledged this, but said the UN was neither configured, nor capable, nor mandated for such a contest. By the spring of 1995, as the Cessation of Hostilities Agreement was ending, none of governments of Europe or America seemed to be interested in what happened next.

Smith's favourite metaphors were 'too many parts moving in the clock' and getting his team to work by 'stepping stones'. He knew that there were too many parts moving on the battlefields of Croatia and Bosnia for the UN to cope, and UNPROFOR might have to withdraw. He told his team that the summer would be like a chain gang trying to cross a fast-flowing stream by stepping stones: sometimes they succeeded in getting halfway across, but then might be forced back and have to try again. So it proved. Smith was to have to absorb more reverses than any other in UN command in Bosnia.

The first major piece to move in the clock was an attack by the Croats on the Serb-held pocket of Western Slavonia round Pakrac. This was a rehearsal for Operation STORM, the operation to recover the entire Krajina territory seized by the Serbs – Knin, the capital of the region, home to Serbs for centuries, fell in August. The Croatian army had been fashioned and tooled under the tutelage of a variety of American and other specialist advisers, including those from US consultancy Military Professional Resources Inc. The Croat offensive put around 150,000 Serbs to flight, amid widespread accusation of Croat atrocities. By mid-August it was clear that the Croats and Muslims in Bosnia were bent on driving Serbs from northern Bosnia, in a sweeping operation towards Prijedor and Banja Luka.

In spring 1995 General Mladic and his Serbs claimed to hold 70 per cent of Bosnian territory – but his forces were stretched thin, and were short of food and materiel. For this reason they could no support the Serb militias in the Krajina. Mladic worked like a boxer, ducking and feinting, trying to pick off opportunity targets.

In May it was the turn of Sarajevo. Tanks and artillery began shelling the centre of town (according to some they were firing phosphorus rounds), and a party of Muslims was mortared at the entrance to the escape tunnel under the airport. Smith threatened air strikes. The Serbs seized weapons from the UN collection sites, and Nato bombed – this time hitting ammunition dumps near the mountain political HQ of the Serbs at Pale. The Serbs retaliated by seizing UN hostages, showing some on video chained to military targets as a warning for Nato to stop bombing. To Smith's relief, the Serbs overplayed their hand. They seized some 400 hostages, which made the crisis international. The capitals of Europe and America and the UN headquarters would have to get involved now.

Among the hostages seized were twenty-eight men from A Company of the Royal Welch Fusiliers, whose release was negotiated with President Milošević in Belgrade. They travelled out of Bosnia via Serbia, and a few weeks later rejoined the battalion. The story of the battalion was as dramatic as any British unit in Bosnia. It is told elegantly in the regimental magazine *Y Draig Goch* (*White Dragon*), the 1996 edition graced by the diary notes of the CO, Lieutenant Colonel Jonathan Riley, an accomplished historian who was awarded the DSO for his leadership in Goražde. 'My concept was to operate according to peacekeeping principles,' he wrote, 'but to be prepared to use force in self defence, and to plan for various contingencies.'

Among the contingencies was the preparation of shelters and hides in the woods away from Goražde as the town came under siege, with twenty-six days of continuous heavy bombardment. Supplies of fuel and food were choked by the Serbs, so the Fusiliers patrolled on foot and used mules. The battalion never lost its grip, though its soldiers based in town had to spend weeks in deep bunkers, with only lightning patrols to check on their observation posts. In August they shot dead two marauders from Muslim special forces as they tried to ransack the British camp – as they had already done at the Ukrainian camp in the town.

In the final act of the drama, the Fusiliers showed the same measure of cunning and daring. From mid-August they realized there was little more to be done as they would largely be hostage material for both sides, so they decided to 'thin out' and go home via Belgrade. Radio signals were conducted in Welsh to avoid eavesdropping on their plans. On the 28 August the last Fusiliers broke out, though the locals tried to stop the convoy, firing their weapons in the air. Once they were across the border in Serbia, General Smith knew he could turn the key to start Nato bombing again without fear of hostages being taken.

The story of the regiment is told with laconic charm in their journal. 'As his cover, a house, was slowly destroyed around him, Sgt Timmons, his interpreter and Fusilier Kevin Duhig kept their heads down and returned fire when they could.' On another occasion a patrol came under fire as it was trying to bring a woman in labour to hospital. 'All vehicles, though battle damaged, arrived in Goražde 800 rounds lighter, and the lady gave birth to a healthy baby girl.'

As the battle for Goražde built up in June, Mladic tried his duck-and-weave tactics further east with a stealthy concentration of forces on Srebrenica, where 40,000 Muslims were confined. British forces played only a marginal part in the collapse of the enclave, the rounding up and subsequent murder of some 7,000 unarmed Muslim males. A team of three British JCOs had watched, and warned, of the Serb offensive and the skirmishing between them and Muslim forces round Srebrenica. The team made good their retreat disguising themselves as Dutch forces after the collapse, and a member of the SAS, who has not been named, won a Military Cross for his deeds.

The Serb attack on Srebrenica was the catalyst to the final moves by the international community to end the war in Bosnia. The Serb leadership acted from opportunism and panic, though the murders were premeditated by the leadership – they had ordered seventy buses to the scene to take the hostages away, most to be murdered. The UN had shown a familiar pattern of lack of coordination. In the end national agendas had prevailed, and the Dutch government had ordered their men to surrender, and later crucial evidence appears to have been destroyed; this is still a matter for national and international investigation.

The crisis led directly to an emergency conference in London – where again national agendas seemed to prevail. The French wanted to counter-attack, either to retake Srebrenica or relieve Goražde, using the new UN Rapid Reaction Force, which they dominated. Britain sent 24 Airmobile Brigade, though it was never to deploy fully from Croatia, and the battle group formed by the 1st Battalion of the Devonshire and Dorset Regiment, one of the two infantry battalions then deployed to Bosnia, prepared to lead 'Alpha Force' of the UN RRF to clear roads to Sarajevo. In all the muddle the London talks achieved two things: they opened the way for serious negotiations led by the US diplomat Richard Holbrooke, and they gave the UN military commanders, and not the civilian officials, the key to order Nato strikes over Bosnia.

On his return from London General Smith succeeded in negotiating the withdrawal of some 10,000 Muslim refugees from the Zepa enclave, eyeballing Mladic in person to achieve this, but even so several Muslims were murdered, including the community leader. Like General Rose, Rupert Smith was to receive the DSO for his leadership, in his case a bar to the one he had been awarded for the Gulf campaign.

Smith's ace was the preparation of a UN artillery force, made up by French Foreign Legion 155mm howitzers, Dutch 120mm mortars and alternating batteries of 105mm L118 Light Guns from 19th Regiment Royal Artillery to be positioned on the forward slopes of Mount Igman. Their role, drowned by the noise and publicity attending the Nato air strikes, was to prove vital in ending the siege of Sarajevo.

On 28 August a salvo of mortars was fired in Sarajevo, one hitting the Markale market again, killing thirty-seven. UN investigators concluded that it was fired from Serb positions, but it was kept secret for two days while the Royal Welch Fusiliers got away from Goražde. Turning the key for Nato attacks fell to General Smith, as his superior General Janvier was on leave.

On the morning of 30 August, according 19th Regiment's journal *The Highland Gunners*, 'the eerie silence [on Mt Igman] was shattered by the deafening roars of F-16s racing towards their targets. 'TAKE POST! Prepare 30 rounds HE . . . Load! rounds fire for effect . . . There was just time for everyone to realise they had made history before shells from every gun and mortar landed on the Serb mortar position and OP.' In all 600 rounds were fired in the first seventy-five minutes of fire missions. The siege of Sarajevo, which had lasted more than 1,000 days, longer than the siege of Leningrad, was coming to an end.

The bombing enabled Richard Holbrooke to hammer out a ceasefire on 14 September, though the Croat–Muslim offensive continued in the north into October. In November the peace settlement was negotiated at the Wright-Patterson Air Force Base at Dayton, Ohio, and was signed formally in Paris in December.

UNPROFOR was wound up. British troops swapped their blue berets and helmets for their more familiar regimental and tactical headgear, as they changed from serving the UN to becoming part of the Nato-led 'implementation force', IFOR.

The first IFOR British contingent was led by Major General Mike Jackson, GOC 3rd UK Division. He moved his HQ from Gornji Vakuf to a factory outside the largest Serb town of Banja Luka.

In Sarajevo, Lieutenant General Sir Michael Walker was the Operations Commander of the new IFOR. He had to deal with Serb militants who beat a retreat from Sarajevo burning five villages and suburbs in mid-March. They were voting with their feet on becoming part of a new multinational capital under the Dayton peace blueprint; in the village of Ilidza they even exhumed their dead from the churchyard to take with them.

British troops, special forces among them, have proved robust keepers of the peace for first IFOR, and its successor SFOR (Sustaining Force). They have helped community projects, built schools and bakeries, helped out with medical and veterinary care. They have been involved in the arrest of the most wanted on the list of war criminals indicted by the Hague International Tribunal. The skills and resolve of the troops were admired by friend and foe alike – they were to be tested again in the Balkans in the crisis over Kosovo.

Kosovo, 1998

Kosovo has been disputed ground between Serbs and ethnic Albanians for centuries. The site of the Battle of Kosovo Polje in June 1389, a defining moment for Serbian nationalism, it was also home territory for Albanian folklore and history. After the Congress of Berlin in 1878 the League of Prizren put in a claim for an independent Albania with Prizren, now in Kosovo, as its capital. Kosovo was intimately caught up in the Balkan Wars of 1912 and 1913 and the two world wars. Tito granted it autonomy, but President Milošević revoked this in 1989. The Kosovar Albanians ran their own unofficial schools and universities, had their own parliament and elected their own 'president', Ibrahim Rugova.

Tension between Serb and Kosovar Albanian was compounded by demography. In 1946 according to official figures 498,242 Albanians lived in the province and 171,911 Serbs; by 1991 this had risen to 1,607,690 Albanians and 195,301 Serbs. On the eve of the Kosovar rebellion in 1998 the figures were roughly 2 million Albanians to more than 200,000 Serbs (including military and police). On projections from 1998 Serbs would become a minority to non-Serbs, Albanians, Slav Muslims and Hungarians in Serbia and Montenegro, the rump Yugoslav Federation, within twenty-five years.

In 1998 a loose coalition of Albanian nationalists calling itself the

Kosovar Liberation Army (KLA), with roots in Albanian communities across the Balkans and the Kosovar community of some 700,000 in northern Europe, raised the flag of rebellion. For three years previously the KLA had claimed responsibility for sporadic attacks on police posts and security forces. In March 1998 Serb paramilitary police attacked the village of Donji Prekaz, stronghold of the clan leader Adem Jasheri; fifty-one villagers including Jasheri and women and children were killed in the fighting.

Throughout the summer fighting raged across Kosovo, and the KLA had early success in liberating whole tracts of the central Drenica plateau. From July the Serb police, backed by the Serb army, struck back, and more than 200,000 Kosovar refugees fled to the hills. After the massacre of an Albanian family of twenty-three hiding in woods at Gornje Obrinje, the international authorities demanded restraint from Belgrade. A monitoring mission from the OSCE (Organisation for Security and Cooperation in Europe) was agreed in October – but it was almost doomed to failure from the first; the monitors were unarmed and depended on the goodwill of the Serb authorities.

The discovery of forty-five Albanian bodies at the village of Racak in January 1999 triggered the international community, led by America, to call a conference at Rambouillet in France. There the Belgrade regime was effectively presented with an ultimatum: withdraw the army (VJ) and allow Nato and UN to monitor, or face Nato bombing. After a resumption of talks at Paris, the Serbs rejected the demands. The OSCE monitors were withdrawn and Nato began bombing Yugoslavia on 24 March 1999 – the alliance's first war.

British forces were heavily involved in the campaign. GR7 Harriers of the RAF attacked from Gioia del Colle in Italy, though they had difficulty targeting in cloud. The submarine HMS *Splendid* launched Tomahawk cruise missiles from the Adriatic. The bombing lasted seventy-eight days – amid controversy; the Americans insisted on delivering from 15,000 feet; two refugee convoys, the Chinese Embassy and the television station in Belgrade were hit.

British forces were deployed with the Nato Allied Rapid Reaction Corps under Lieutenant General Sir Mike Jackson in Macedonia (FYROM). They were to implement any peace deal for Kosovo, but while they were waiting they had to deal with hundreds of thousands of refugees fleeing the province. Another formation under the Ace Mobile Force command of Major General John Reith coped with the 400,000 refugees who arrived in Albania – Nato's first humanitarian mission.

After seventy-eight days Belgrade agreed to terms, and General Jackson signed the technical terms for Serb withdrawal and Nato's entry into Kosovo at an airfield outside Kumonovo in Macedonia. On 11 June, as Nato forces prepared to move into Kosovo, they heard the Russians were sending a contingent from their peace force in Bosnia to occupy Pristina airport. The Supreme Allied Commander, General Wesley Clark, told Jackson to fly forward a force of British and French paratroopers to oppose the Russians. Apocryphally Jackson is said to have told Clark he was 'not prepared to start World War Three for this.' Washington, London and Paris conferred and declined to move. The incident shows again that rarely does an international commander in Nato or the UN have full operational command and ability to change the mission. He merely has operational control for the agreed mission and operational command remains with the national capitals.

On 12 June Nato forces moved into Kosovo under UN Security Council resolution 1244. Of the eleven battalions commanded by Mike Jackson, five were British. The 1st Battalion The Parachute Regiment, The King's Royal Hussars and the Irish Guards headed for Pristina, where they were met by cheering crowds and festooned with flowers. The Paras shot dead a drunken policeman threatening them with a pistol on the day of their arrival, and shot dead two KLA militia firing weapons on the Flag Day celebrations in July. The paras brought order to the capital, and successfully held off the mafia mobsters arriving from Albania trying to take over the city. Both Jackson and Lieutenant Colonel Paul Gibson, CO of 1 Para, were awarded the DSO.

Peacekeeping has not come easy for the British troops in Kosovo, as the Hussars, paras and Gurkhas quickly discovered. The first casualties were Lieutenant Gareth Evans and Staff Sergeant Balaram Rai of the Gurkha Independent Engineer Squadron; they were clearing Nato ordnance from a village near Malisevo when it blew up.

The biggest difficulty has been the vagueness of the terms of the Resolution 1244 – it does not say what the future status of Kosovo should be – and the wave of revenge attacks on the isolated Serb communities in the province. Among the Albanians mafia activity has been endemic.

The town of Mitrovica, under French control, became a flashpoint in early 2000, with the Serbs occupying a ghetto north of the River Iber which divides the town. In February a company of 2nd Battalion The Royal Green Jackets under their CO, Lieutenant Colonel Nick Carter, held back a crowd from a march of 70,000 Albanians just south of the main bridge merely by linking arms and talking to the leaders – the French gendarmerie meanwhile resorted to riot shields, helmets and CS gas.

In the early summer the Serb monastery village of Gračanica became a focus of revenge attacks, and the Royal Regiment of Fusiliers were called in to restore order. During a riot, the Commander British Force, Brigadier Richard Shirreff, Commander 7th Brigade, went to survey events. It was a considerable risk as rioter a drew a pistol and fired at him; later a grenade was rolled under his command jeep.

The British commitment to Bosnia and Kosovo looked open ended by the close of 2000. At least a brigade of troops was involved, some 7,000 between the two areas, plus support from the RAF and Royal Navy and auxiliary services. Twelve months after arriving in Kosovo, it looked likely to last for years.

Notes

The World in 1945: The View from 2001

1. For a full discussion of this very complex subject see Alice Hills, *Doctrine, Criminality, and Future British Army Operations: a Half Completed Understanding*, Strategic and Combat Studies Institute Occasional Paper Number 39.

2. Hills, op. cit., pp. 14–15.

3. John Keegan, *Spectator*, 24 March 2001, pp. 39–40.

4. Carl von Clausewitz, *On War*, edited and translated by Michael Howard and Peter Paret (Princeton University Press, 1984), p. 119. 'Everything in war is very simple, but the simplest thing is difficult. The difficulties accumulate and end by producing a kind of friction that is inconceivable unless one has experienced war.'

5. *Observer*, Sunday 18 February 2001, Editorial, 'How to create a Woman-Friendly Army'.

6. William Darryl Henderson, *Cohesion: The Human Element in Combat* (National Defense University Press, Washington DC, 1986), p. 164.

7. Martin van Creveld, *Fighting Power: German and US Army Performance, 1939–1945* (Greenwood Press: Westport Conn: USA, 1982), pp. 163–4.

8. Henderson, op. cit., p. 8.

9. Correlli Barnett, *The Lost Victory: British Dreams and British Realities 1945–1950* (Macmillan, 1995), p. 3.

10. France, China and the USSR were also recipients of Lend-Lease.

11. Barnett, op. cit., p. 50.

12. James Morris, *Farewell the Trumpets: an Imperial Retreat* (Penguin, 1979), p. 463.

13. In fact the British army left Dublin in 1922 on the setting up of the Irish Free State.

14. Morris, op. cit., p. 462.

15. Ibid., pp. 472–3.

16. Quoted in Lawrence James, *Raj: the Making and Unmaking of British India* (New York: Little, Brown & Company, 1997), pp. 560–61.
17. Ibid., p. 607.
18. Andrew Roberts, *Eminent Churchillians* (Phoenix, 1995), Chapter 2, 'Lord Mountbatten and the Perils of Adrenalin'.

1. Netherlands East Indies, 1945–1947

1. The most detailed and careful analysis of Mallaby's death is by John Springhall, 'Disaster in Surabaya: the Death of Brigadier Mallaby during the British occupation of Java, 1945–46', *The Journal of Imperial and Commonwealth History*, vol. 24, no. 3, September 1996, pp. 422–43.
2. Imperial War Museum, Lieutenant General Sir Philip Christison, 'Memoirs', p. 188.
3. Major-General S. Woodburn Kirby, *The War against Japan*, vol. 5, *The Surrender of Japan* (HMSO, 1969), p. 336.
4. Anthony Reid, 'Indonesia: Revolution without Socialism', in Robin Jeffrey, ed., *Asia – The Winning of Independence* (London: Macmillan, 1981), p. 144.
5. Report on the Activities of 5 Parachute Brigade Group in Semarang, January–May 1946, copy in Darling papers, Imperial War Museum.
6. An examination of the tortuous interplay of military–political considerations over the NEI is beyond the scope of this chapter. I have discussed this question at length in *Troubled Days of Peace: Mountbatten and South East Asia Command, 1946–47* (Manchester: Manchester University Press, 1987).

2. Palestine, 1945–1948

1. CO733/371/1, Sir Harold MacMichael to Malcolm MacDonald, 29 July 1938.
2. IWM/004550/05 Middle East British Military Personnel, 1919–1939, Major-General H. E. N. Bredin, p. 40.
3. Aviv Shlaim, *The Iron Wall: Israel and the Arab World* (London: Allen Lane The Penguin Press, 2000), p. 13.
4. FO371/68854, Transjordan – A Possible Forecast of Events in Palestine, Brigadier John Bagot Glubb, 13 May 1948; Chaim Herzog, *The Arab–Israeli Wars* (London: Arms and Armour Press, 1984), p. 24.
5. J. R. Hill, 'The Realities of Medium Power, 1946 to the Present', in *The*

Oxford History of the Royal Navy (Oxford: Oxford University Press, 1995), p. 383.

6. CAB131/2, Meetings of the Cabinet's Defence Committee, 8 and 9 March 1946.

7. Naomi Shepherd, *Ploughing Sand: British Rule in Palestine 1917–1948* (London: John Murray, 1999), p. 225.

8. Correlli Barnett, *The Lost Victory: British Dreams, British Realities 1945–1950* (London: Macmillan, 1995), p. 61; Shepherd, op. cit., p. 223.

9. Nigel Hamilton, *Monty: The Field Marshal 1946–1976* (London: Hamish Hamilton, 1986), pp. 664–6.

10. Shepherd, op. cit., p. 228; Air Chief Marshal Sir David Lee, '*Wings in the Sun*': *A History of the Royal Air Force in the Mediterranean, 1945–1986* (London: HMSO, pp. 20–21); Nicholas Bethell, *The Palestine Triangle: The Struggle Between the British, the Jews and the Arabs 1935–1948* (London: André Deutsch, 1979), pp. 280–81.

11. David A. Charters, *The British Army and Jewish Insurgency in 'Palestine' 1945–1947* (London: Macmillan Press in association with King's College, London, 1989), p. 63.

12. Hamilton, op. cit., p. 697.

13. Ibid., p. 696.

3. Malaya, 1948–1960

1. John Coates, *Suppressing Insurgency: An Analysis of the Malayan Emergency, 1948–1954* (Westview, Boulder, 1992), p. 18; conversation, Chin Peng with author, Canberra, February 1999.

2. Conversation, Chin Peng with author, Canberra, February 1999.

3. A good discussion of the forces on both sides is Anthony Short, *The Communist Insurrection Malaya 1948–1960* (London: Frederick Muller, 1975), pp. 95–112, 113–48.

4. Arthur Campbell, *Jungle Green* (London: George Allen and Unwin, 1953), pp. 9–10.

5. Coates, op. cit., pp. 40–41.

6. Ibid., pp. 190–202.

7. Short, op. cit., p. 235.

8. Coates, op. cit., pp. 40–41.

9. Ibid., p. 83.

10. Karl Hack, 'Corpses, Prisoners of War and Captured Documents: British

and Communist Narratives of the Malayan Emergency, and the Dynamics of Intelligence Transformation', *Intelligence and National Security*, 14:4, Winter 1999, p. 237n., p. 39.

11. This is the burden of argument in Karl Hack, 'British Intelligence and Counter-Insurgency in the Era of Decolonisation: The Example of Malaya', *Intelligence and National Security*, 14:2, Summer 1999.

12. Cited in Coates, op. cit., p. 113.

13. John Cloake, *Templer: Tiger of Malaya. The Life of Field Marshal Sir Gerald Templer* (London: Harrap, 1985), p. 262; Richard Stubbs, *Hearts and Minds in Guerrilla Warfare: The Malayan Emergency 1948–1960* (Singapore: Oxford University Press, 1989).

14. Cloake, ibid., p. 265–77.

15. John Leary, *Violence and the Dream People: The Orang Asli and the Malayan Emergency 1948–1960* (Athens: Ohio University Press, 1995).

16. Conversation, Chin Peng with author, Canberra, February 1999.

17. Little has been written on naval activities in Malaya. For a brief general discussion see Jeffrey Grey, *Up Top: the Royal Australian Navy in Southeast Asian Conflicts, 1955–1972* (Sydney: Allen and Unwin, 1998), pp. 24–41.

18. Richard Miers, *Shoot to Kill* (London: Faber, 1959), p. 32.

19. There is episodic mention of the Fijian battalion in M. C. A. Henniker, *Red Shadow over Malaya* (Edinburgh: William Blackwood and Sons, 1955). Henniker commanded the 63rd Gurkha Infantry Brigade in Malaya.

20. Miers, op. cit., p. 37. Miers served with the 1st Battalion, South Wales Borderers.

21. For a useful discussion of developments in British thinking culminating in the ATOM pamphlet, see Tim Jones, 'The British Army and Counter-Guerrilla Warfare in Transition, 1944–1952', *Small Wars and Insurgency*, 7:3, Winter 1996.

22. For a discussion of this involvement, and of operations in the last years of the Emergency, see Peter Dennis and Jeffrey Grey, *Emergency and Confrontation: Australian Military Operations in Malaya and Borneo, 1950–1966* (Sydney: Allen and Unwin, 1996).

23. Kumar Ramakrishna, 'Content, Credibility and Context: Propaganda, Government Surrender Policy and the Malayan Communist Terrorist Mass Surrenders of 1958', *Intelligence and National Security*, 14:4, Winter 1999.

24. Short, op. cit., p. 503.

5. Kenya, 1952–1956

1. Marshall S. Clough, *Mau Mau Memoirs: History, Memory and Politics* (Boulder, Col.: Lynne Rienner Publishers, 1998), p. 129.
2. Paul Maina, *Six Mau Mau Generals* (Nairobi: Gazelle Books, 1977), pp. 36–50.
3. Marshall S. Clough, op. cit., p. 155, quoting from Kahinga Wachanga, *The Swords of Kirinyagga* (Nairobi: East Africa Literature Bureau, 1975).
4. Frank Kitson, *Gangs and Counter-gangs* (Place: Barrie and Rockcliff, 1960), pp. 73–8, 91–5, 122, 170–171.
5. Terence Gavaghan, *Of Lions and Dung Beetles* (Ilfracombe: Arthur H. Stockwell Ltd, 1999), p. 217.
6. Charles Douglas-Home, *Evelyn Baring: The Last Proconsul* (London: Collins, 1978), pp. 258–9, 264, 272–3.

6. The Canal Zone and Suez, 1951–1956

1. Cmd 5360, *Treaty of Alliance between His Majesty, in respect of the United Kingdom, and His Majesty the King of Egypt and a Convention Concerning the Immunities and Privileges to be enjoyed by the British Forces in Egypt, London, August 26, 1936* (London: HMSO, 1937).
2. Michael Ionides, *Divide and Lose, The Arab Revolt of 1955–1958* (London: Geoffrey Bles 1960), p. 12.
3. FO 371/90115, Telegram from Sir Ralph Stevenson, British Ambassador, Cairo, to Foreign Office 26 August 1951.
4. FO 371/90115, Secret letter from Sir Ralph Stevenson to R. J. Bowker at the Foreign Office, 5 October 1951.
5. FO 371/90116, BBC Monitoring Report of a broadcast by General Erskine, C-in-C British Troops, Egypt, on British Forces Radio, 7.30–7.45 p.m., 16 October 1951.
6. Unpublished manuscript, Imperial War Museum.
7. FO 371/96858.
8. It was at Tel El Kebir that the British forces defeated the Egyptian nationalists in 1882.
9. FO 371/96863.
10. WO 236/8, Erskine Papers: Problems in the Canal Zone after the Abrogation of the 1936 Treaty, Lecture notes prepared by Lieutenant General Sir

George Erskine KBE CB DSO – General Officer Commanding British Troops in Egypt C1954.

11. FO 371/96986, Confidential report on a dinner held by the British Military Attaché 18 September 1952.

12. FO 371/96985, PM Personal Minute from Churchill to Eden 9 March 1952. Eden's Top Secret reply 10 March 1952.

13. Information compiled by the late Colonel P. S. 'Pip' Newton MBE for submission to John Spellar MP, 19 March 1998, in support of the campaign for a medal.

14. CAB 128/30, Conclusions of a Cabinet Meeting held at 10 Downing Street 17 July 1956.

15. CAB 128/30 Confidential Annexe to a Cabinet Meeting held at 10 Downing Street 23 October 1956.

16. The existence of the Israeli copy of the secret agreement was made public in Britain in a BBC TV documentary televised on the fortieth anniversary of the Crisis in 1996. The agreement was signed by David Ben-Gurion, the Israeli Prime Minister; on Britain's behalf by Patrick Dean, Chairman of the Joint Intelligence Committee; and by Christian Pineau, the French Foreign Minister.

17. *Hansard*, Commons, vol. 560, col. 1518, 20 December 1956.

8. Muscat and Oman 1958–1959

1. The Trucial Oman States were a British Protectorate of seven sheikhdoms located to the north and west of Muscat and Oman, with which state they had no political connection; they federated as the United Arab Emirates in 1971. Muscat and Oman was renamed Oman, formally the Sultanate of Oman, in 1970. See also Chapter Eleven, 'Dhofar, 1965–1975: The Unknown War', pages 255ff, for further background on the British involvement in Oman.

2. Consisting of the Northern Frontier Regiment (NFR), Desert Regiment (DR), and Muscat Regiment (MR).

3. Later General Sir Frank Kitson.

4. Frank Kitson, *Bunch of Five* (London: Faber and Faber, 1977), p. 171.

5. Ibid., p. 178.

6. Deane-Drummond, *Arrows of Fortune* (London: Leo Cooper, 1992), p. 166.

7. Later Lieutenant General Sir John Watts, Commander of the Sultan's Armed Forces.

8. Lieutenant; later General Sir Peter de la Billière.
9. Kitson, op. cit., p. 201.

9. Brunei and Borneo, 1962–1966

1. For a variety of reasons, including the difficulty encountered by journalists filing their stories, and just moving around the battlefield, there were no cases of security breaches caused by members of the media actually with the Falklands Task Force. The indiscretions, of which there were several, emanated from government ministers in Whitehall.

10. South Arabia and Aden, 1964–1967

1. Formed October 1959; from July 1968 part of The Light Infantry.
2. AIR 23/8637, MEAF in Aden, 1964.
3. FCO 8/220 and FCO 8/221, Thomson visit to Aden, 1967.
4. FCO 8/257, Crater and the Argylls.
5. DEFE 13/627, Minister's Office.
6. FCO 8/257, Crater and the Argylls.
7. DEFE 13/627, Minister's Office.
8. Julian Paget, *Last Post—Aden 1964–67* (London: Faber & Faber, 1969).

11. Dhofar, 1965–1975

From this point forward in the narrative metric units are used as British forces began to adopt metric in conformity with NATO practice.

1. Oman, formally the Sultanate of Oman, was called Muscat and Oman until 1970. See Chapter Eight, 'Muscat and Oman, 1958–1959: Seize the Green Mountain', page 189.

12. Northern Ireland, 1969–2000

1. Report of the Tribunal Appointed to inquire into the Events on Sunday 30 January 1972 which led to loss of life in connection with the Procession in Londonderry on that day, HC220 (London: HMSO, 1972), conclusions.
2. Account based on interview by the author of the corporal in the Royal Green Jackets who was involved in this action.

13. The Falklands, 1982

1. This consisted of around 450 infantry, six 105mm howitzers, plus logistic and transport sub-units. The Amphibious Commando Company was ninety-two strong, and the beach reconnaissance sub-unit the Buzos Tacticos consisted of twelve men.

2. Nick Barker, *Beyond Endurance; An Epic of Whitehall and the South Atlantic Conflict* (London: Leo Cooper, 1997), pp. 184–5.

3. Admiral Sandy Woodward, *One Hundred Days; The Memoirs of the Falklands Battle Group Commander* (London: HarperCollins, 1992), p. 133.

4. Michael Clapp and Ewen Southby-Tailyour, *Amphibious Assault Falklands: The Battle of San Carlos Water* (London: Leo Cooper, 1996), p. 136.

5. Field Marshal Slim once remarked that tactics are for amateurs, while logistics are for professionals, so the professionals might be interested in the logistics of moving guns and ammunition in 1982, in war, as opposed to in a classroom. A battery consists of six guns, and to move each gun takes one Sea King sortie. To move 480 rounds per gun for one battery alone takes sixty Sea King sorties, or a hundred and twenty Wessex sorties, or twenty Chinook sorties. To this must be added six Sea King sorties for the men, and two for half-ton vehicles solely for battery charging (they will not drive anywhere in the Falklands). So to move a battery and enough ammunition for one night of fighting takes around seventy-four Sea King sorties. If the guns were not moving, the bill for ammunition alone was sixty Sea King sorties. There were four batteries supporting the 3rd Commando Brigade alone.

6. The Carrier Battle Group had to remain in various forms until the full air defence system, including Phantoms, was ready, some six months later.

7. David Brown, *The Royal Navy and the Falklands War* (London: Leo Cooper, 1987), p. 336.

Index